THE DAZED DECADES

RANKIN
1990 - 2016

FEEL IT/TV IS BORING/ACCEPT NO
IMITATIONS/EMPEROR'S NEW CLOTHES/
ABSOLUTELY FLAWLESS?

RANKIN

I came to photography quite late. I had begun an accountancy degree at Brighton Polytechnic when, at 20, I picked up a camera for the first time. Whether it was hanging out with art students or a love of taking pictures, I quickly realised that photography was what I wanted to do. Much to my parents dismay, I dropped accountancy and went back home to restart my A-levels in the arts.

After a year working as a porter in a hospital and combining night classes in film and English with a BTEC in photography, in 1988 I was accepted into The London College of Printing [now London College of Communication] to do a BA in photography.

Little did I know, that the course I had chosen was ridiculously semiotics driven, which meant lots of discussing encoding and decoding. To be fair, it did leave me loving a good concept and wanting my photographs to mean something, but it didn't teach me much about the actual technical bits around taking good pictures.

What made me the photographer I am today came from trial and error and not being afraid to just experiment.

Walking into LCP on my first day, I ran into a student handing out copies of a magazine. With a copy in my hand, I asked them who published this and their answer was "we do". That blew my mind, the students had made this very polished and very readable magazine. On so many levels it opened up a whole new world to me. I realised you didn't need to be a multi-million dollar publishing house and I could learn to do things like that myself.

I immediately got involved with the student union, just to be part of the college magazine. Eventually I became the Communications Officer, in charge of putting together a team for the college mag. My first task was putting up signs around campus asking people if they wanted to get involved. In typical "buddy movie" style, Jefferson Hack, my now long-time collaborative partner, was the only person who turned up.

Along with a graphic design student, Ian Taylor, our first collaboration together was the student union magazine *Untitled*, which went on to win "Best Design" and "Best Photography" at the Guardian Student Media Awards.

Making *Untitled* definitely gave us the confidence to want to start something truly independent ourselves. So we thought about a name for ages and came up with *"Dazed & Confused"*, which was how we felt back then. The rest is history.

Full of youthful determination we got *Dazed* published. In true "London creative tradition" we survived by promoting nightclubs and tried to create our very own network of talent. We put together "nights", to get a couple of hundred quid, and that would be enough to get us through to the next week. All while helping us build and create a community of friends and collaborators.

In all honesty, back then, I didn't think we would last more than a few issues. Now, looking back, I'm pretty amazed as we've already passed *Dazed*'s 30th anniversary, and its readership and influence on culture is well beyond anything we could have imagined.

Those early years were great for experimentation. For me, just starting out, I was like a blank canvas. I was able to try new things, push photography and publishing conventions, and be provocative.

Because we were pretty naively fearless and there weren't financial or corporate constraints on what we were working on, we did things that ended up really changing culture.

You couldn't really feel it at the time, but we were lost in the moment. We were so sure of ourselves - almost blindly so. However, it was really from that time where I learnt that I love what I do, and I fell in love with the people around me - capturing them all on medium format film.

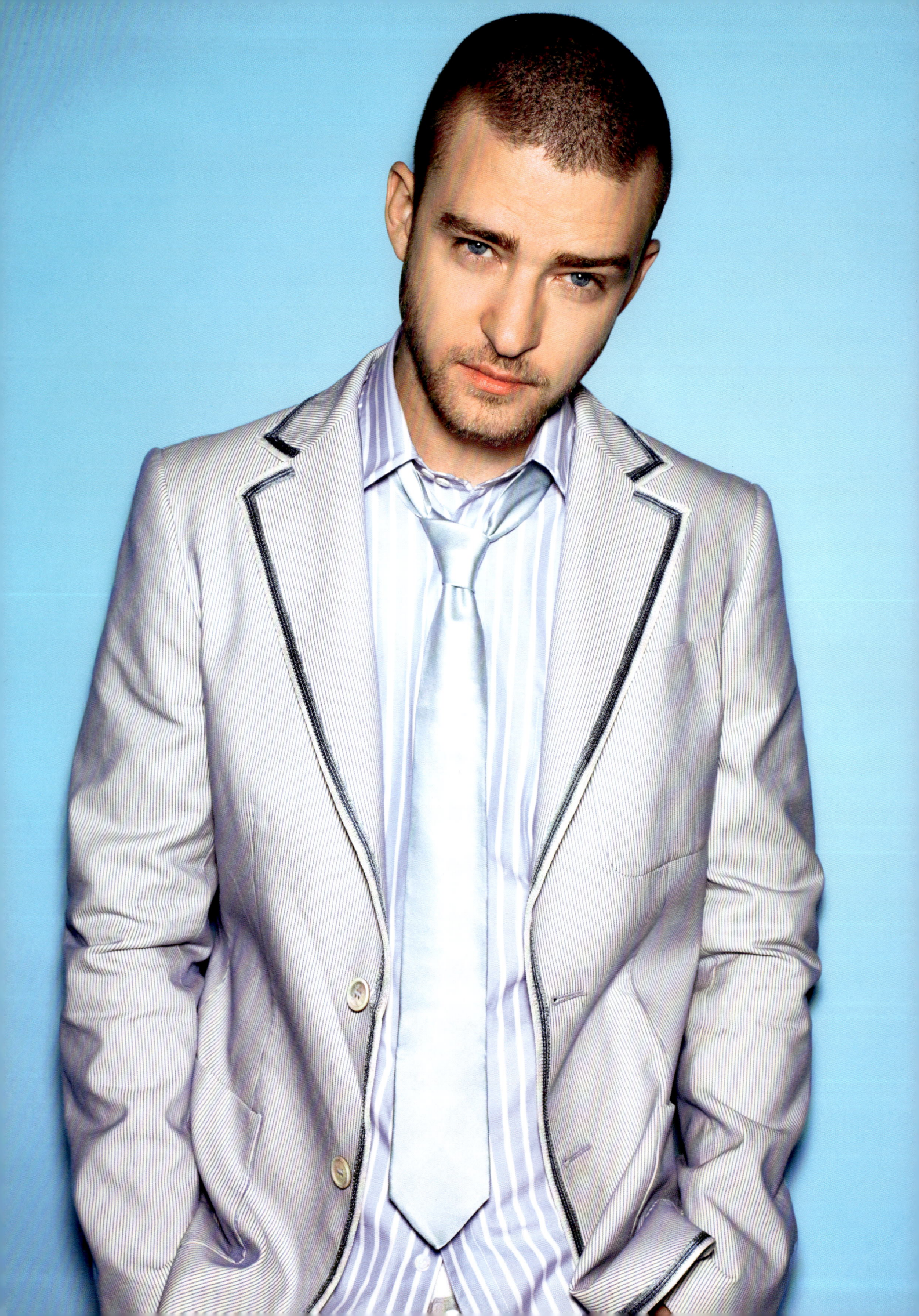

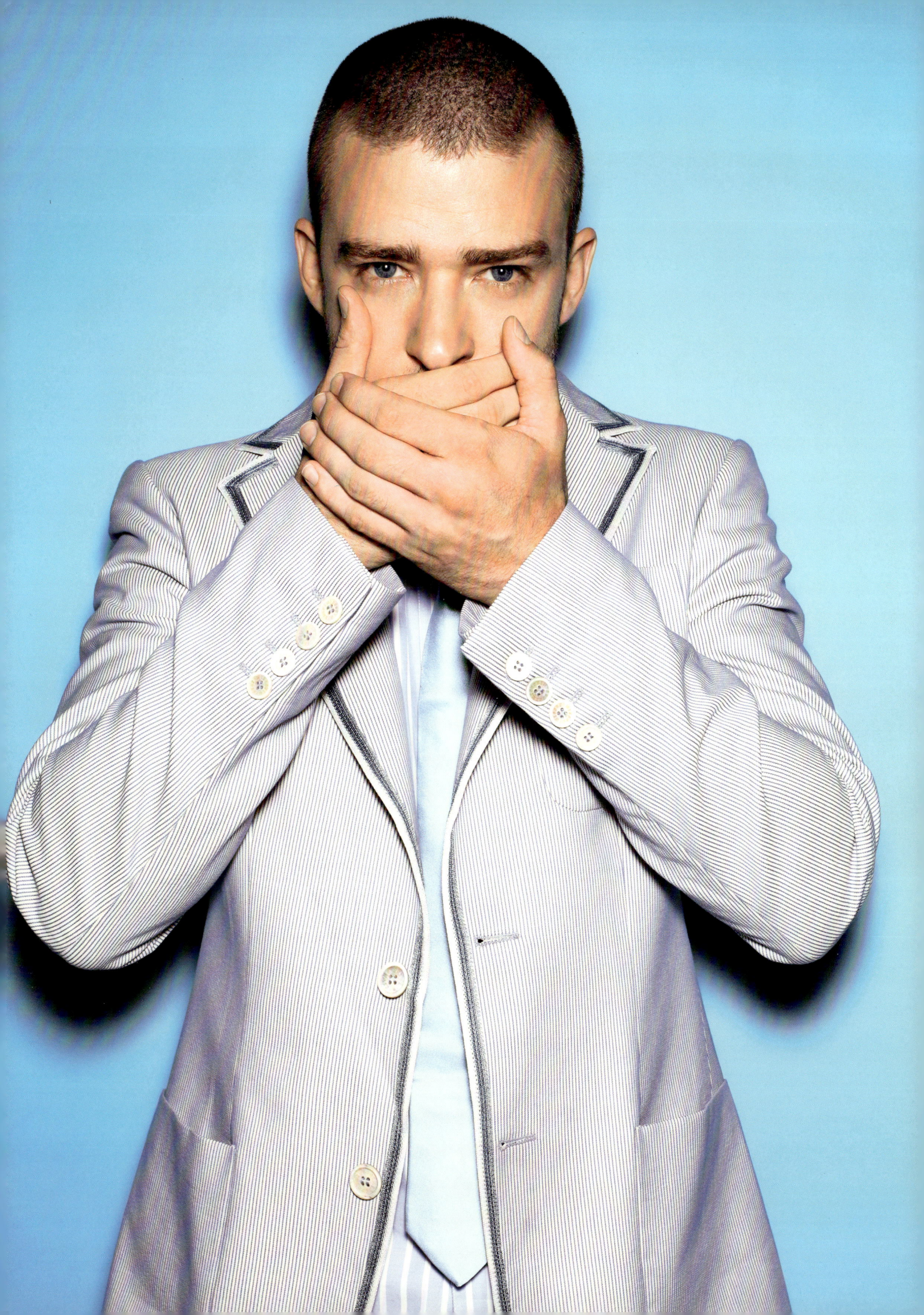

THE DAZED DECADES

BY ELLEN STONE

It says something about Rankin's photography, that after years of working with it, it still has the capacity to surprise me. There is a visceral gut response to opening a folder and finding your teenage idols staring back at you. Surreally they look exactly as you remember them; their eyes, their hair, their fashion, their stance… it takes you back to a moment in time when you thought they were the most important people on the planet.

It is in those moments when reality and fantasy collide. You are forced to realise that Rankin has been the eye behind so many memories. Think of your favourite young actor or pop star, find a picture of them in your head - invariably you are remembering a Rankin photo.

Dazed & Confused has been around for longer than I can remember. And, in its over three decades it has become firmly part of the popular consciousness.

Growing up, *Dazed & Confused* was the realm of friend's cooler older siblings. The type of magazine I imagined I may one-day graduate from the *NME* to reading myself. A status symbol for kids under-represented by the mainstream.

Yet, as an adult, I can see the impact on the minds and souls of the youth in a strangely deeper way. These northern teenagers could soliloquise with an adopted brash, yet romantic, provocatively honest language style - I see now that came, in part, courtesy of Jefferson Hack. They spoke of those London based brothers making sculptures with dildos for noses - Mark Sanders made that introduction. Their clothes looked nothing like the nice working class kids of generations before - Katie Grand and Alister Mackie's hands are evident there.

Dazed & Confused took these things, parts of rarefied culture, and gave them to the people. Indie actors, garage bands, grunge fashion, contemporary art and progressive sexual politics all snuck into the home via subscription.

At its heart though, it was the imagery that excited me first about *Dazed & Confused*: the images pasted on bedroom walls; the strange hot feeling you could get when Kate Moss winked at you from a torn out page; the heart palpitations of catching Justin Timberlake's eye on a news-stand.

I fell in love through Rankin's images. It's hard to look at those photographs and not feel like he fell in love when taking them too.

Every image said something. It said something about the model or it said something about culture. Looking at Alex Leigh biting into an aggressively large bar of chocolate, her clothes clipped onto her tiny frame, you know instantly the message of mistreatment and industry wide starvation of models.

Just as it would be impossible not to look at the *Feel It* cover images, and not immediately understand the celebratory inclusivity that Rankin and *Dazed & Confused* were promoting. Nothing is just surface - unless of course Rankin pointedly wanted it to be.

Rankin remains today a leading photographer; known for his portraiture, fashion shoots, advertising and conceptual works. But it was during his *Dazed* decades where he honed his craft.

Through the pages of *Dazed & Confused* he explored the different elements of his photography and created the personality he is today. To understand his work you need not look any further than the pages of his first magazine, a printed record of his thoughts and reactions to the world around him.

As a collection, these images showcase a unique perspective; one of someone who has seen everything and responded to it. These works form a manifesto about how to view the world, a political statement communicated not with words but with a camera lens. They speak of changing cultural norms and what it is to be famous. It is clear there is a way of seeing which Rankin has been sharing with us for over 30 years.

So here we explore five rules for viewing and acting. Across our chapters, "Feel It", "TV is Boring", "Accept No Imitations", "Emperor's New Clothes", and "Absolutely Flawless?", we share with you Rankin's way of being. Part self-help, part provocation, *The Dazed Decades* are a map for existence expressed through popular culture.

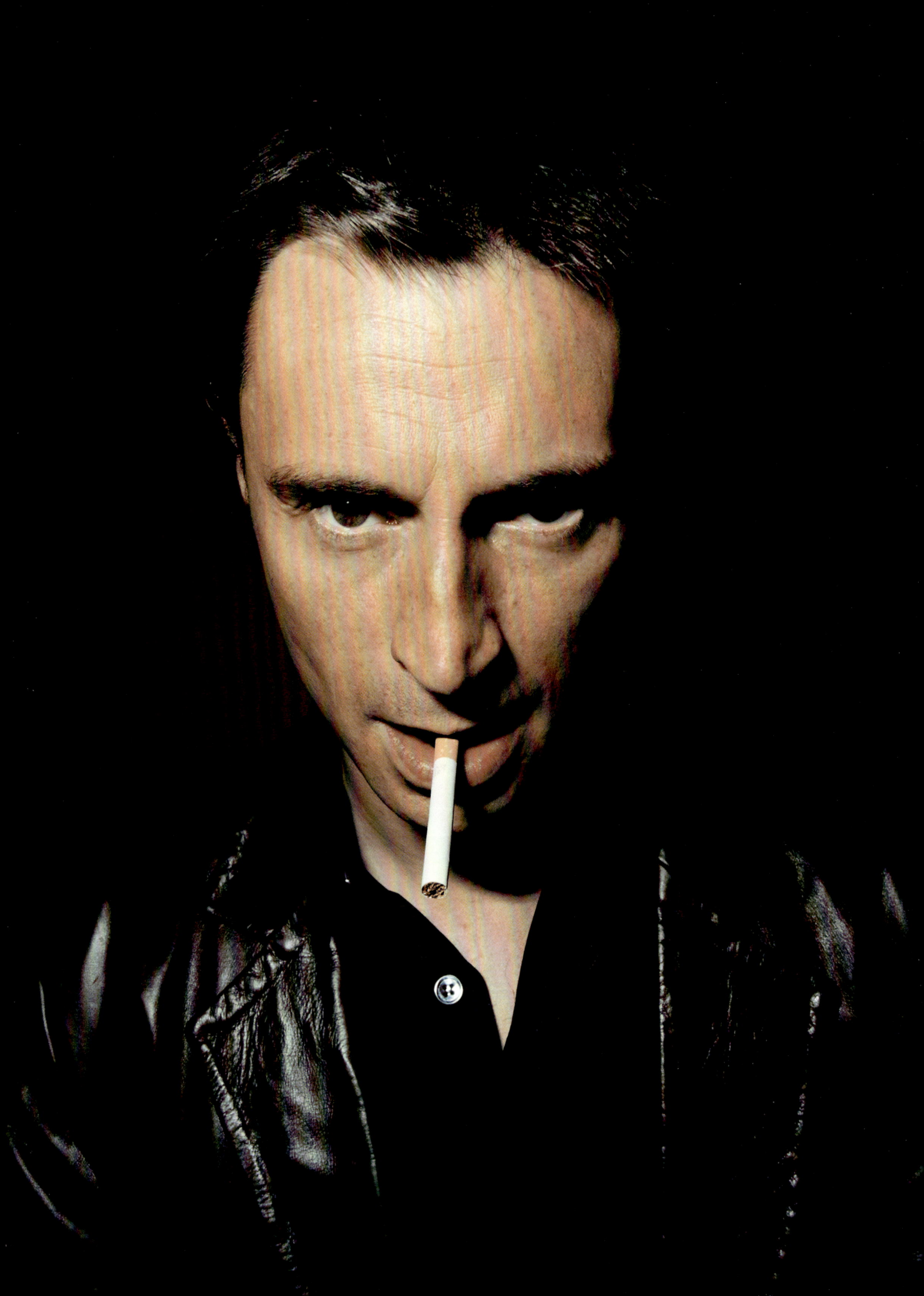

CONTENTS

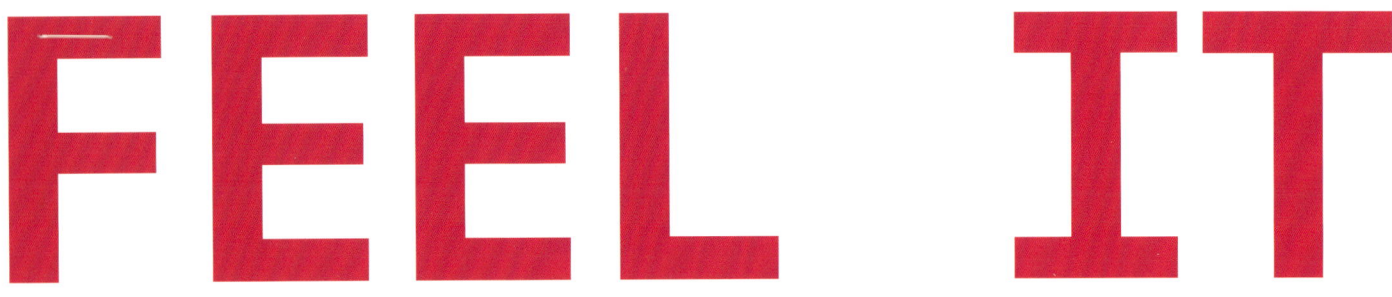

EMOTE/ENGAGE/CRITIQUE/WINCE/ LAUGH/CRY/SEE IT/SAY IT...

FEEL IT

The term "emotive" can suggest a form of acrid sentimentality, reminiscent of images adorning Hallmark greetings cards. But then there is Rankin's take on being emotive. To look at his work is to understand that emotion is not a dirty word.

With the seminal covers of issue 63, Rankin asked the viewer to *Feel It*. With images of boys kissing boys and girls kissing girls, Rankin asked you to feel their passion, but also, to feel the change in the air. It was a dawn of a new millennium, and the dawn of openly liberal social norms. Bold in their simplicity, the images critiqued antiquated notions of what can and should be shown.

But his love affair with emotional resonance did not begin in the year 2000. Emotion links images from far across his photographic career. In 1995 Rankin asked models to cry, a simple reversal of what is expected in a photograph: "say cheese" and smile.

Across the 90's, as models starved themselves and enacted forms of torture to appear hairless, poreless

and "perfect", Rankin put those images centre stage and undercut them against images of real people with extravagant style.

But it is his images of disaffected youth which pack the largest punch for the audience. Starting as Thatcherism bled into Major's government, Rankin and *Dazed & Confused* found the disenfranchised lost boys; whether it was the teens and tweens hanging out in a broken post-industrial Bradford, or David Newby and Jimmy Dixon isolated and alone in the busy streets of London. Their youthful masculinity becomes intertwined with a breakdown of working Britain.

In *Surveillance*, from 1996, two teenage boys, who later would have been called by the tabloid press members of the "ASBO Generation", break into cars and play on the streets. Captured as though through CCTV, Rankin is not asking you to see criminals, but finds instead the moments of camaraderie. These images ask you to remember back to when you yourself were a teenager, and you too revelled in the strength of being seen and treated as an equal by an older sibling or friend.

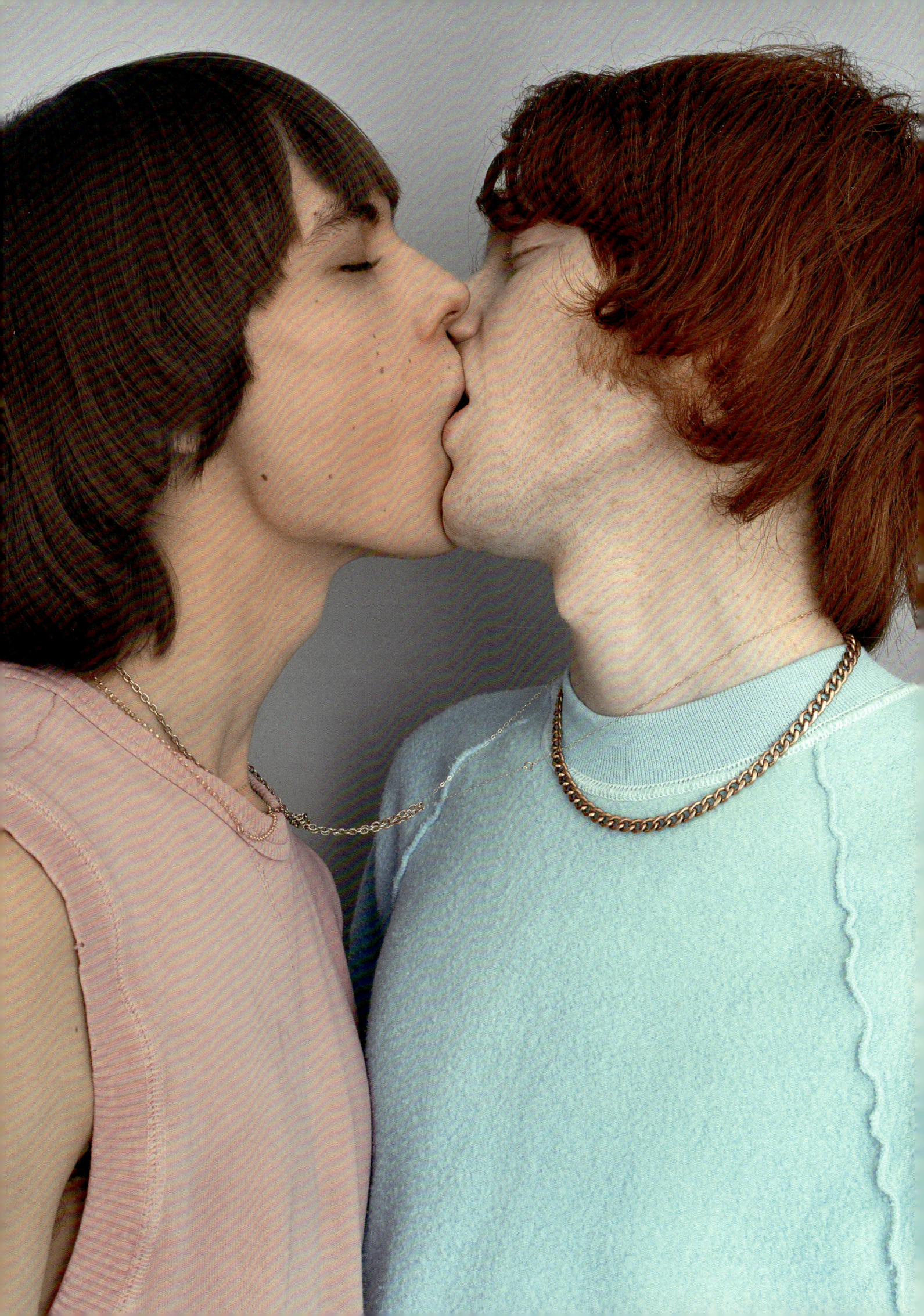

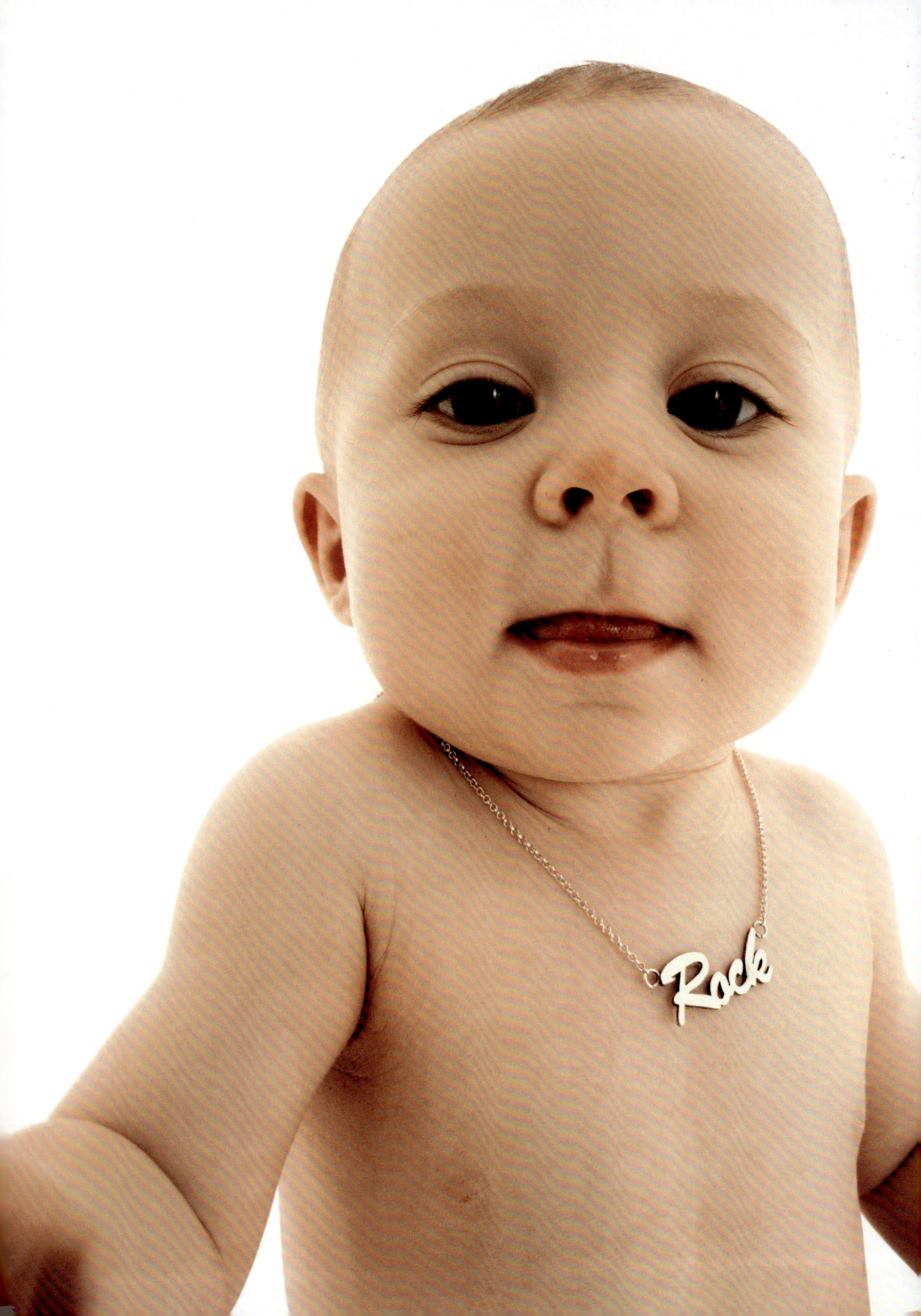

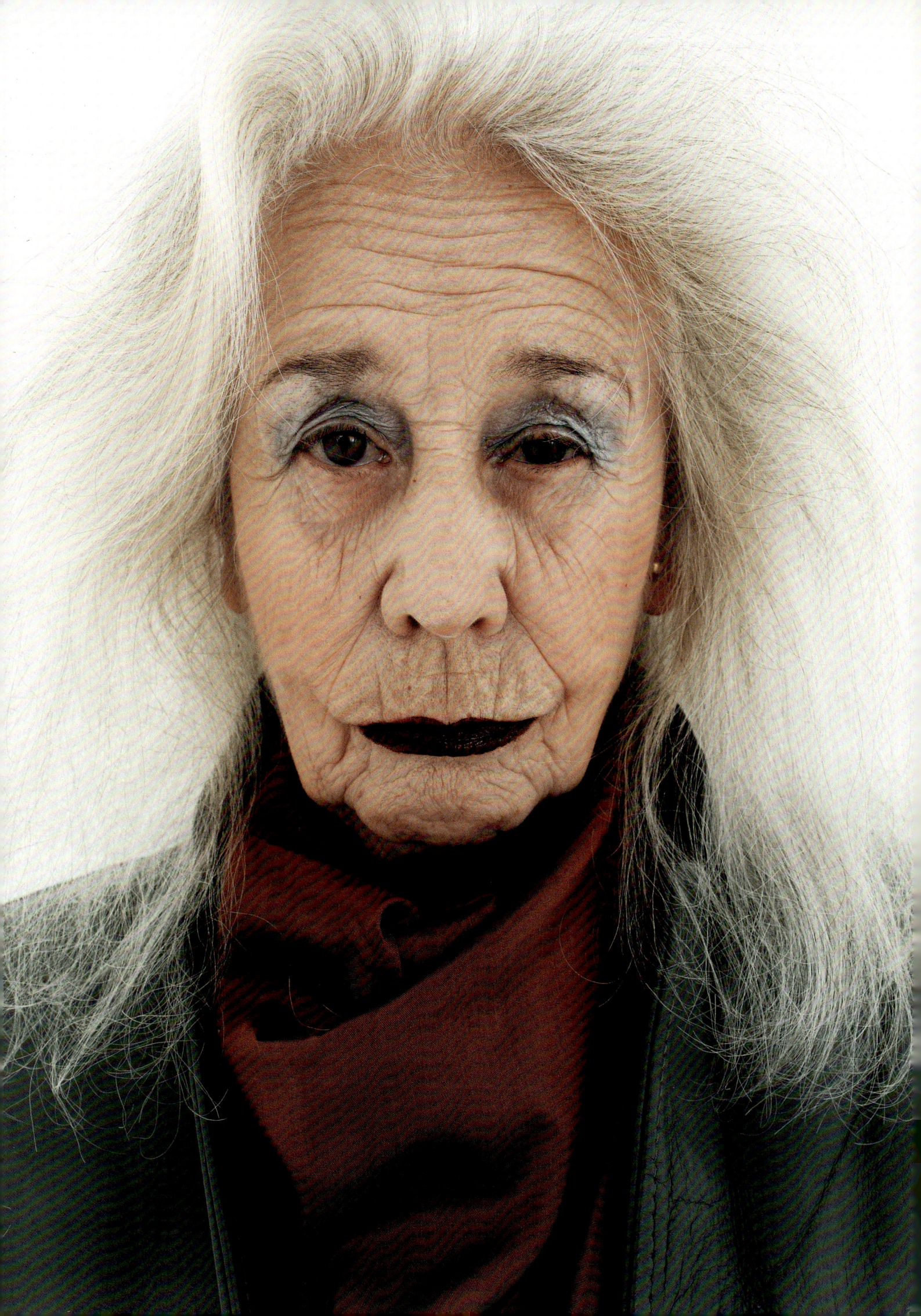

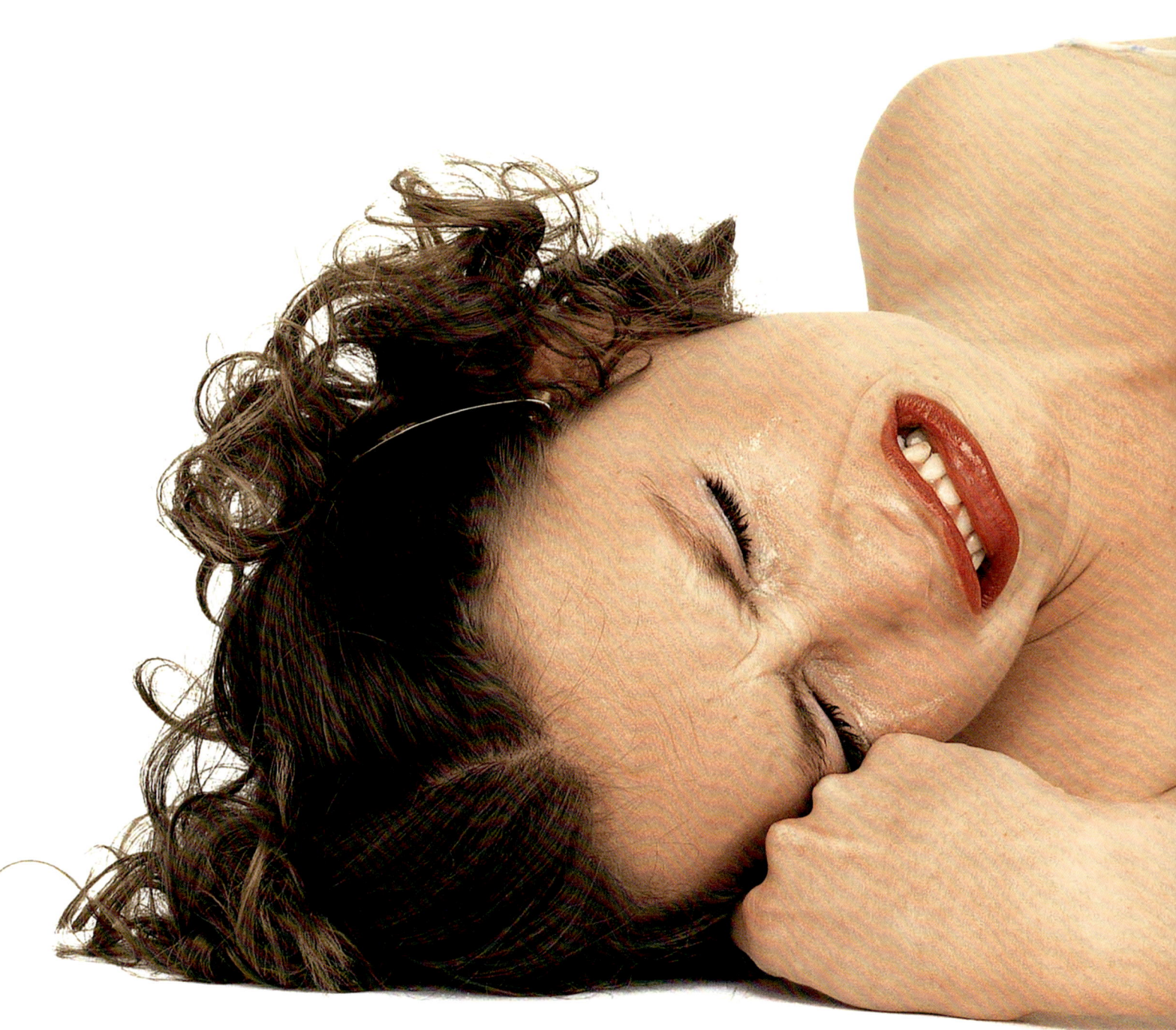

Weep, Issue 10, 1995

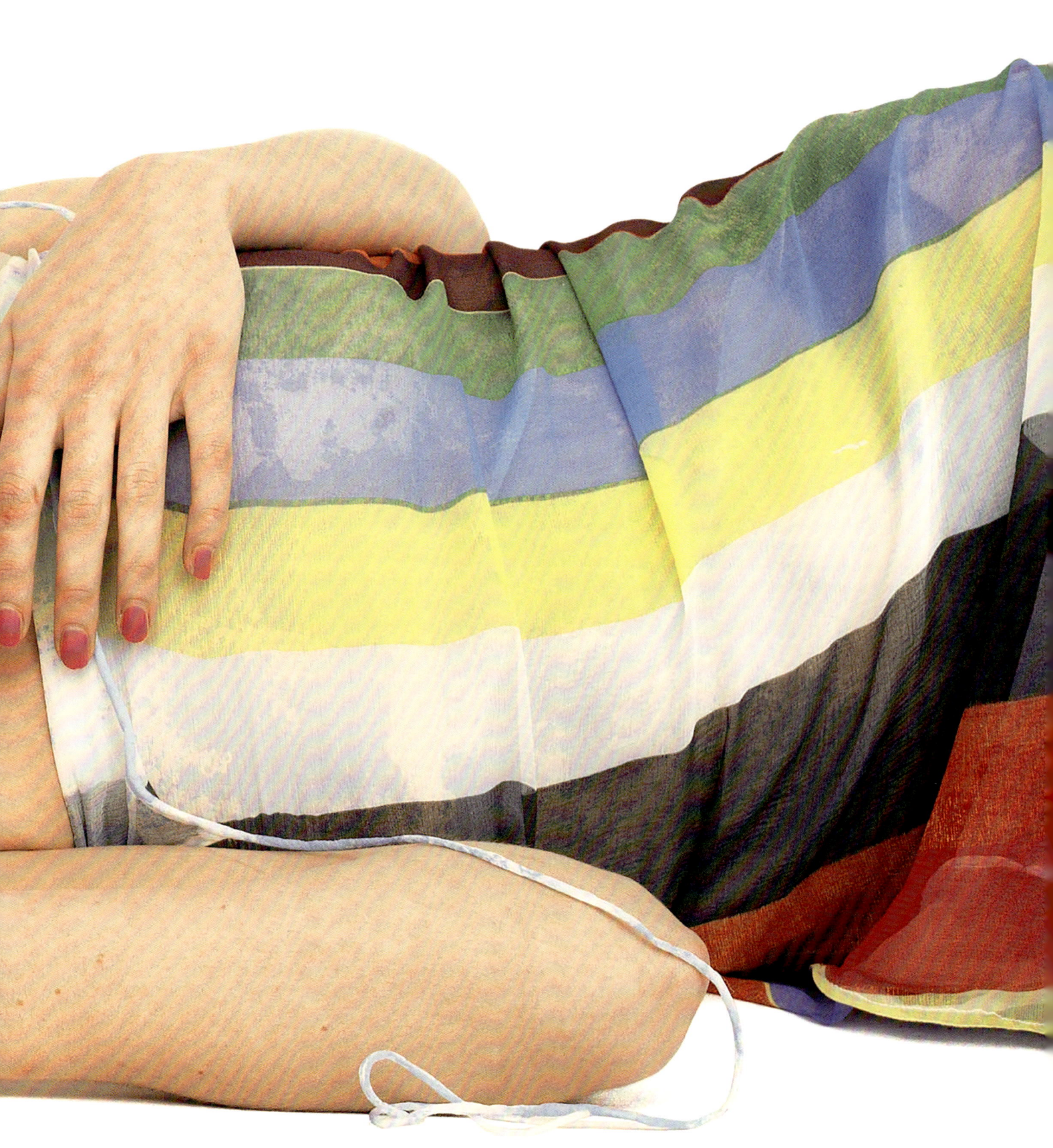

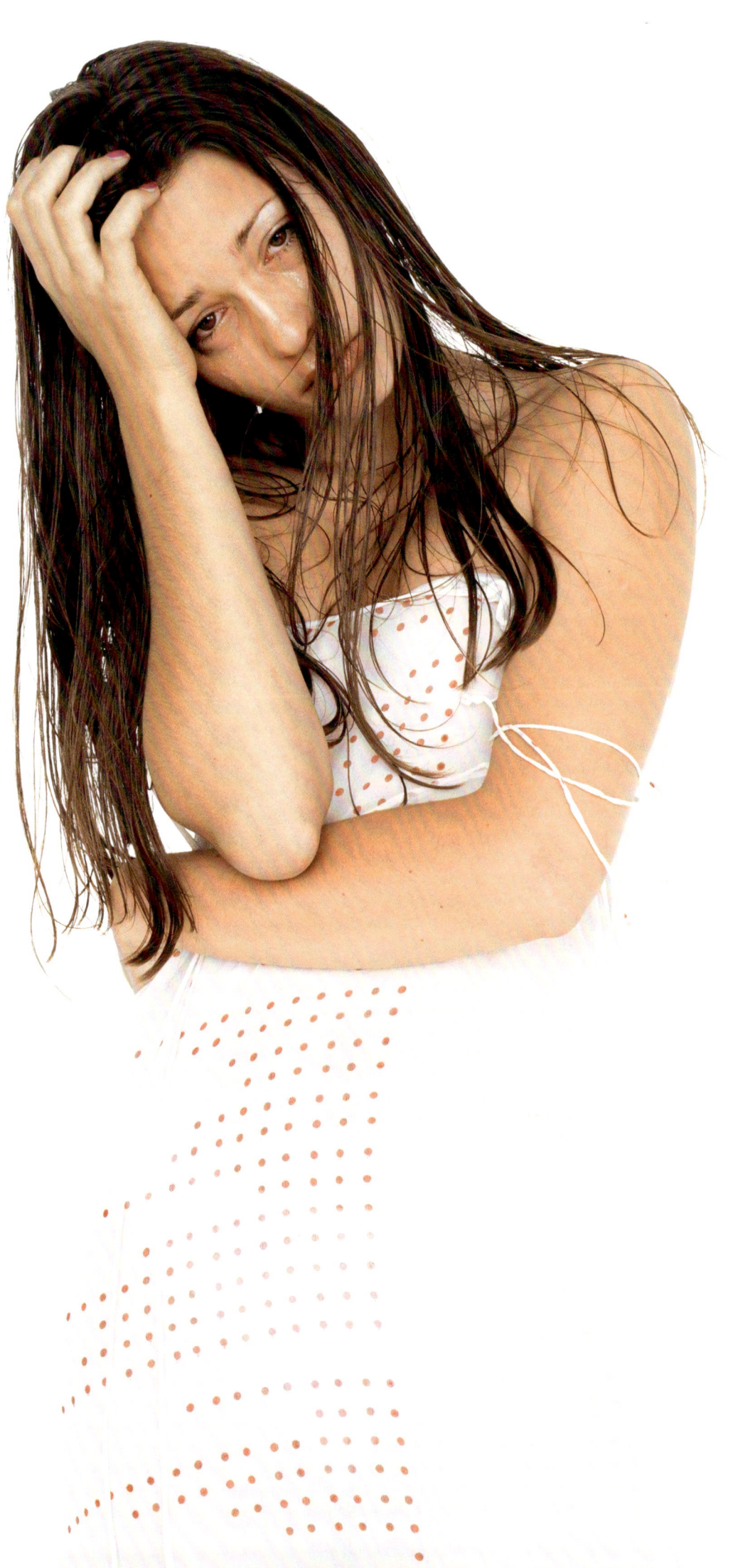

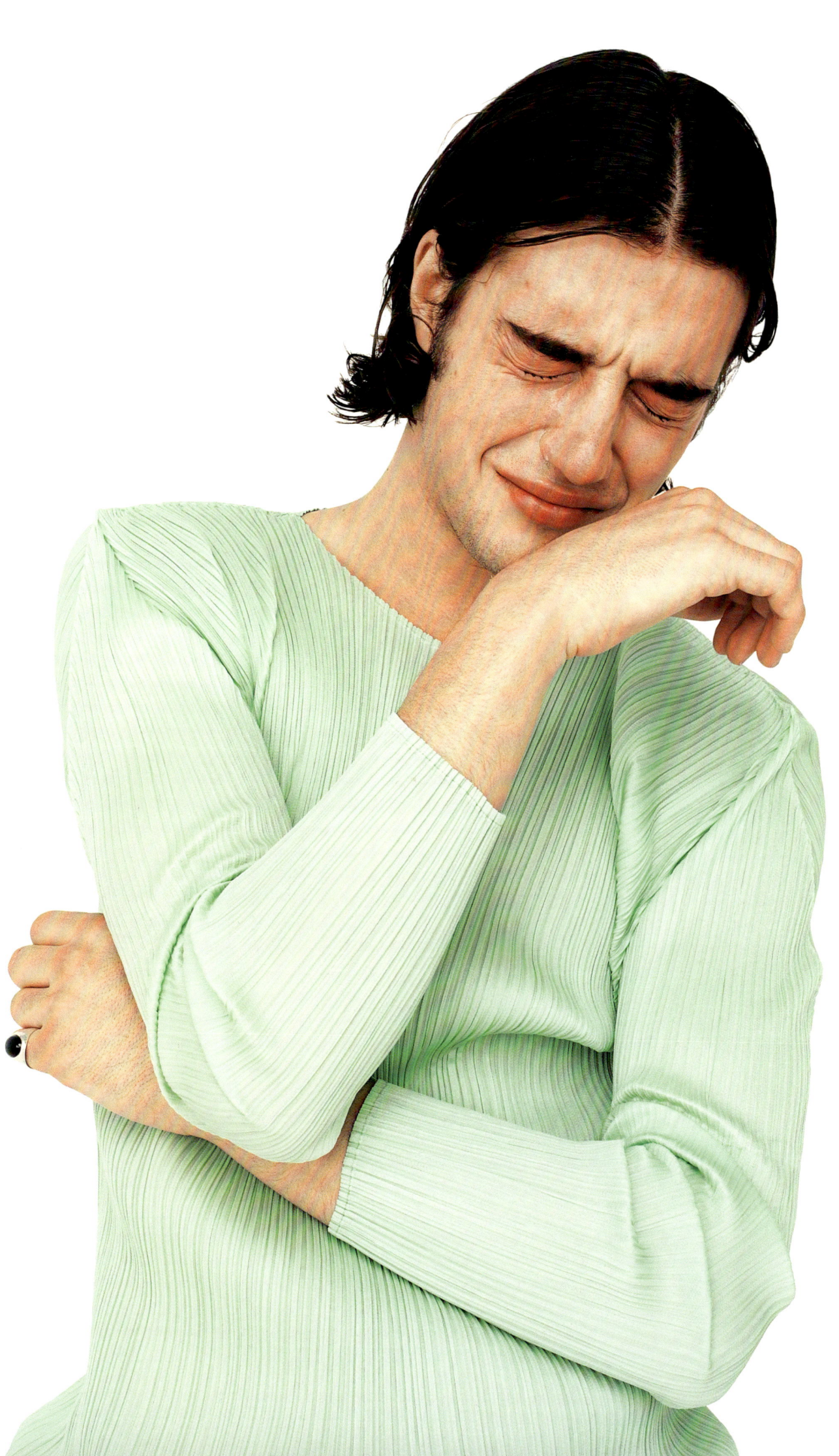

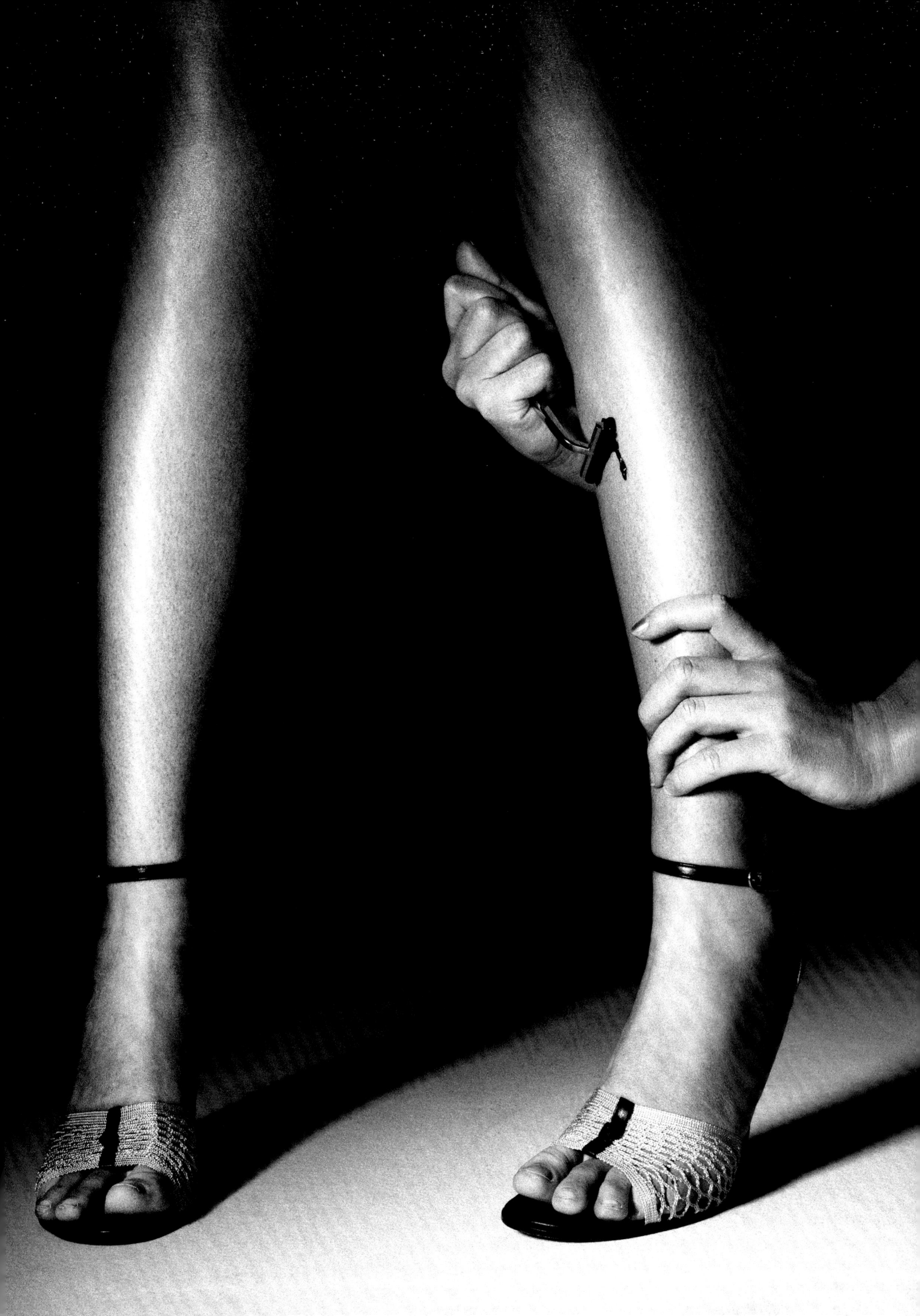

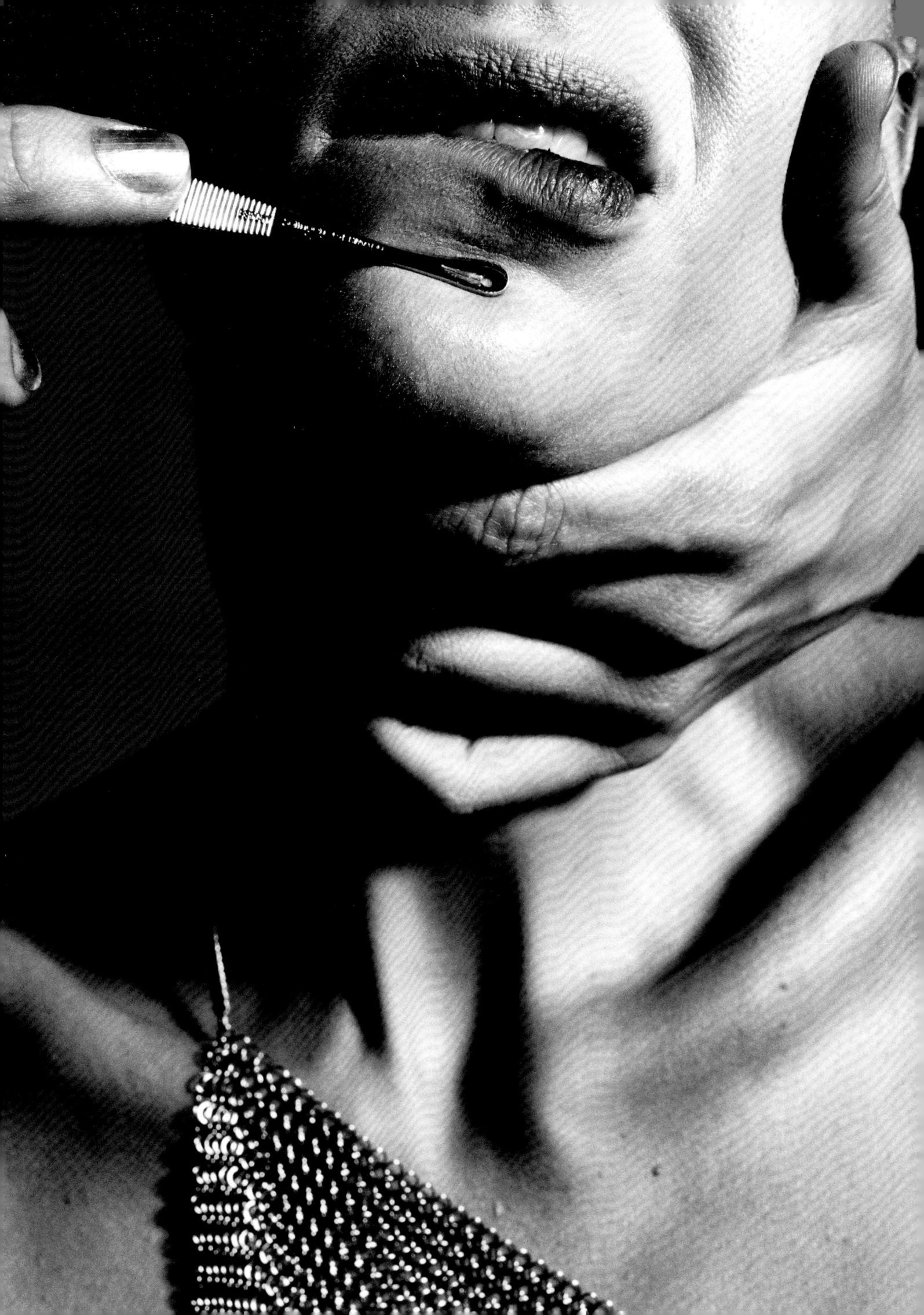

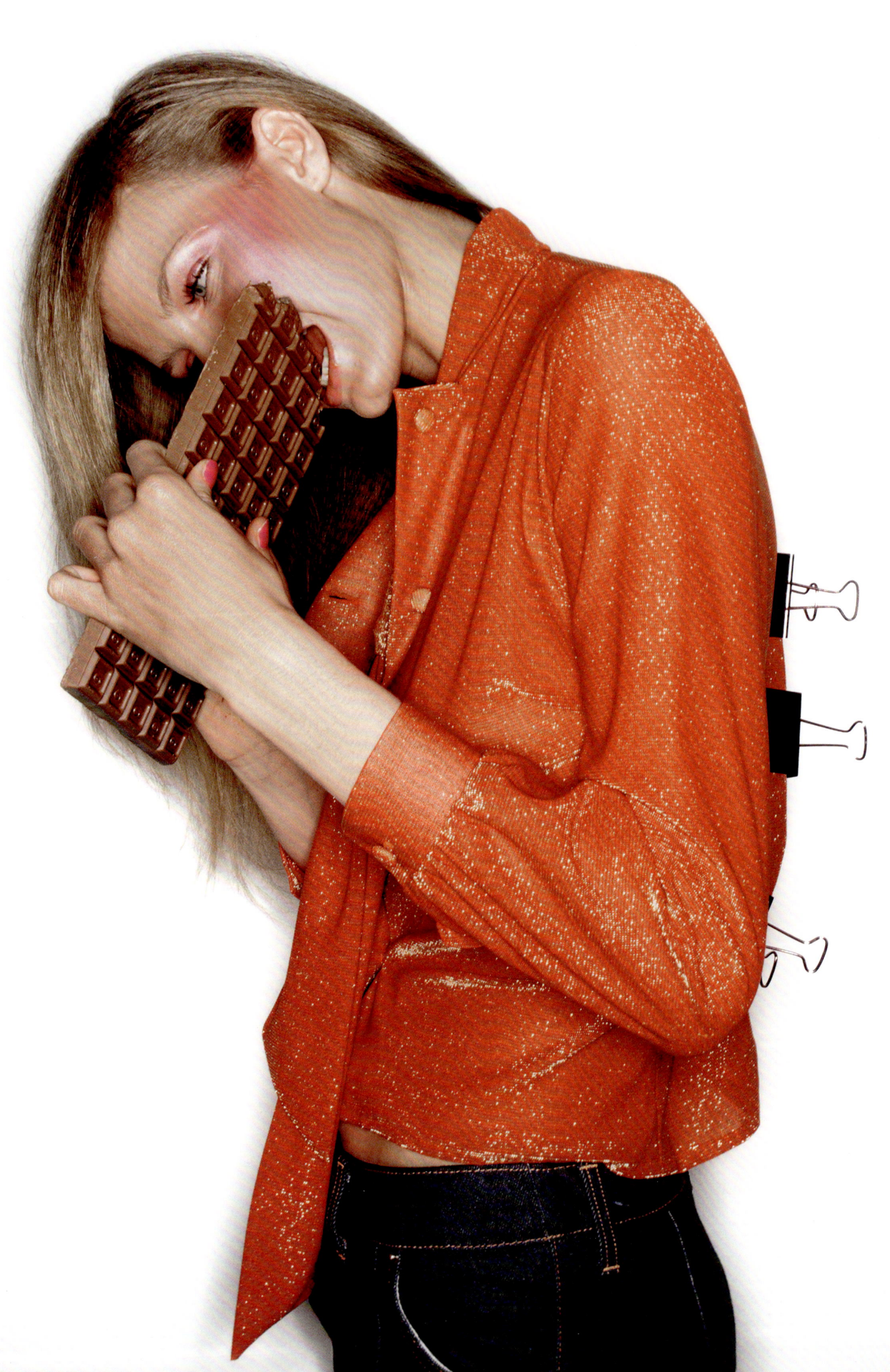

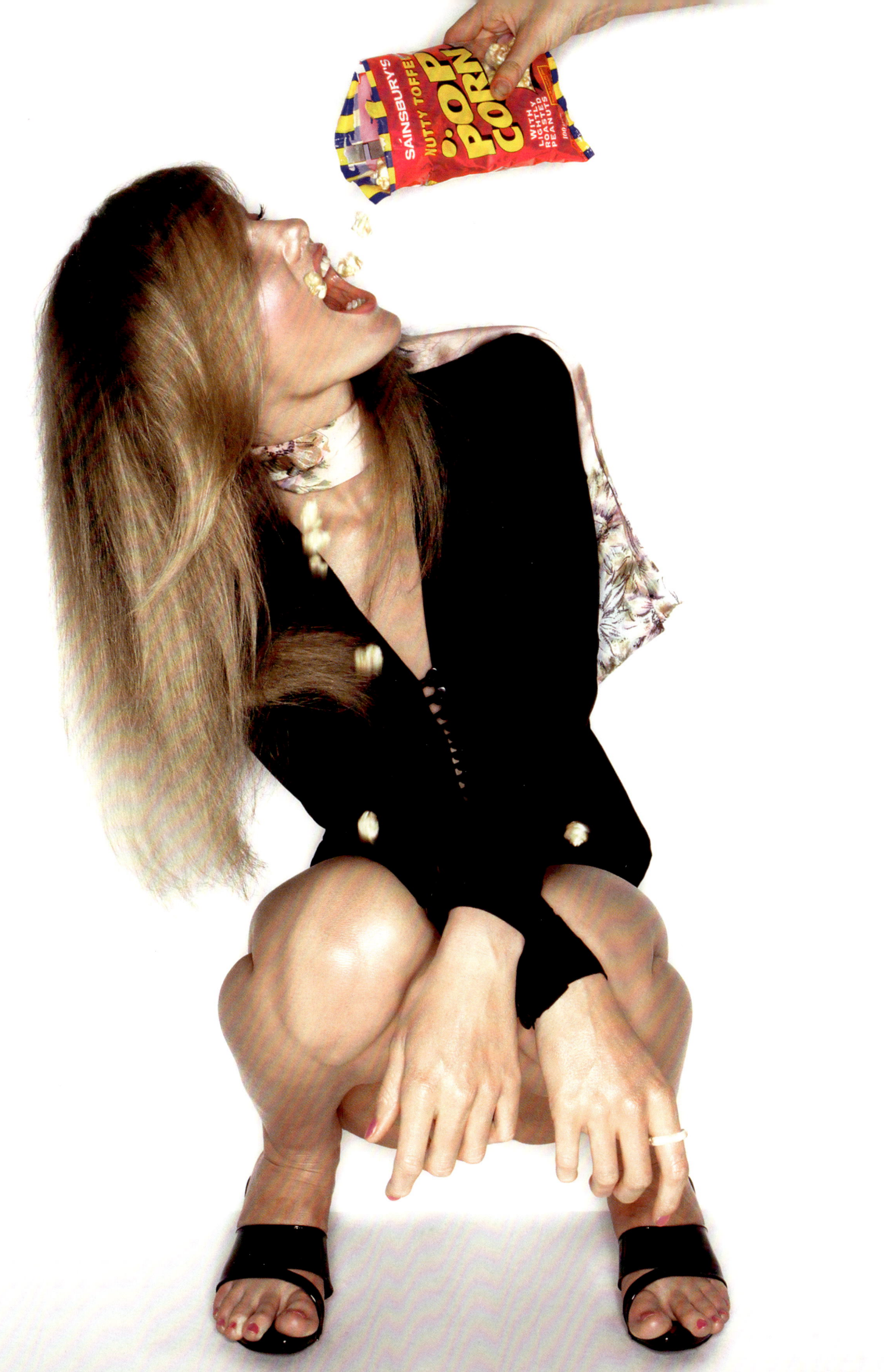

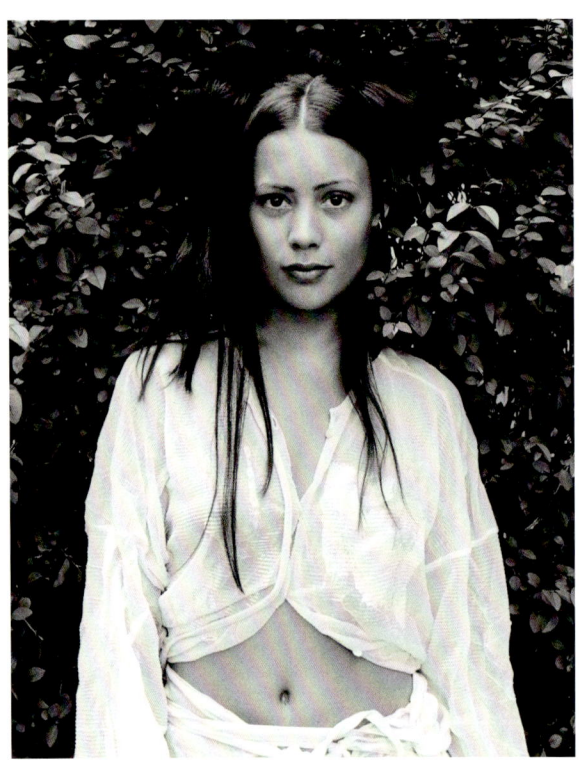

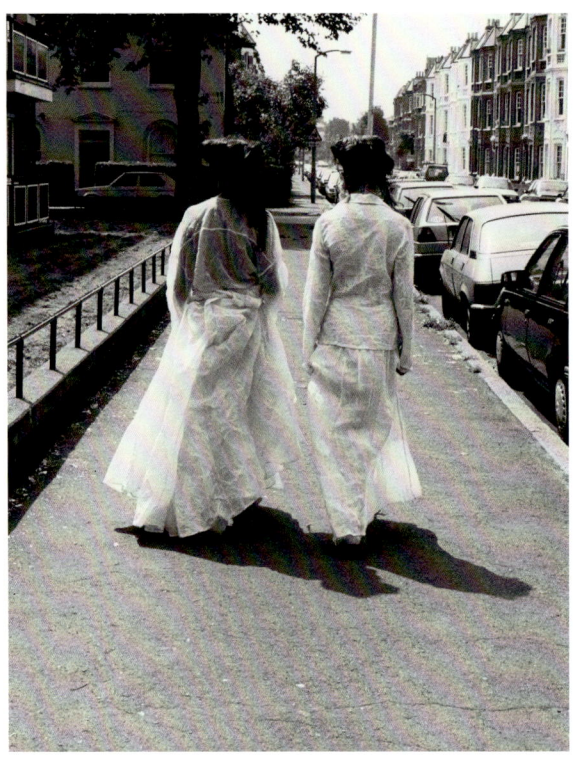

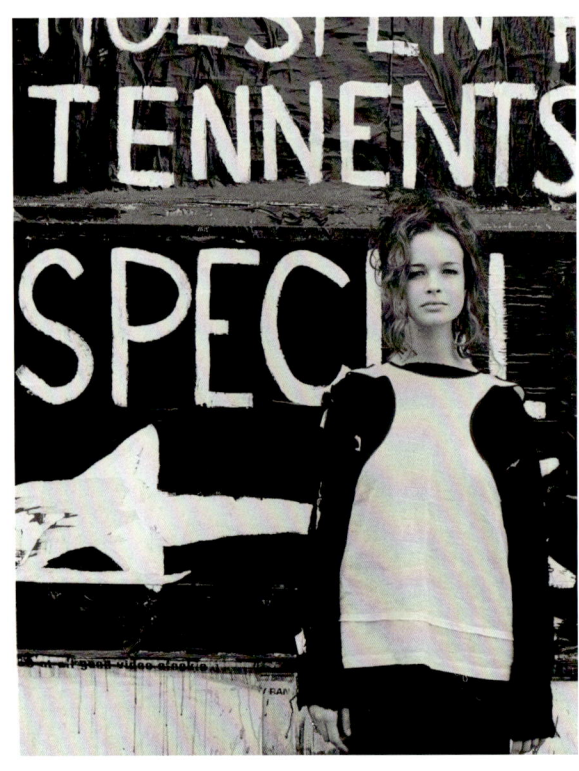

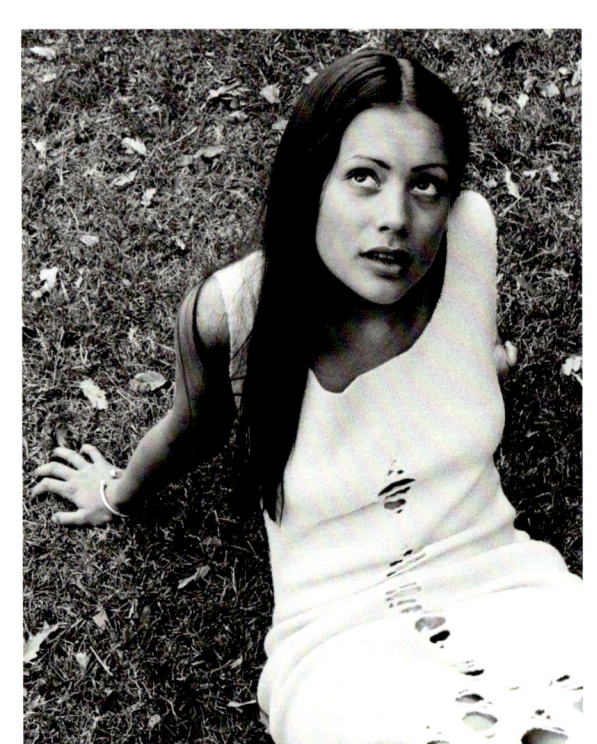

Complete and Unabridged, Issue 5, 1993

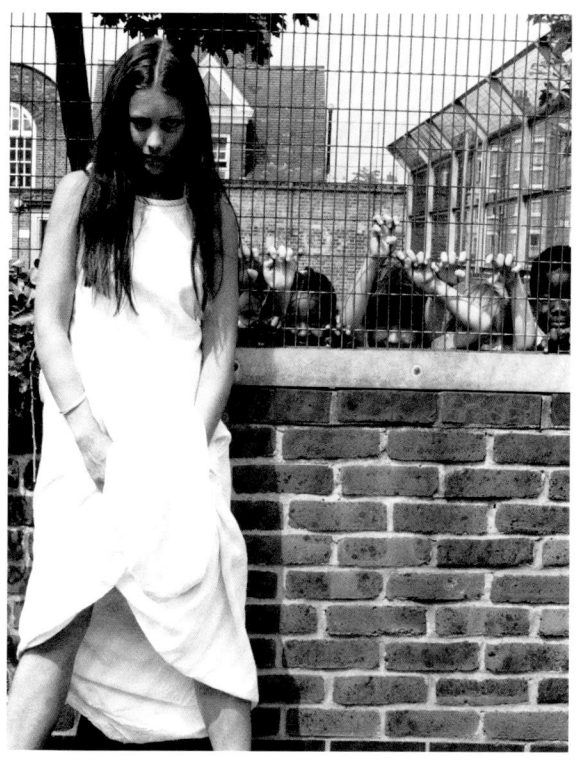

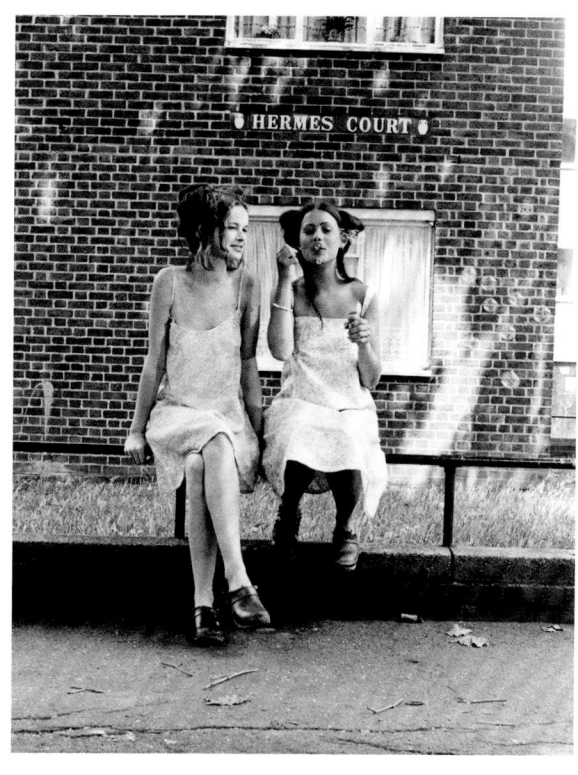

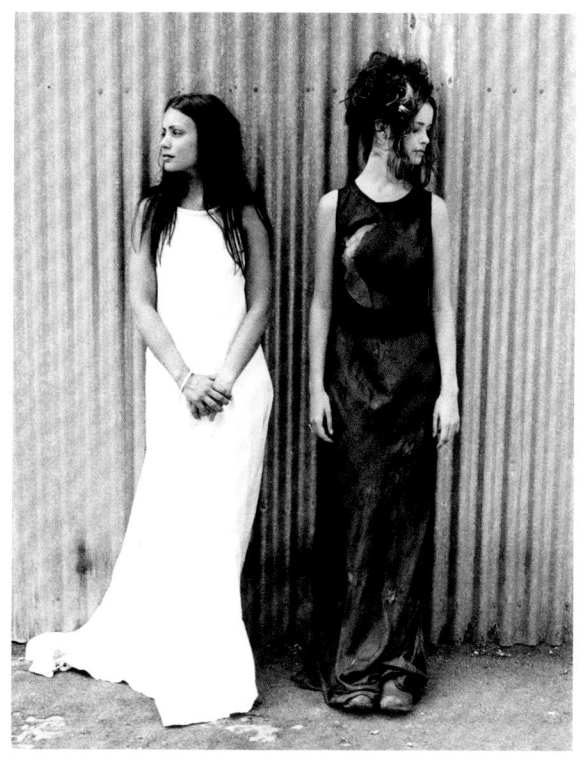

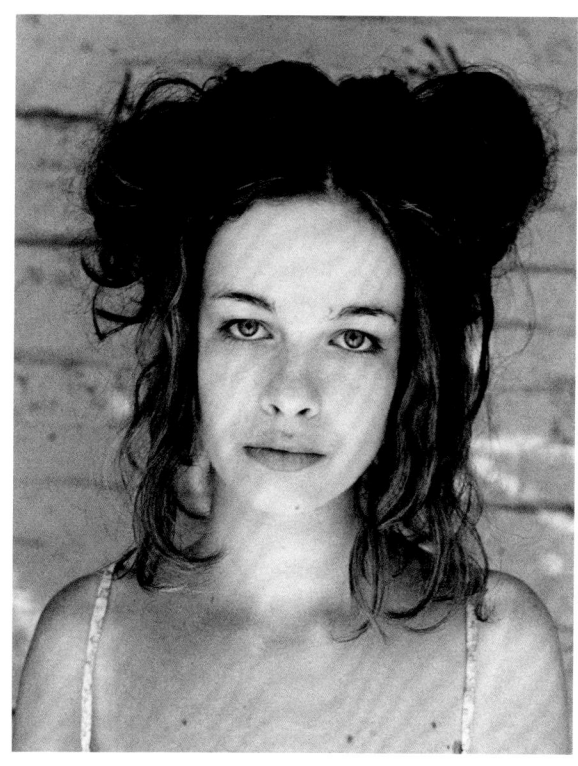

Next Pages - Also Available in Orange, Issue 5, 1993

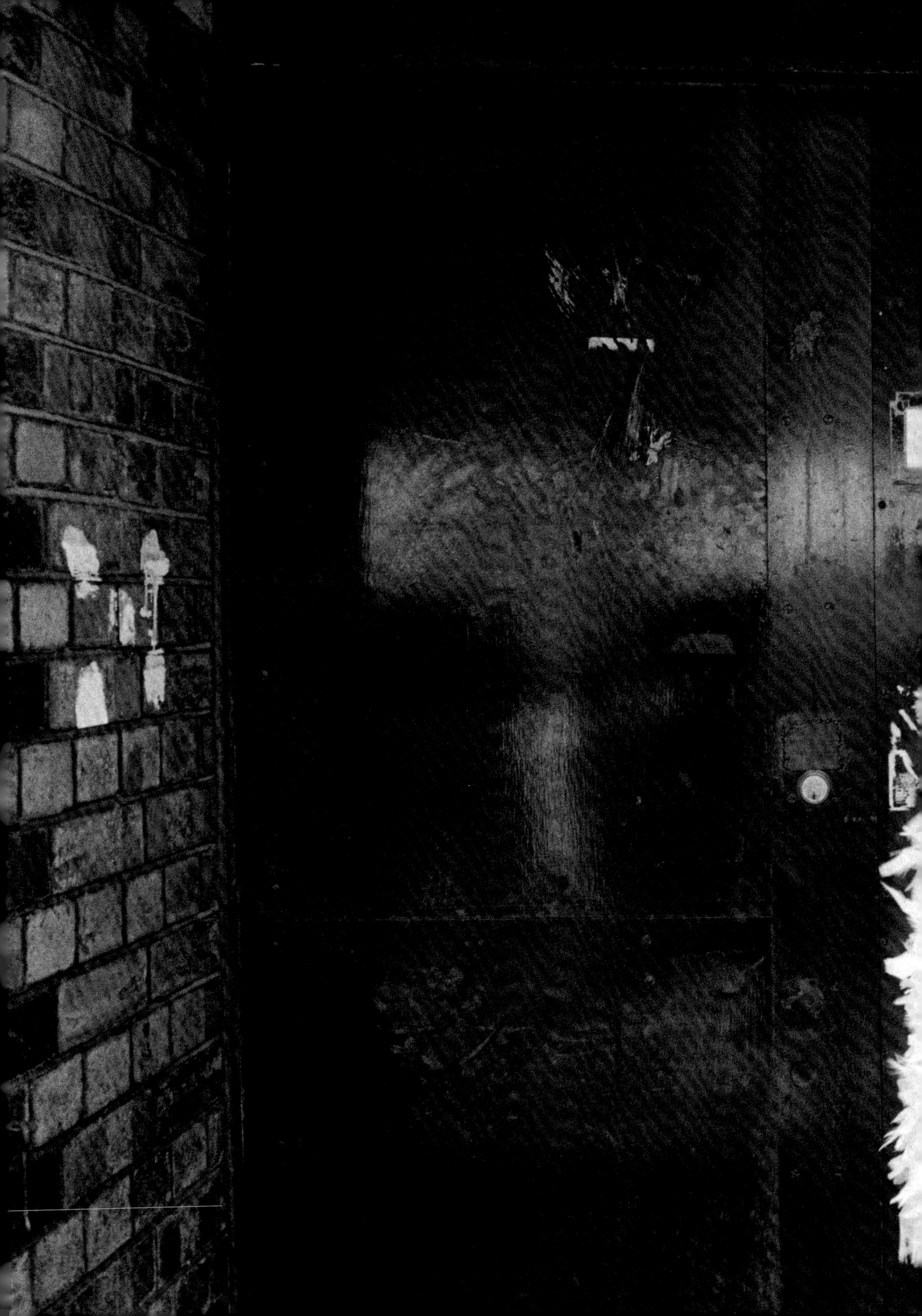

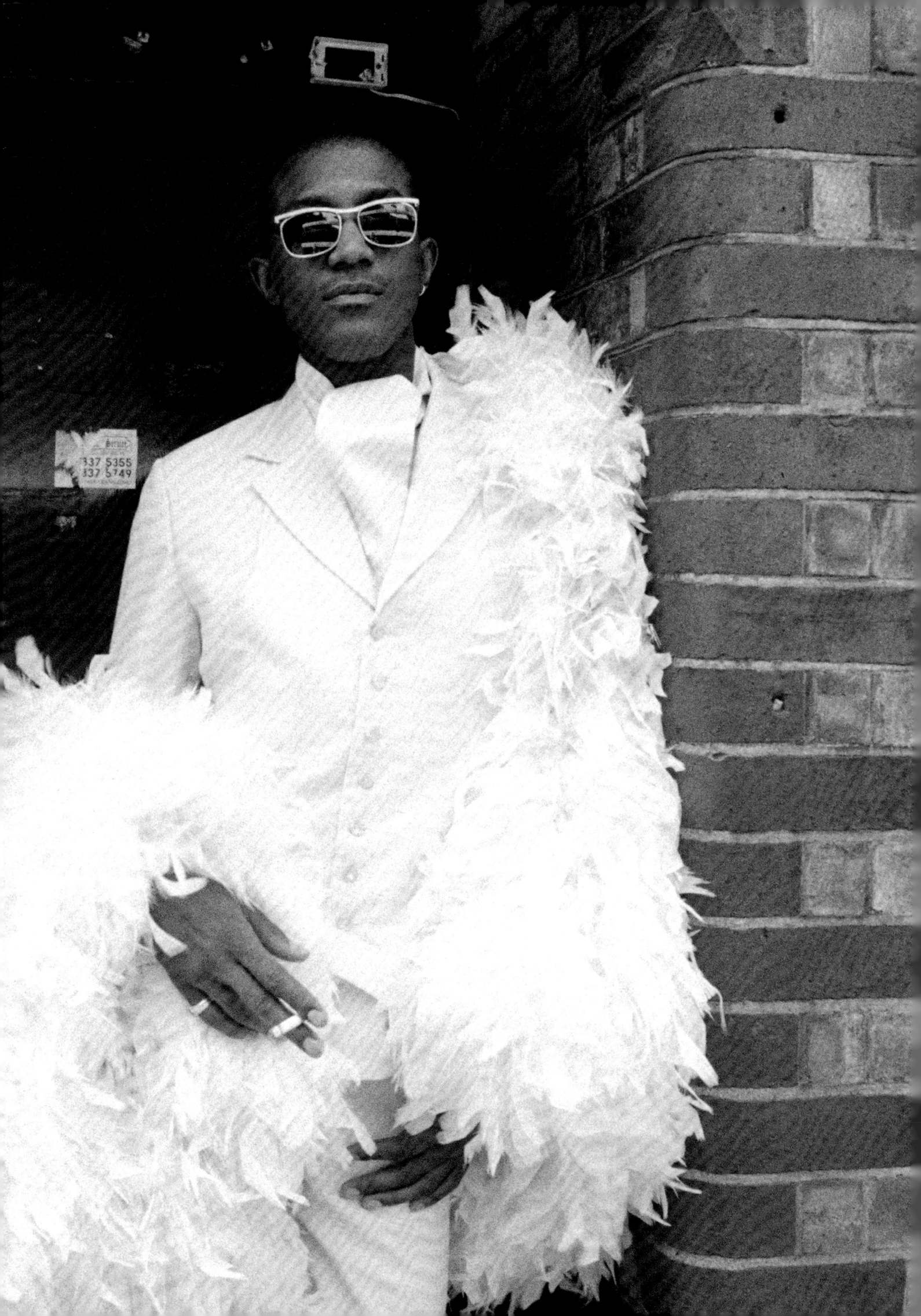

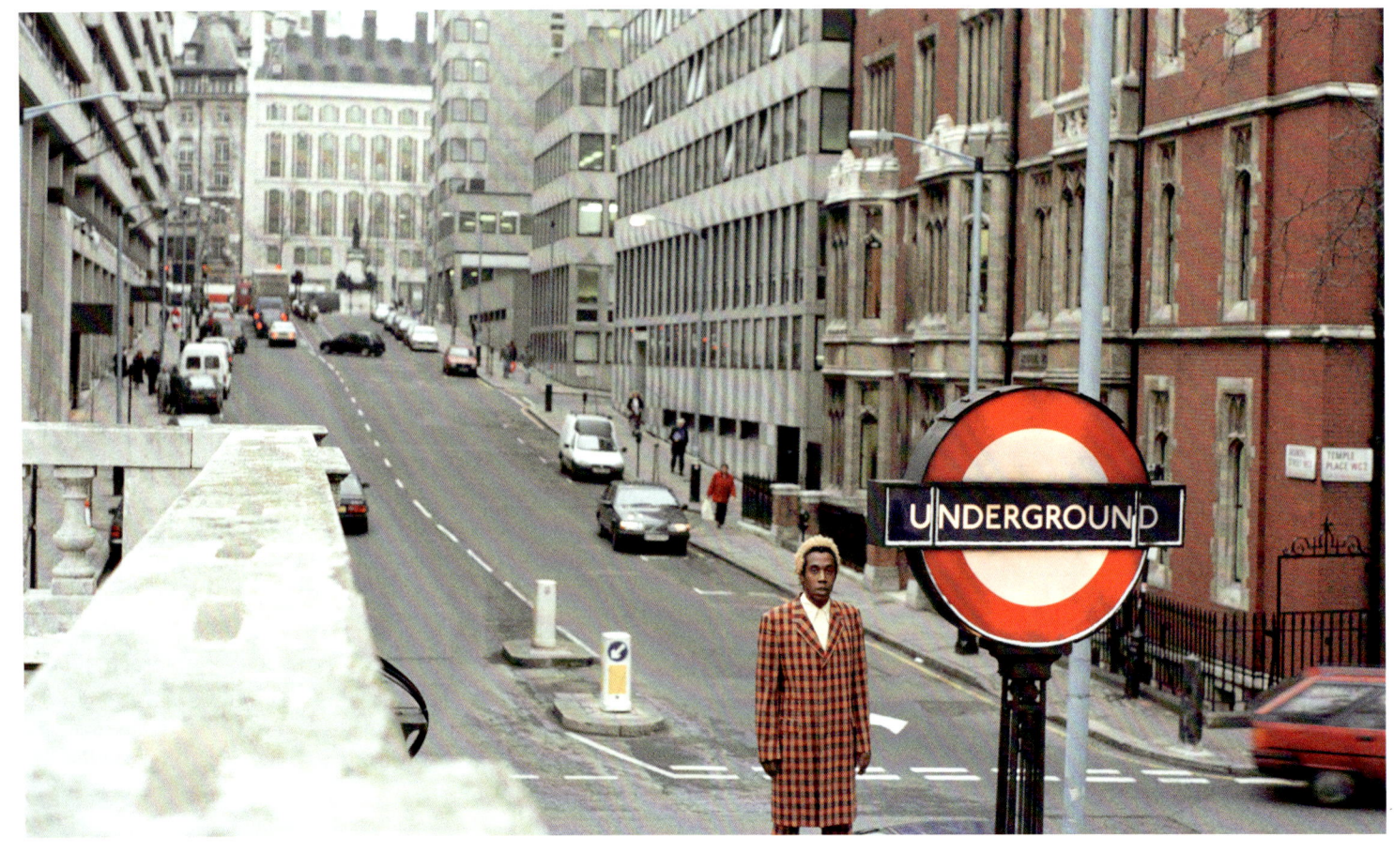

Circle Line, Issue 7, 1994

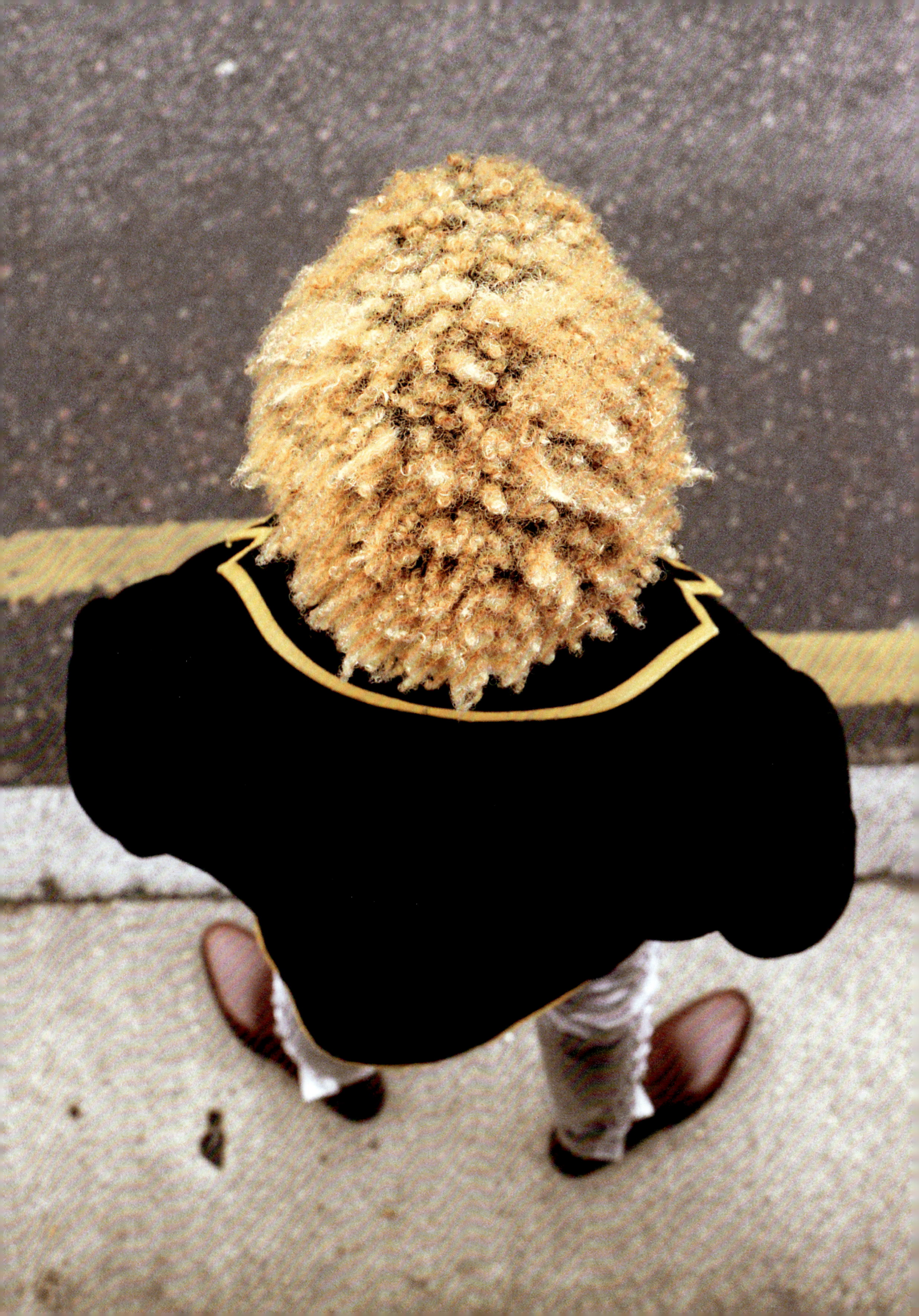

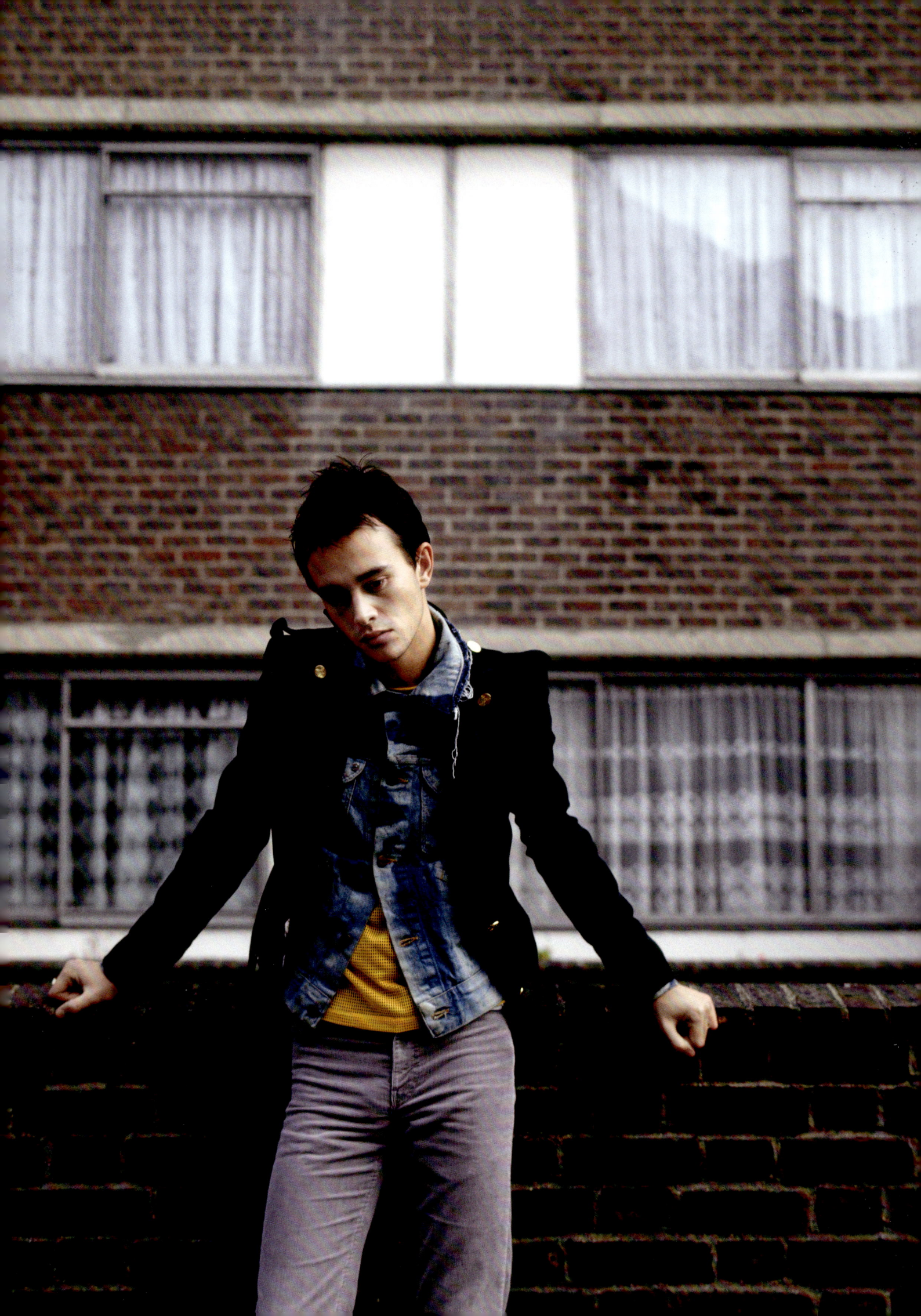

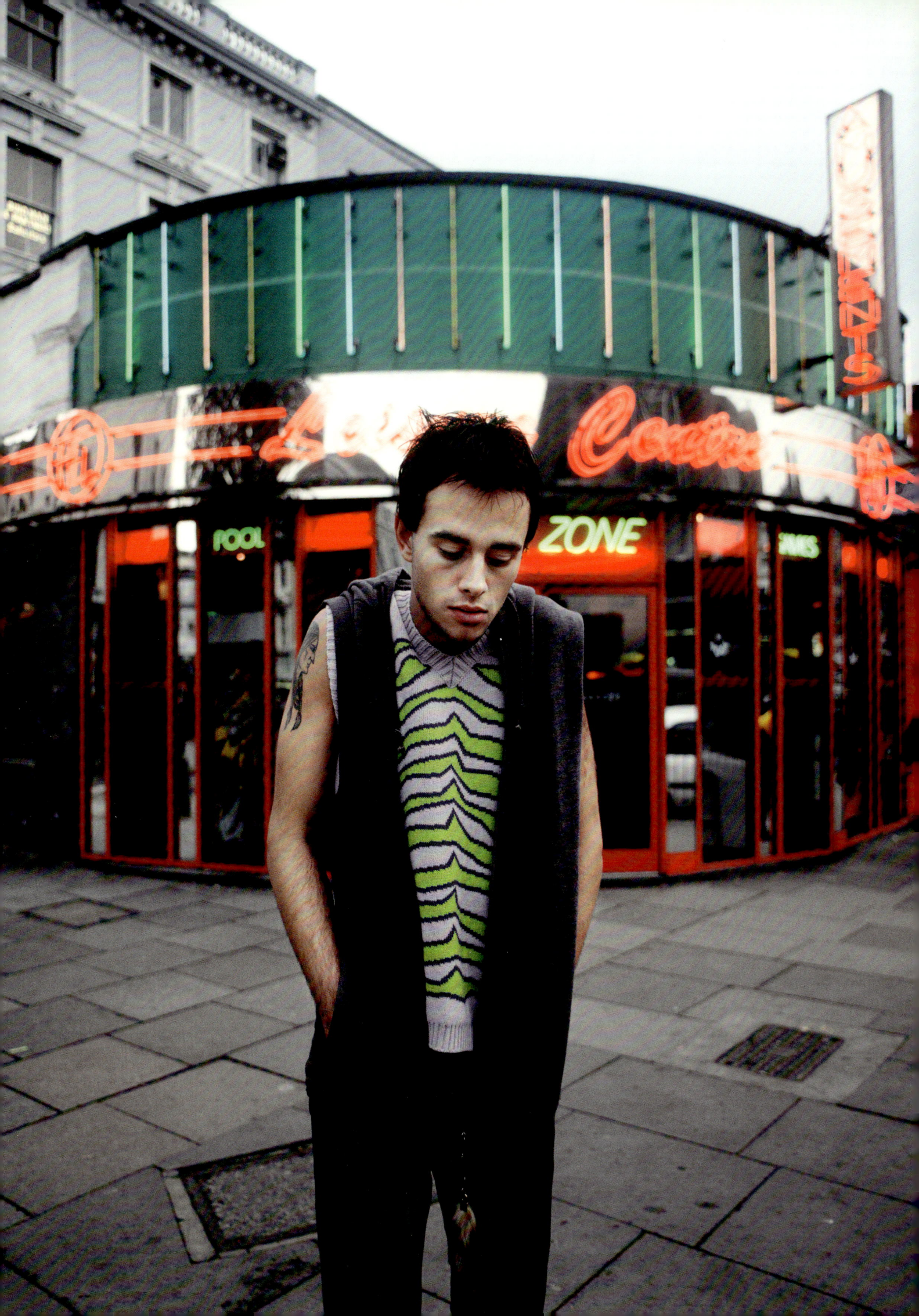

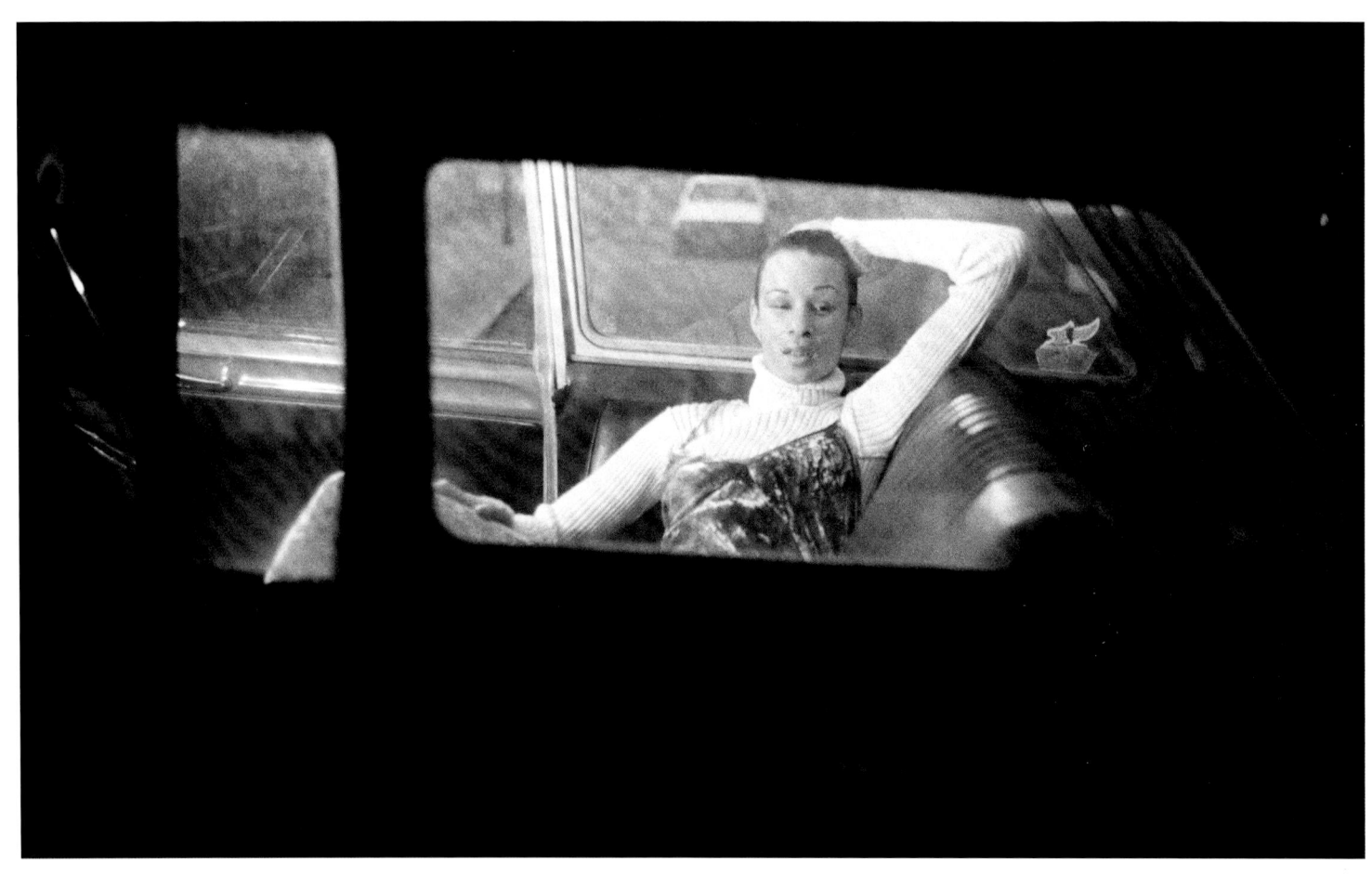

Peeping Tom, Issue 6, 1993

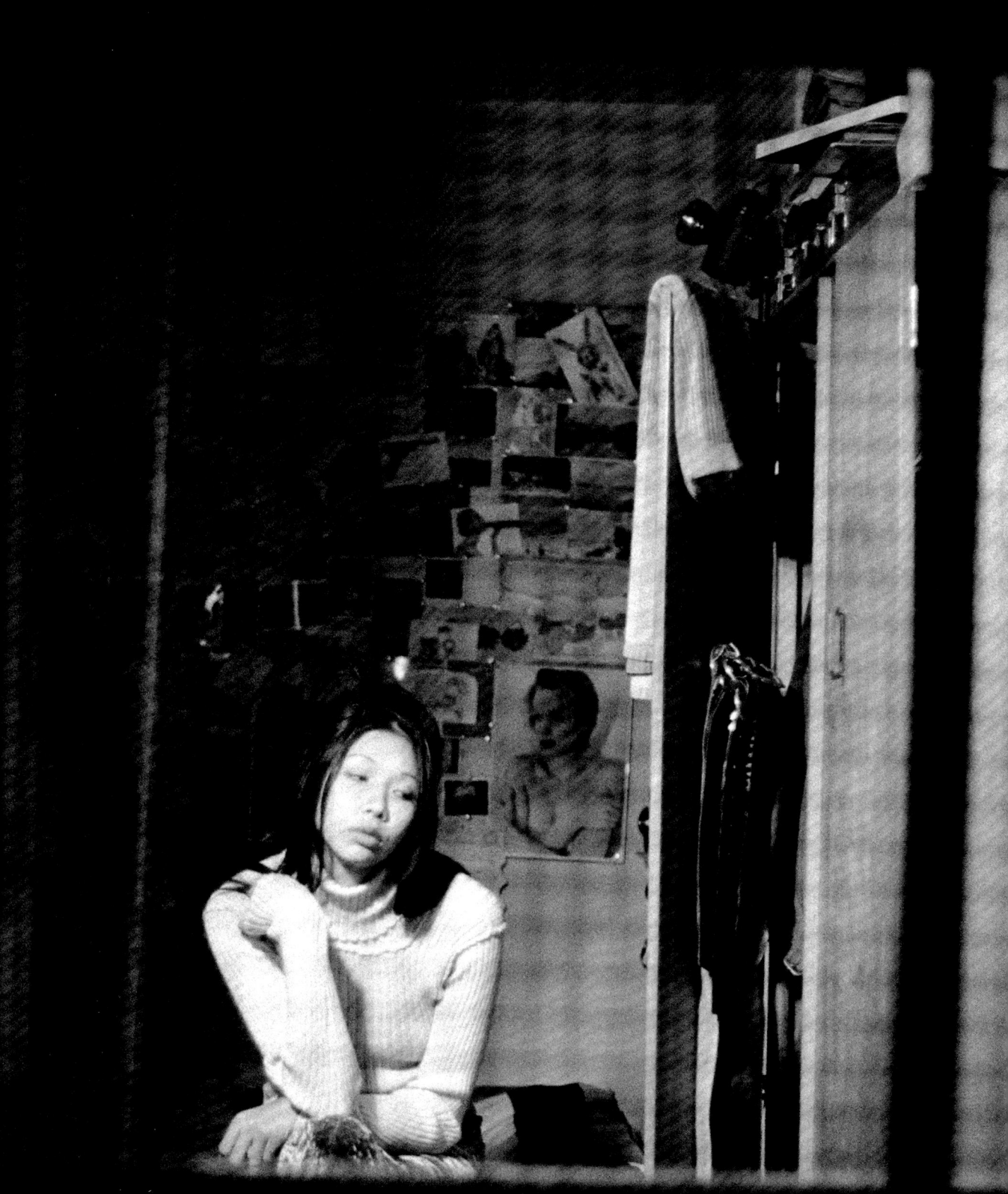

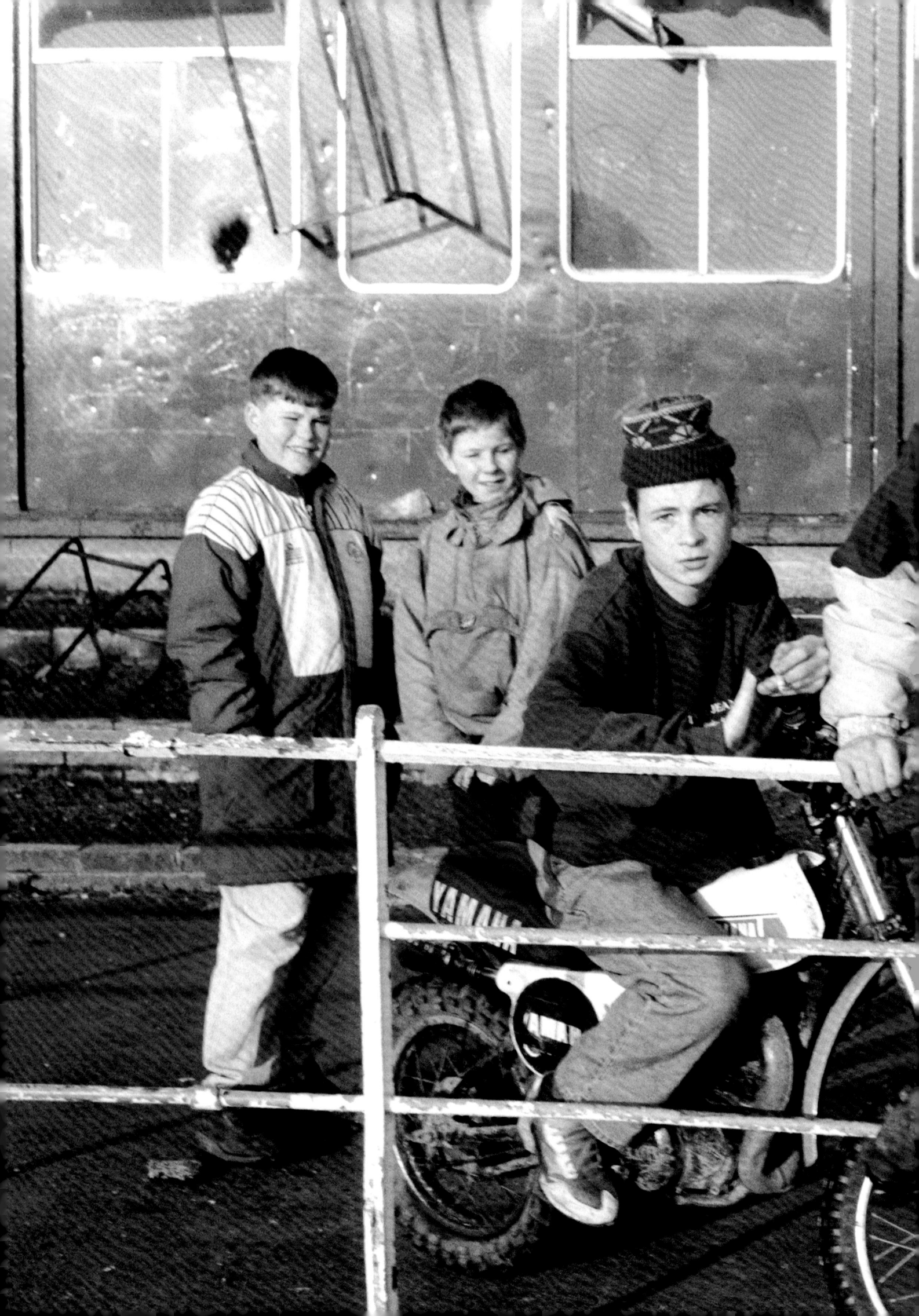

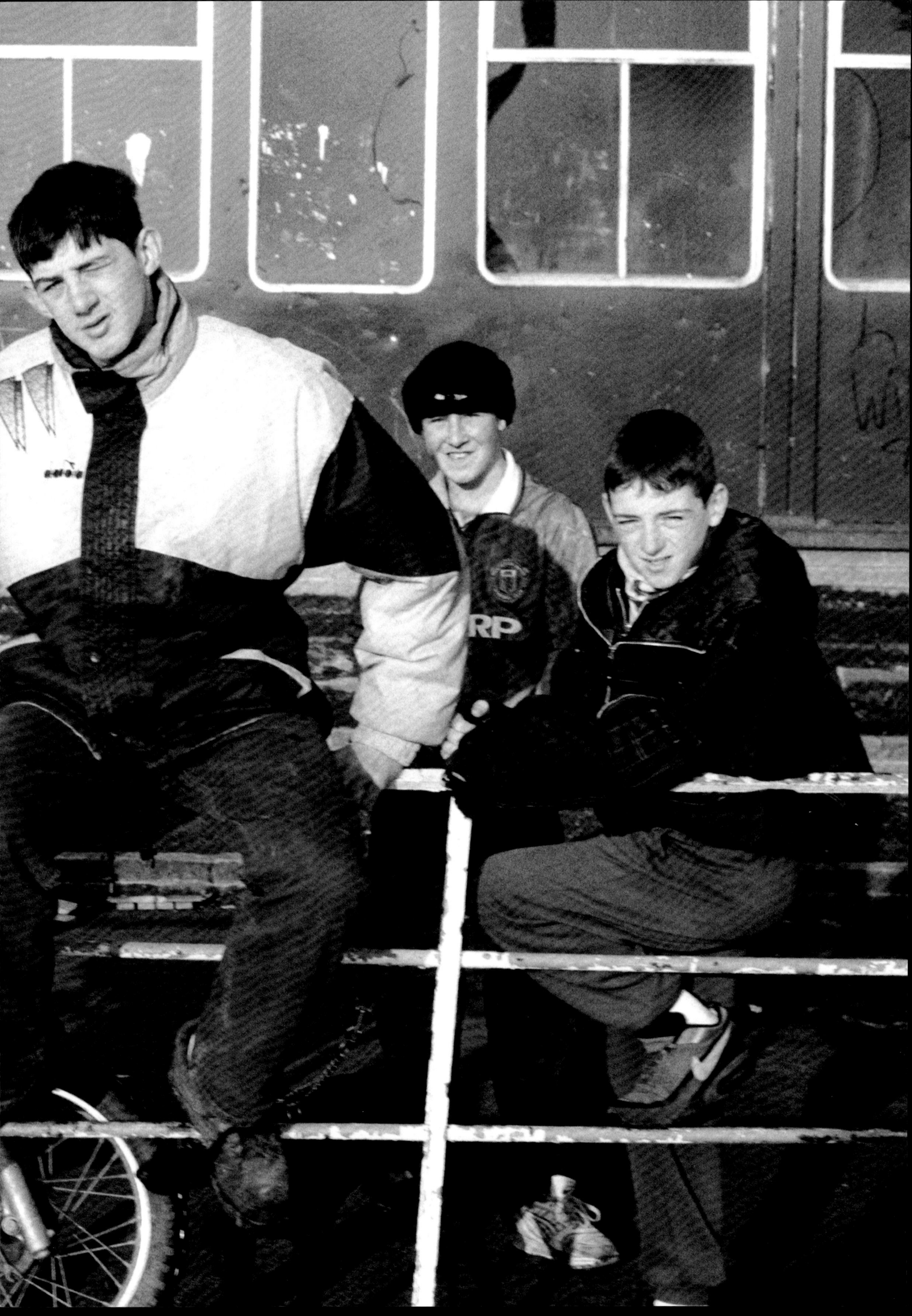

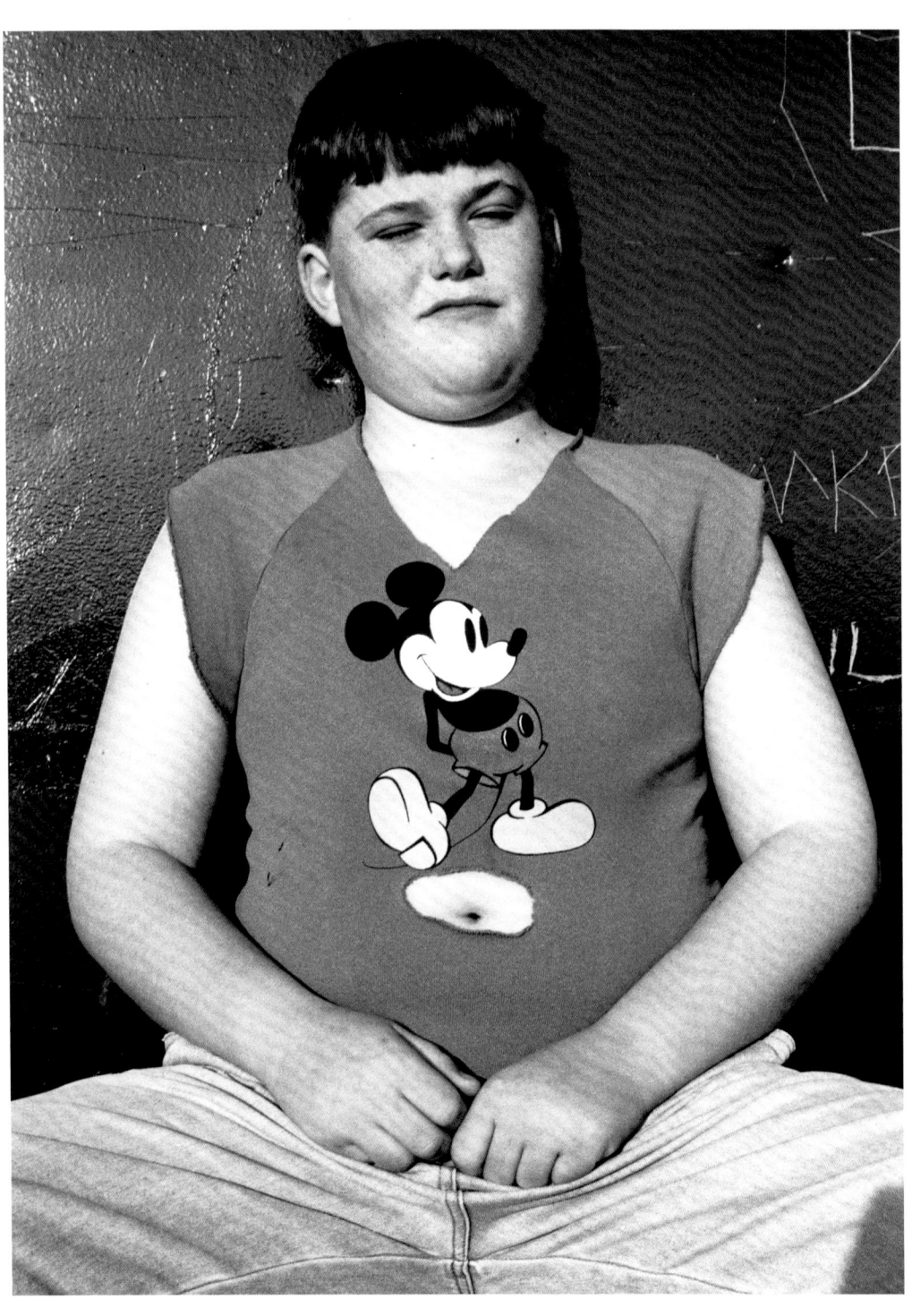

No Future, Issue 7, 1994

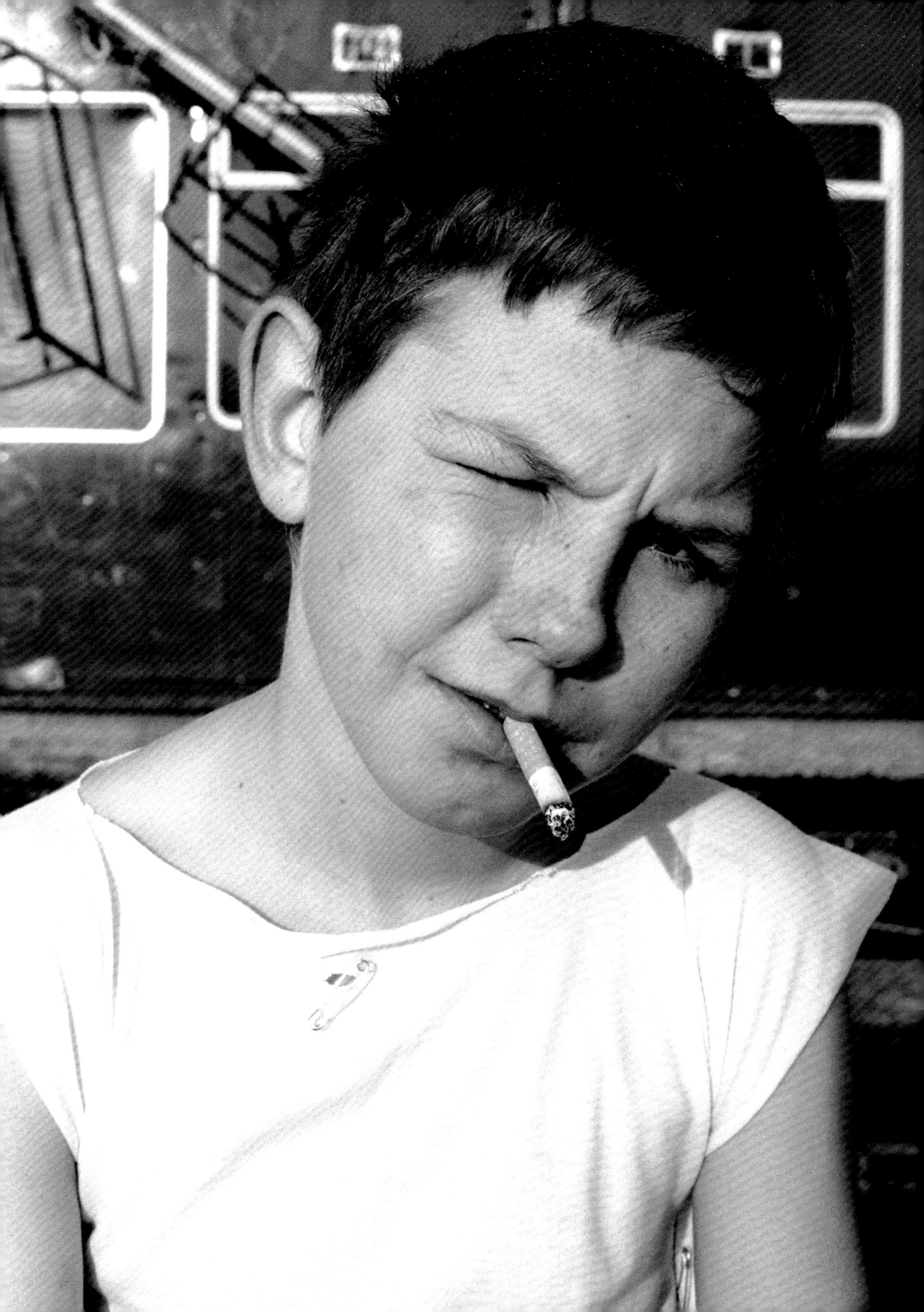

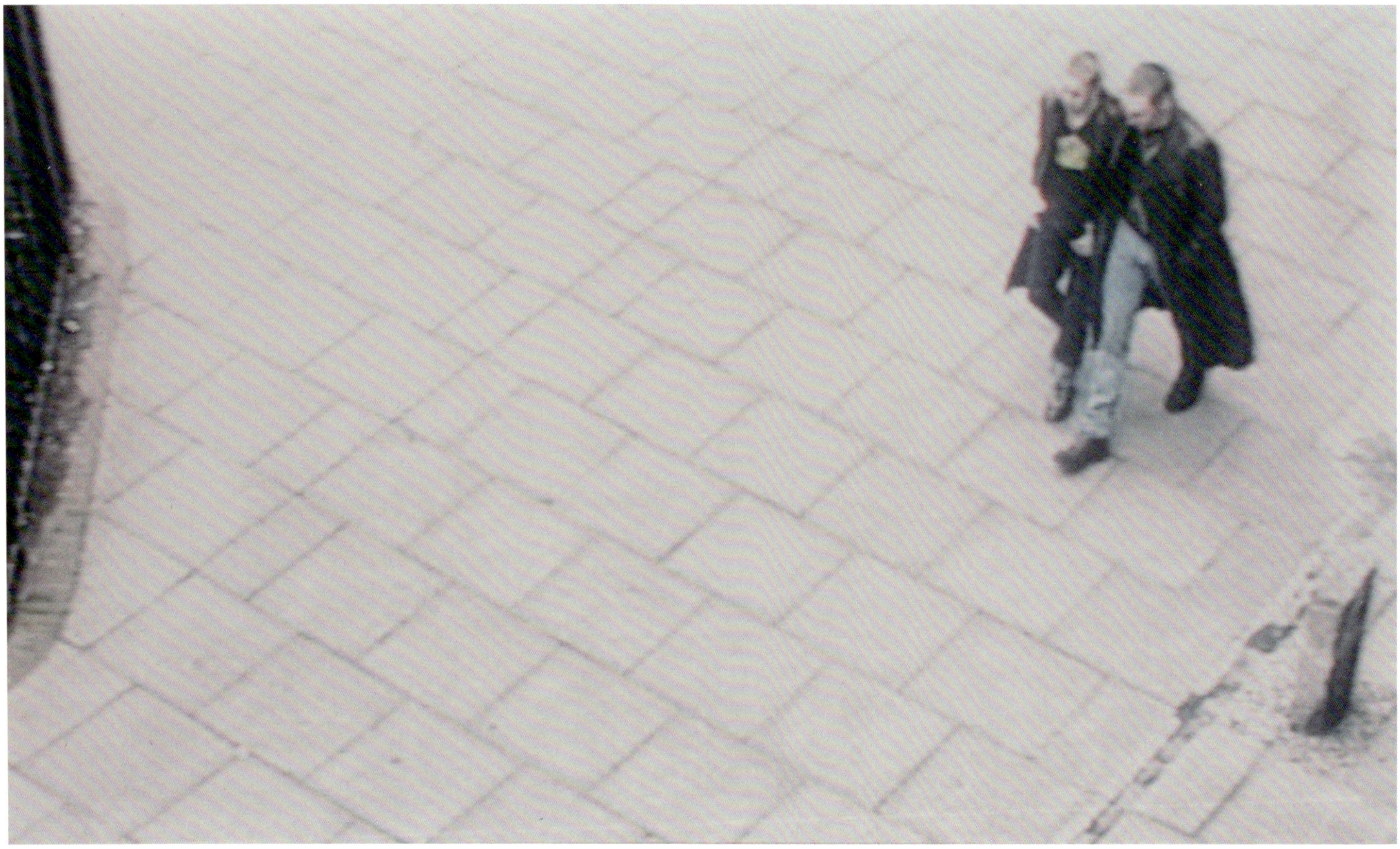

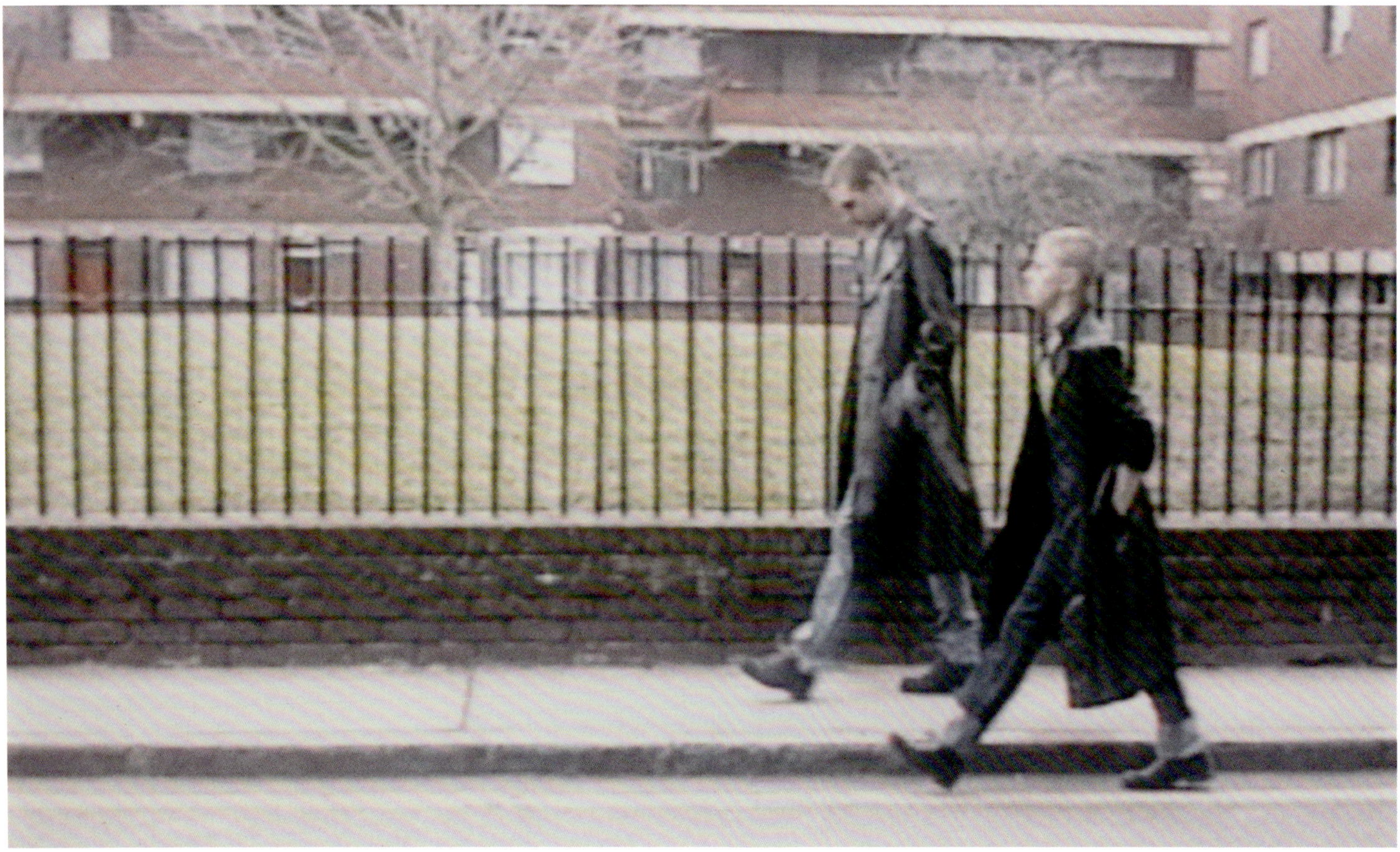

Surveillance, Issue 19, 1996

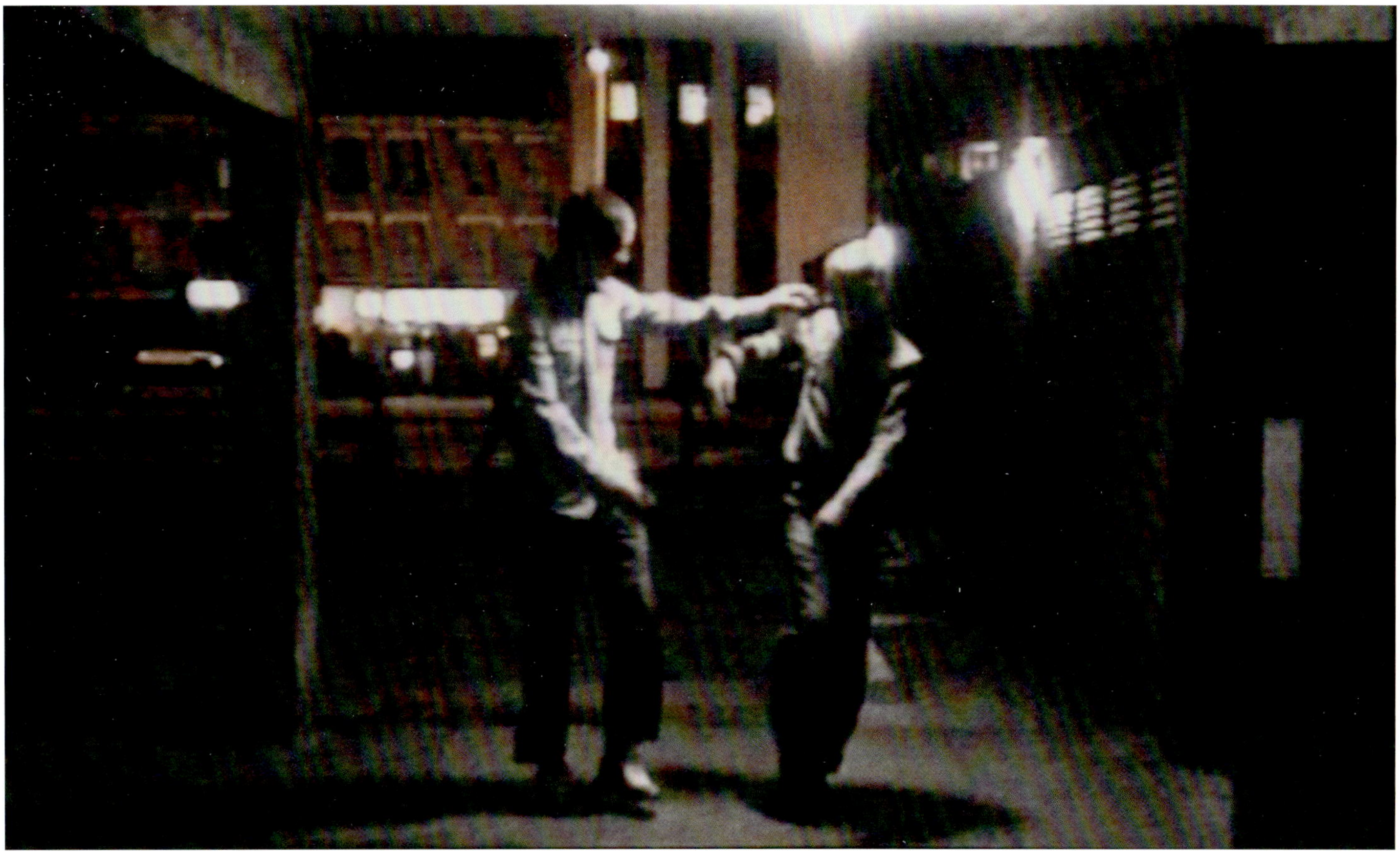

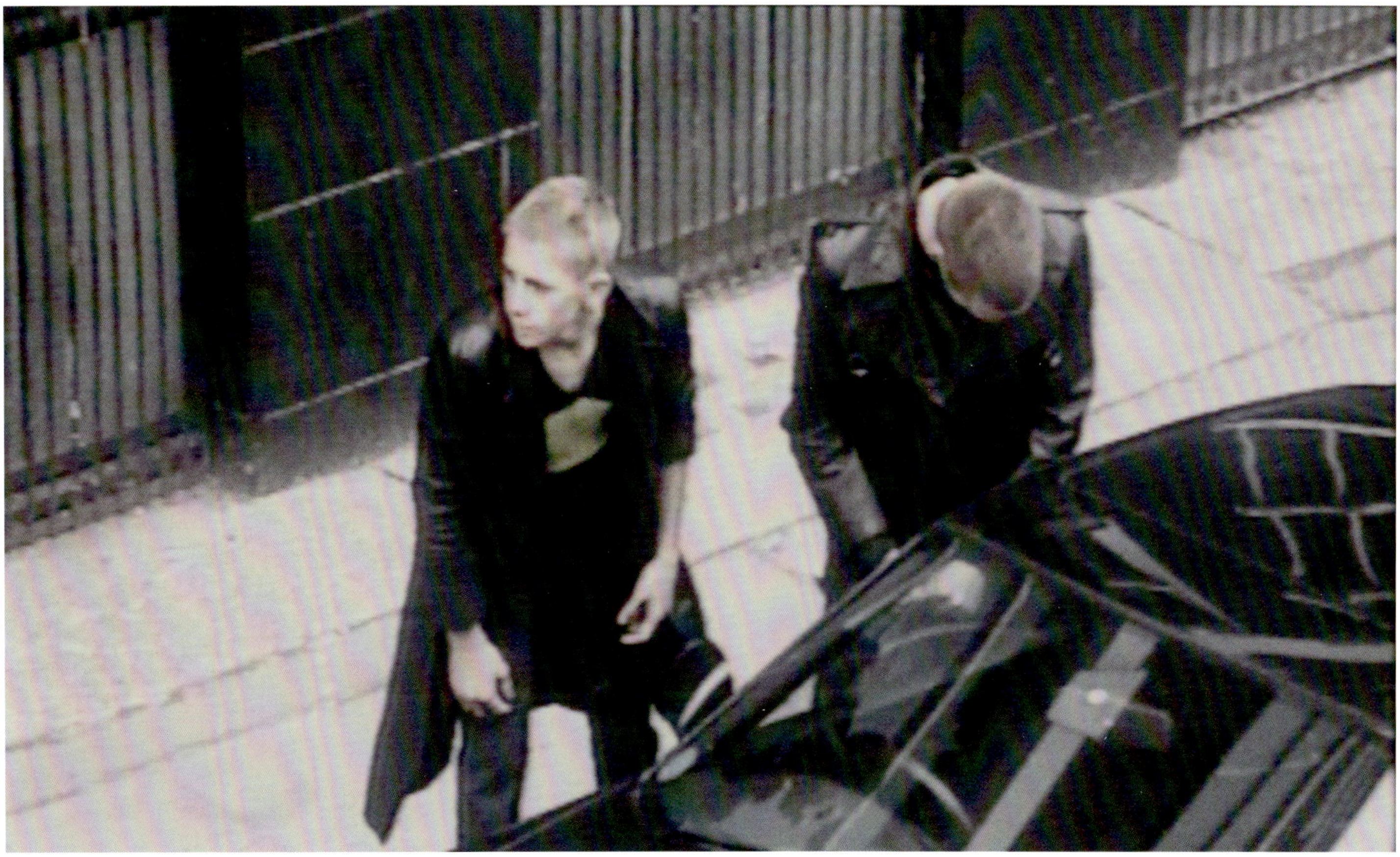

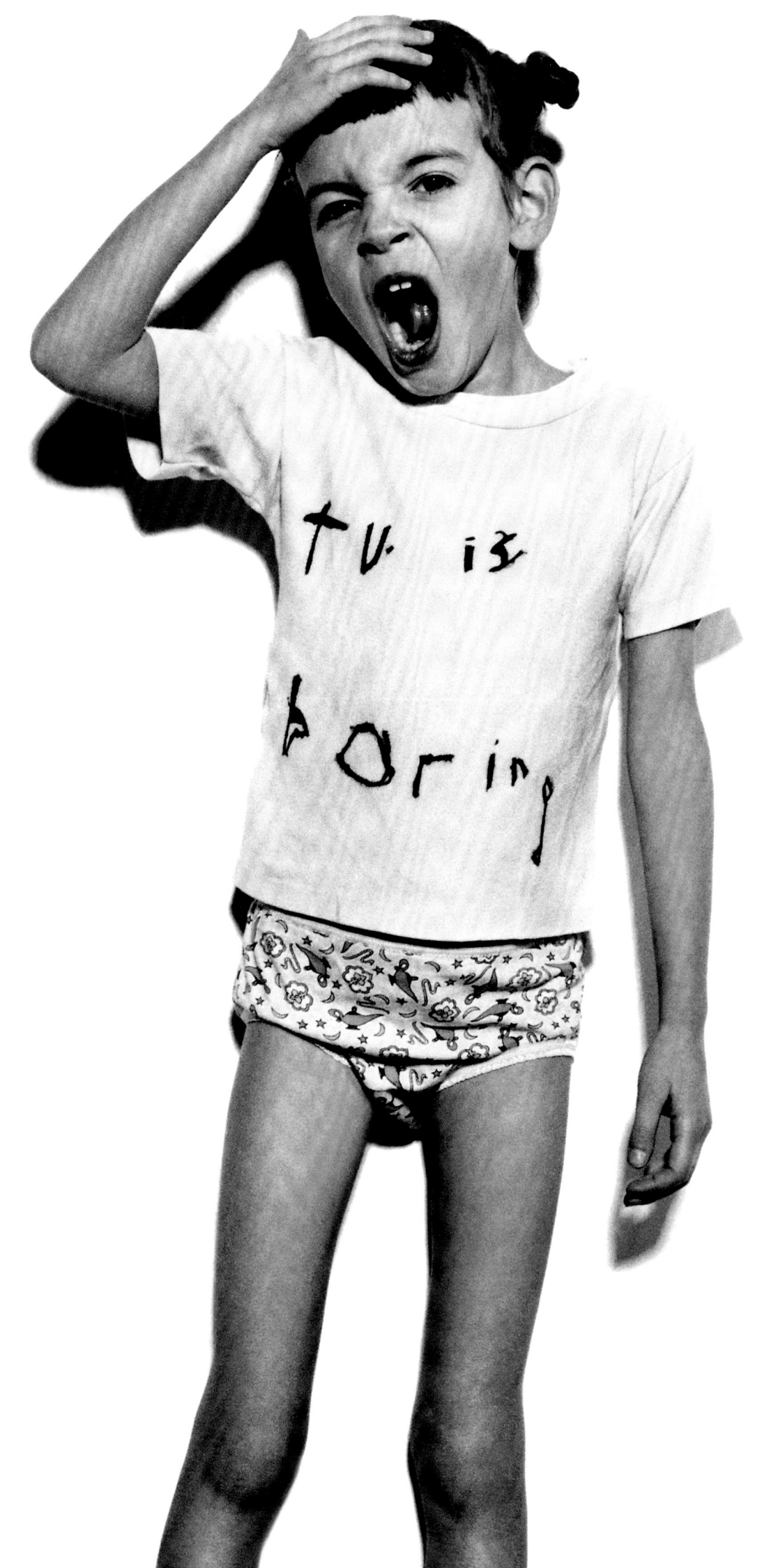

THERE IS MORE THAN THE MAINSTREAM/ CELEBRATE THE UNKNOWN/PROMOTE THE NEW GENERATION/WEIRD PEOPLE MAKE GREAT PARTY GUESTS...

For someone often called a "Celebrity Portrait Photographer", Rankin is ironically someone whose work could often be described as a middle-finger to celebrity culture.

T.V. Is Boring, the cover shoot for issue 7 from 1994, placed an unknown face on news stands plastered with supermodels and rock stars. A mission statement for Rankin's ongoing work: personality is more important than fame.

The title *T.V. Is Boring* came from a t-shirt designed by the child cover-star herself. This artwork acting as an inditing statement on how the youth were tuning out of the mainstream. You can look at these words as the key to many of the *Dazed & Confused* cover stars that followed.

Whether it was Chloë Sevigny, promoting her first ever film, well before the title of cult movie star was bestowed upon her, or Saoirse Ronan, before *Ladybird* made her a household name, Rankin's sitters need not be widely known, but rather have a longevity and atypical allure.

You can see this further in how actors, artists, musicians and film directors all became part of the *Dazed & Confused* and Rankin orbit. Their images are playful, strange, loud and quiet. When Rankin finds a model, he does not take your standard PR shot, instead his work strives for connection. By looking at a Rankin portrait of Thom Yorke or Jarvis Cocker you are not looking at a clean press image, you are looking truly at them.

TV IS BORING

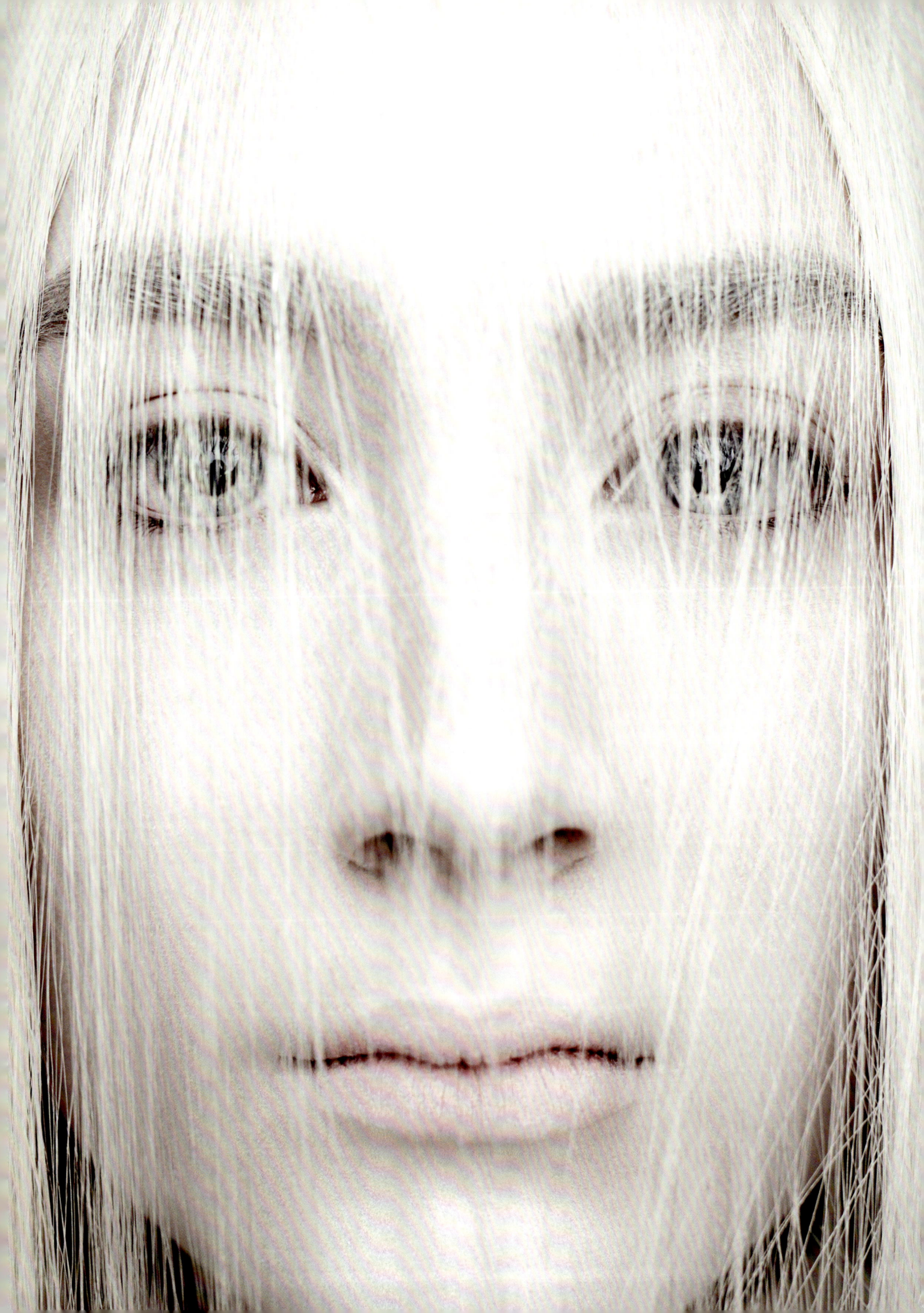

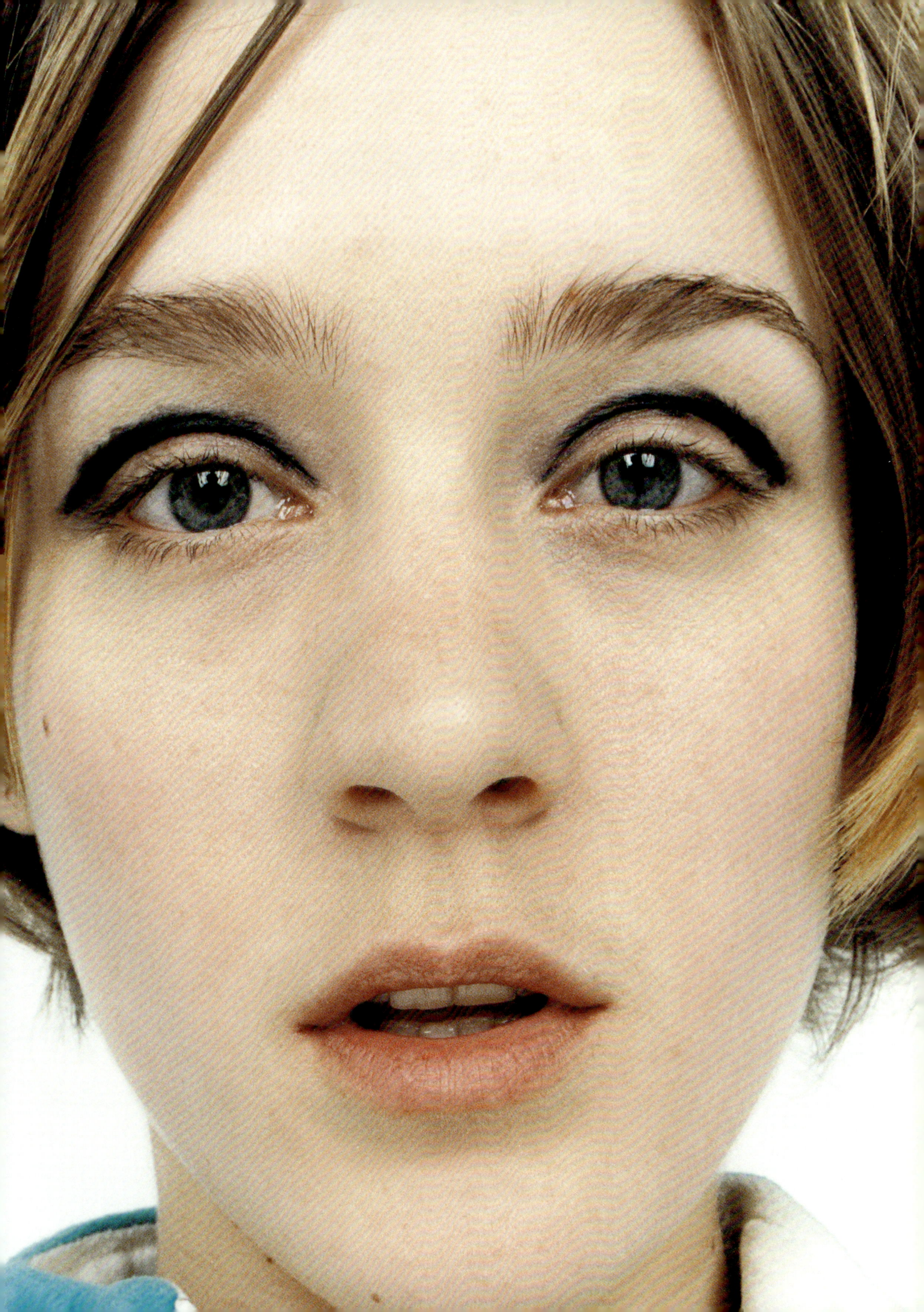

Previous Pages - Born Free, Vol. 3, Issue 20, 2013
                    Who's That Girl, Issue 20, 1996

Opposite Page - Class of '97, Issue 35, 1997

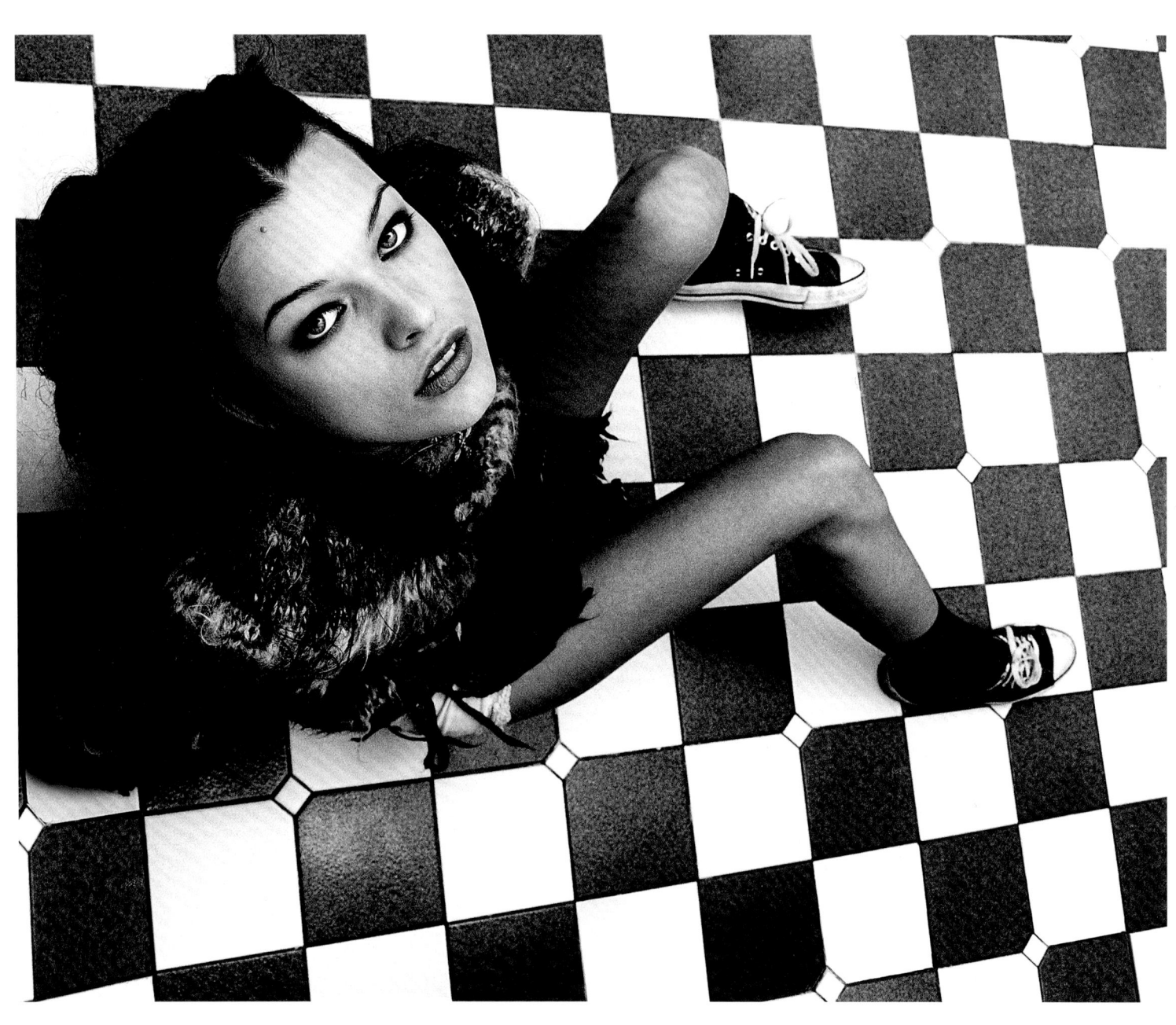

Teenage Dream, Issue 8, 1994

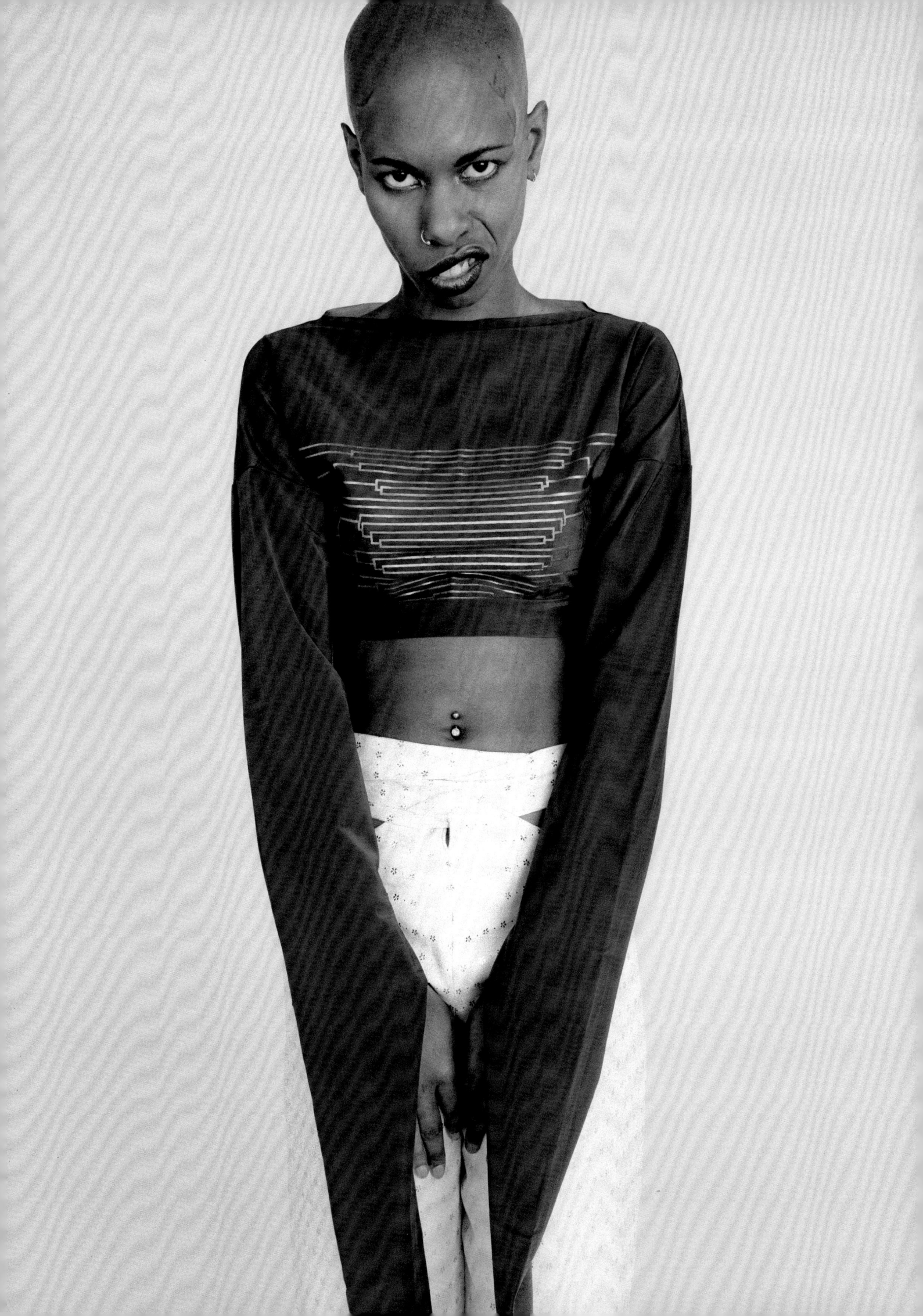

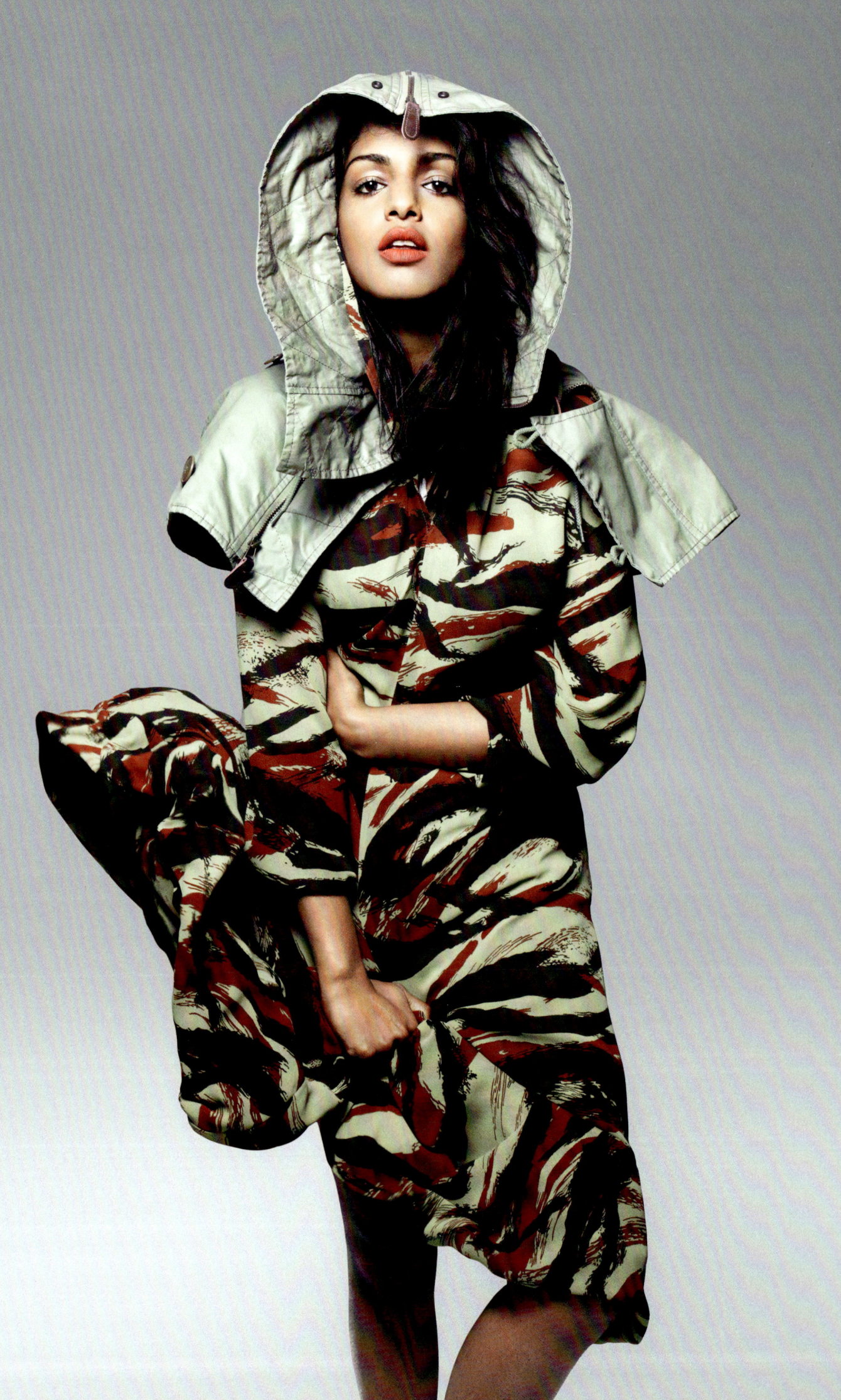

Opposite Page - On the Attack, Vol. 2, Issue 87, 2010
Next Pages - Lost & Found, Issue 25, 1996

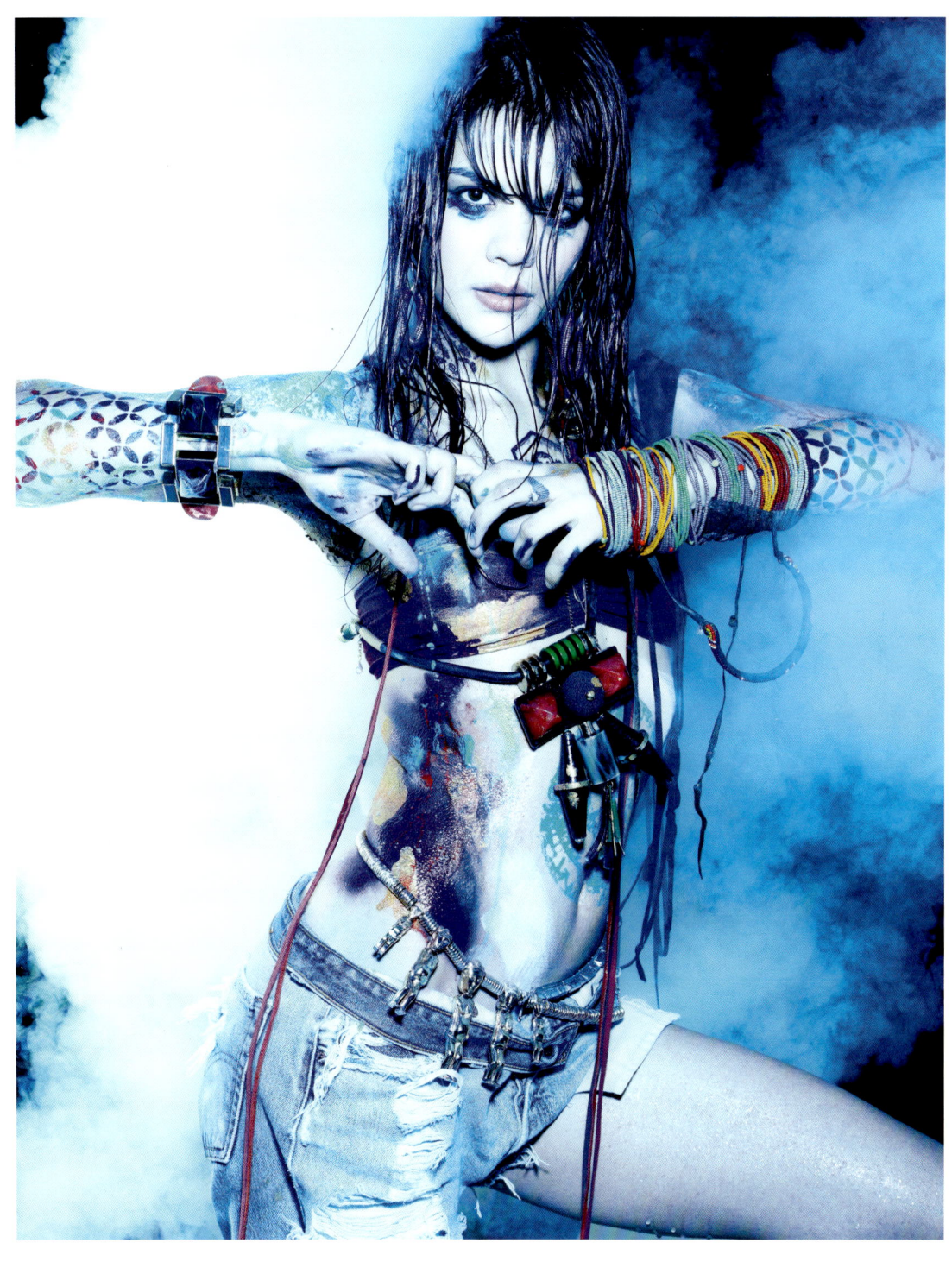

Far Out!, Vol. 2, Issue 70, 2009

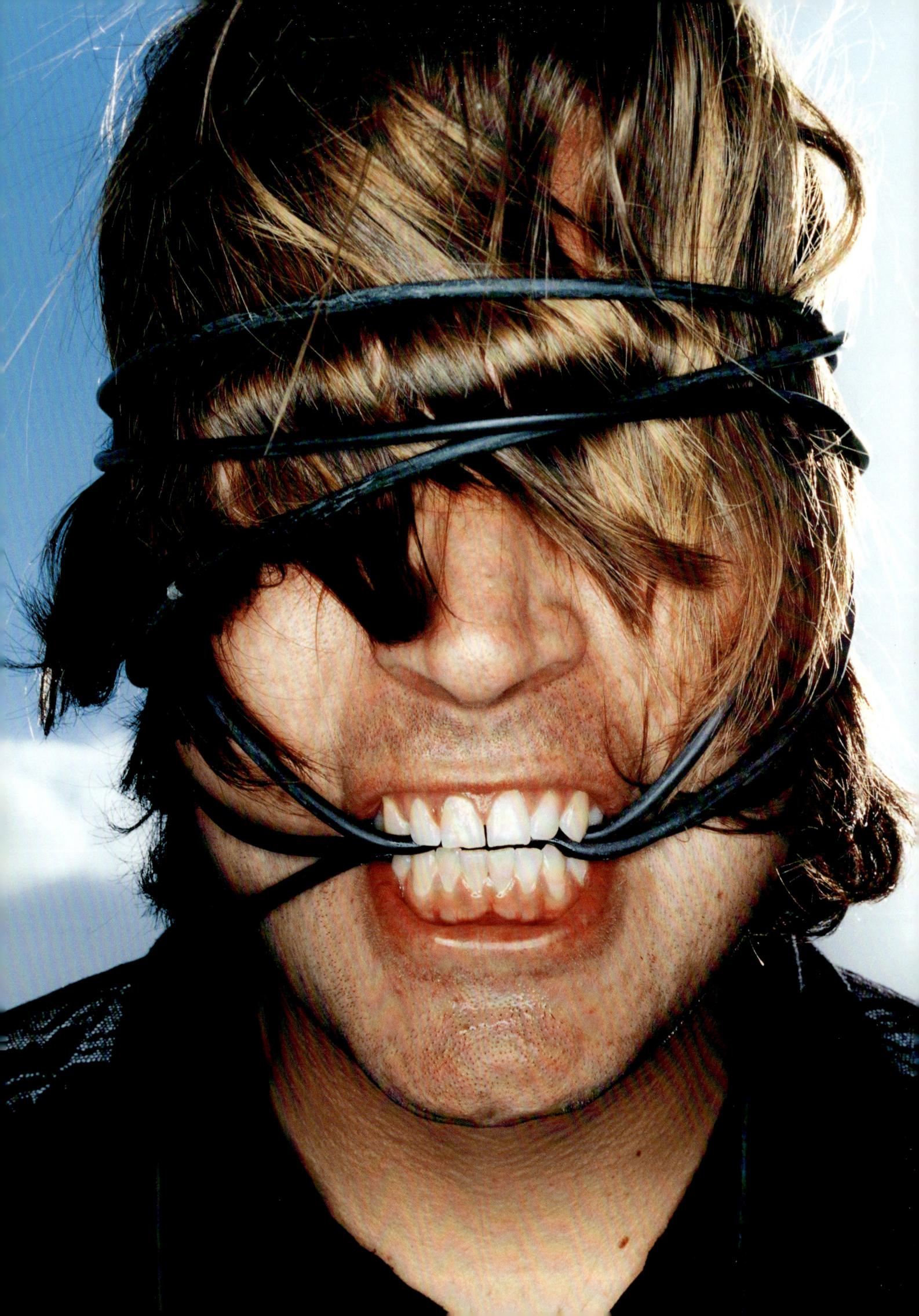

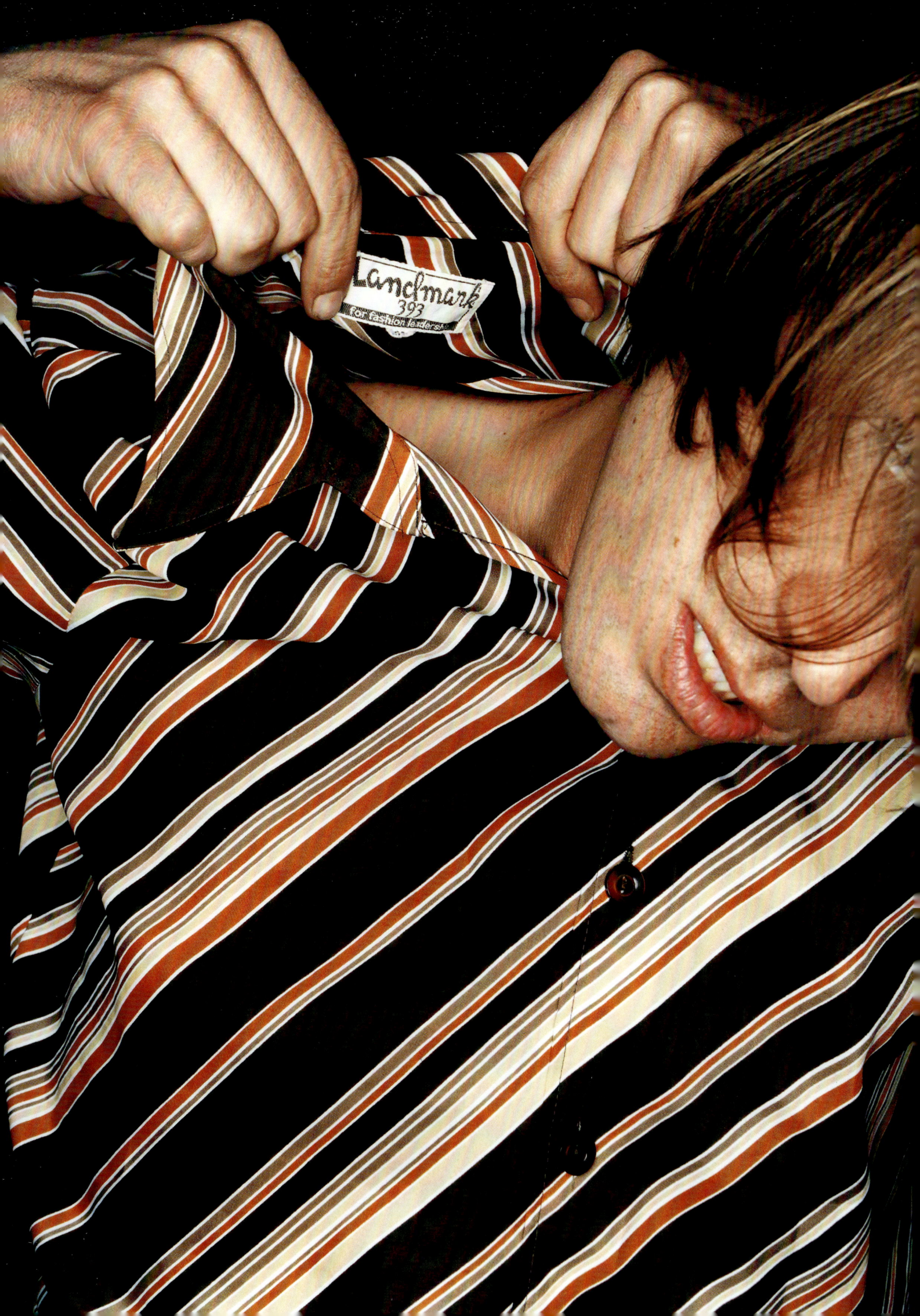

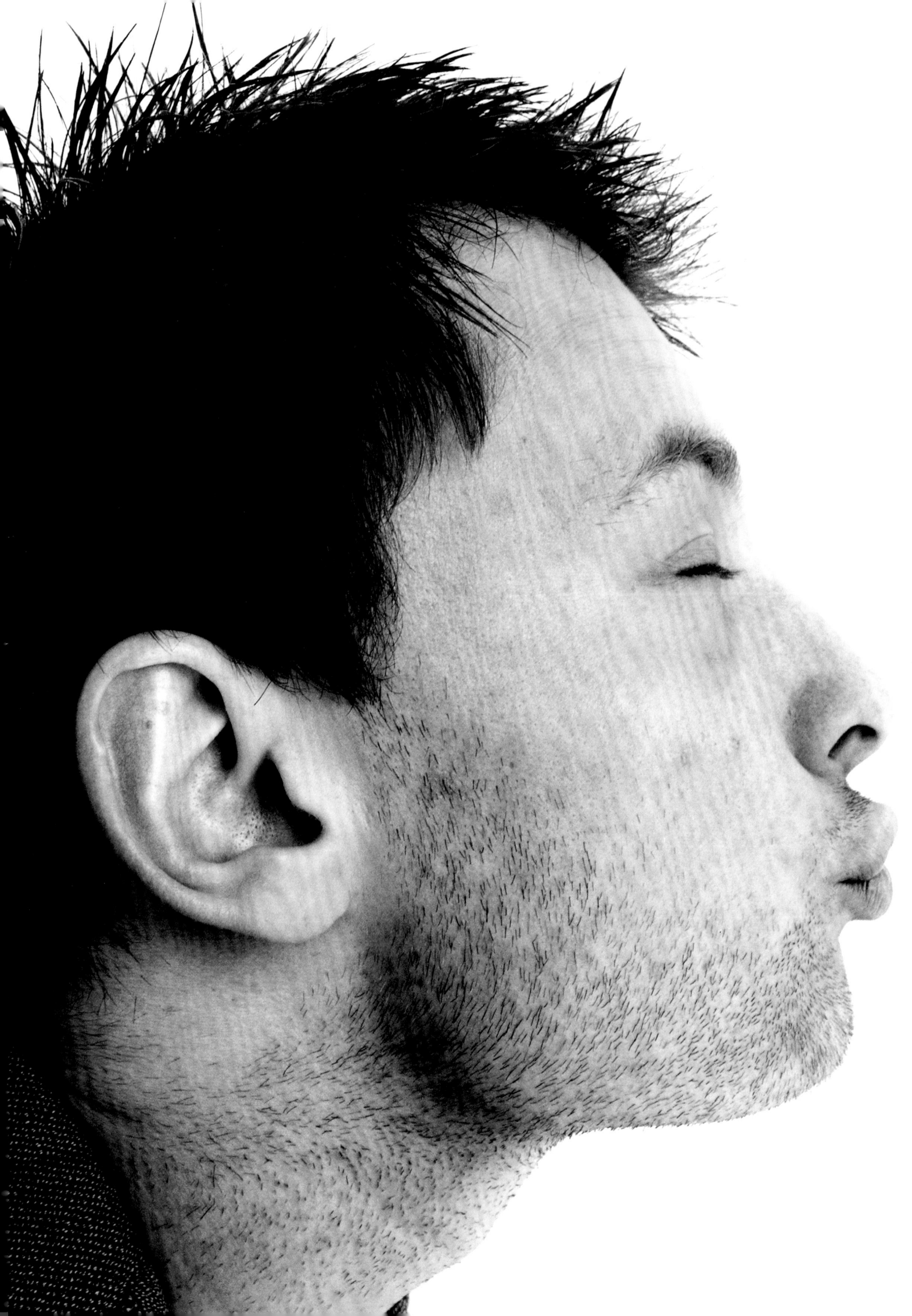

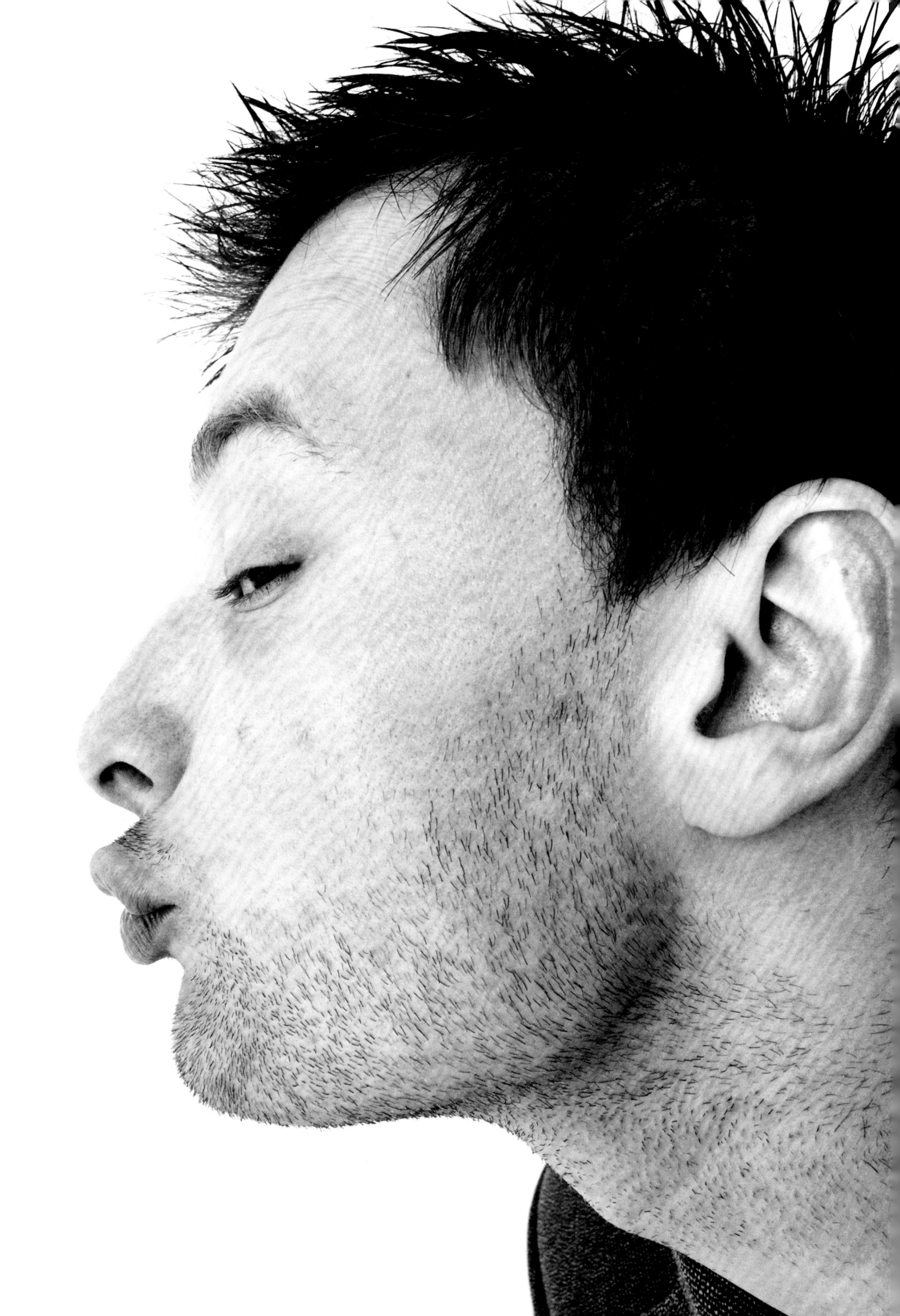

Boys to the Front of the Queue, Issue 98, 2003

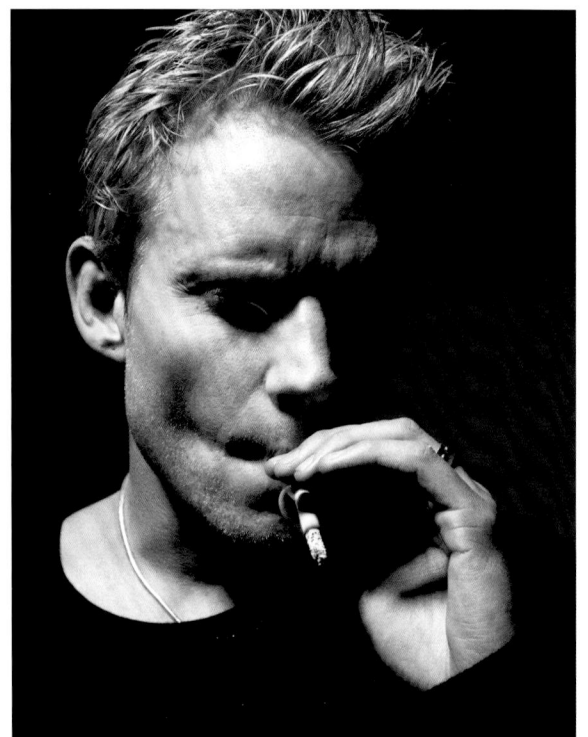
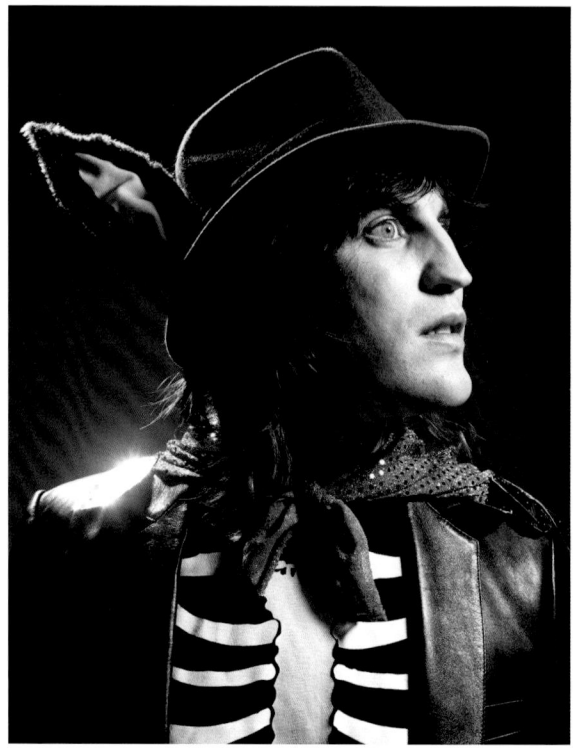
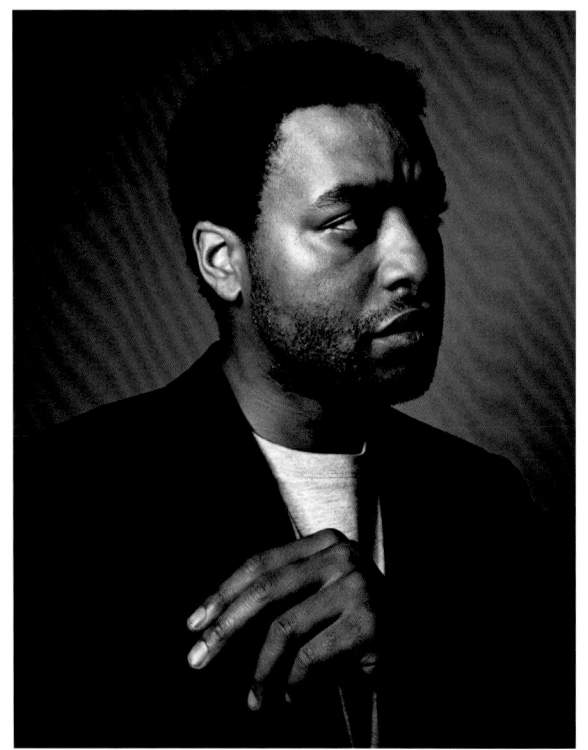
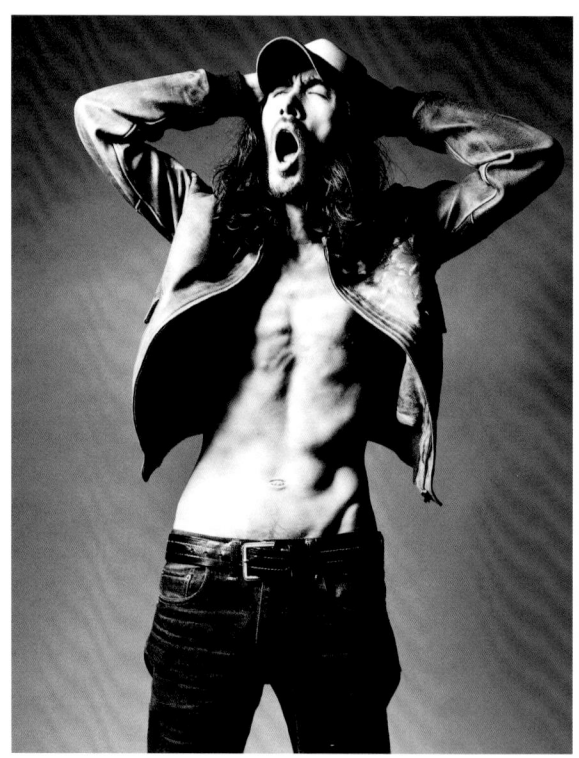

Previous Pages - You Do it to Yourself, Issue 19, 1996

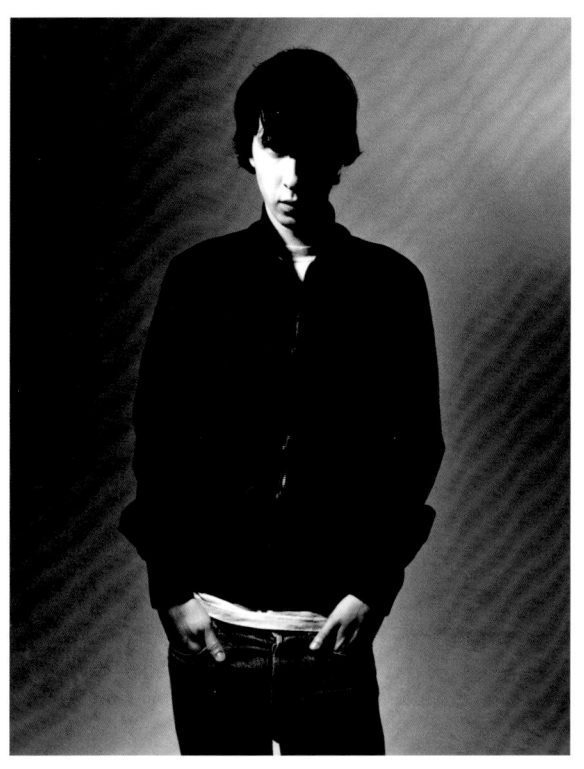

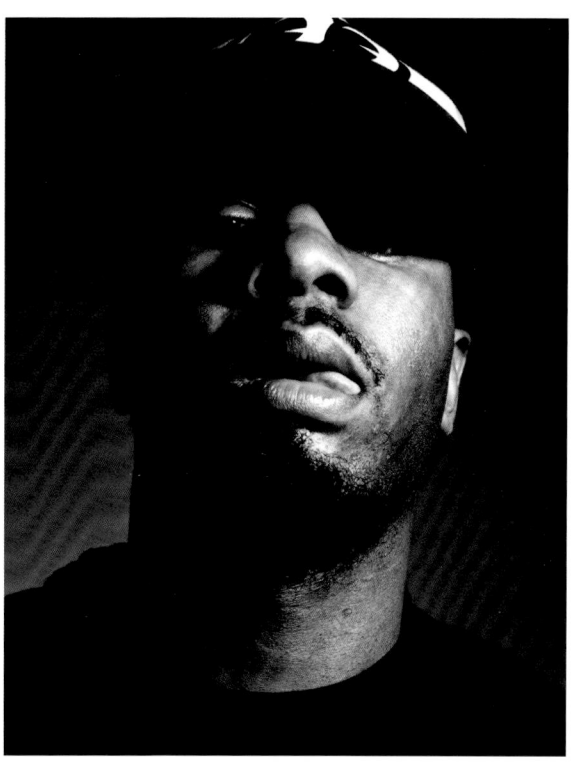

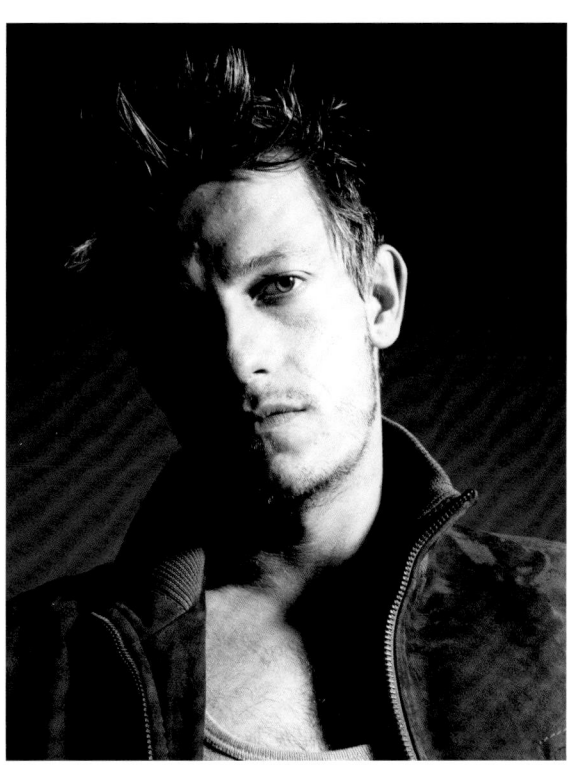

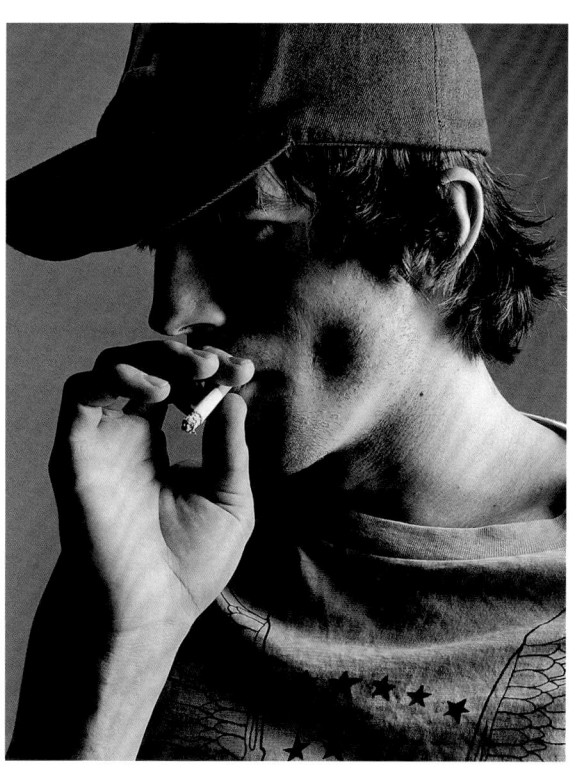

Next Page - 03 Minute Heroes, Issue 35, 1997

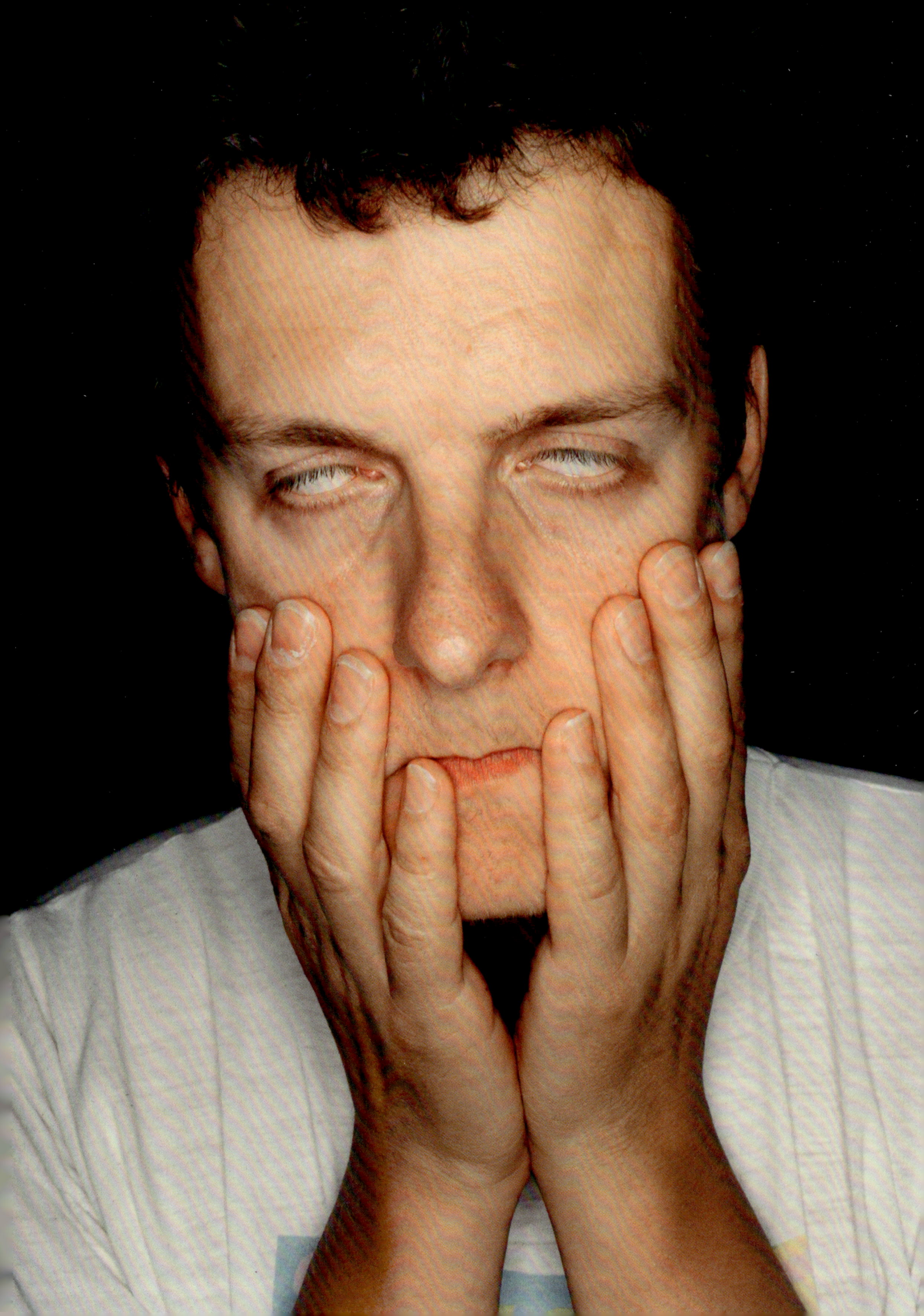

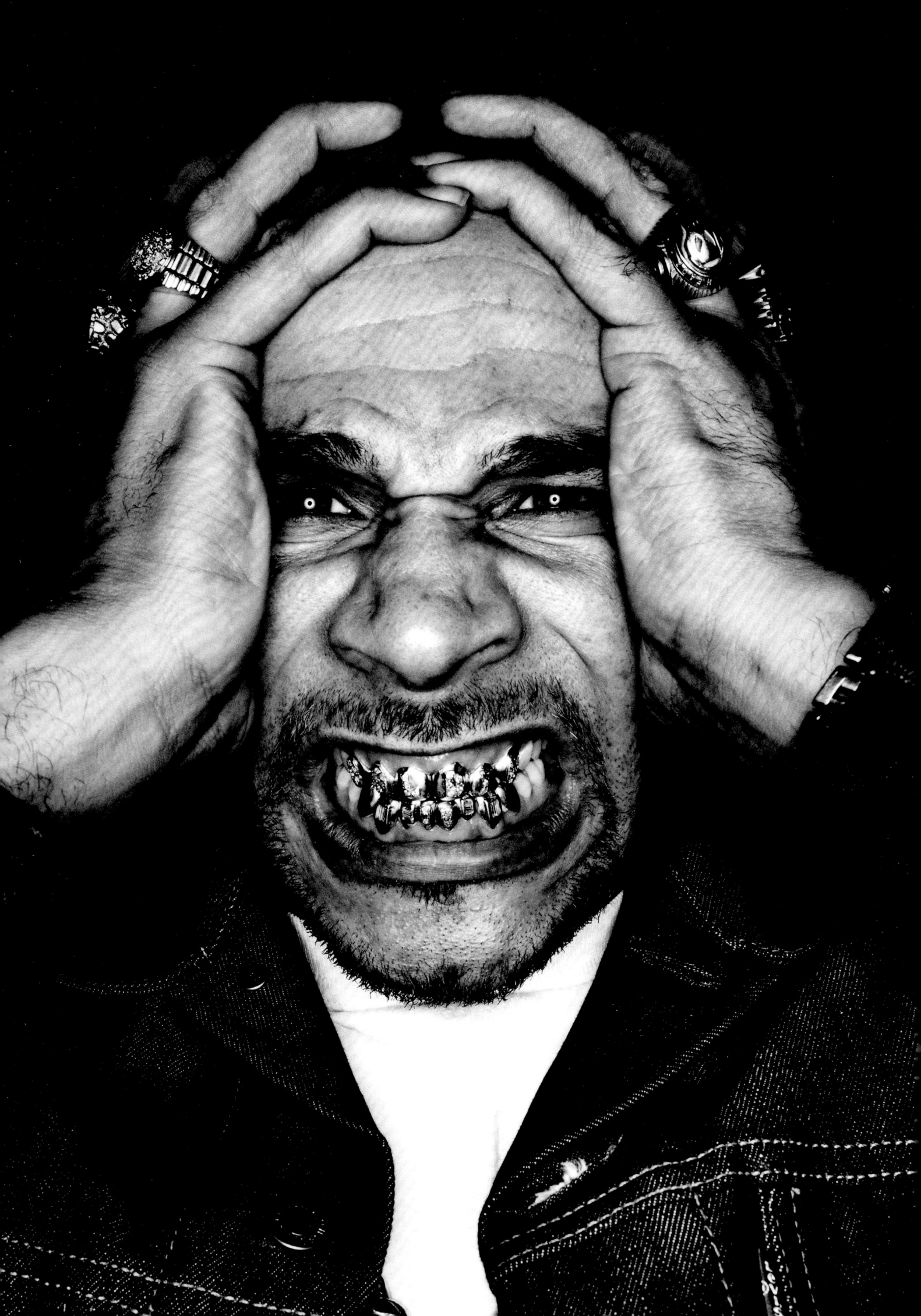

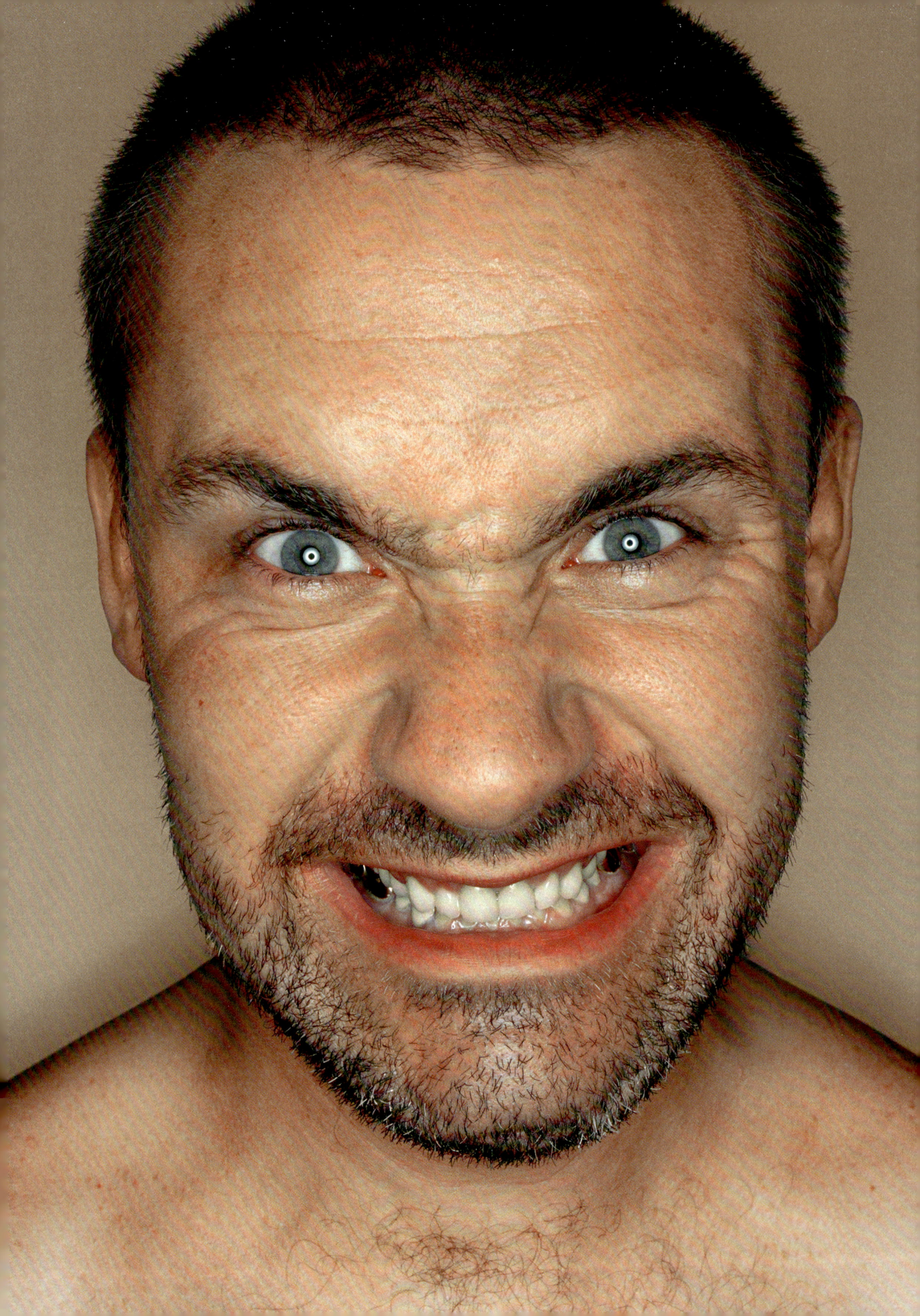

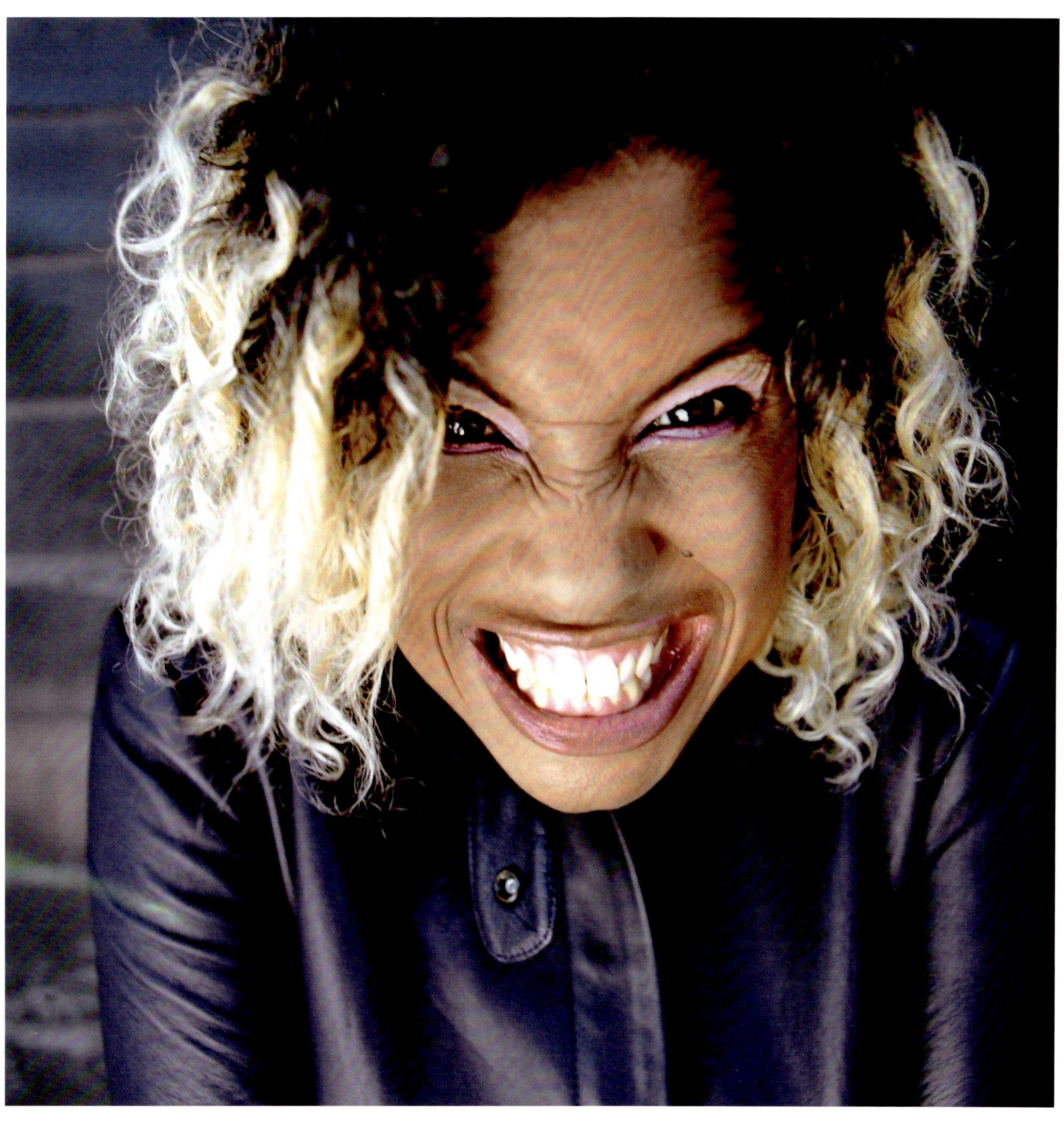

A Private Perspective, Issue 22, 1996

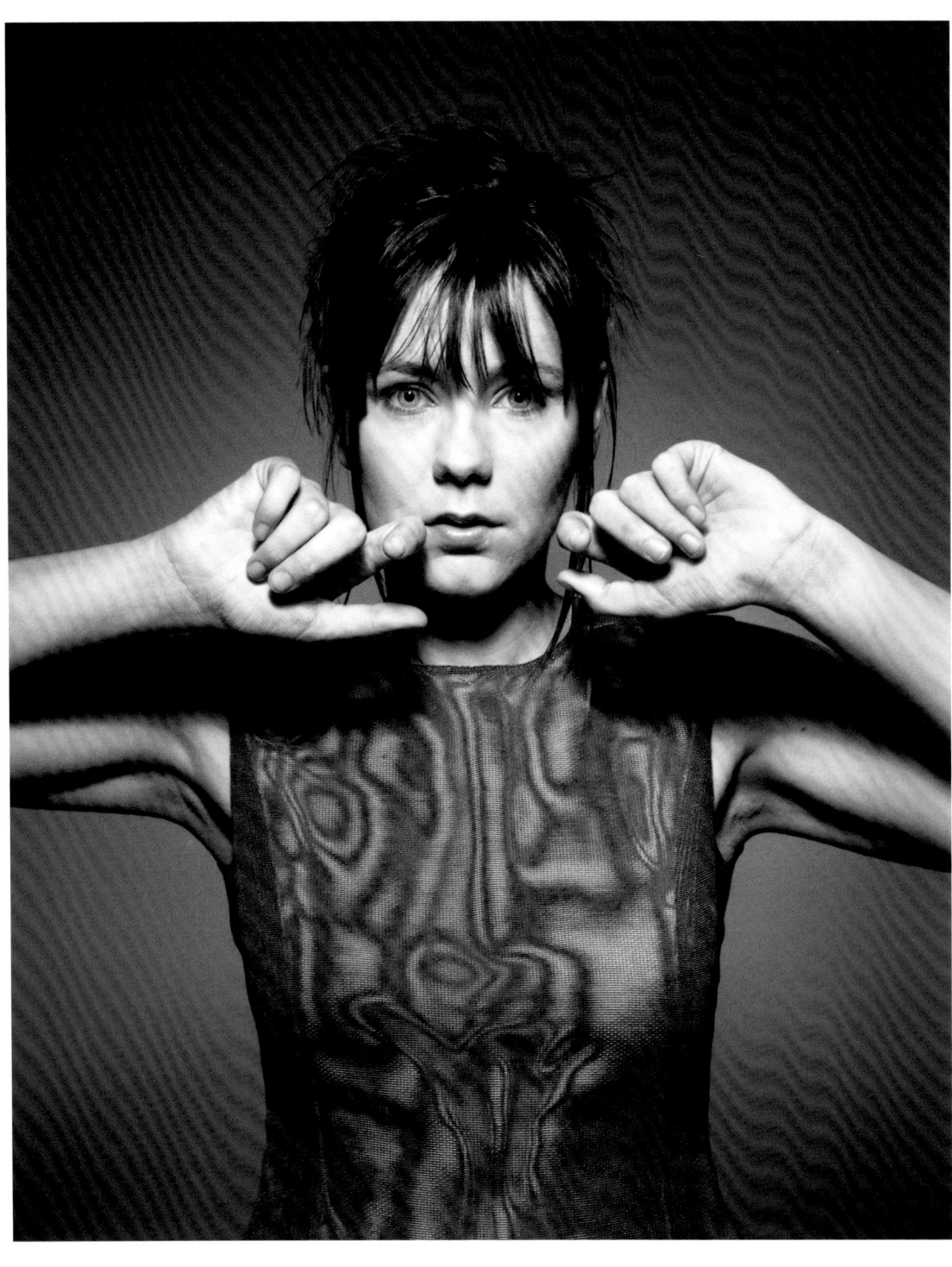

The Spotlight's On..., Issue 39, 1998

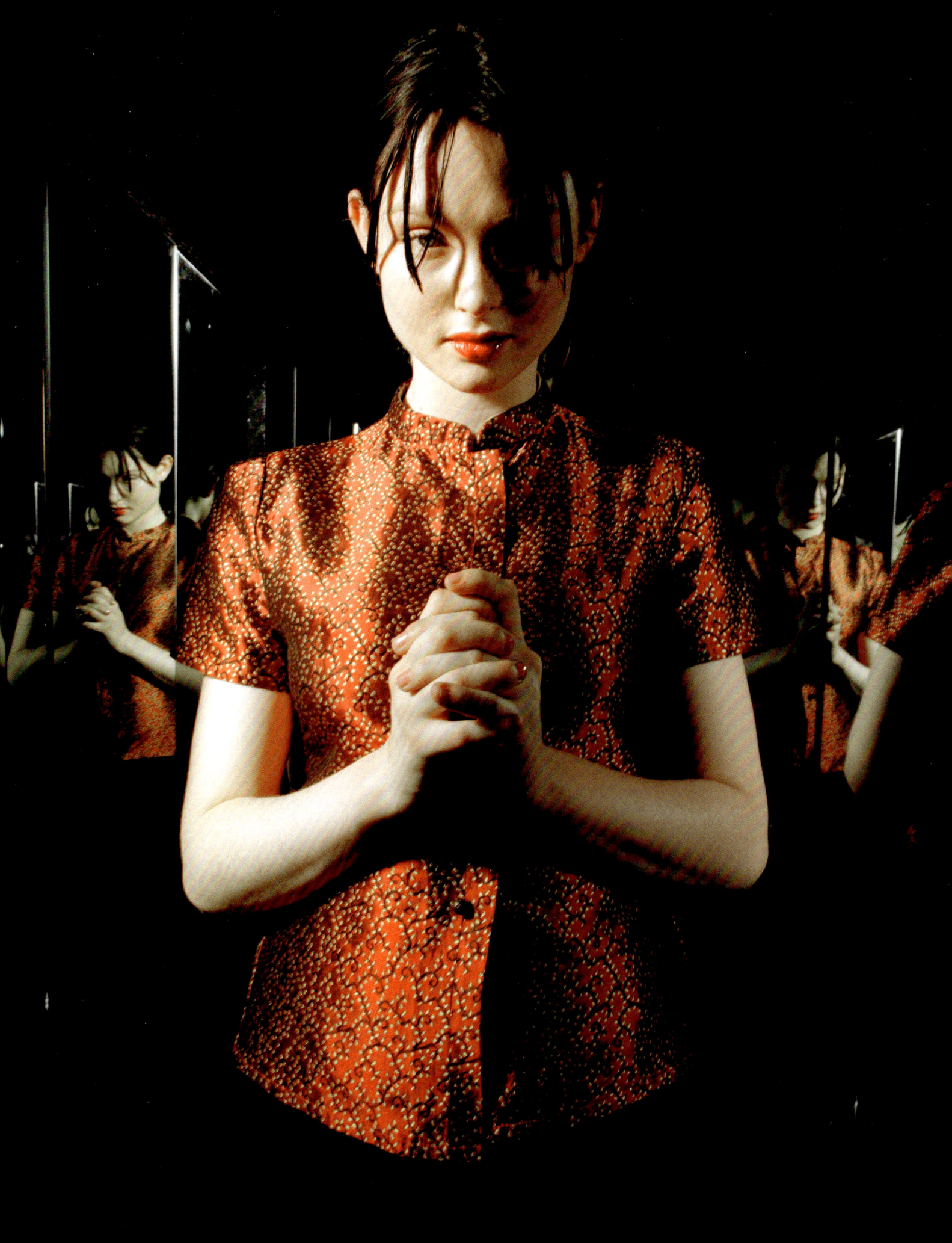

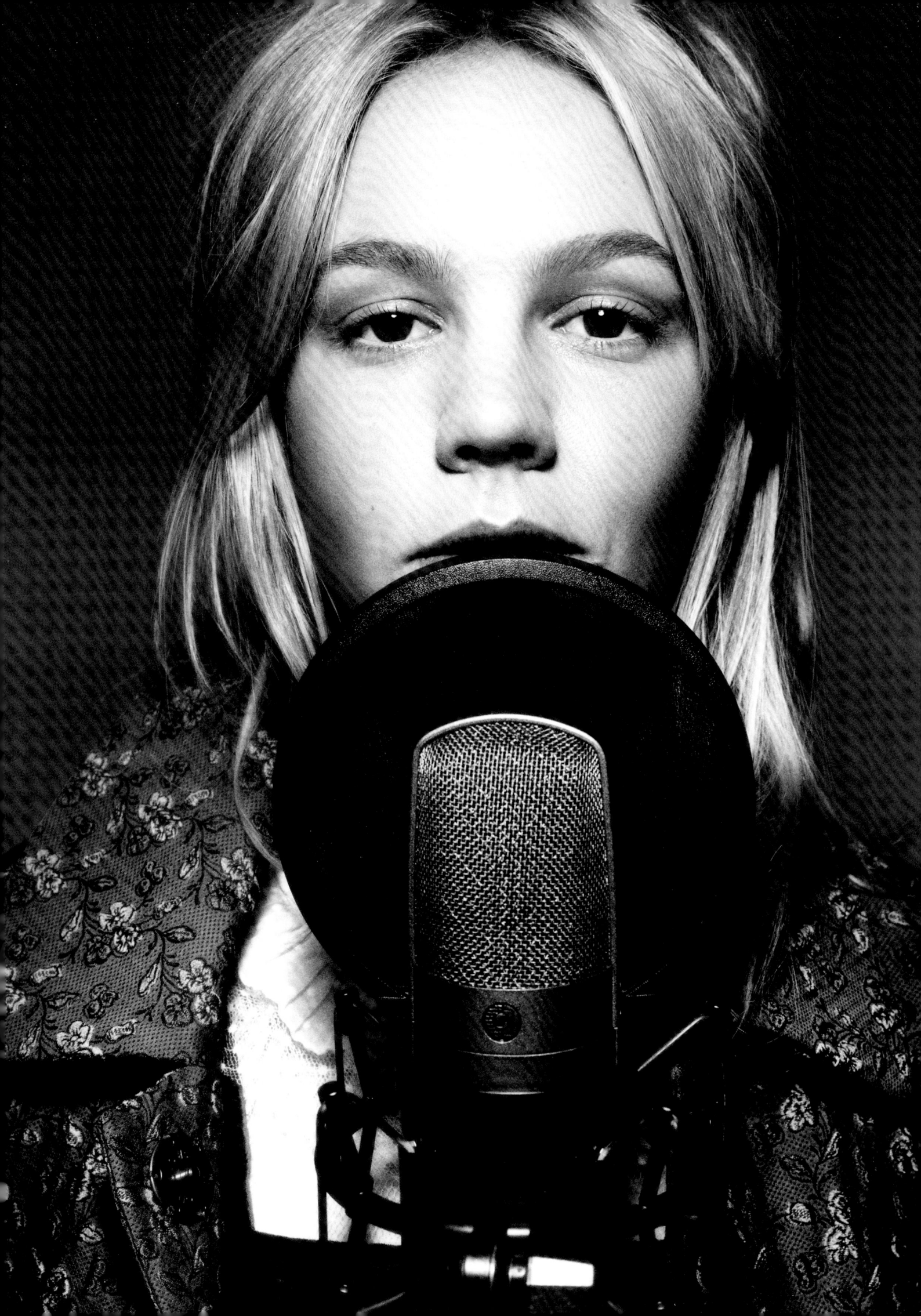

Opposite Page - Wild at Heart, Vol. 3, Issue 29, 2014
Next Pages - Famous Forever, Issue 41, 1998

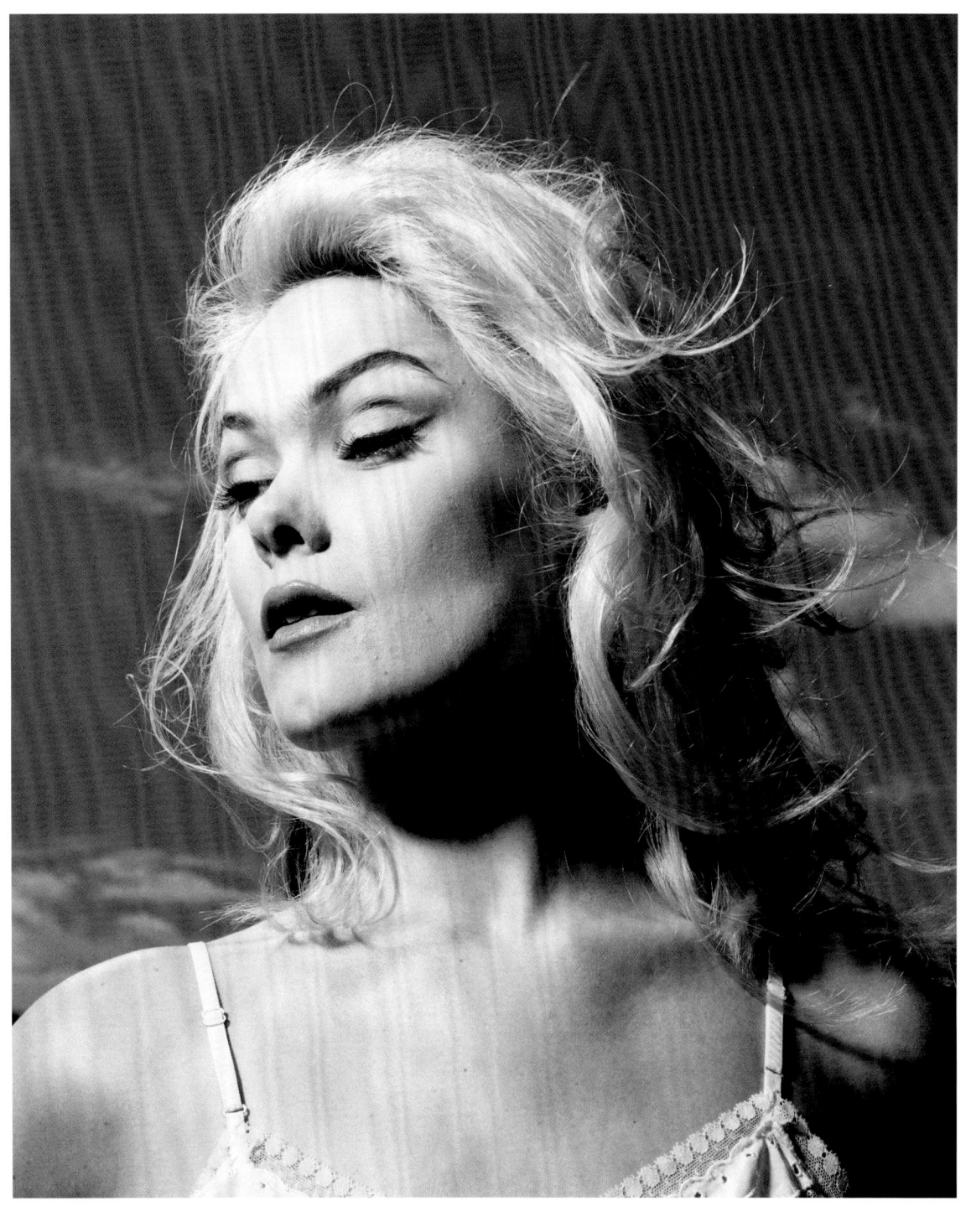

The Mood I'm In, Issue 49, 1998

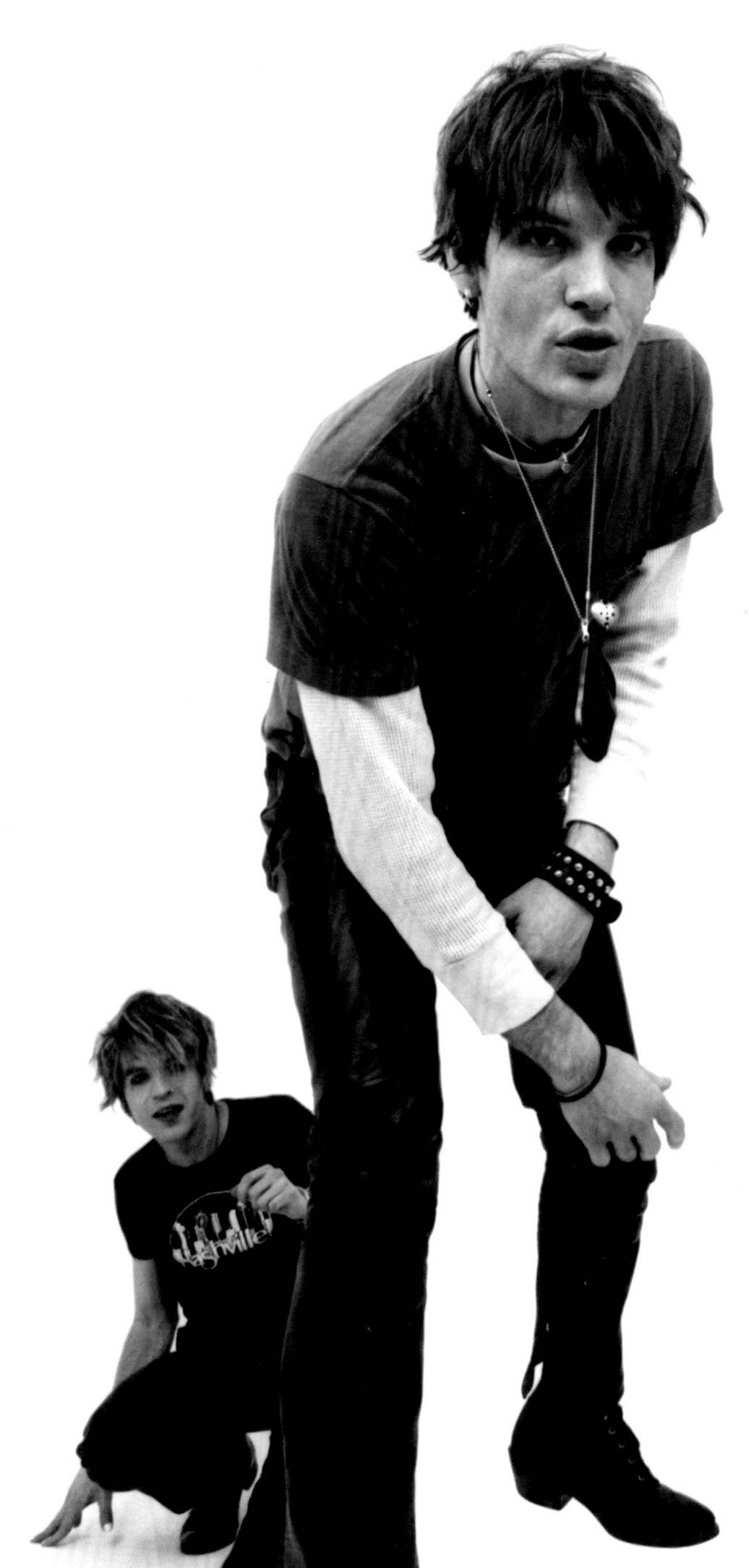

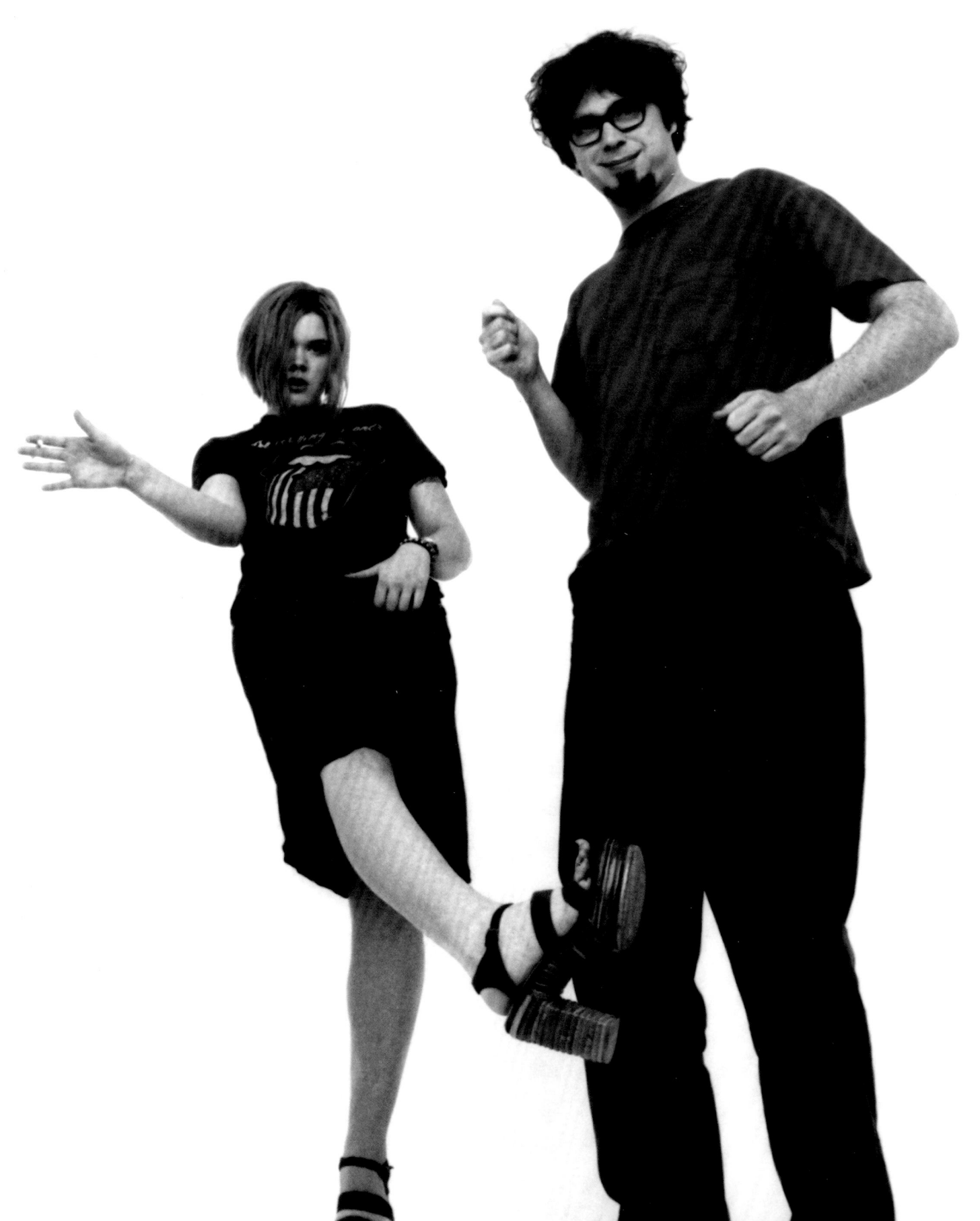

Opposite Page - Ask Me Later, Issue 13, 1995

Next Pages - The Patsy Kensit Affair, Issue 10, 1995
          Get Your Mojo Working, Issue 40, 1998

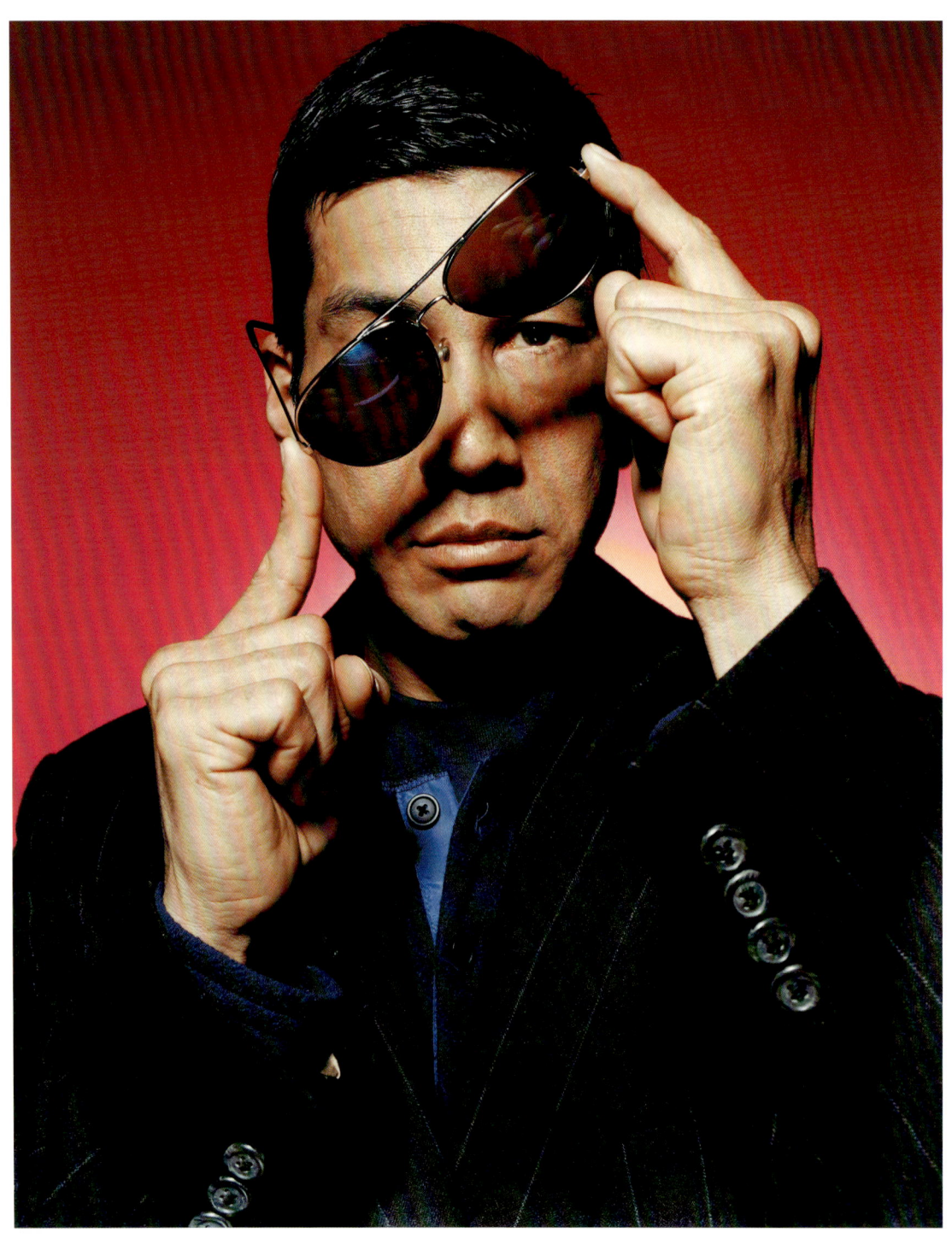

Tell 'em About the Money, Issue 42, 1998

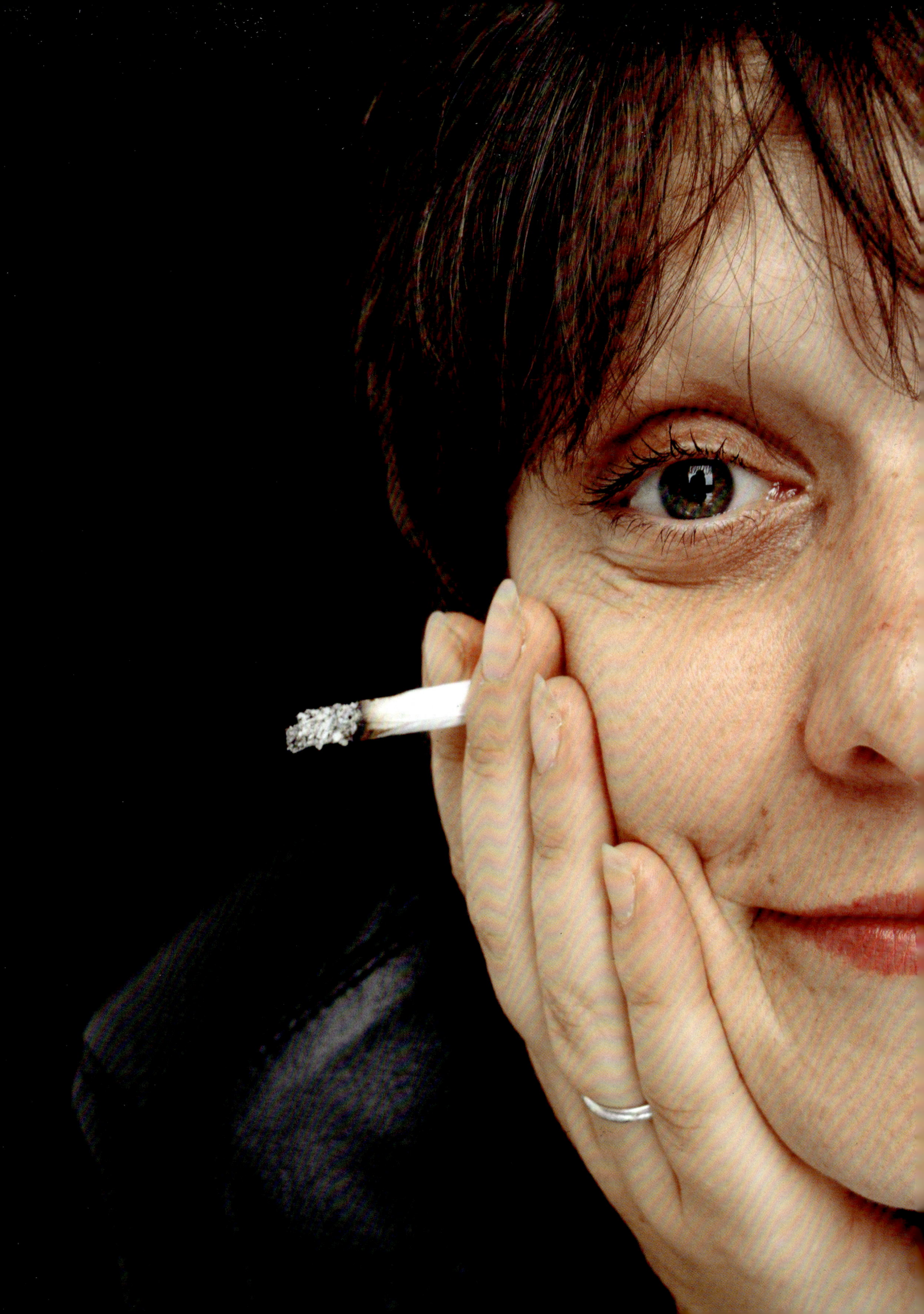

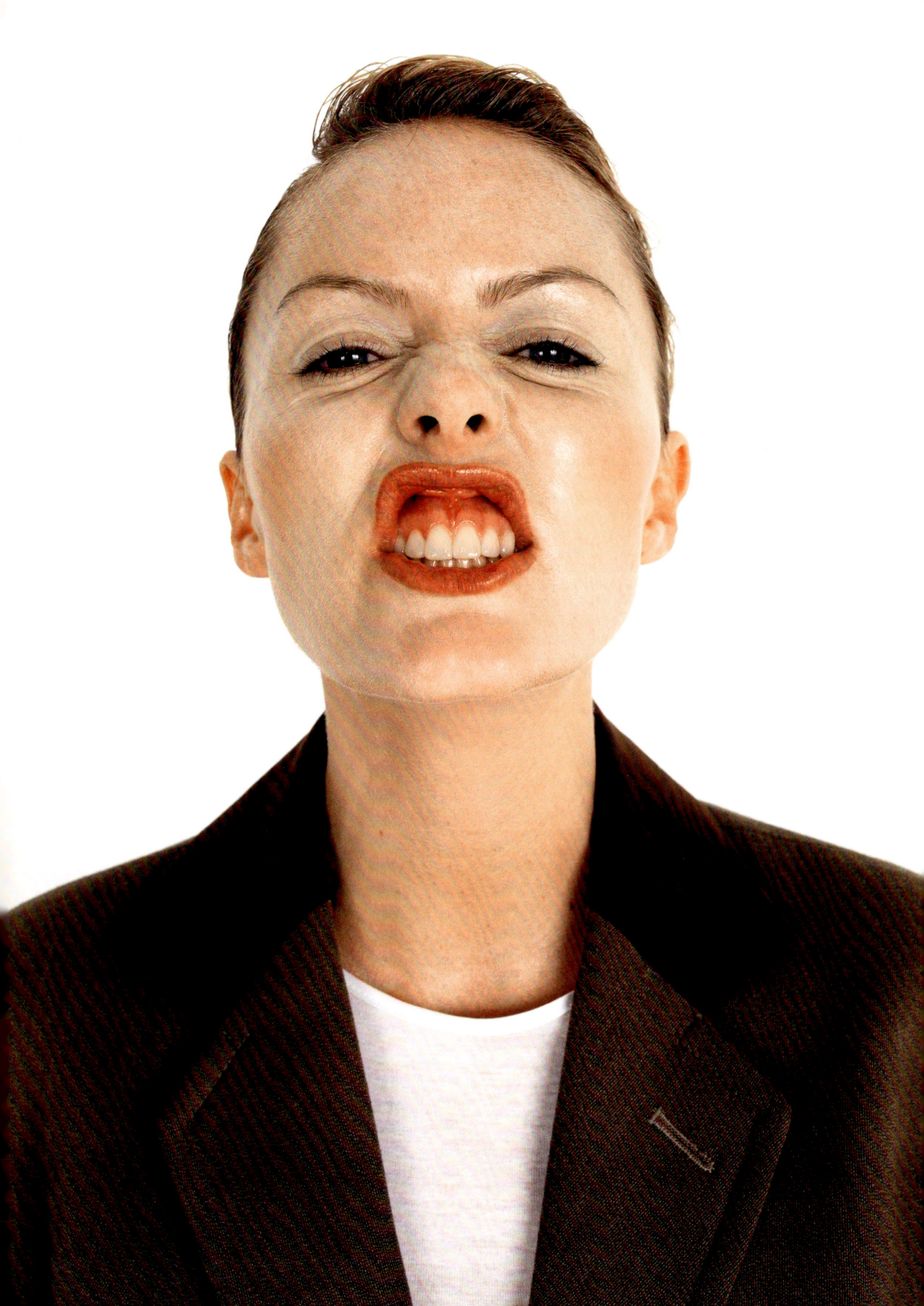

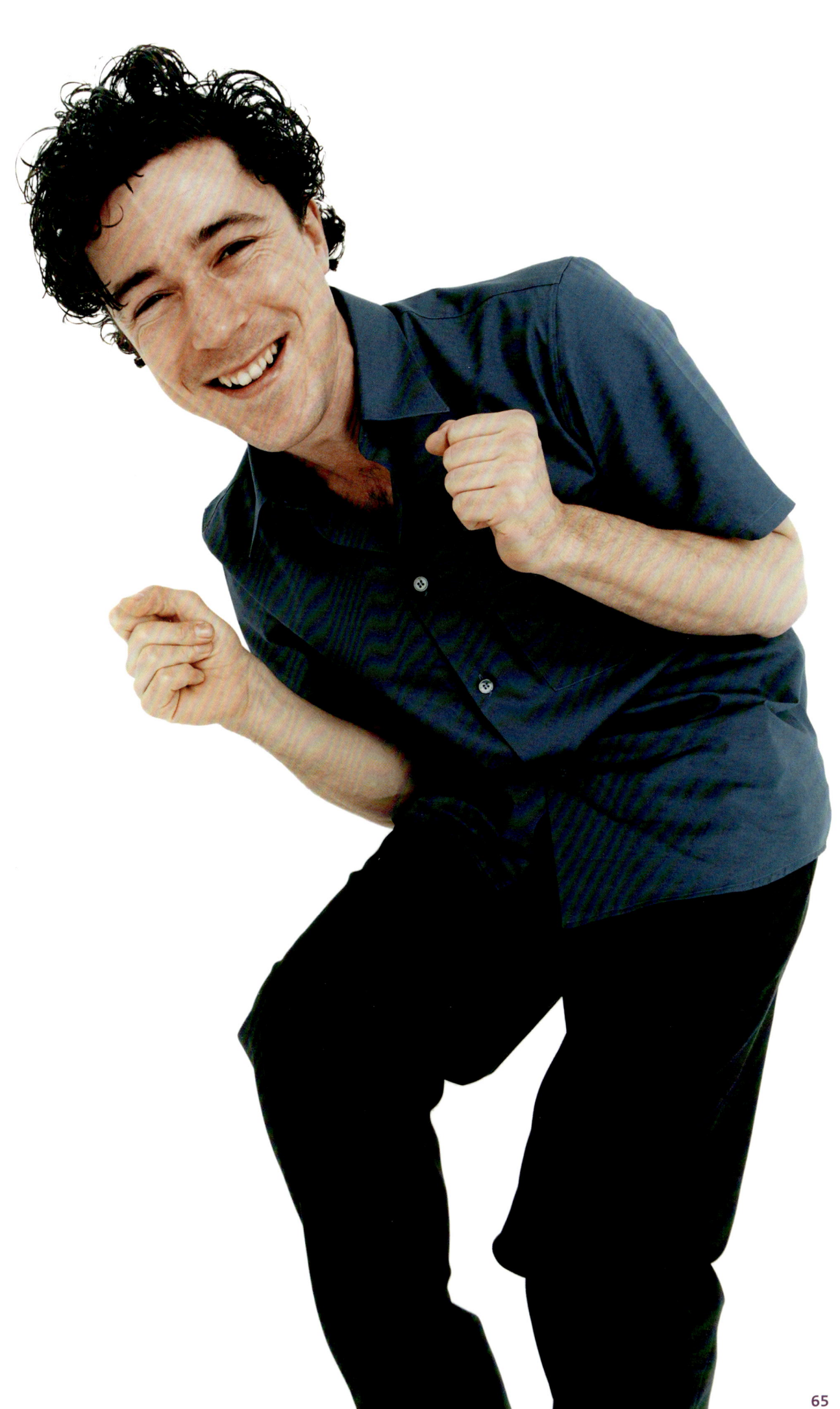

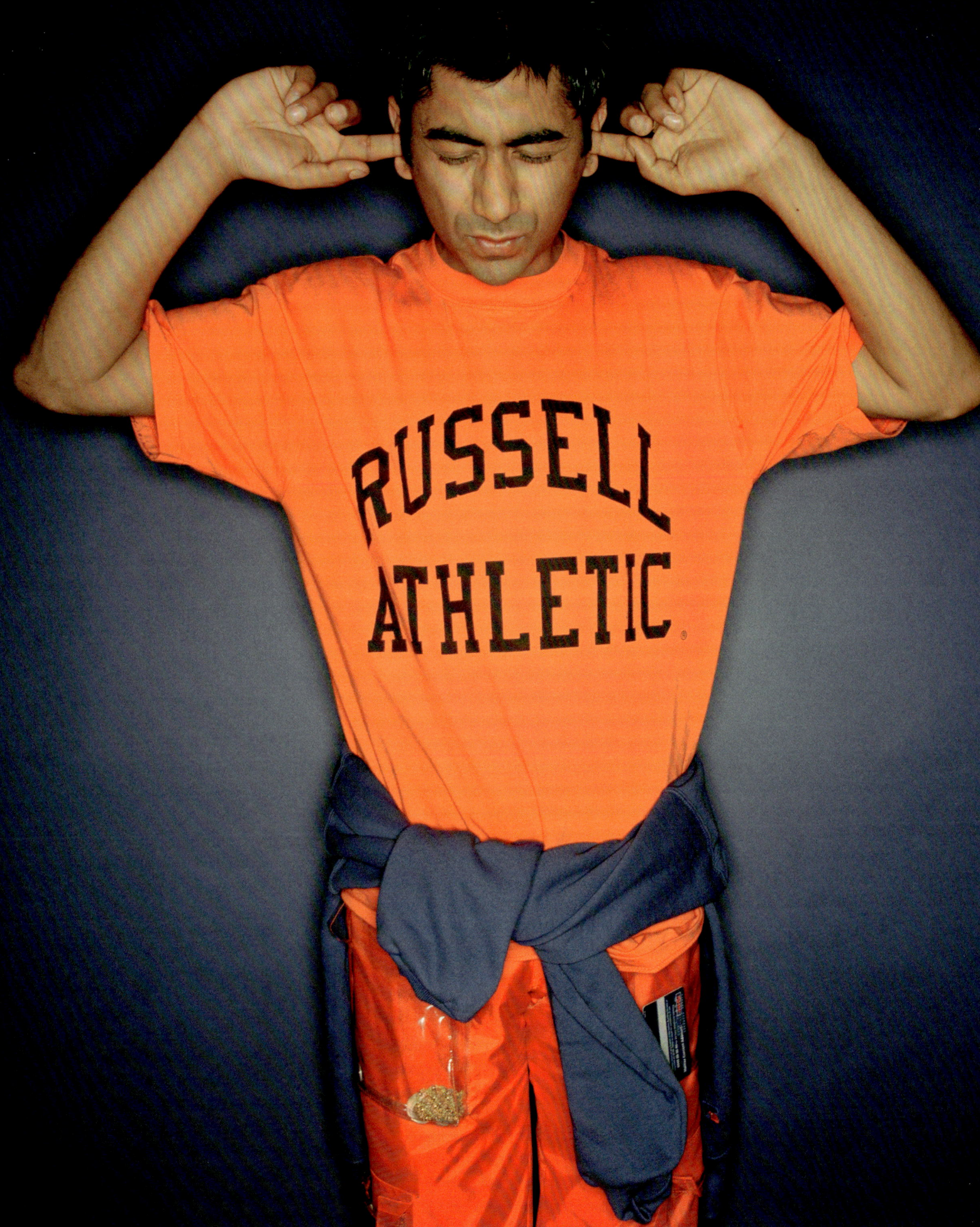

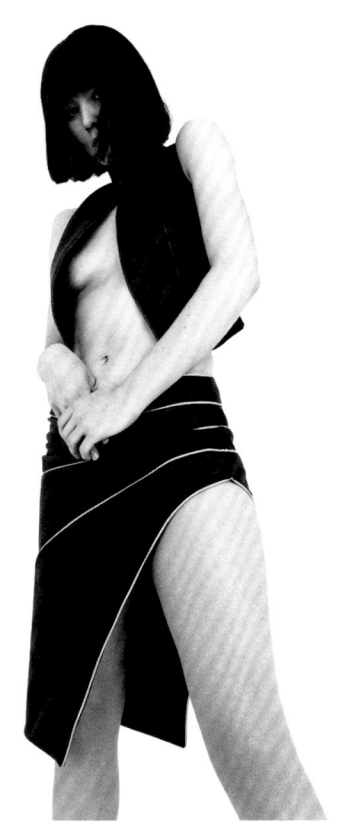

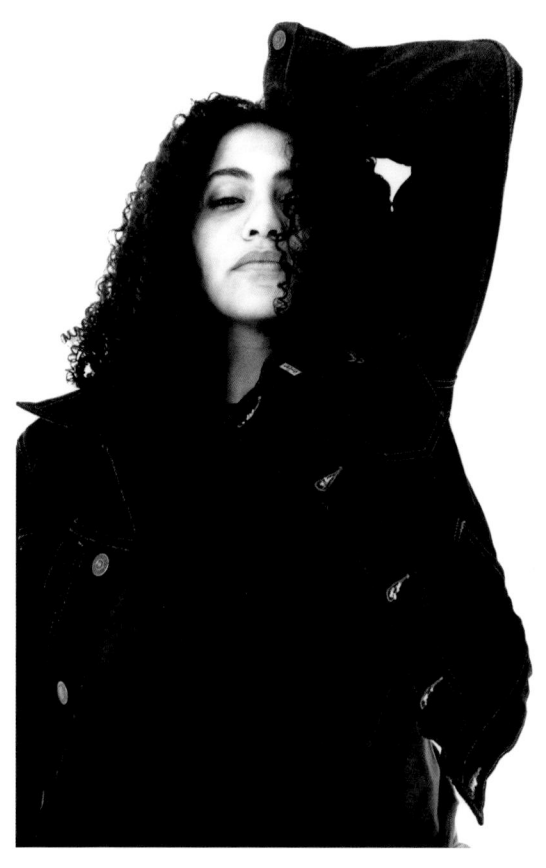

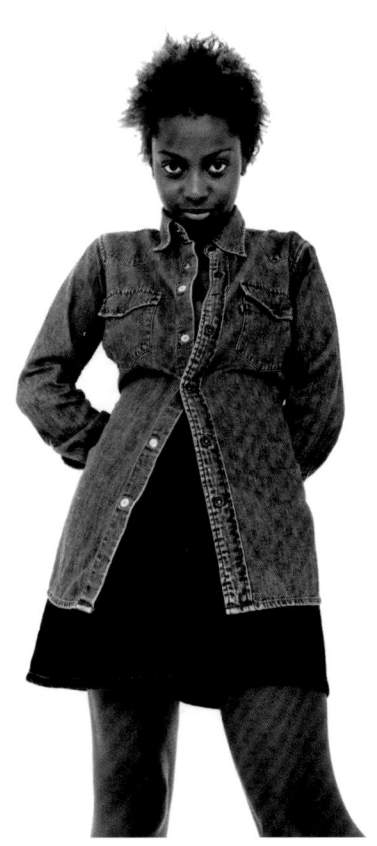

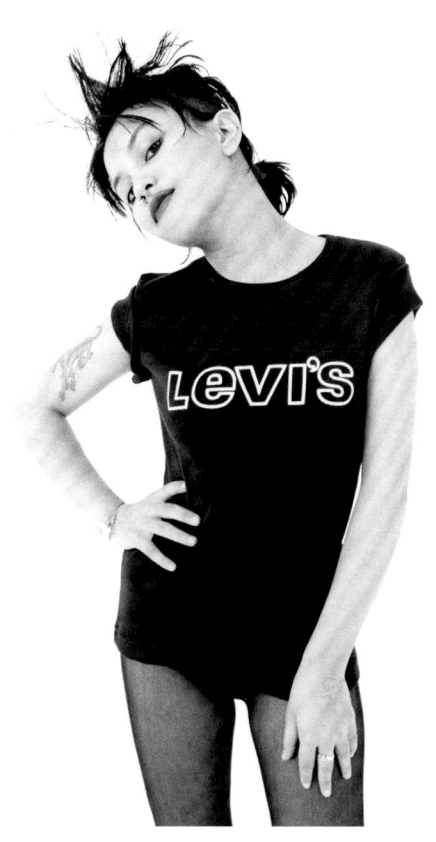

The All-Girl Club, Issue 23, 1996

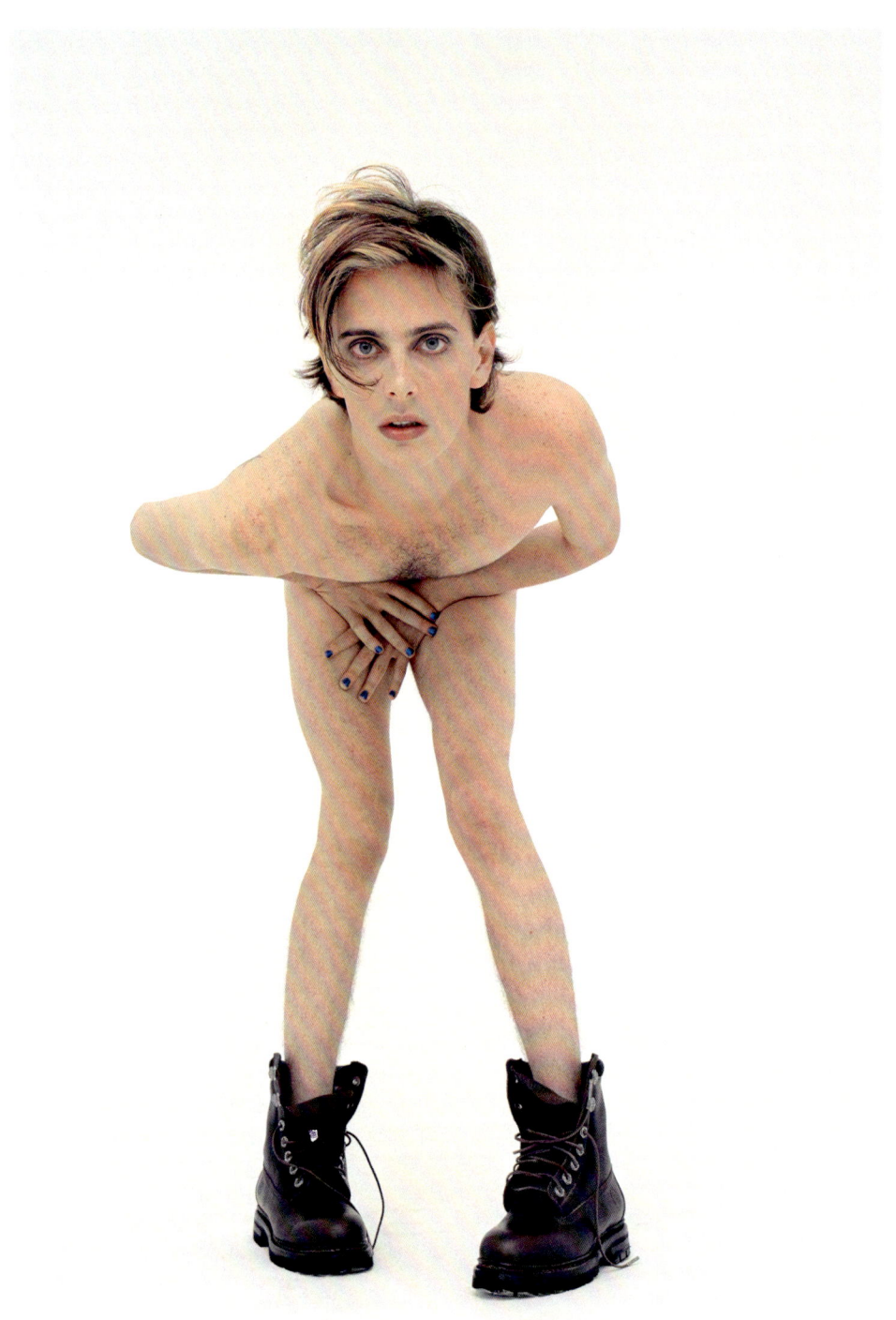

Posh Punks, Issue 9, 1994

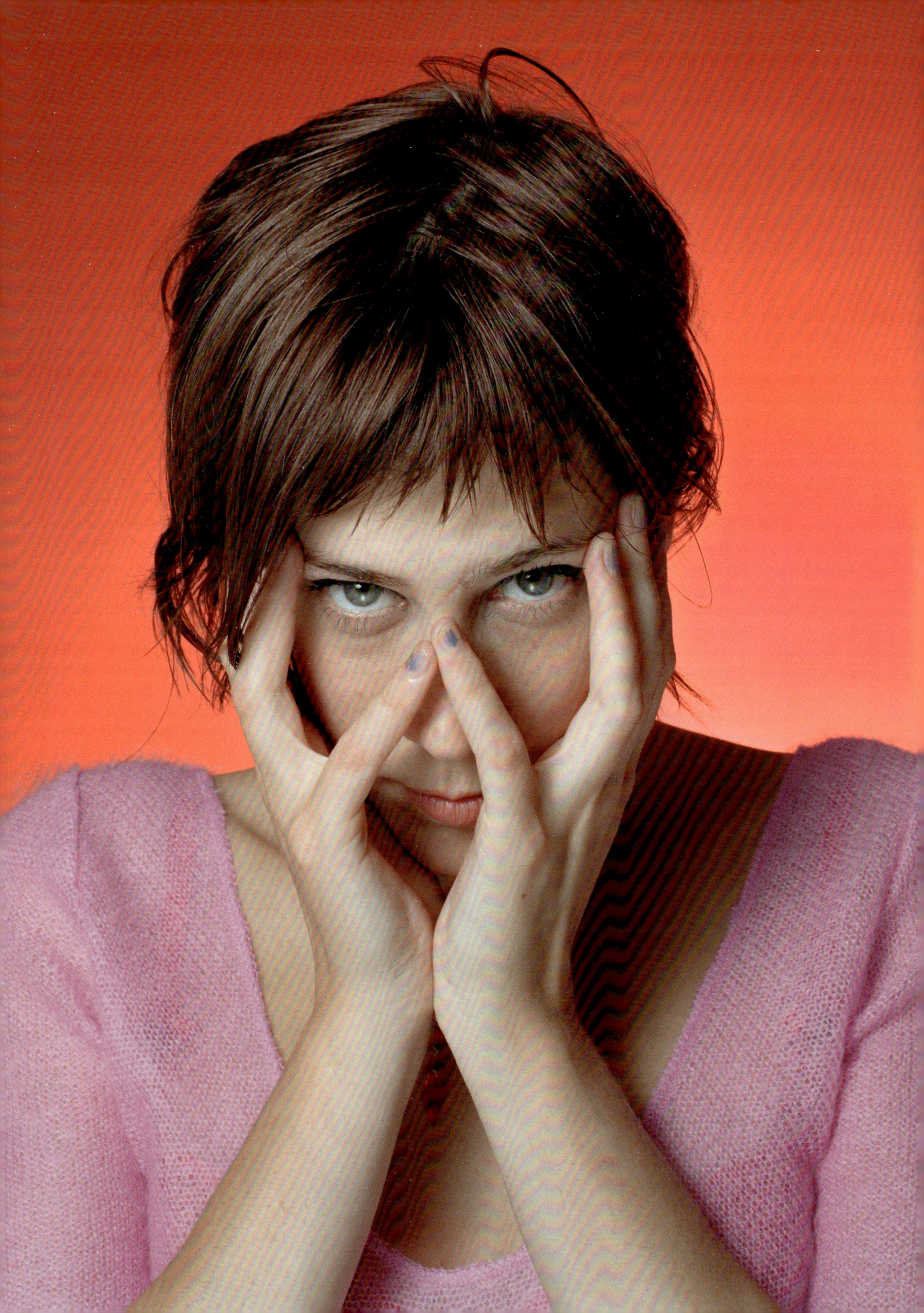

The Cast, Issue 26, 1996

Next Pages - 03 Minute Heroes, Issue 35, 1997
           Out of the Dark, Issue 98, 2003

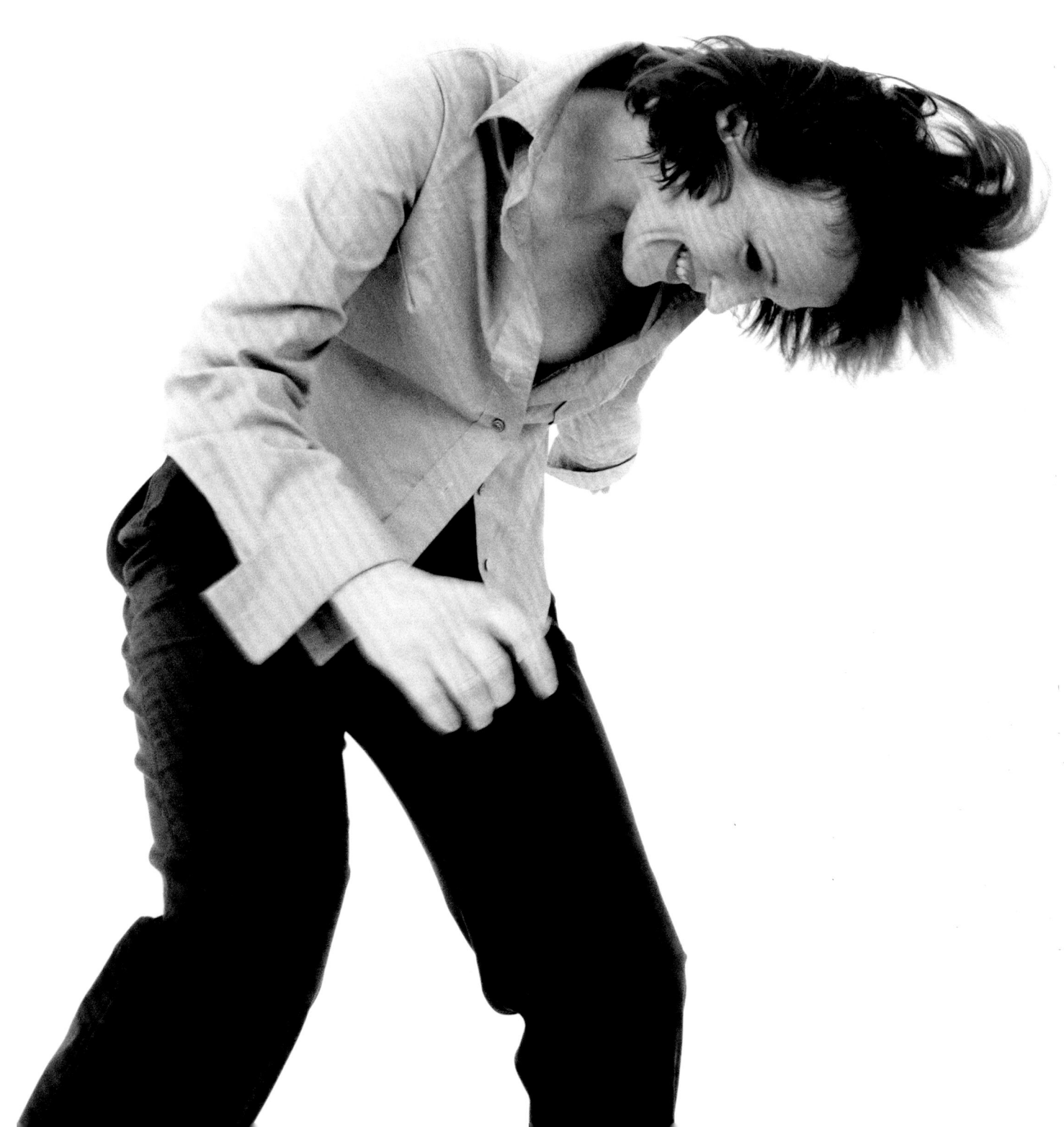

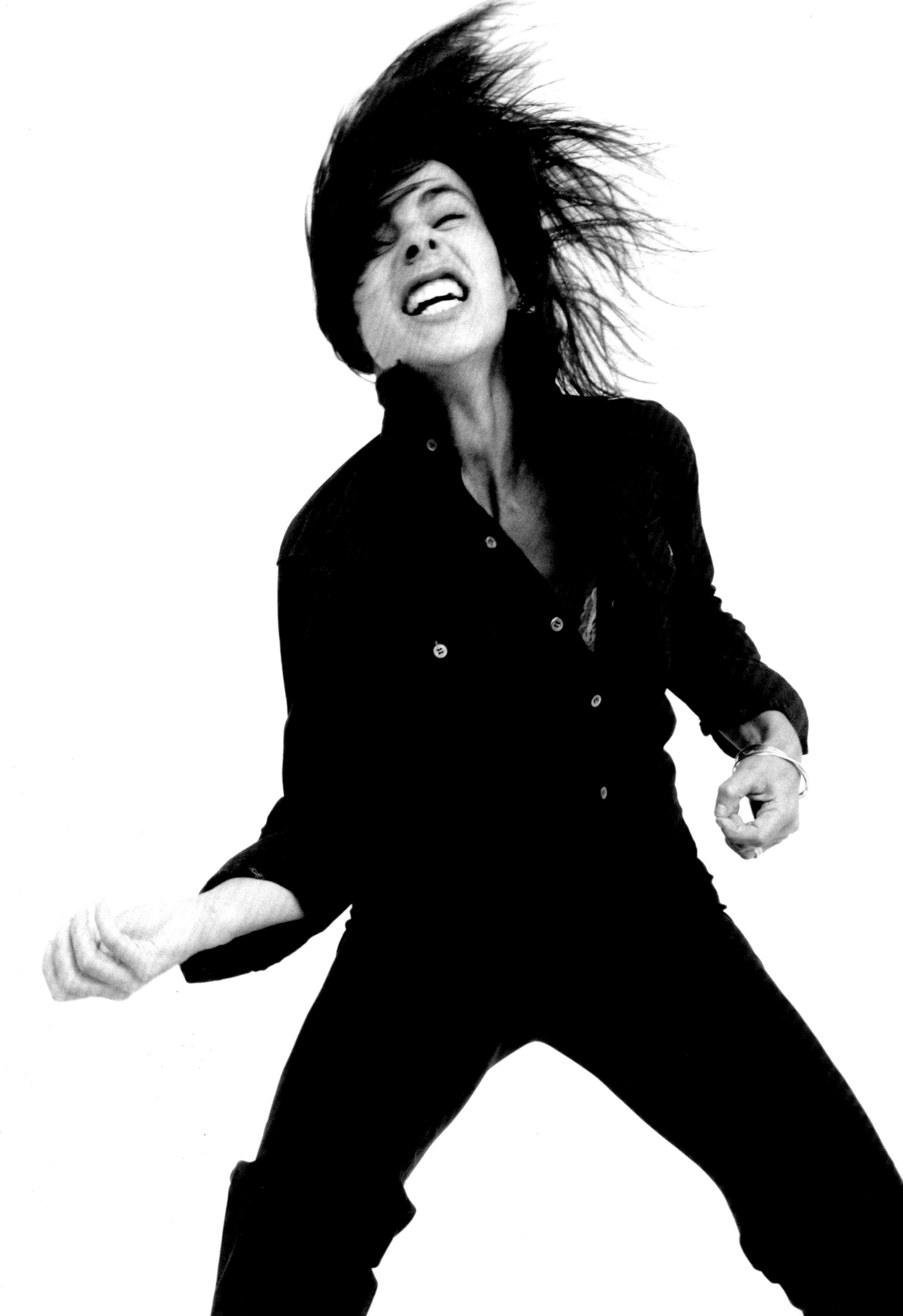

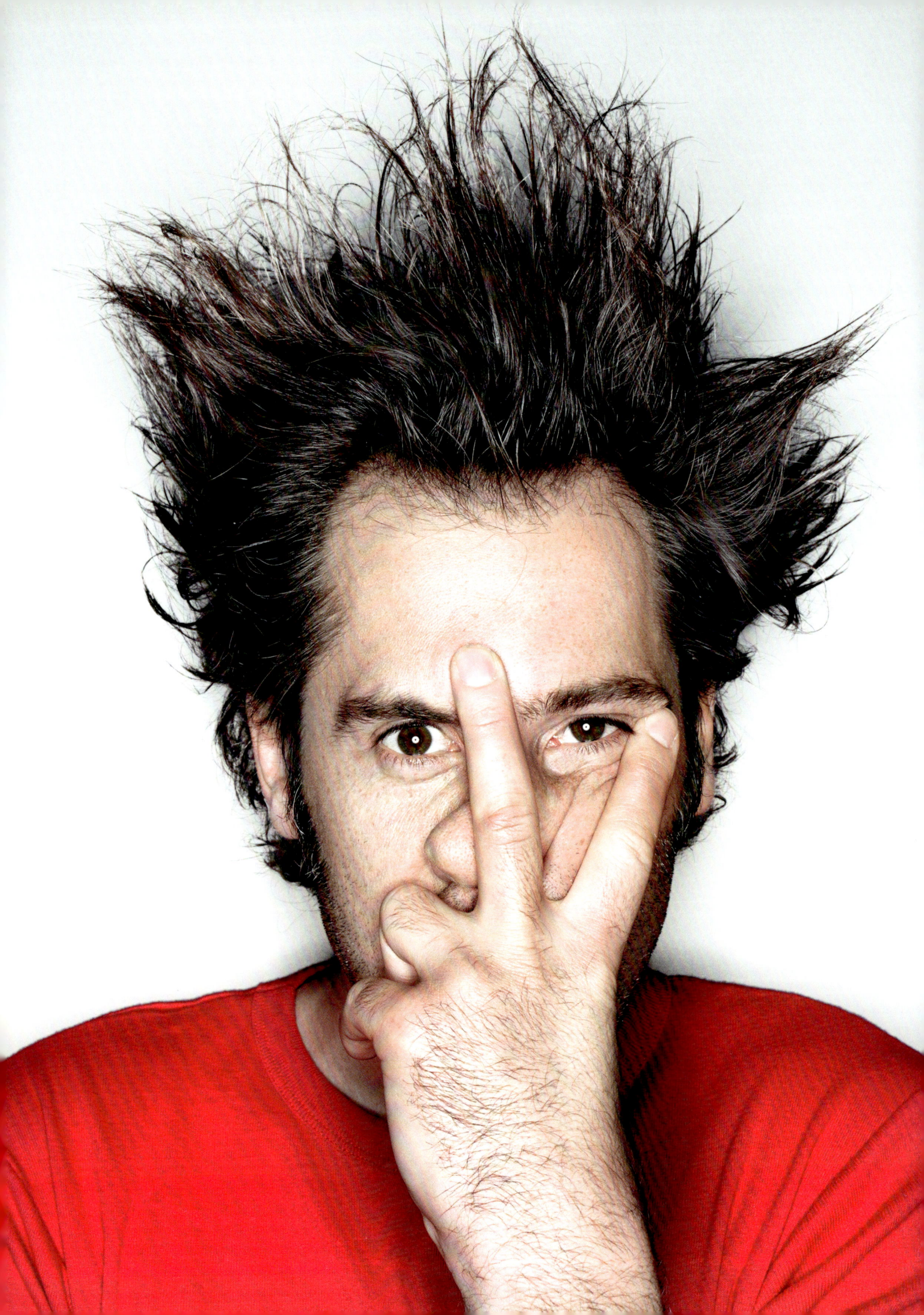

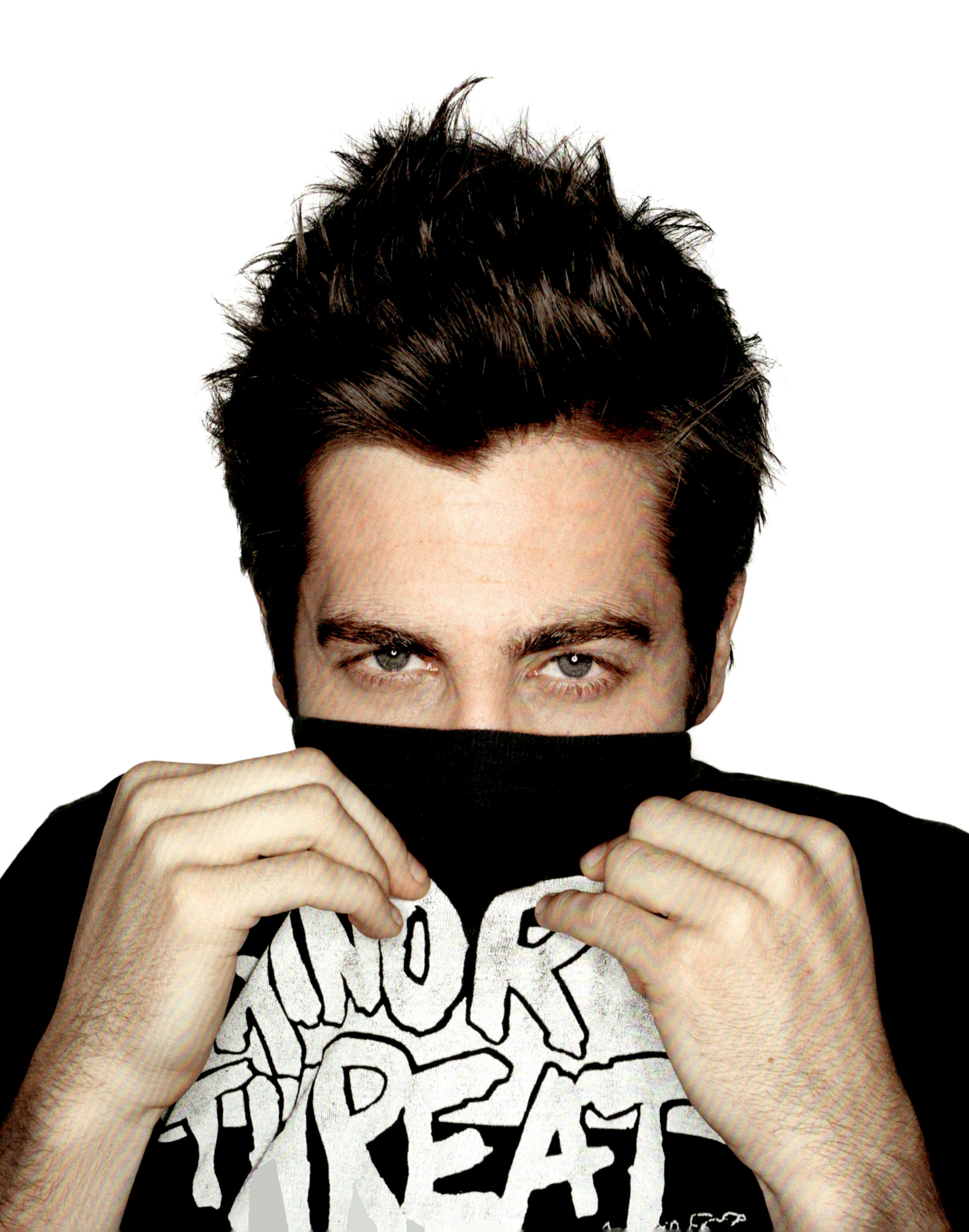

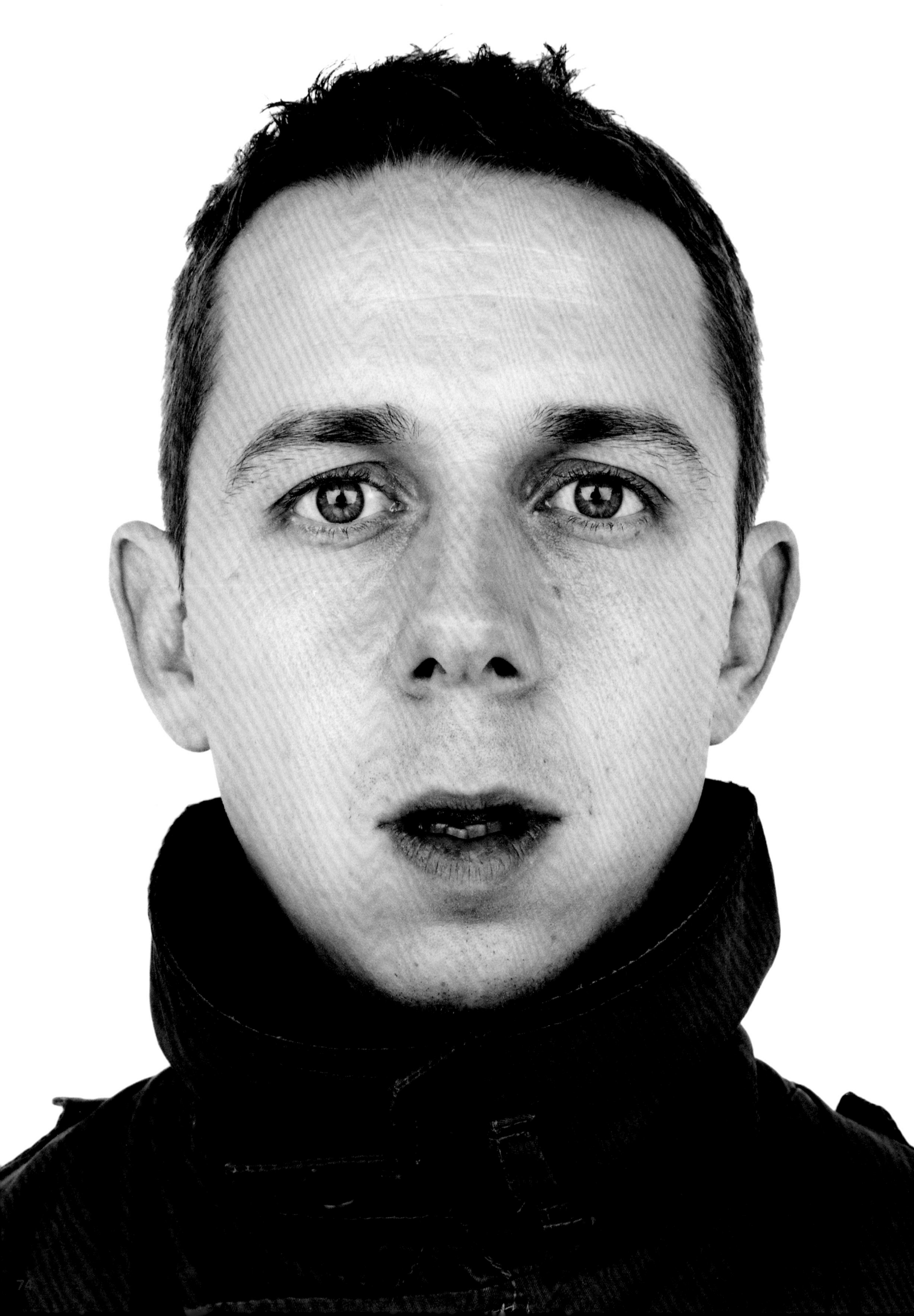

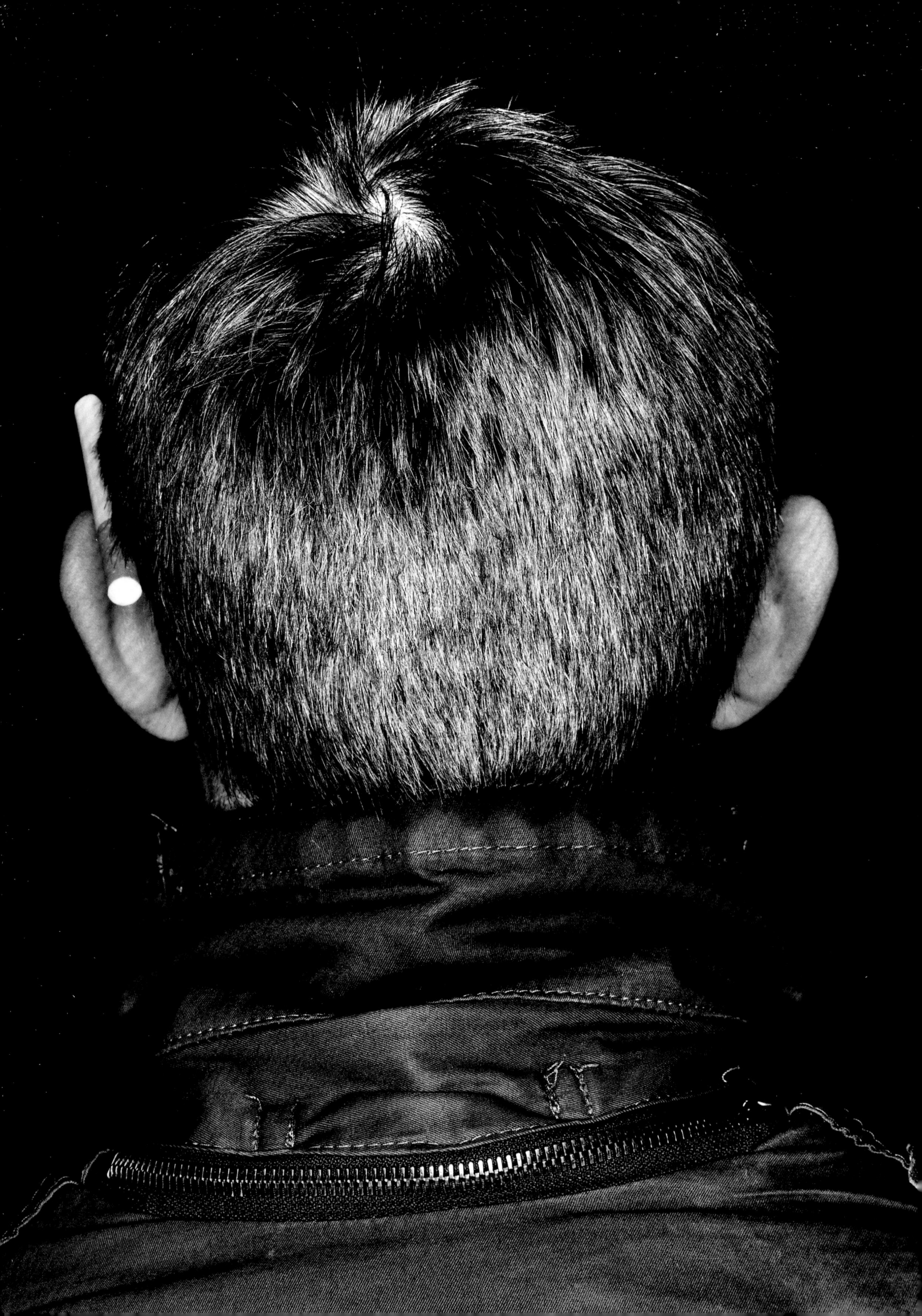

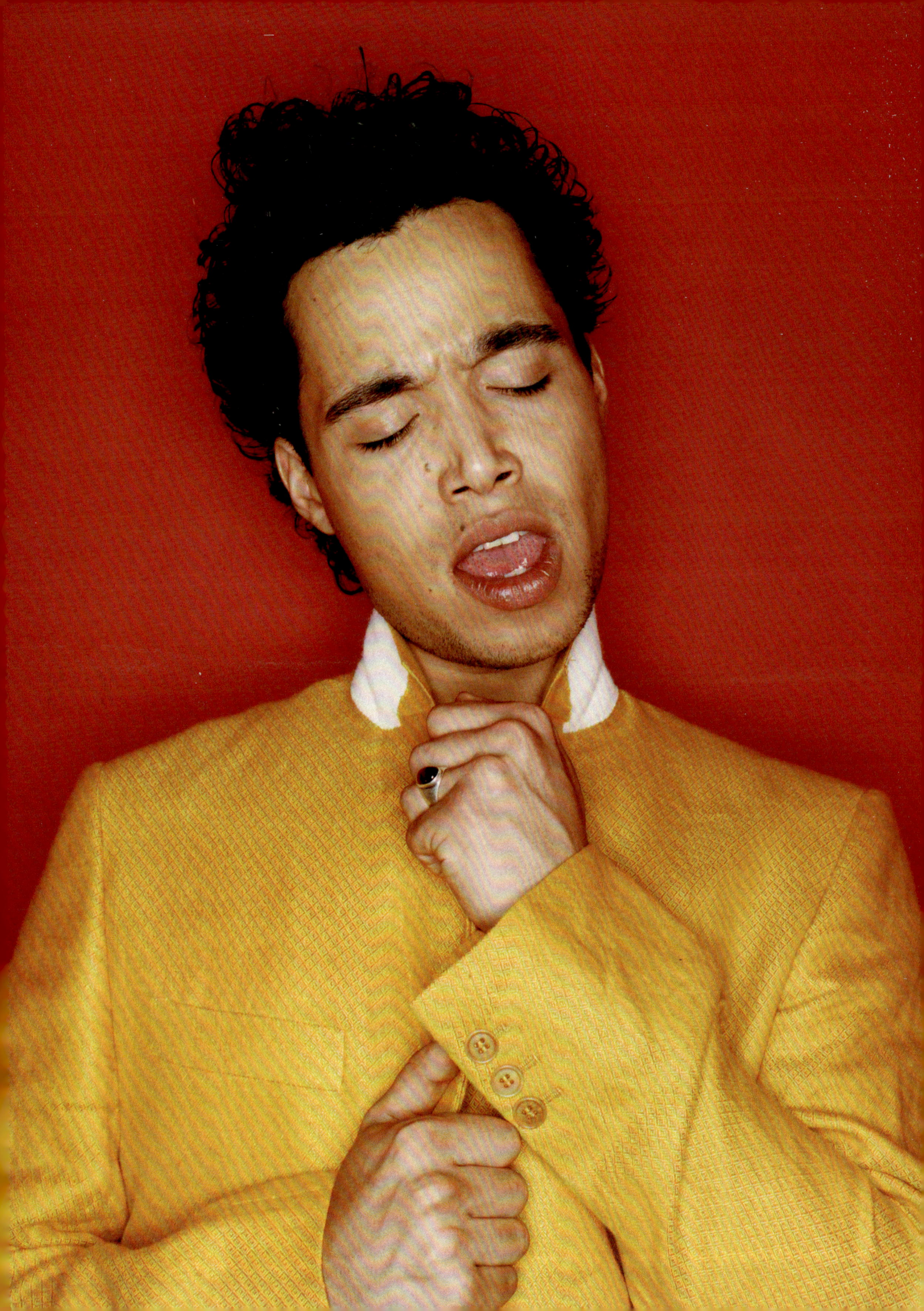

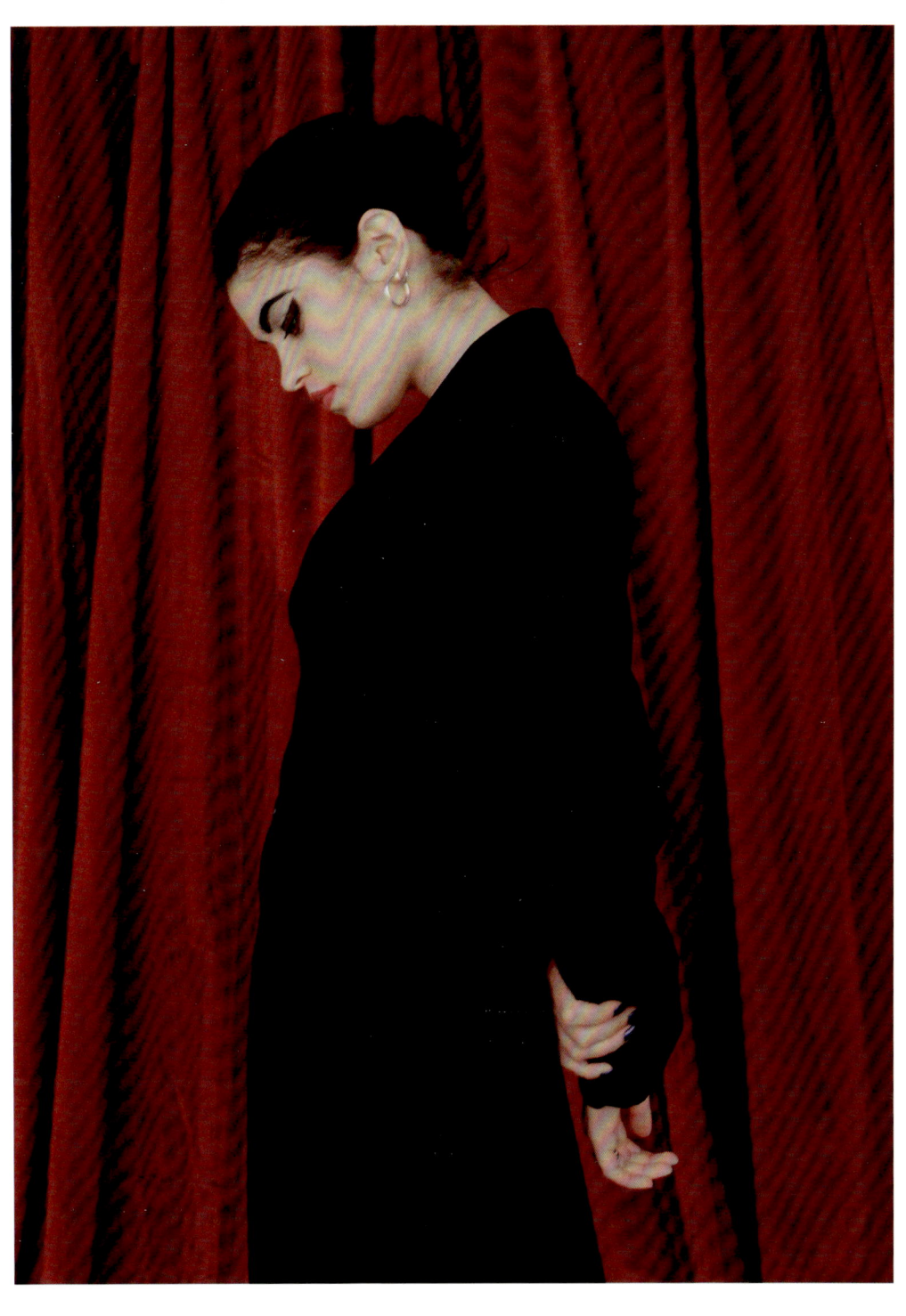

In the Meantime, Issue 27, 1996

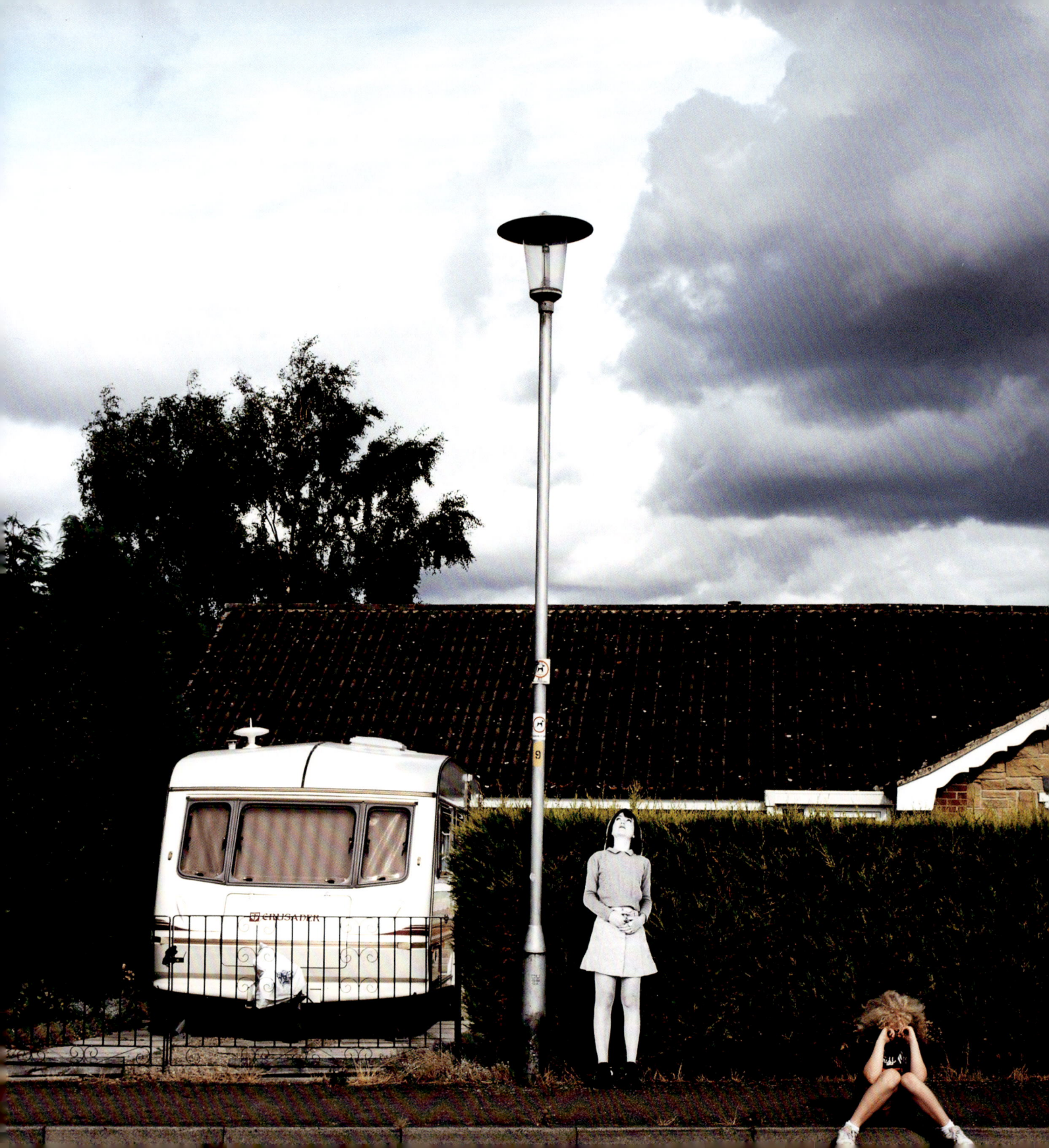

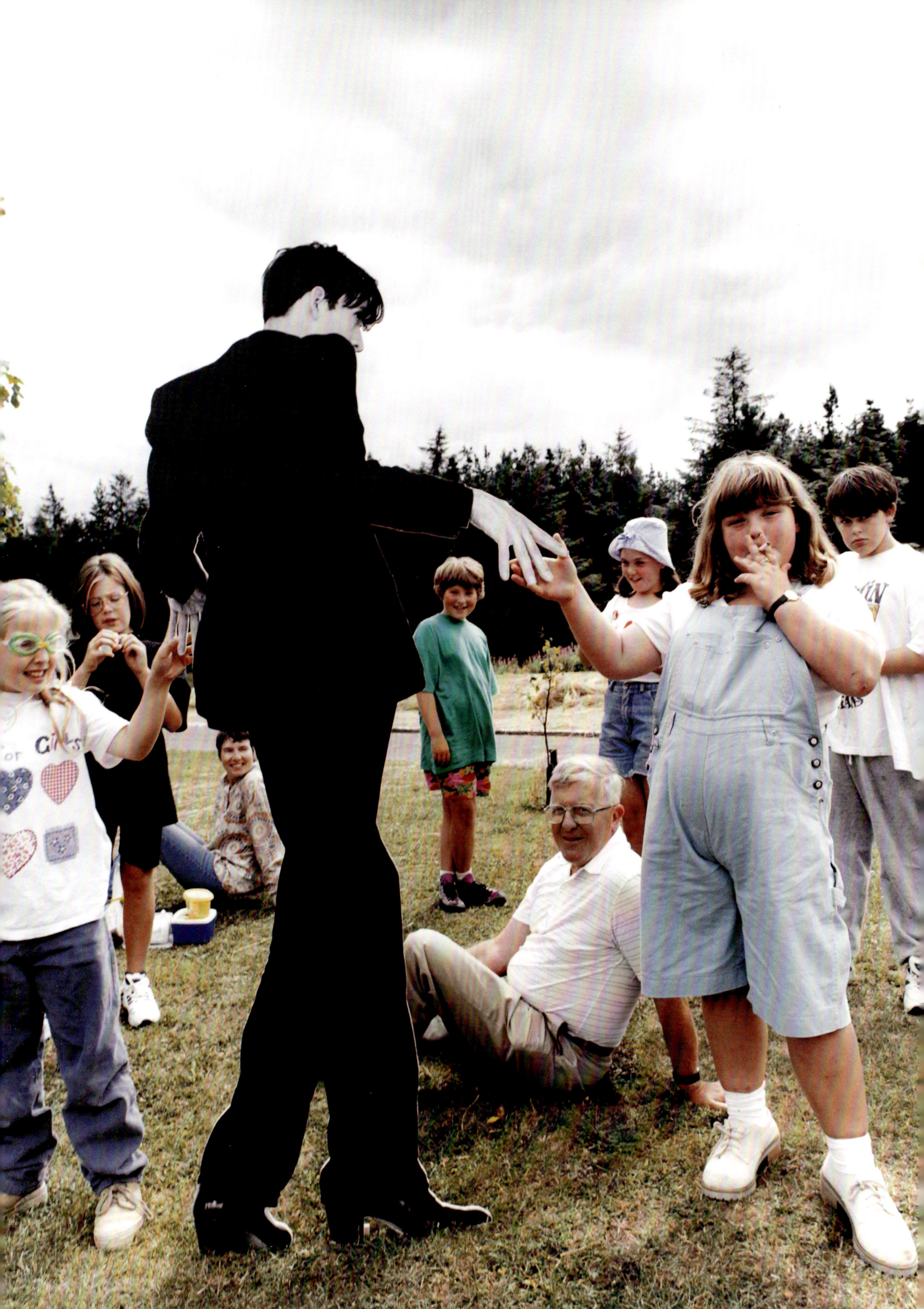

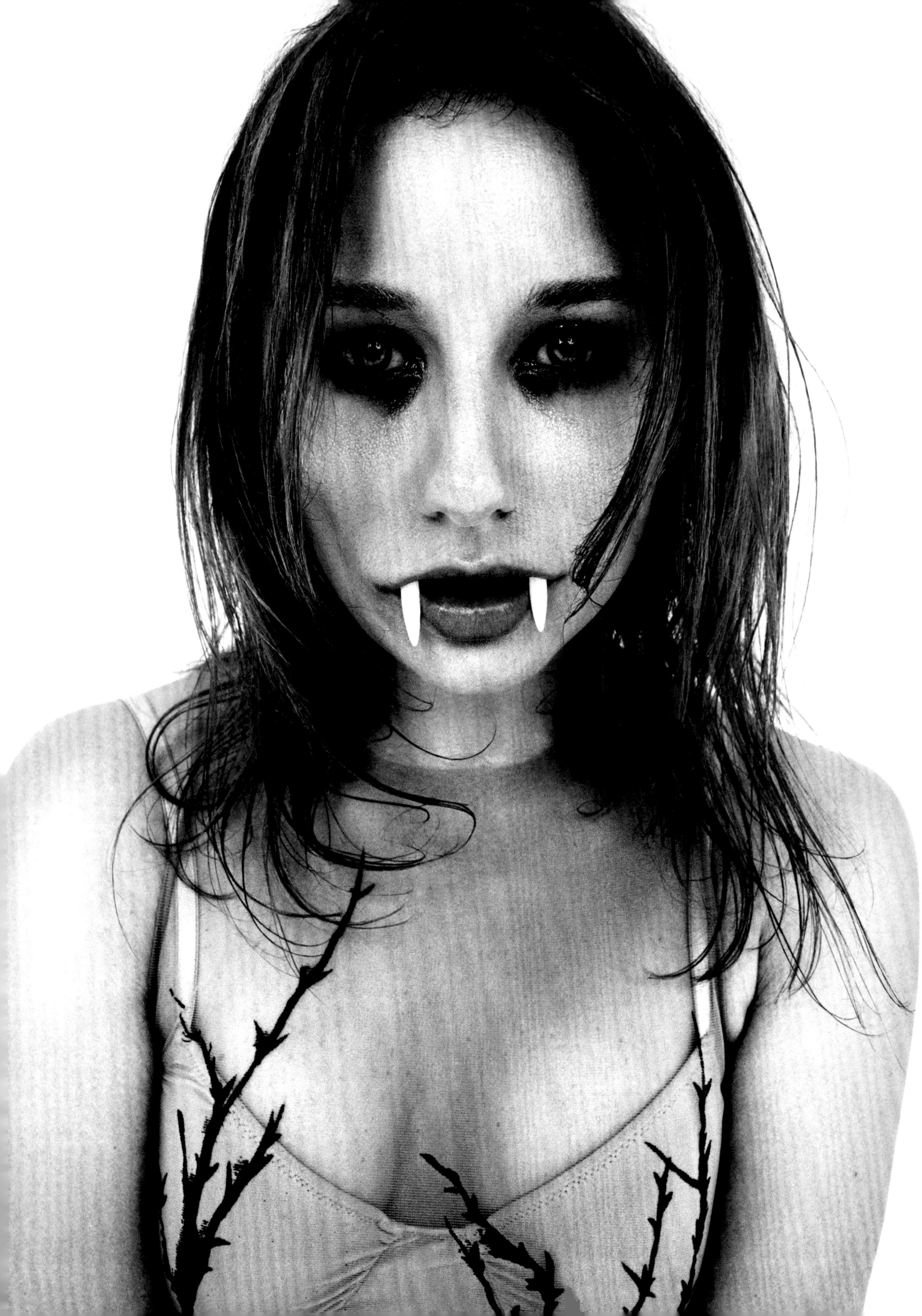

Previous Pages - It's a Wrap, Issue 15, 1995

Opposite Page - Talk of the Devil, Issue 17, 1995

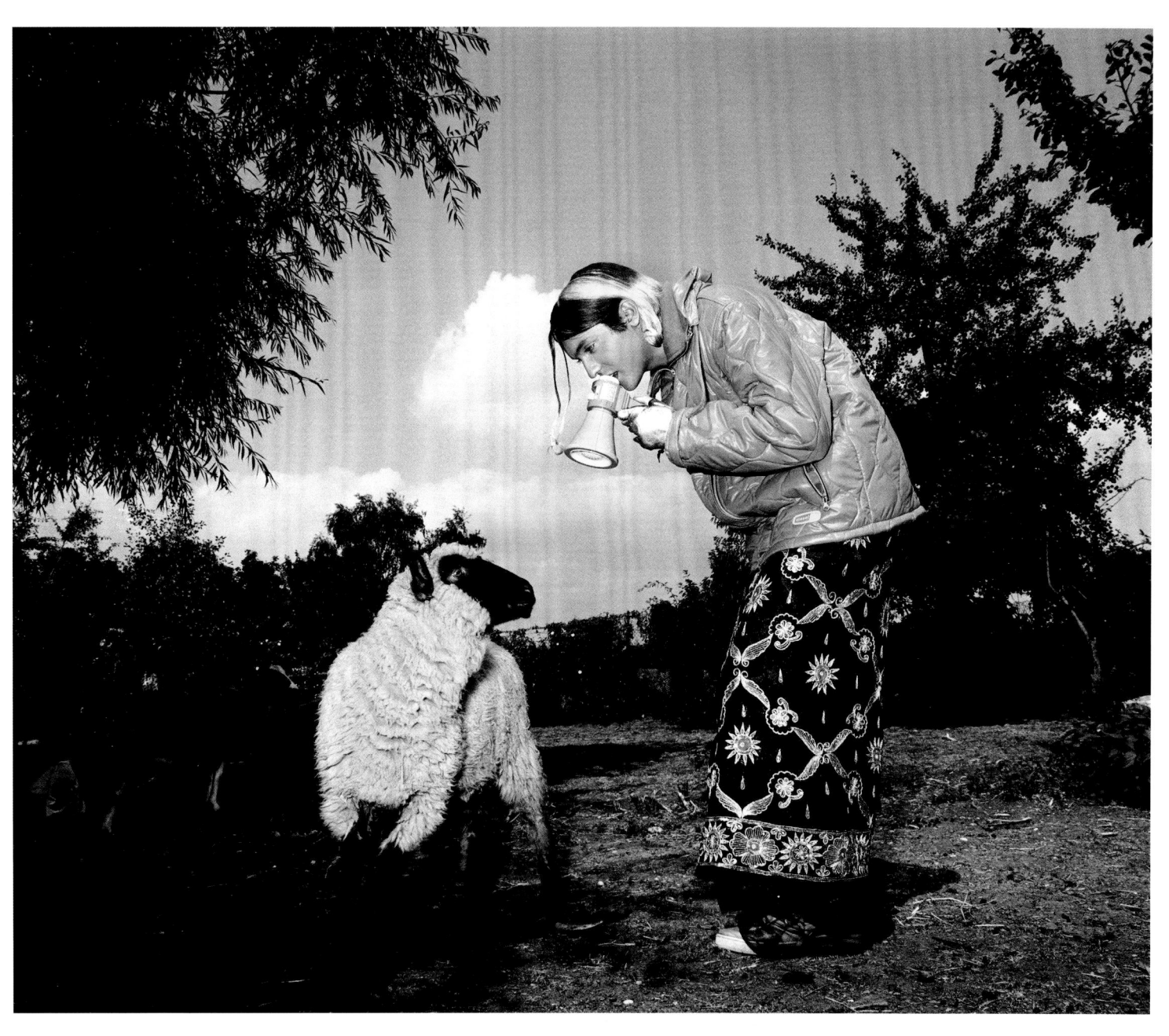

The World According to Jas Mann, Issue 14, 1995

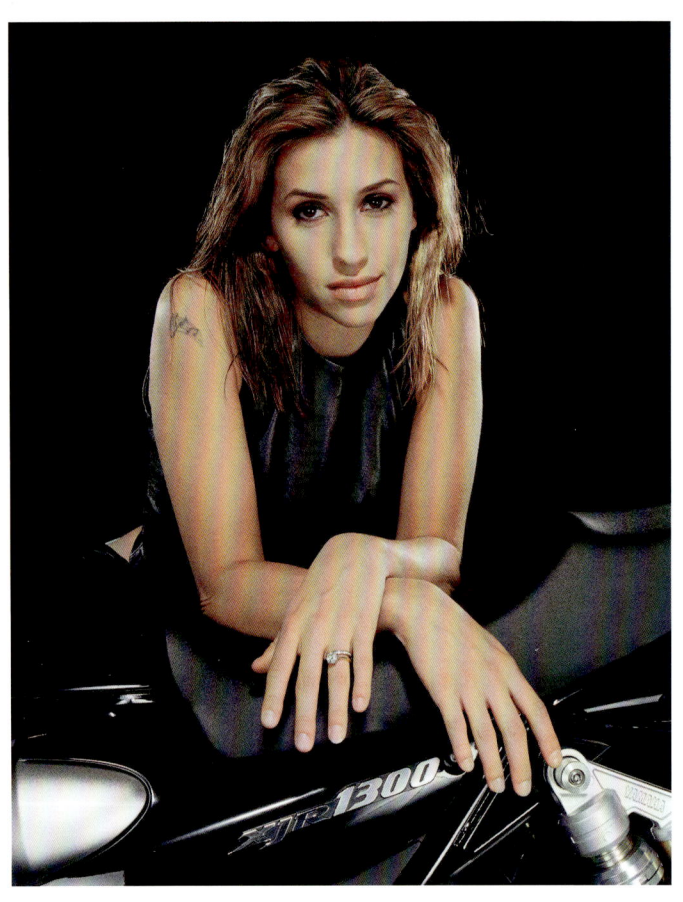
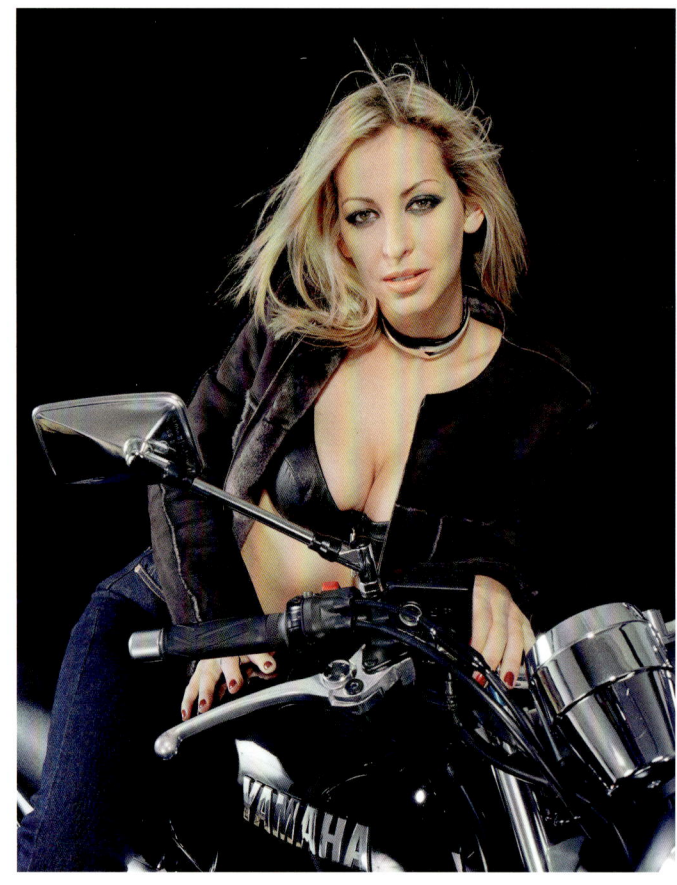
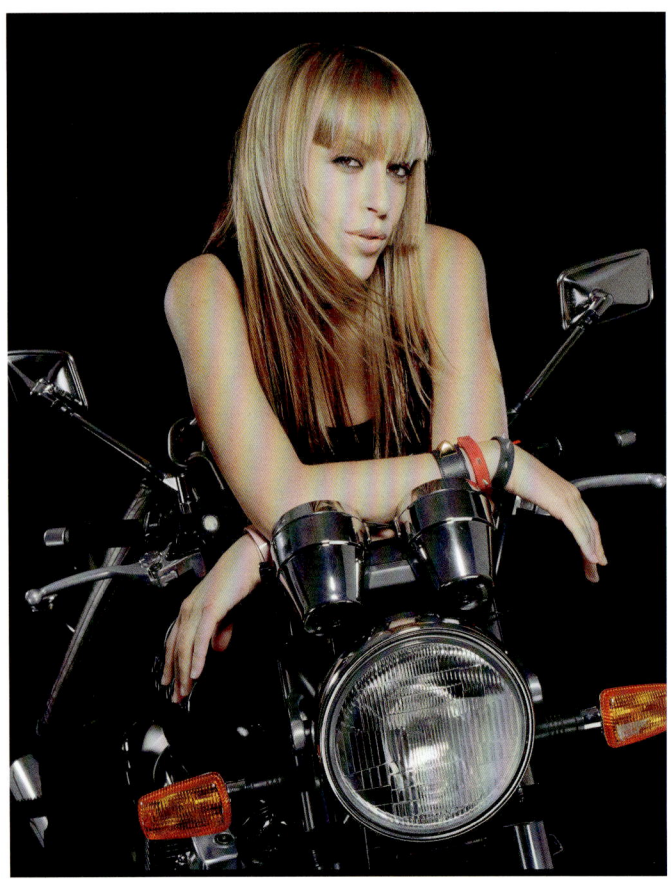
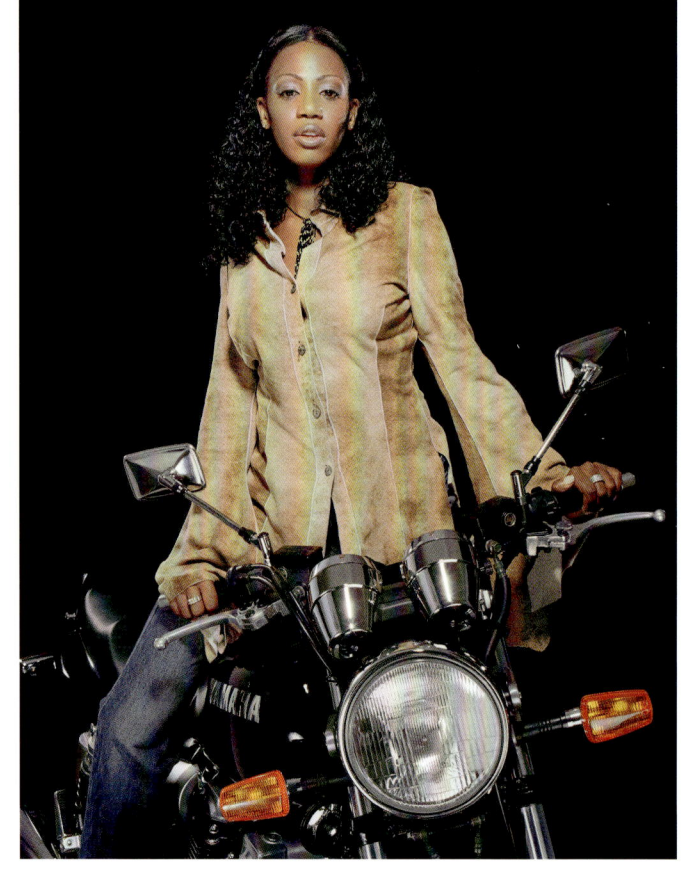

Hell's Angels, Issue 59, 1999

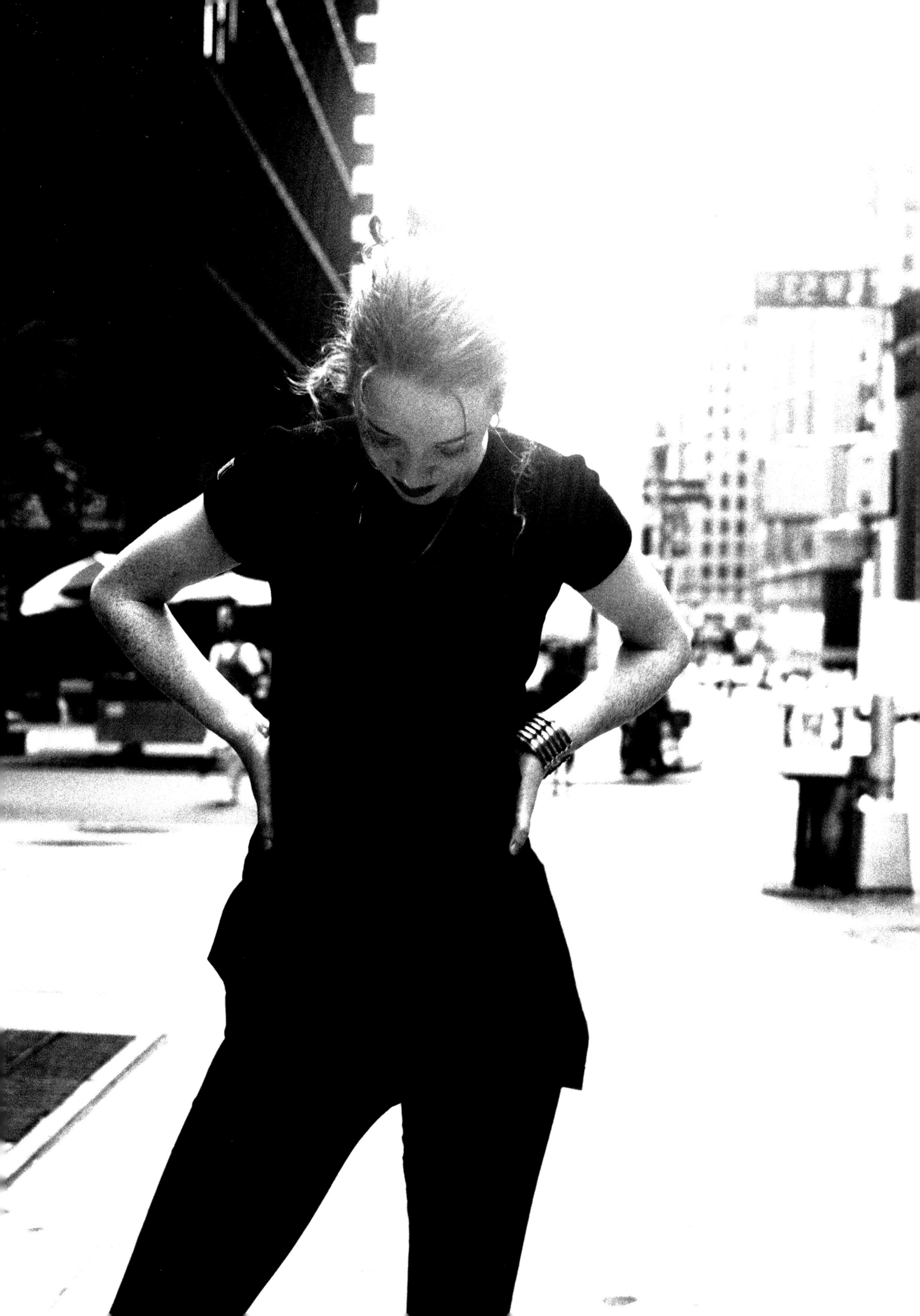

Previous Page - Bright Lights, Big City, Mission Impossible Supplement, 1993

Opposite Page - Talking About a Revolution, Vol. 2, Issue 10, 2004

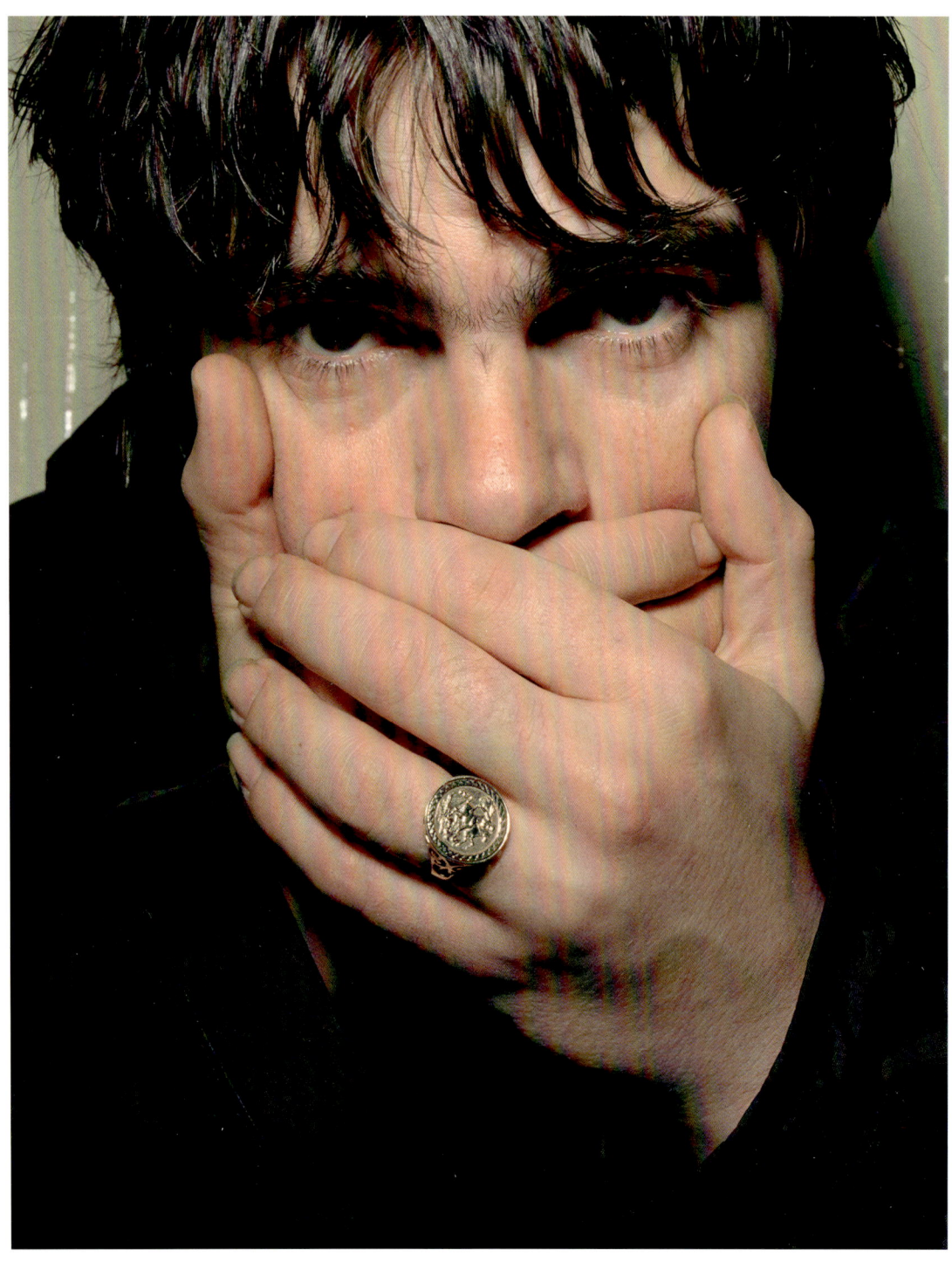

Class of '97, Issue 35, 1997

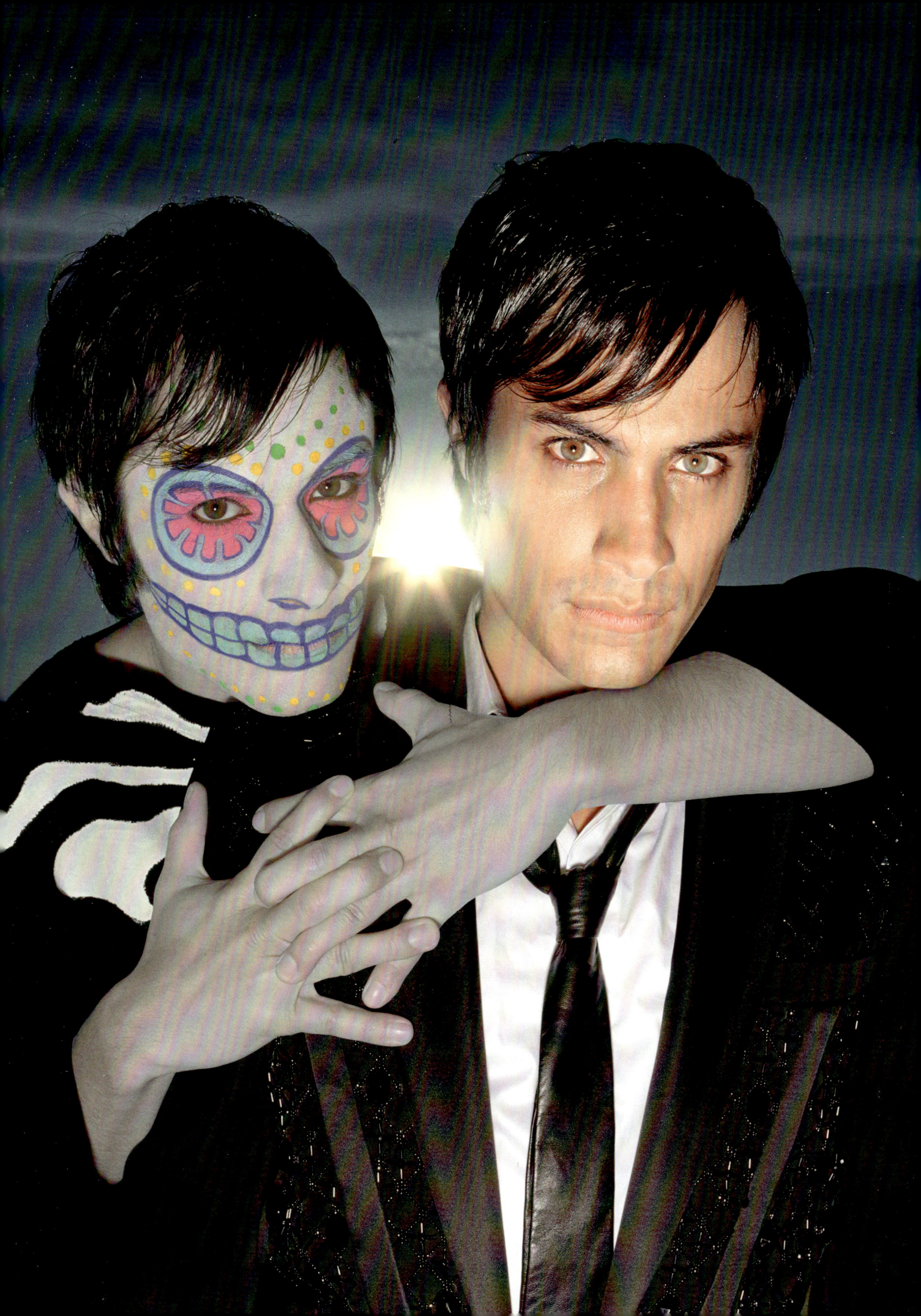

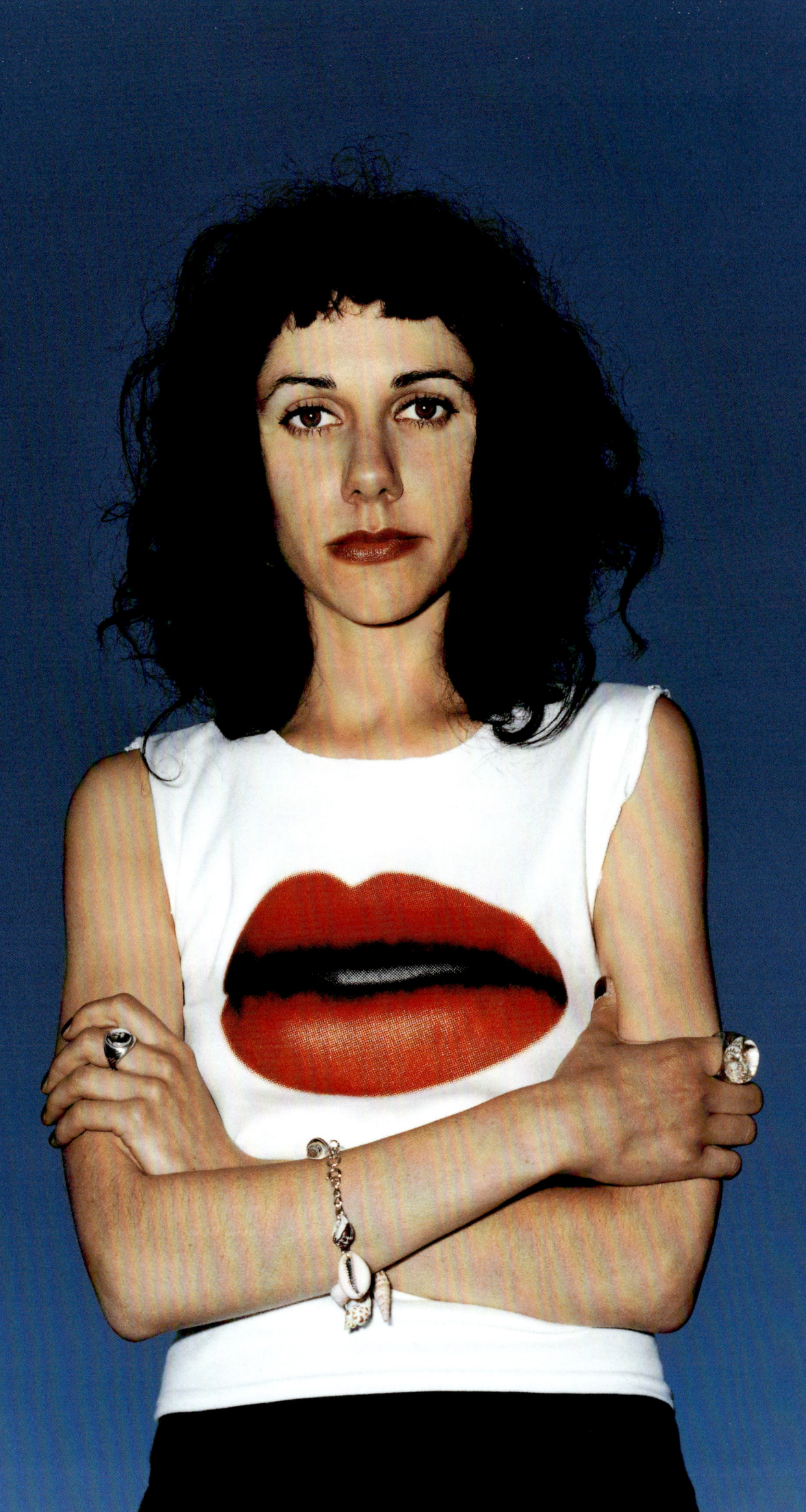

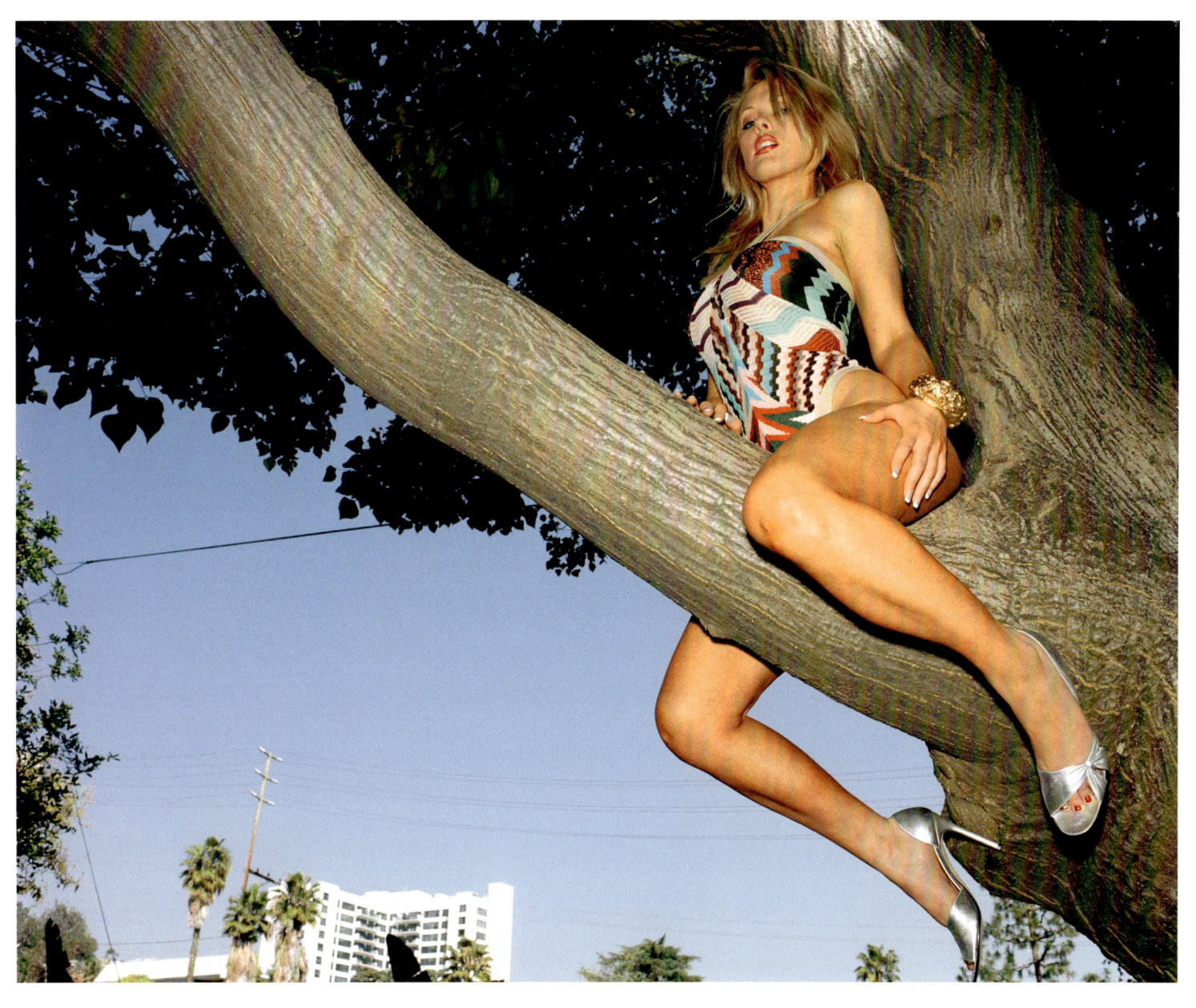

Model, Actress, Whatever, Vol. 2, Issue 3, 2003

HAVE HEROES/OBSESS AND COLLECT/ SHARE MOMENTS/FALL IN LOVE...

ACCEPT NO IMITATIONS

There are some people who are more than the sum of their parts; their impact on popular culture is so ingrained in the zeitgeist that they feel part of you. Rankin's lens has regularly captured those people.

Interestingly though, there is no overt reverence in Rankin's photographic style. The icons he captures are not untouchable, rather the opposite is true. These legends of music, film and television are human beings, worthy of love and obsession, not due to their celebrity aura but rather because of their humanity.

Debbie Harry, eyes closed, captured in a moment of breath and introspection, becomes something existential through Rankin. Eye contact is the expected norm for human-to-human connection, but seeing someone who stares out of posters and from vinyl sleeves closed off brings an intimacy so rarely felt.

Jamie Foxx in profile, photographed in 2005 just after his Oscar win for *Ray,* is a figure of strength. Shot from below, his raised jaw is sculptural, playing on art historical memories of ancient heroes photographed through a modern and politically astute lens.

Then there is Minnie Driver in 1996, post her break-out role and already hailed as a British actor of her generation; she has a cigarette in her mouth, a high slit on her dress, and the image is imbued with sexuality and sensuality. But this is not performed for the viewer, through Rankin's portrait she is a woman in control of her own being, at that moment enjoying just herself.

To look at Rankin's portfolio is to look at hundreds of images just like these. On one hand a clear fan-boy for rock stars and celebrities, on the other a photographer looking to capture something implicit in the human condition.

Opposite Page - No Different From Anyone Else?, Issue 14, 1995

Next Pages - Straight To the Point, Issue 20, 1996
            You're Making Me Hot, Issue 49, 1998

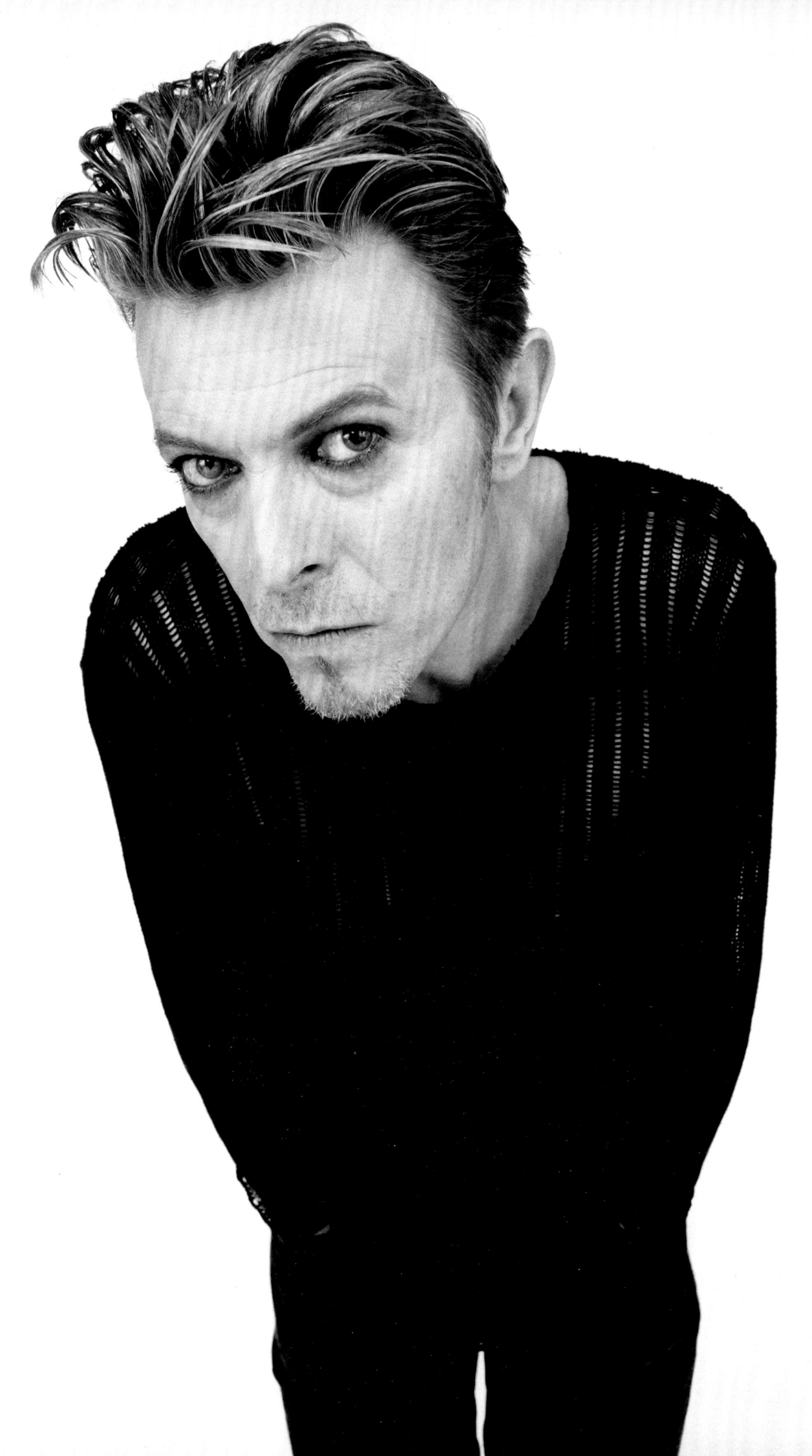

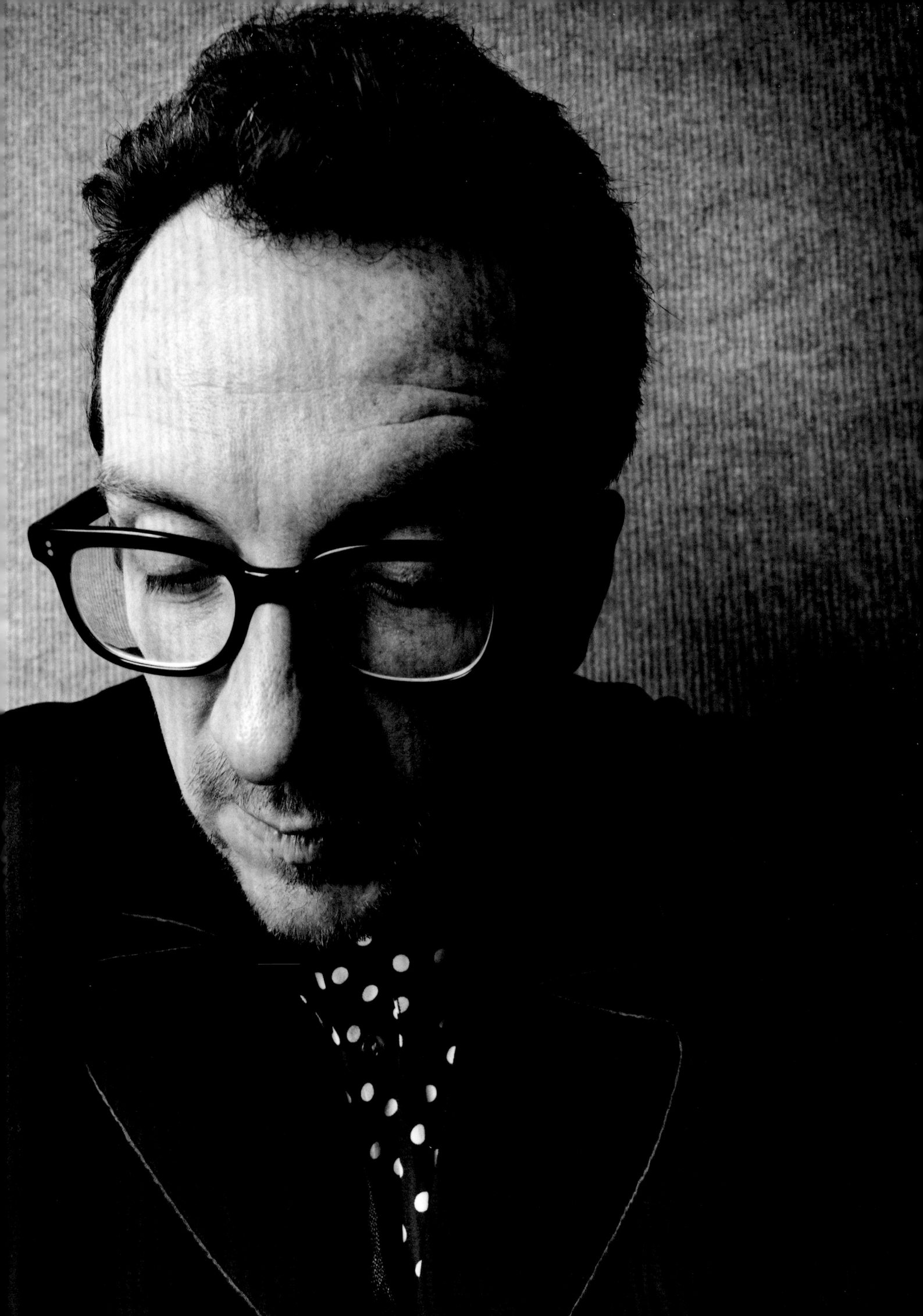

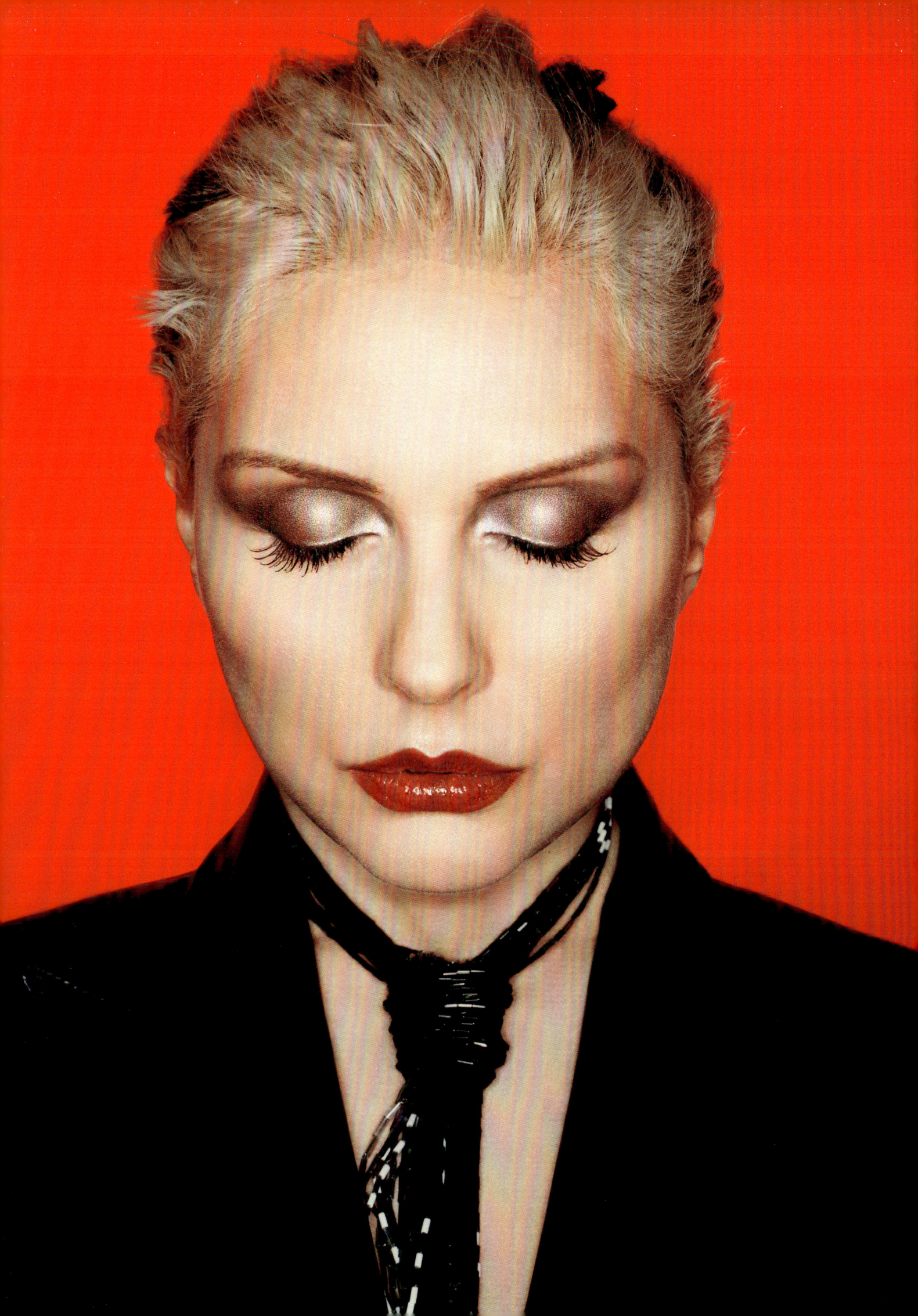

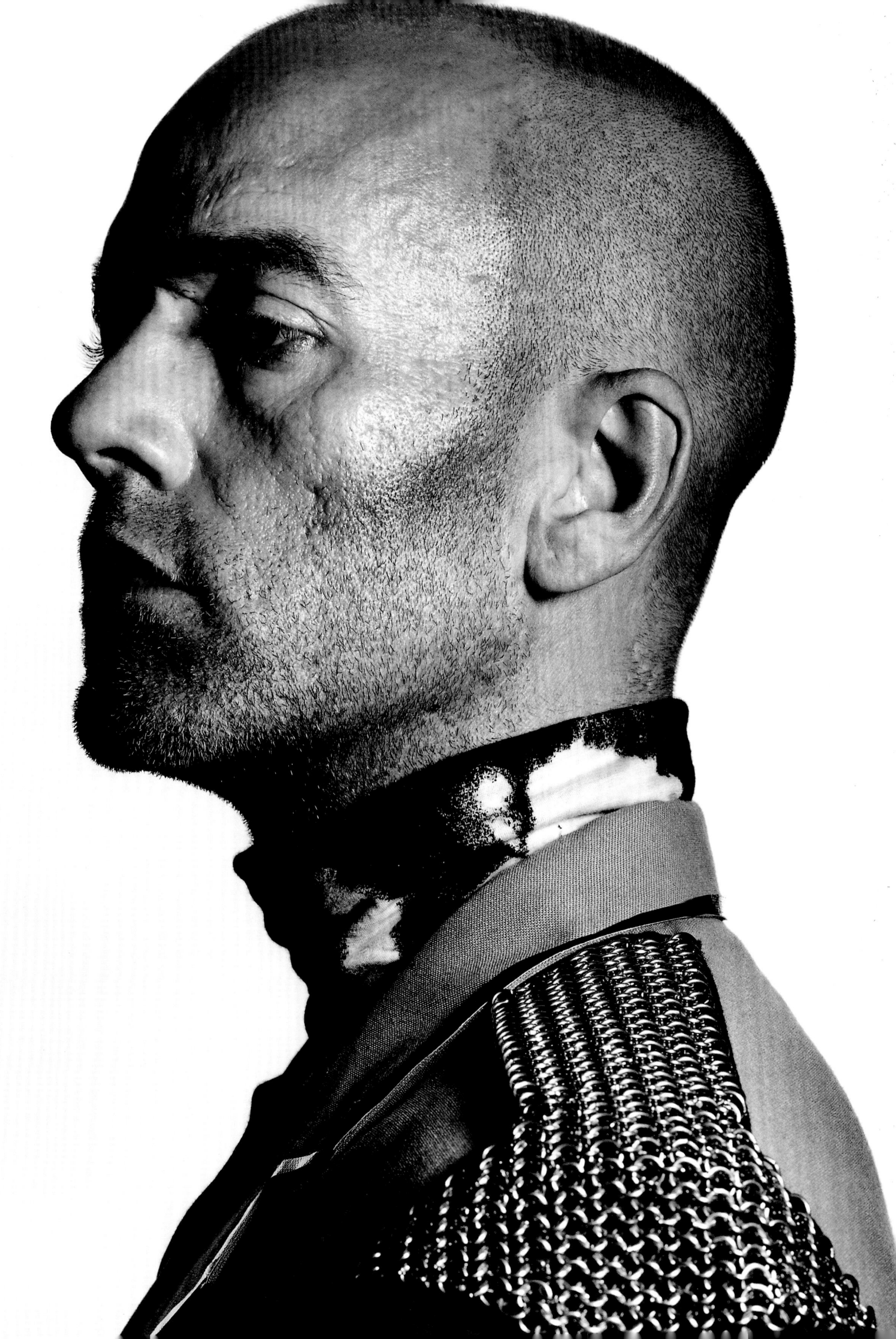

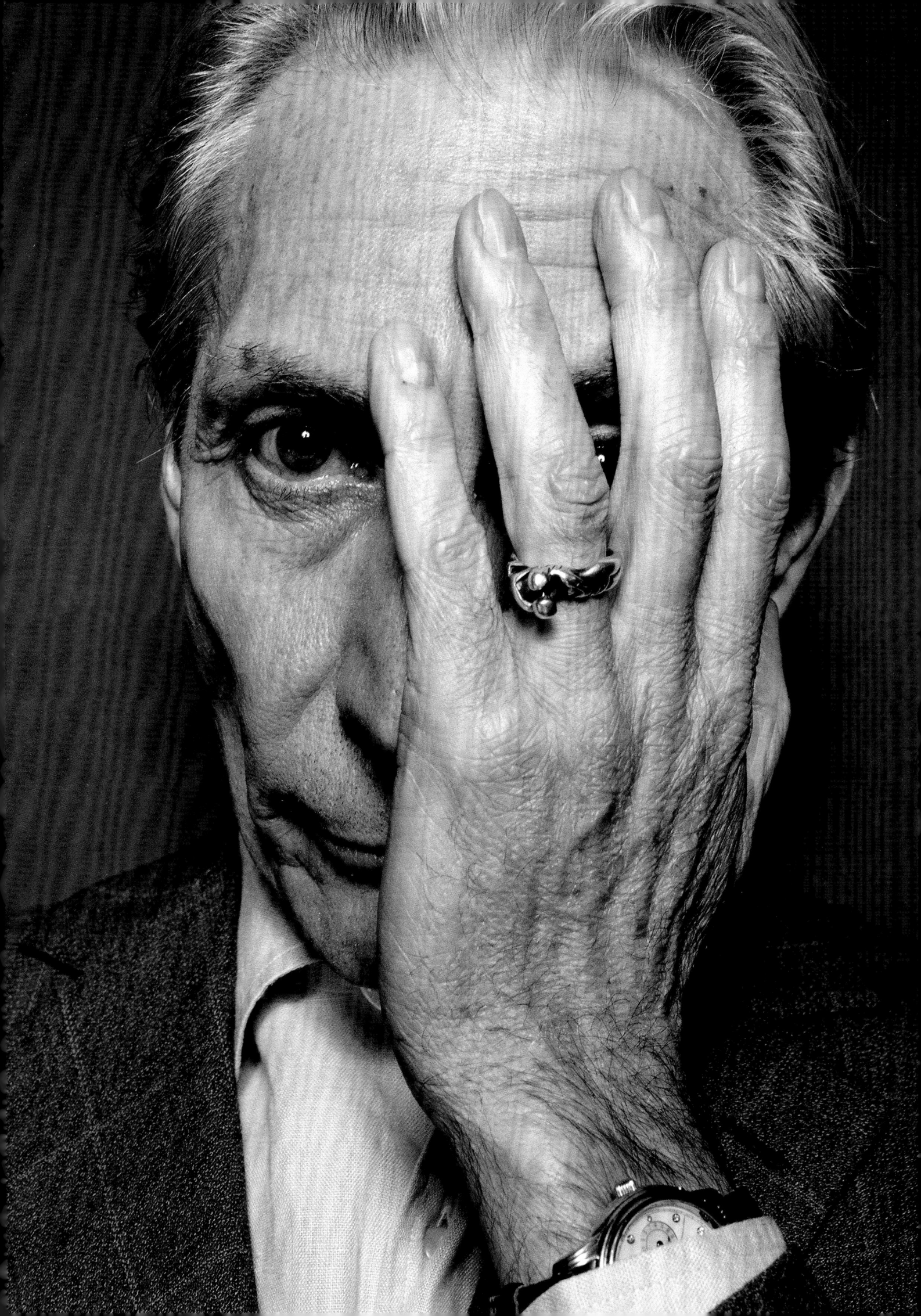

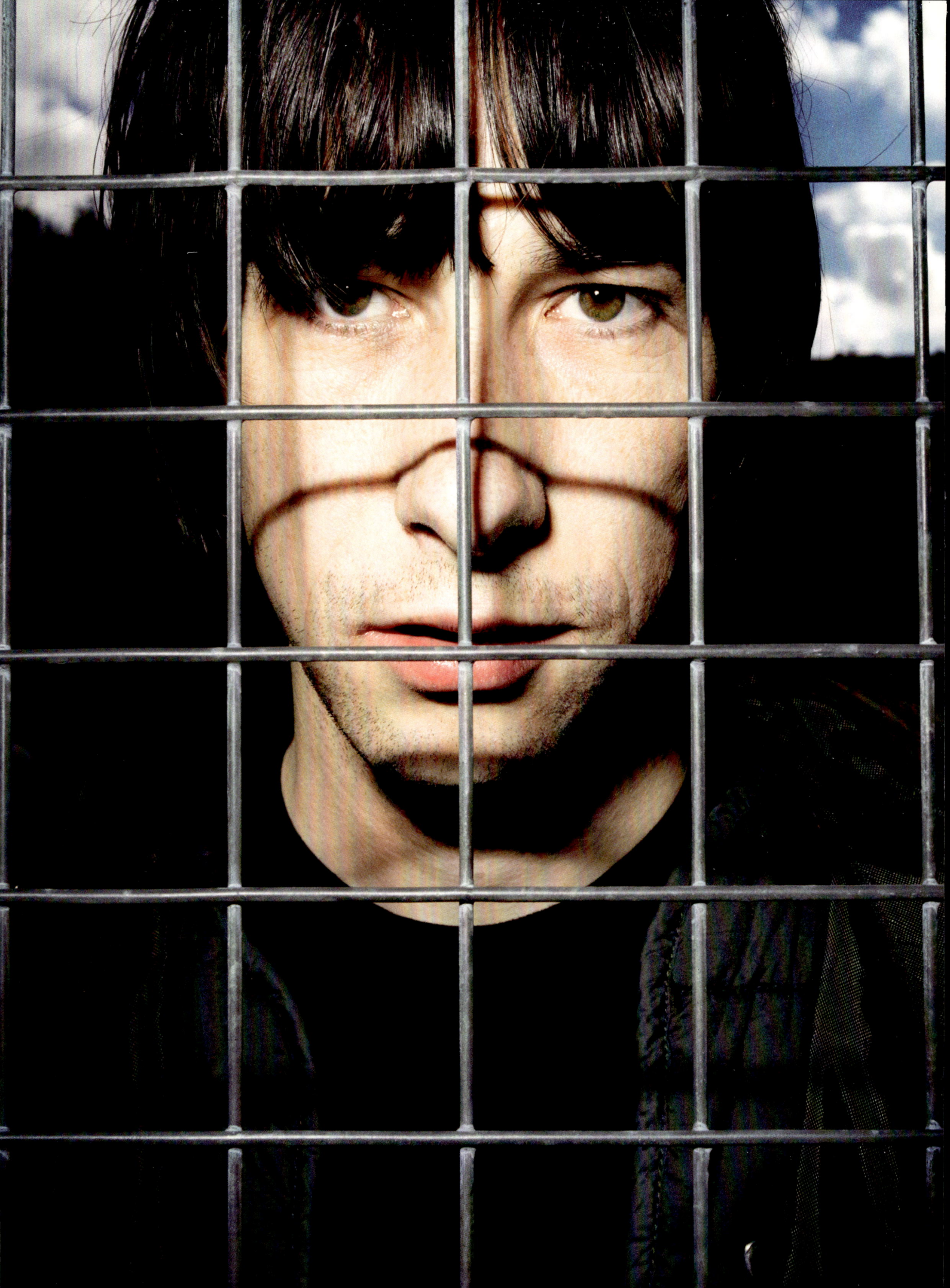

Previous Pages - Revolution in the Head, Issue 68, 2000
Give the Drummer Some, Issue 70, 2000

Next Pages - Tear Along the Dotted Line, Issue 40, 1998
Natalie Imbruglia, Issue 37, 1997

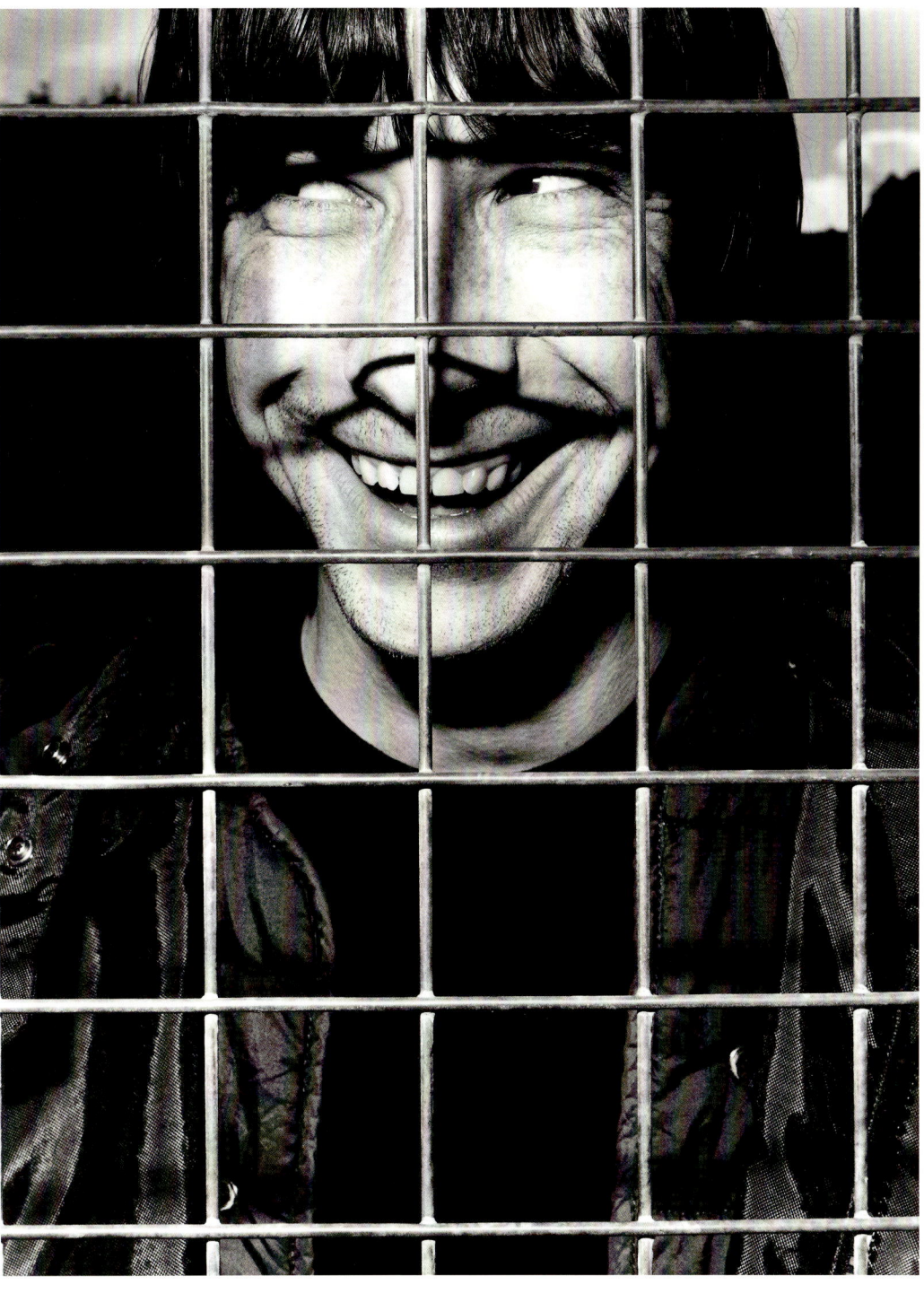

Hide & Seek, Issue 37, 1997

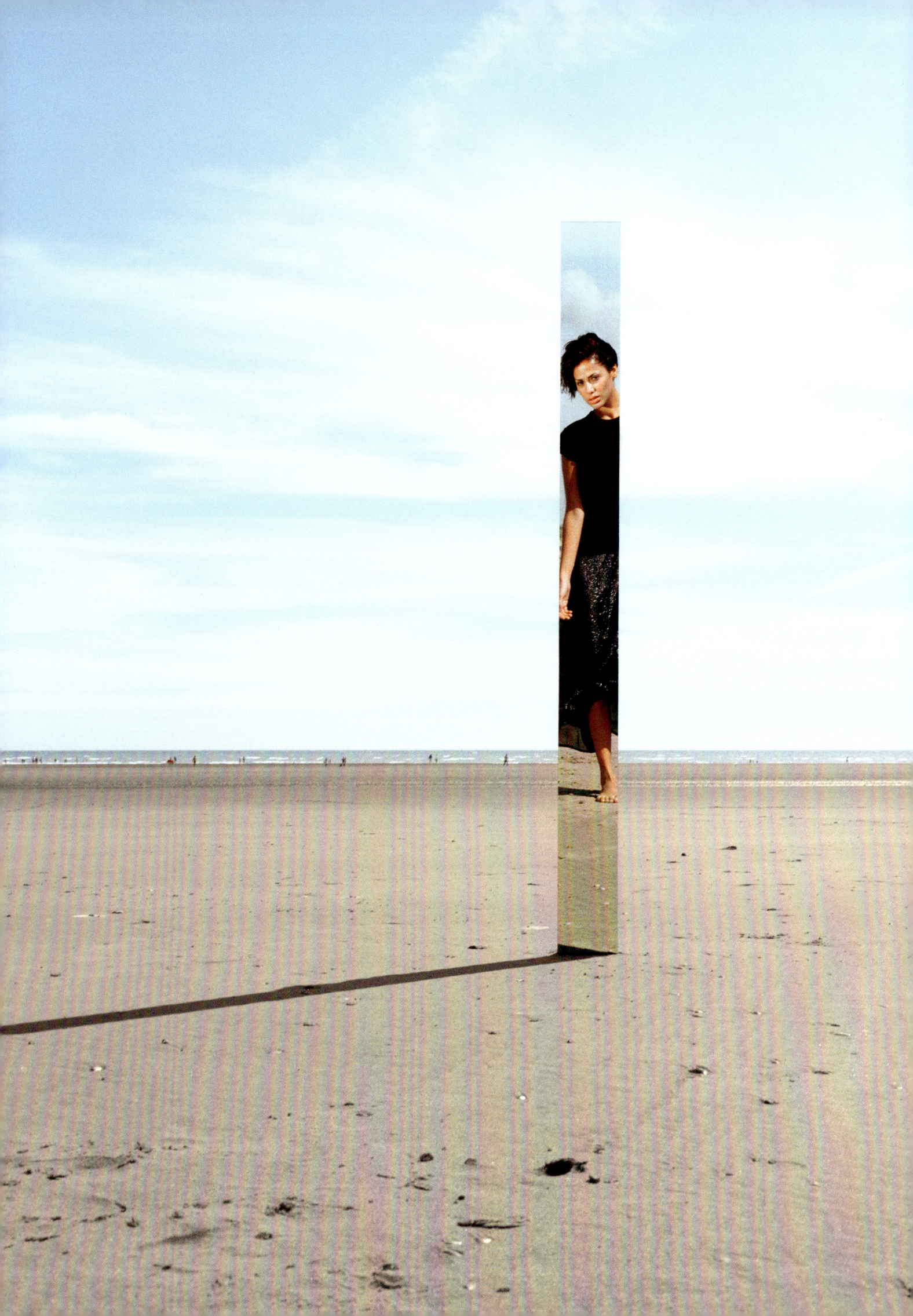

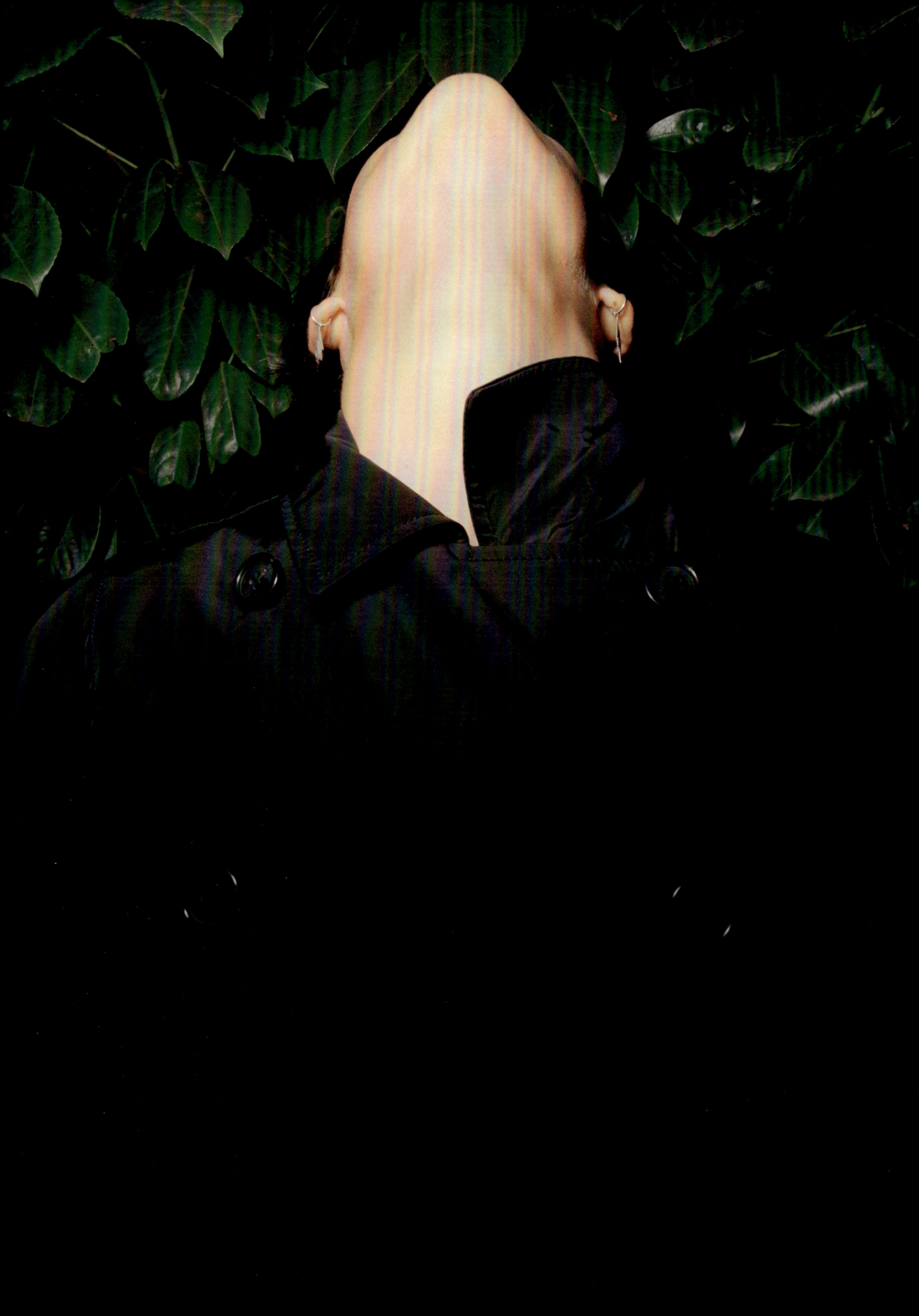

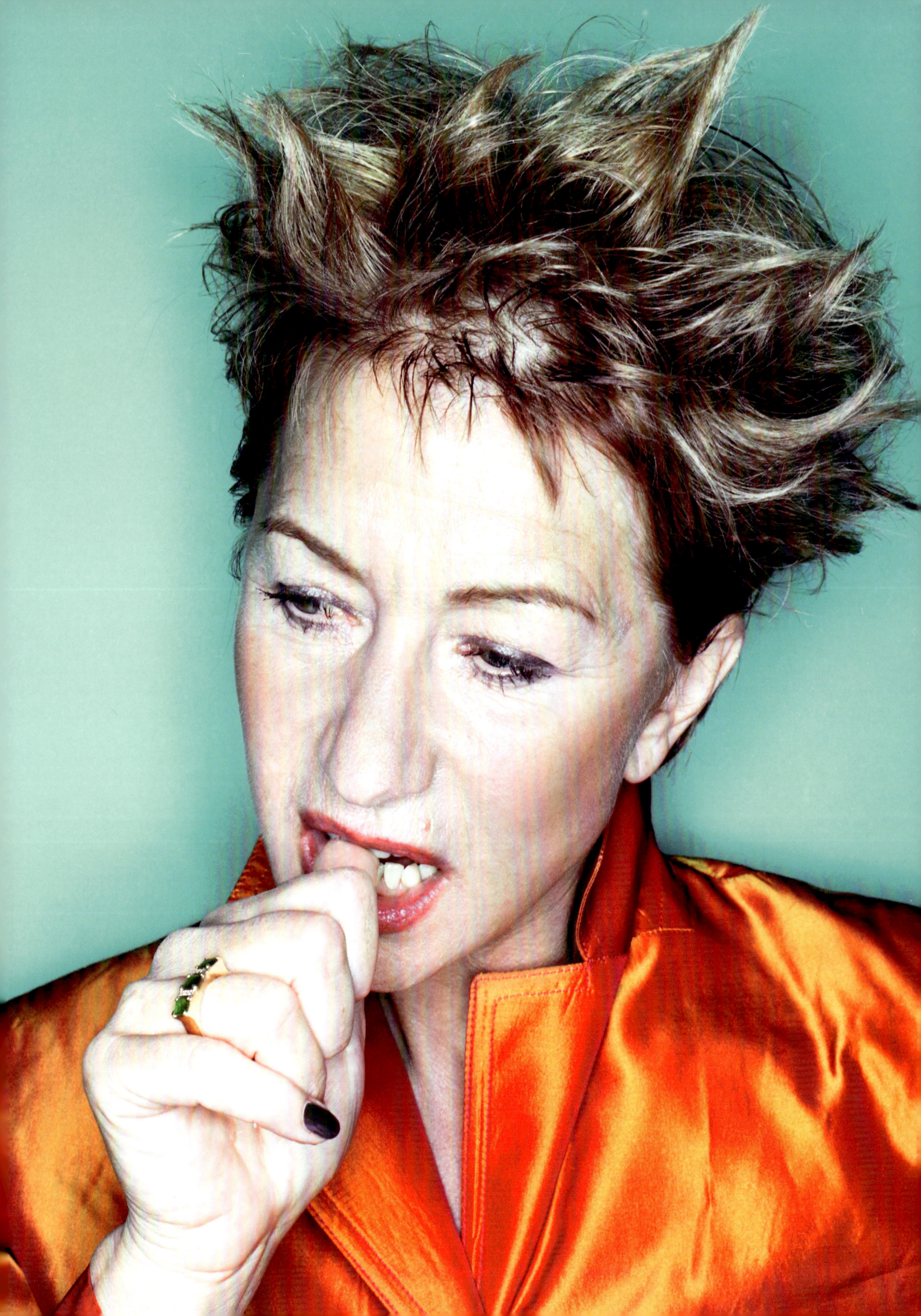

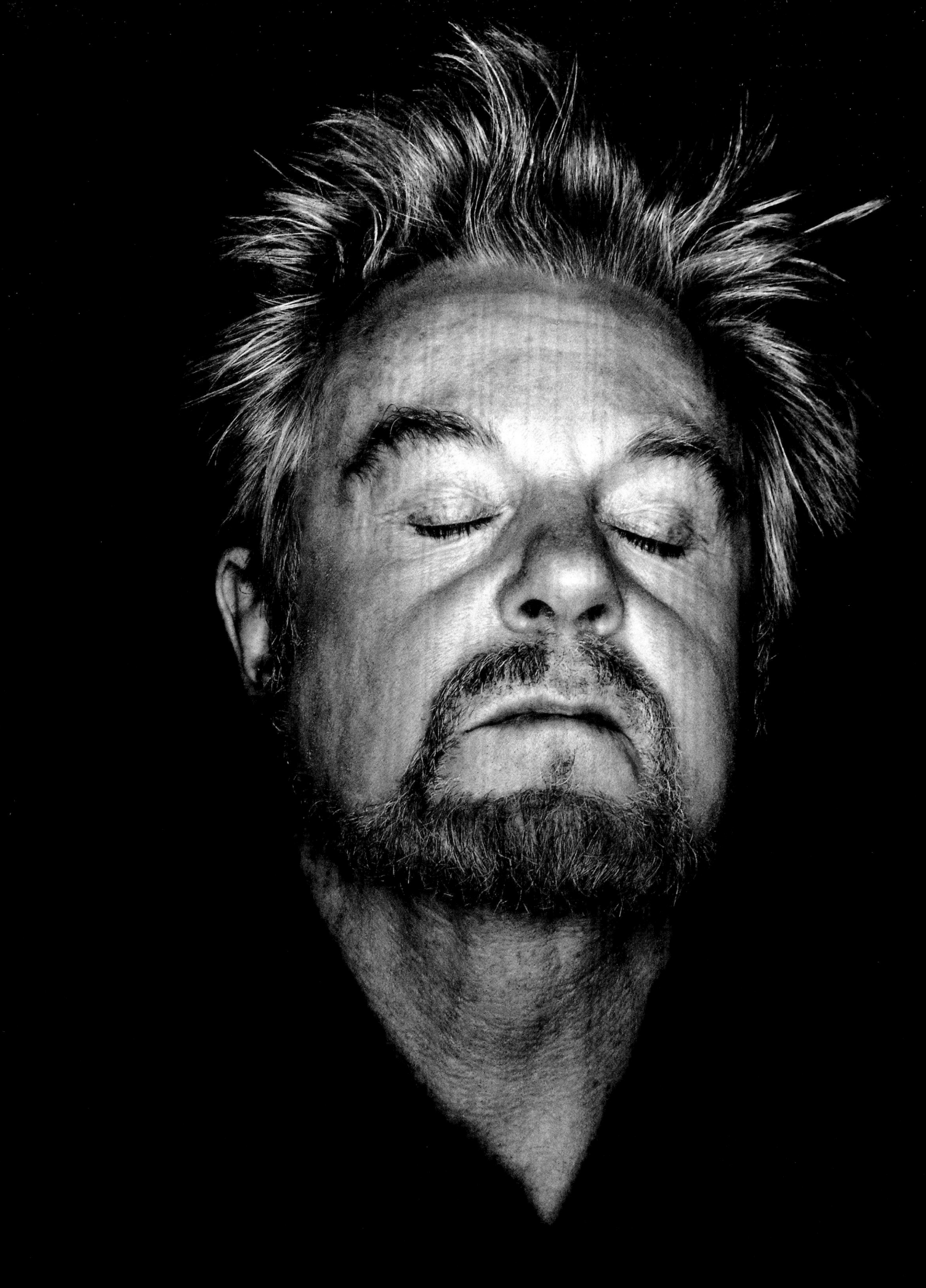

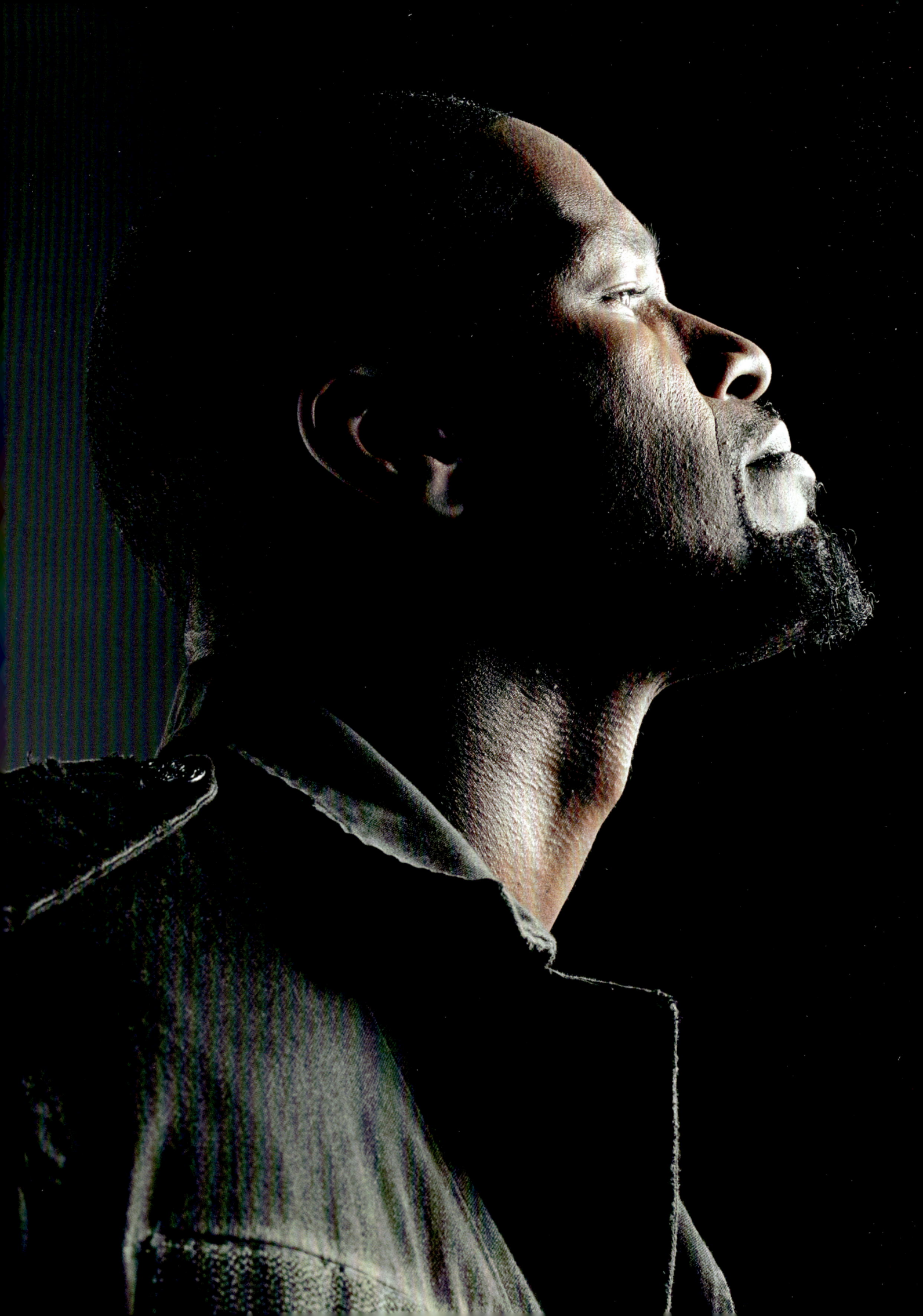

Previous Pages - Mirren Mirren On The Wall, Issue 46, 1998
The Cast, Issue 26, 1996

Opposite Page - Golden Touch, Vol. 2, Issue 32, 2005

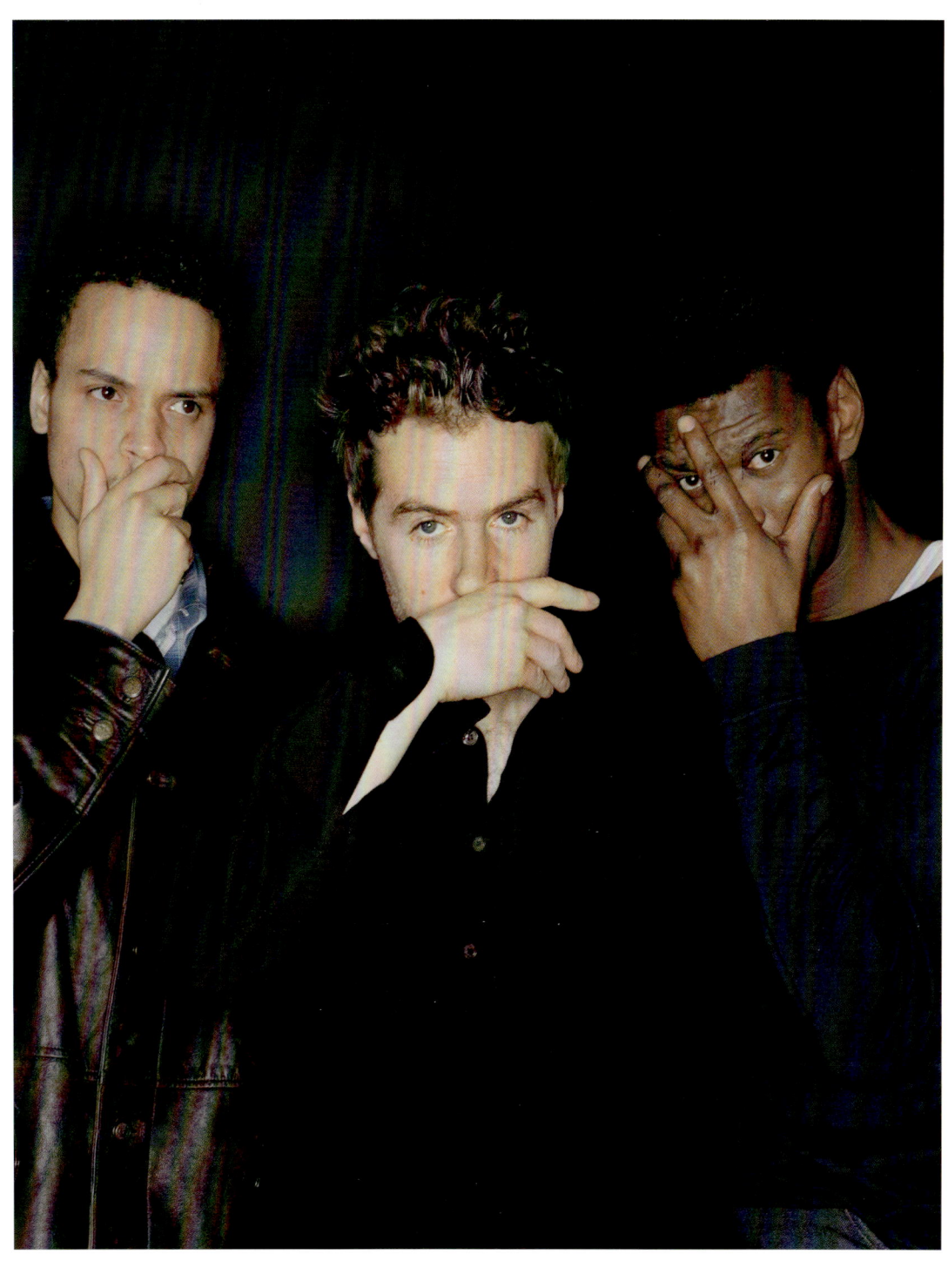

Split Personalities, Issue 39, 1998

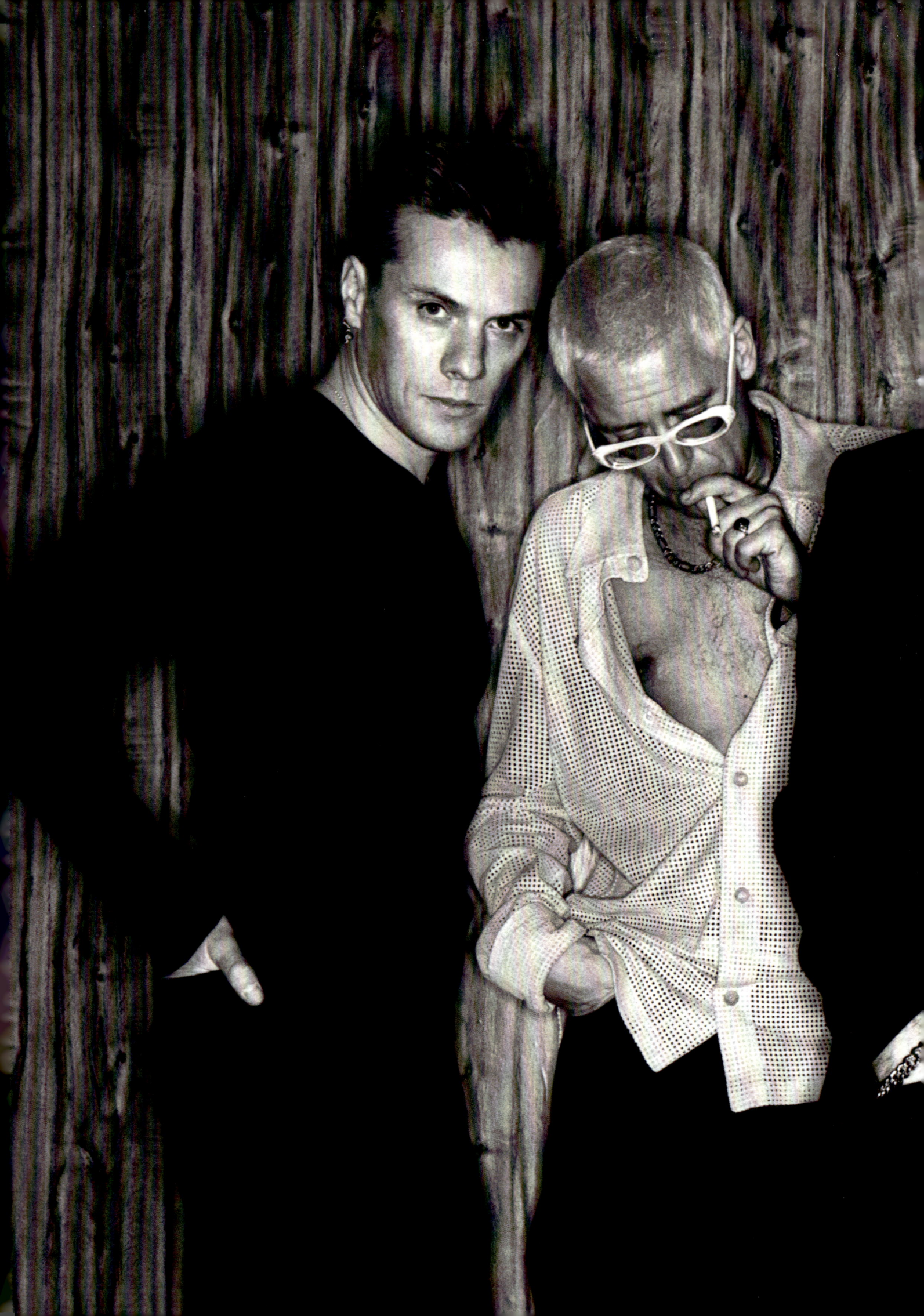

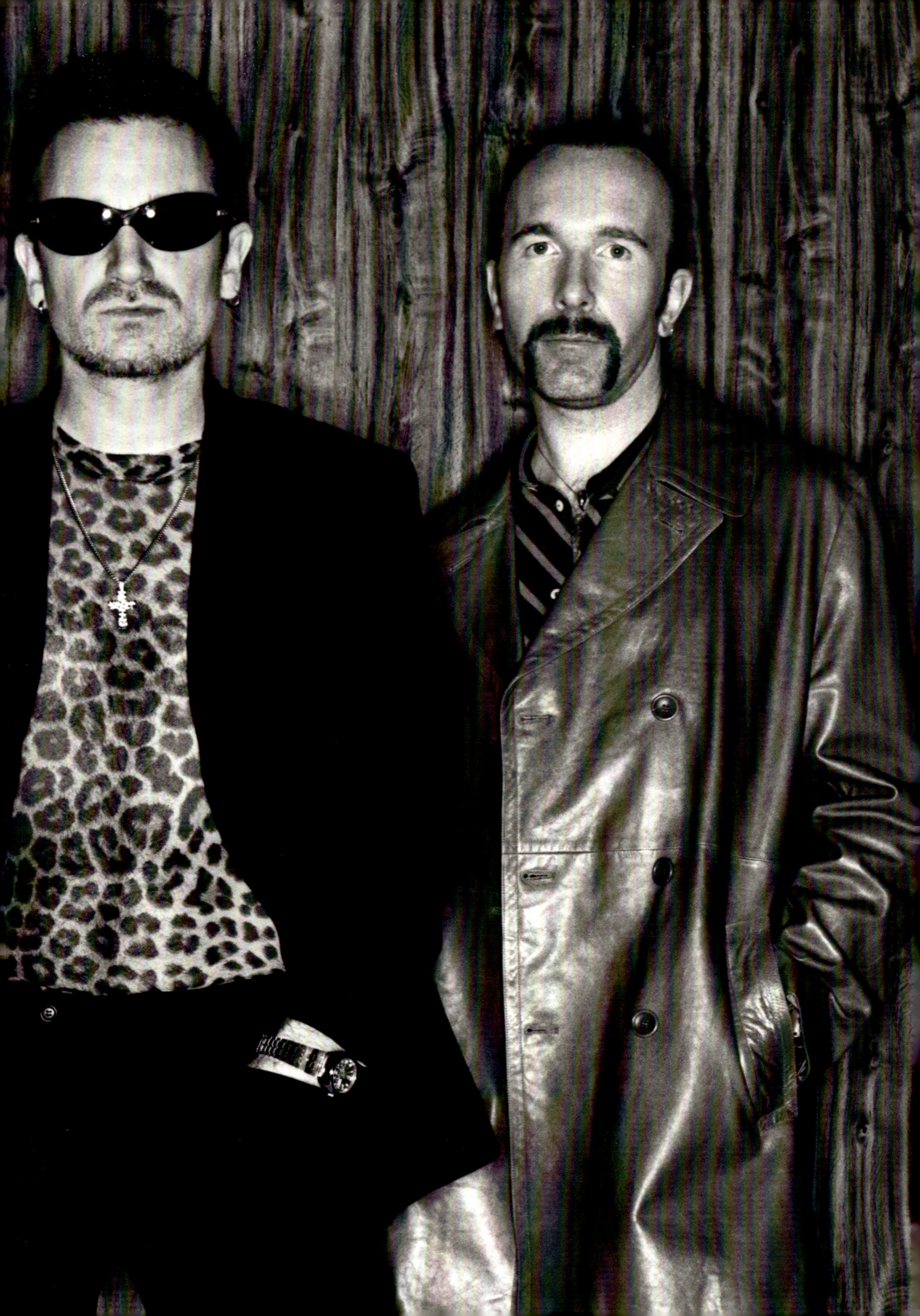

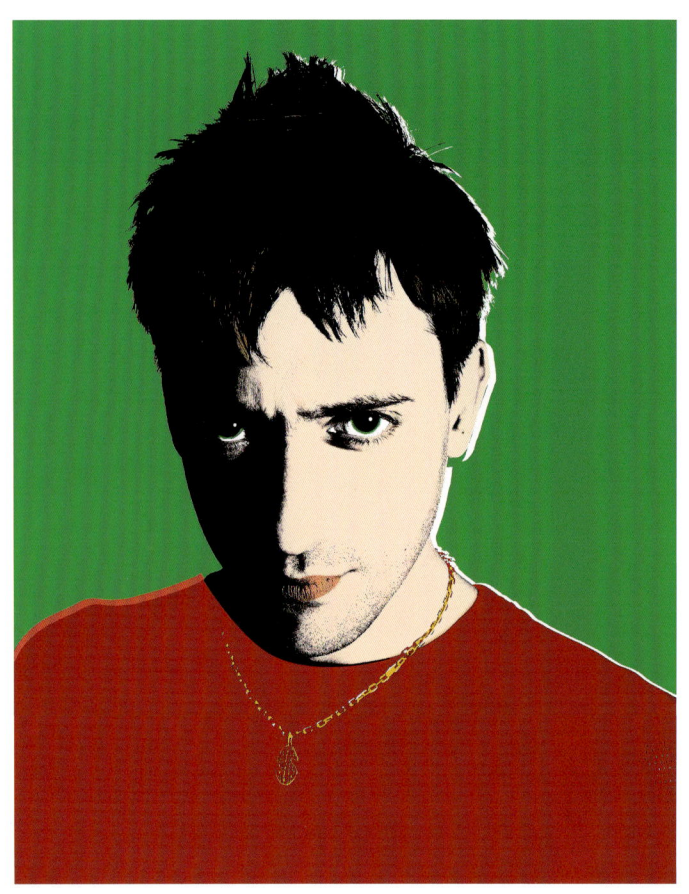
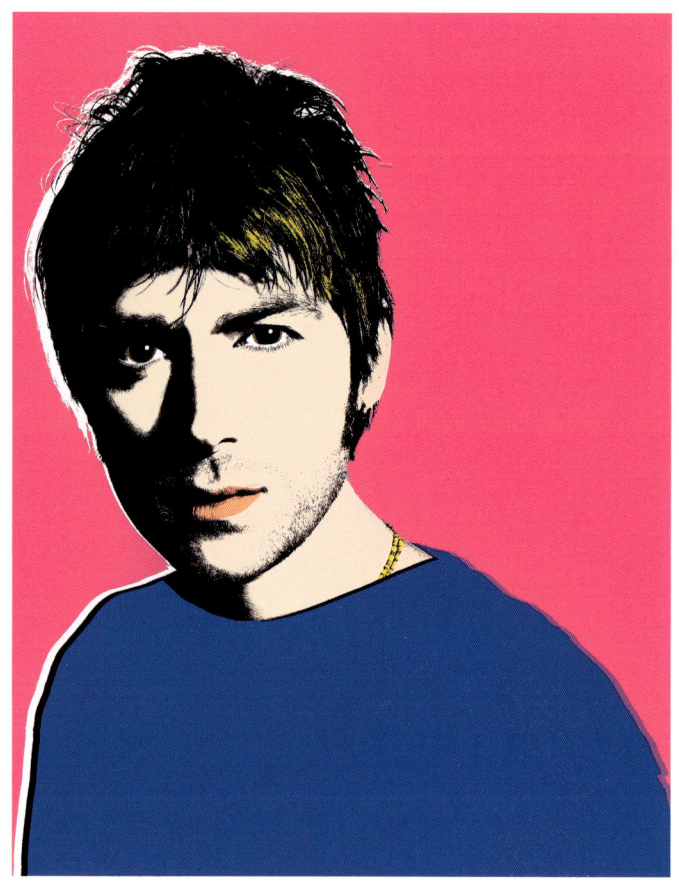
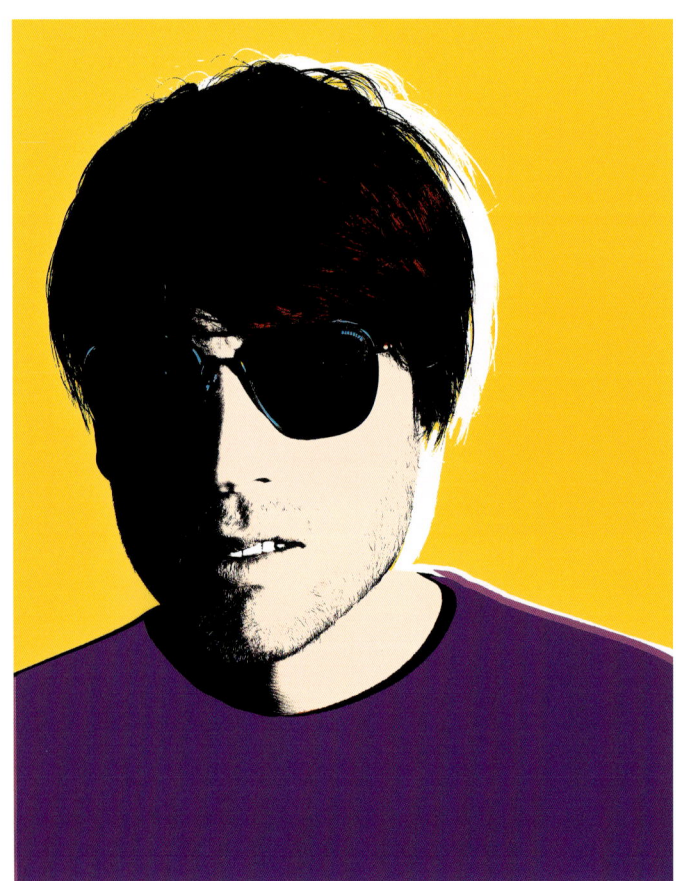
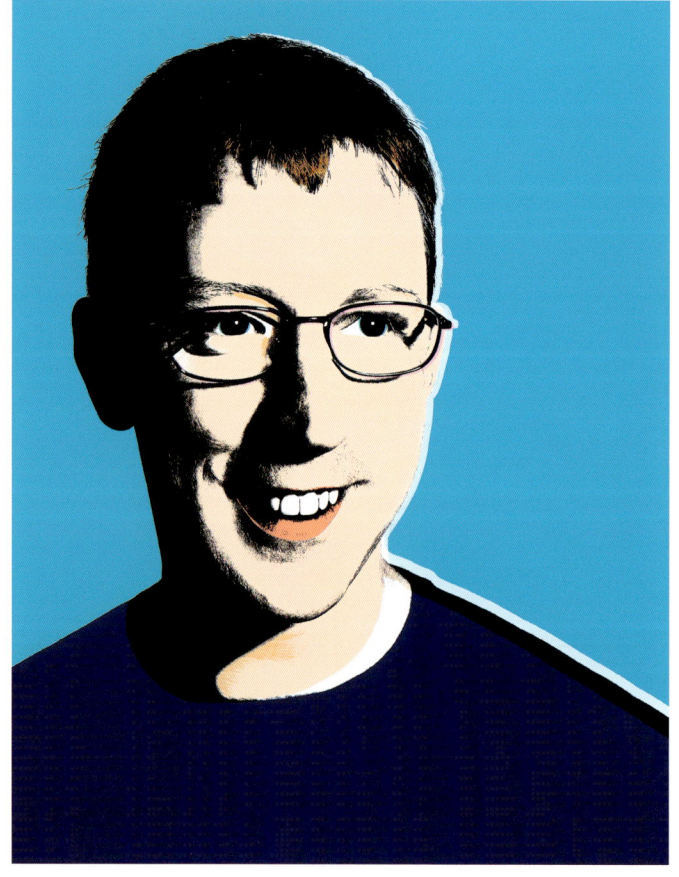

Boys Who Like Girls, Issue 56, 1999

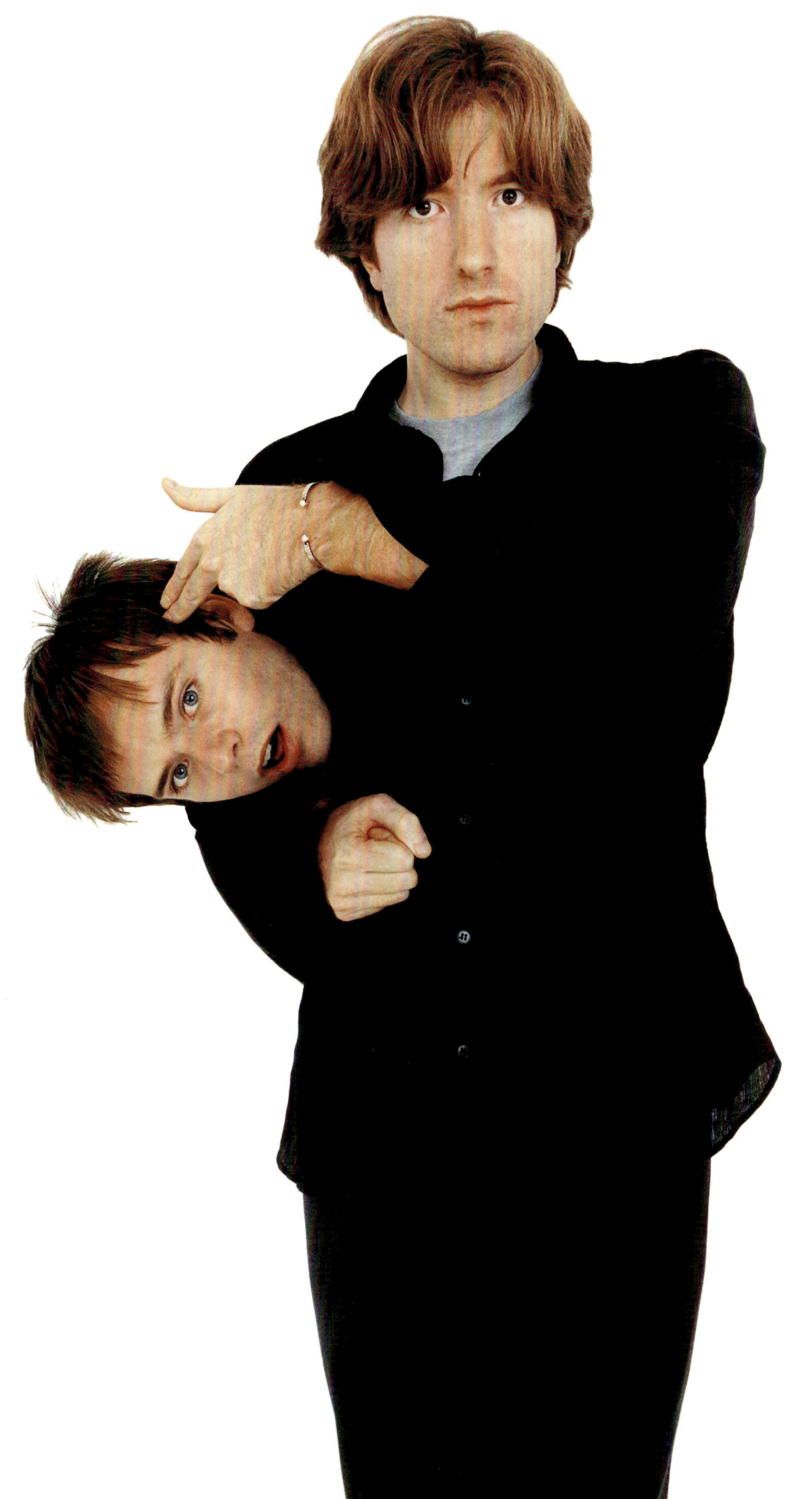

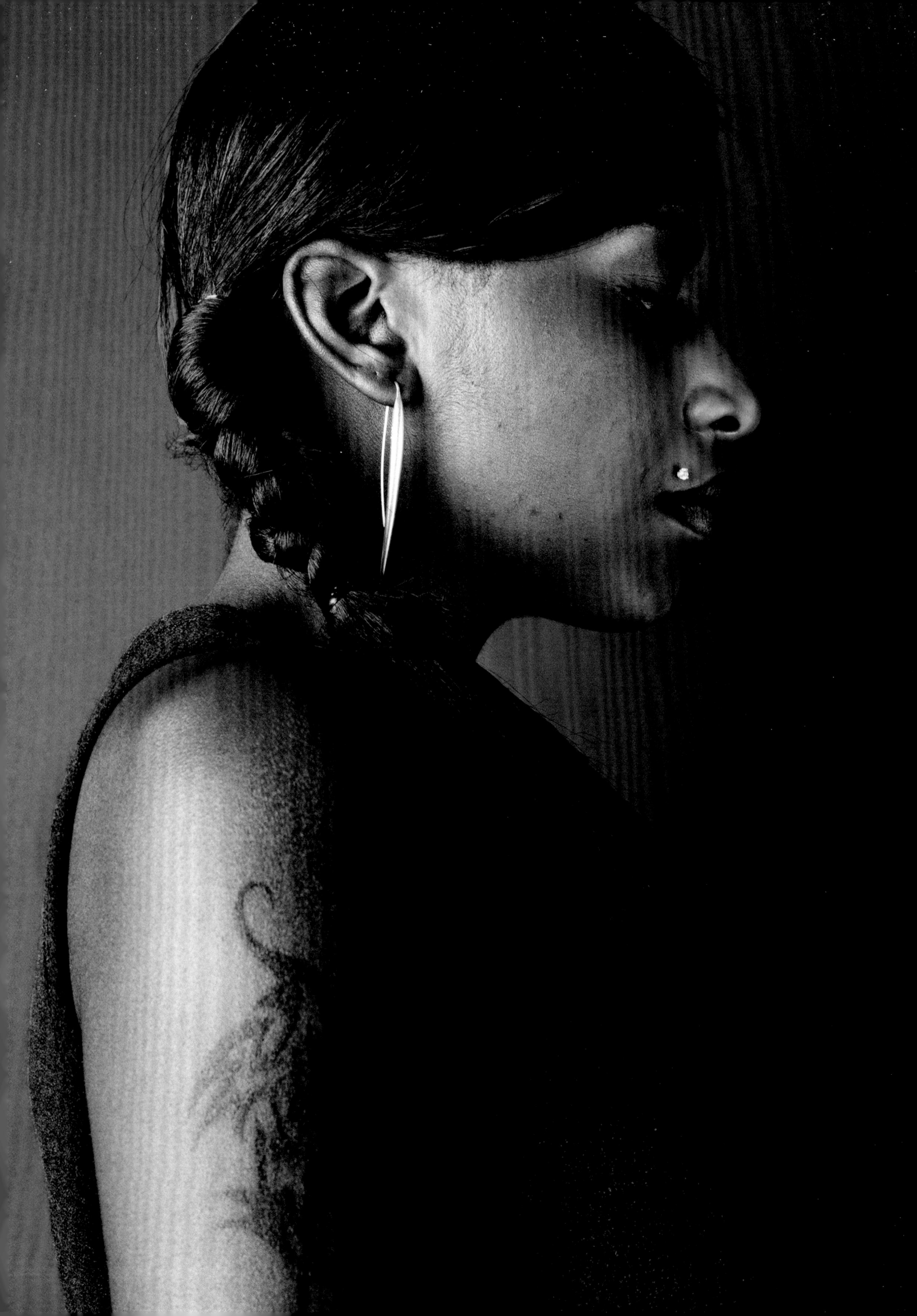

Opposite Page - Everyone's Someone, Issue 46, 1998

Next Pages - Filthy and Gorgeous, Vol. 2, Issue 53, 2007
          The Sun Always Shines on Kirsten, Vol.2, Issue 13, 2004

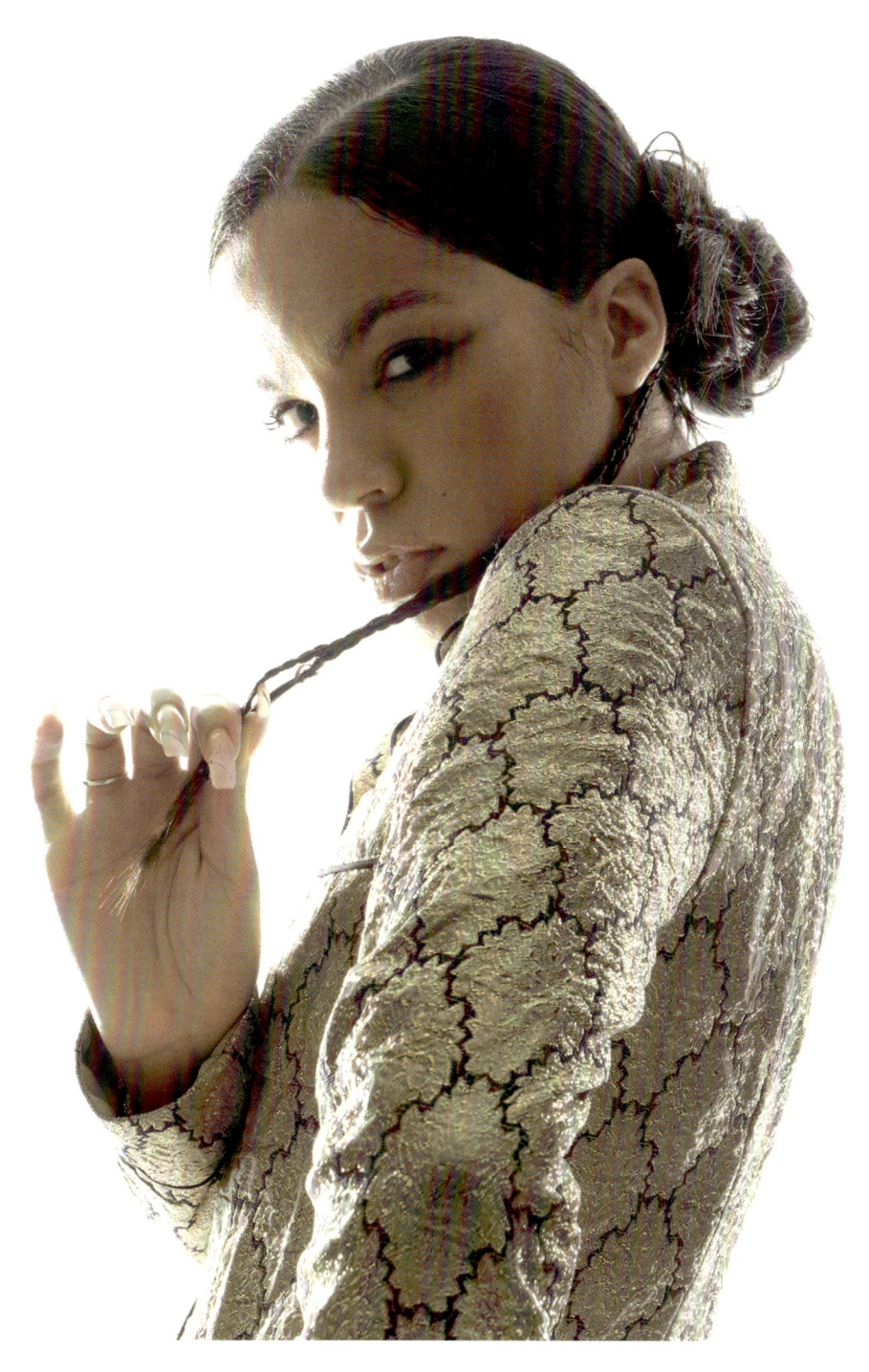

100% of Me, Issue 89, 2002

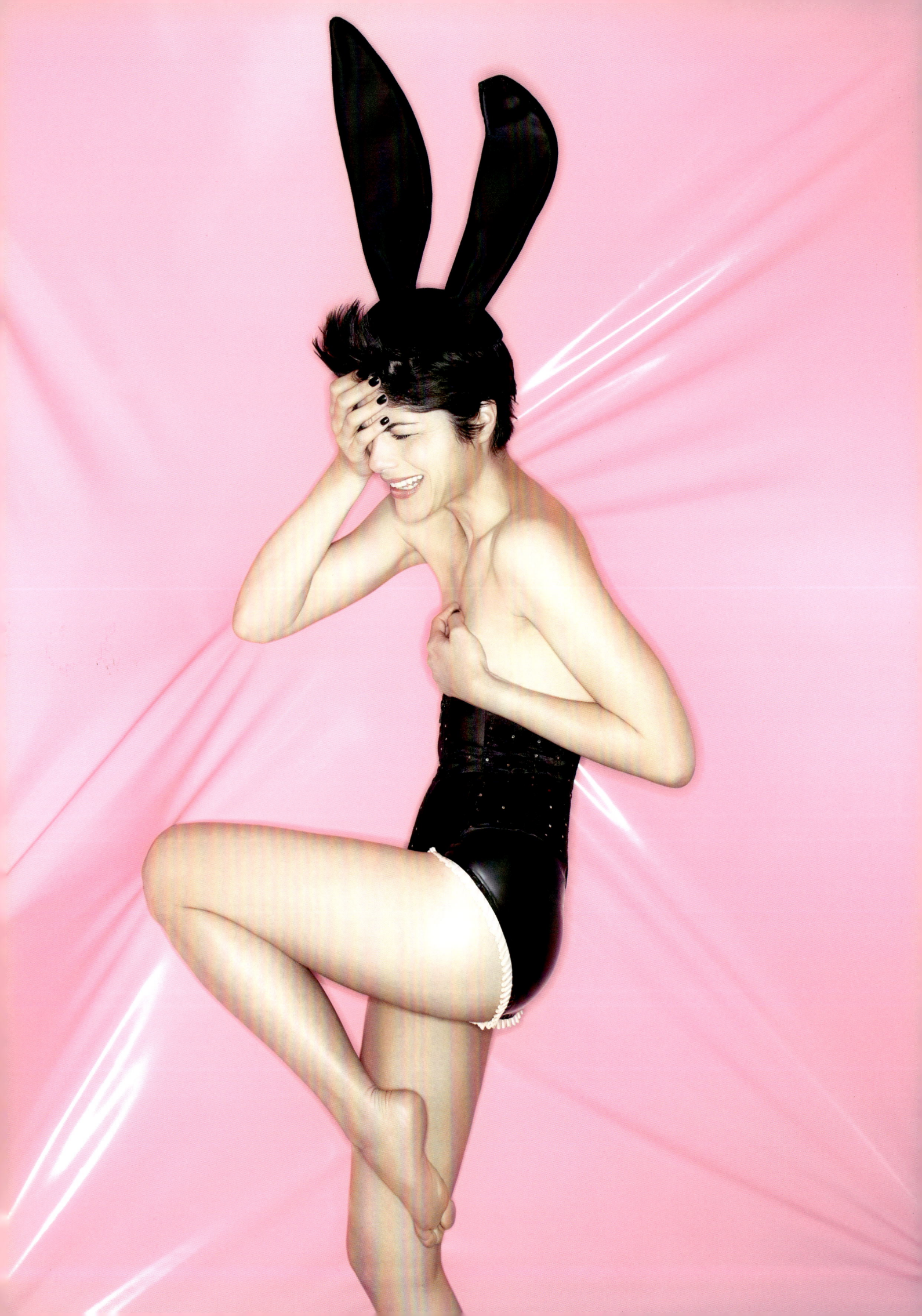

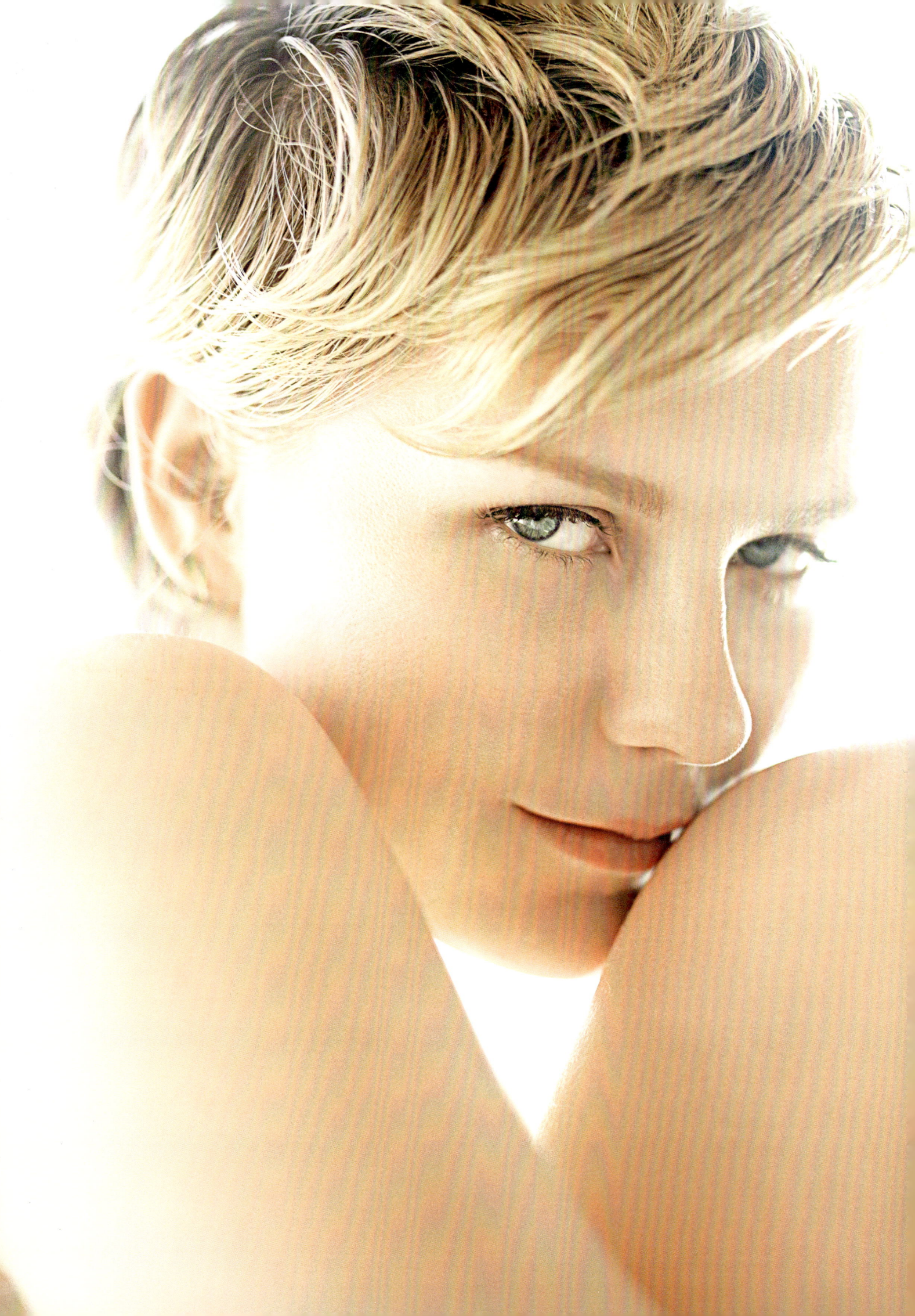

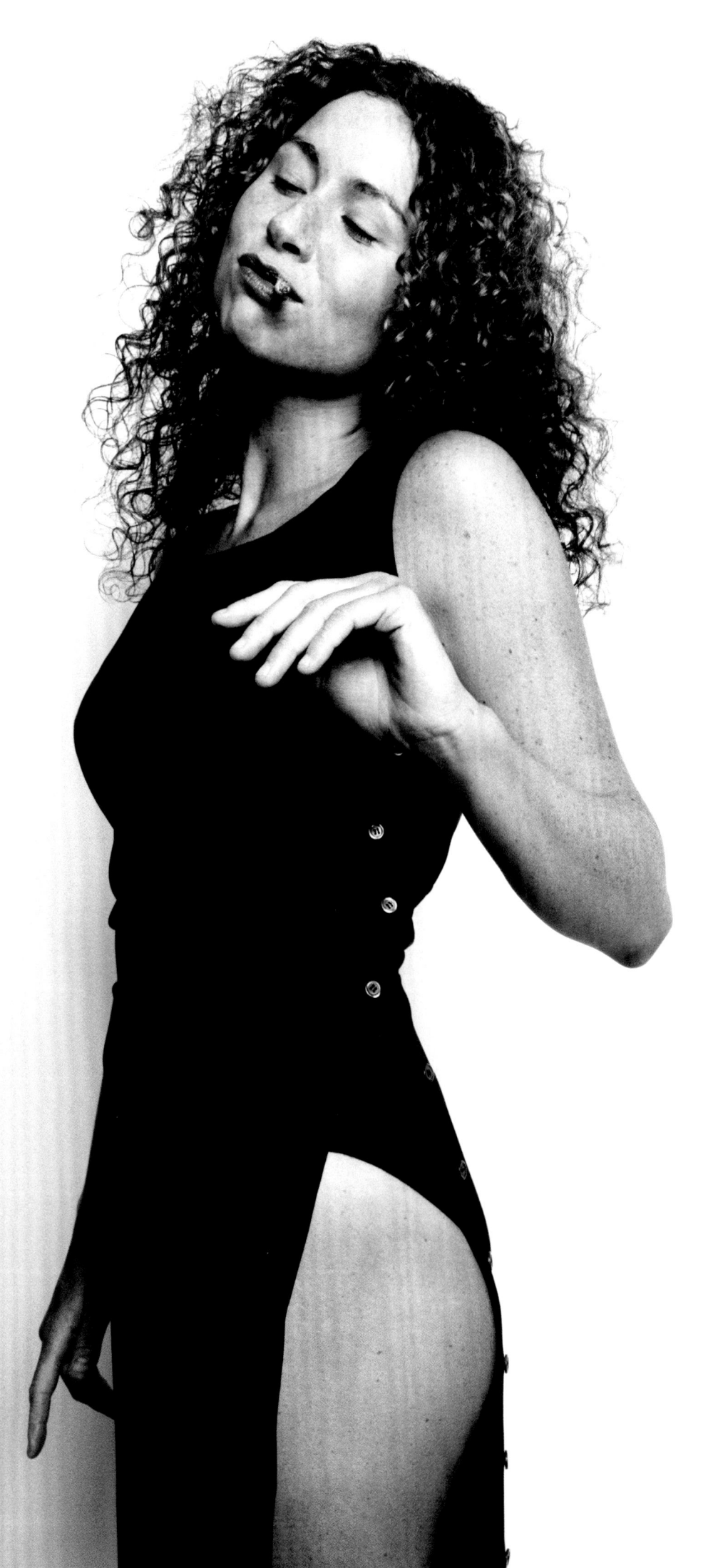

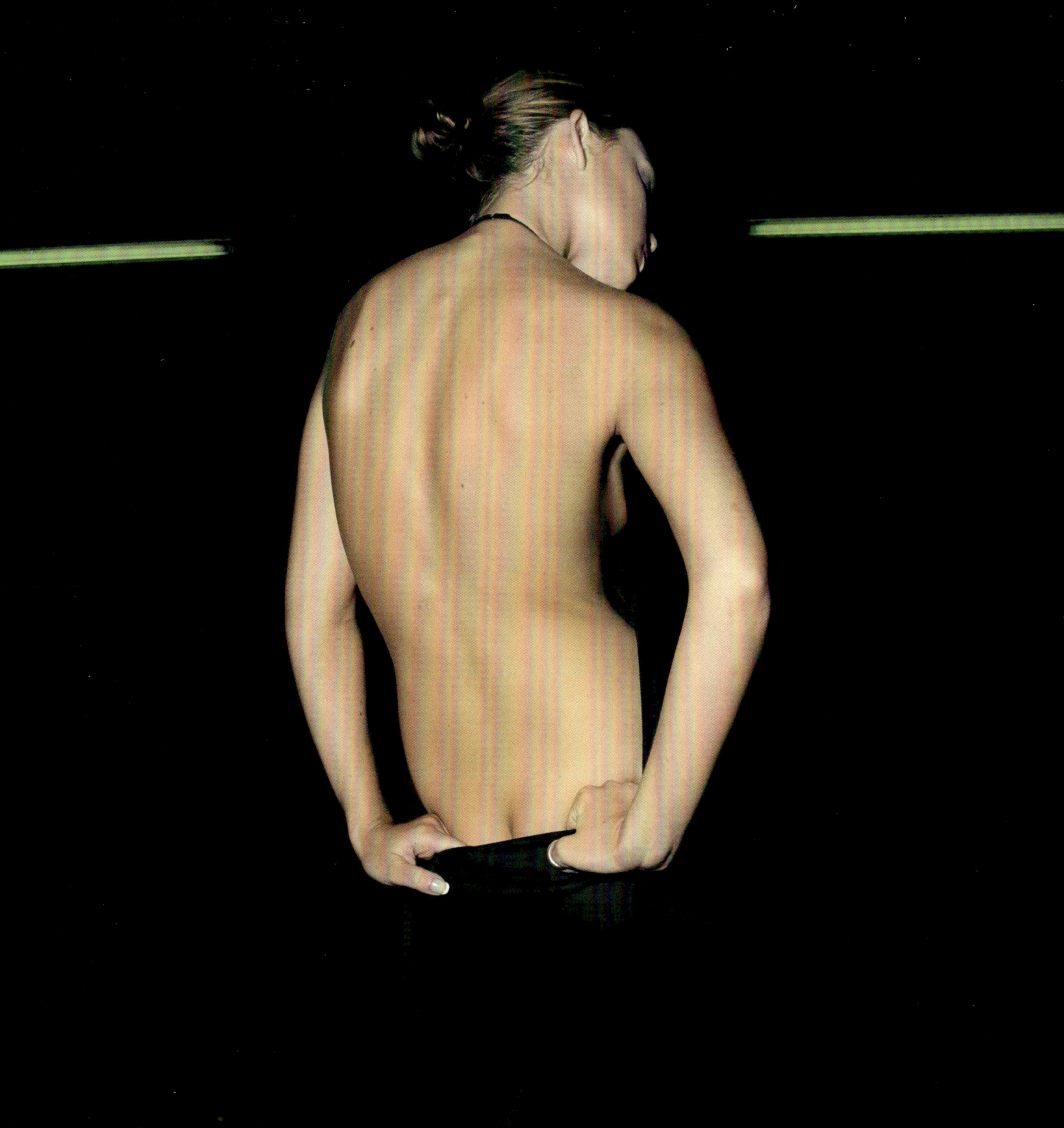

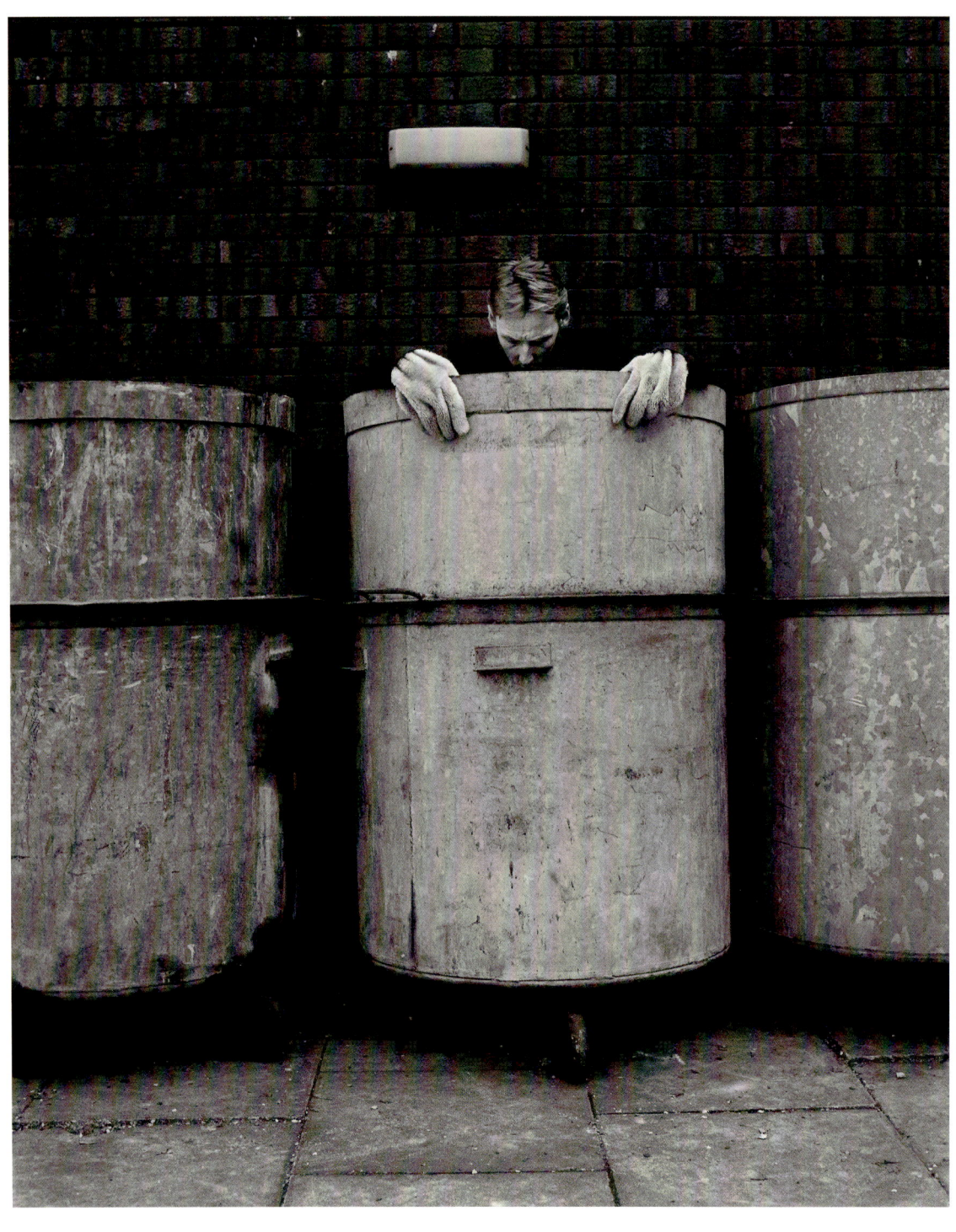

The Cast, Issue 26, 1996

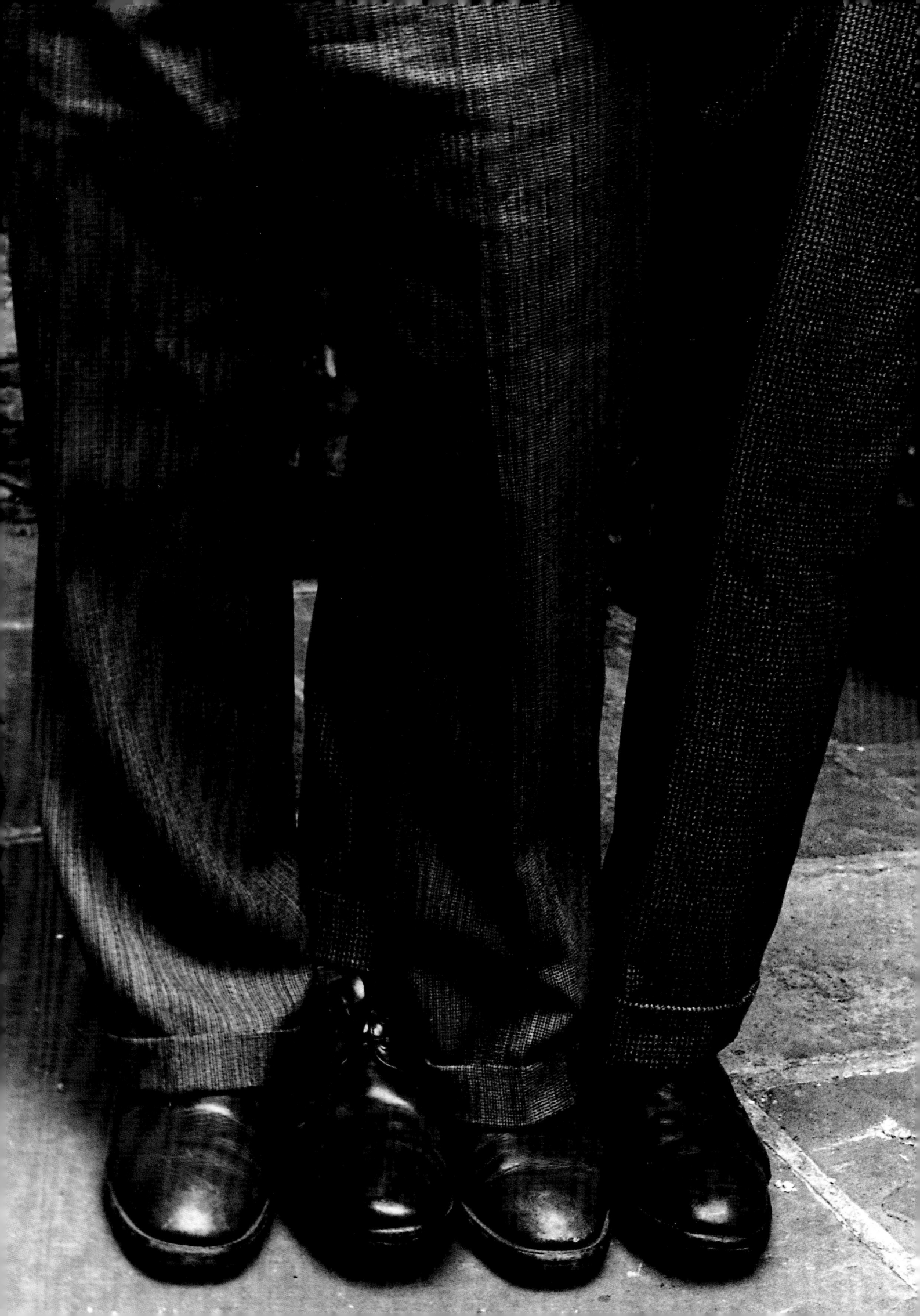

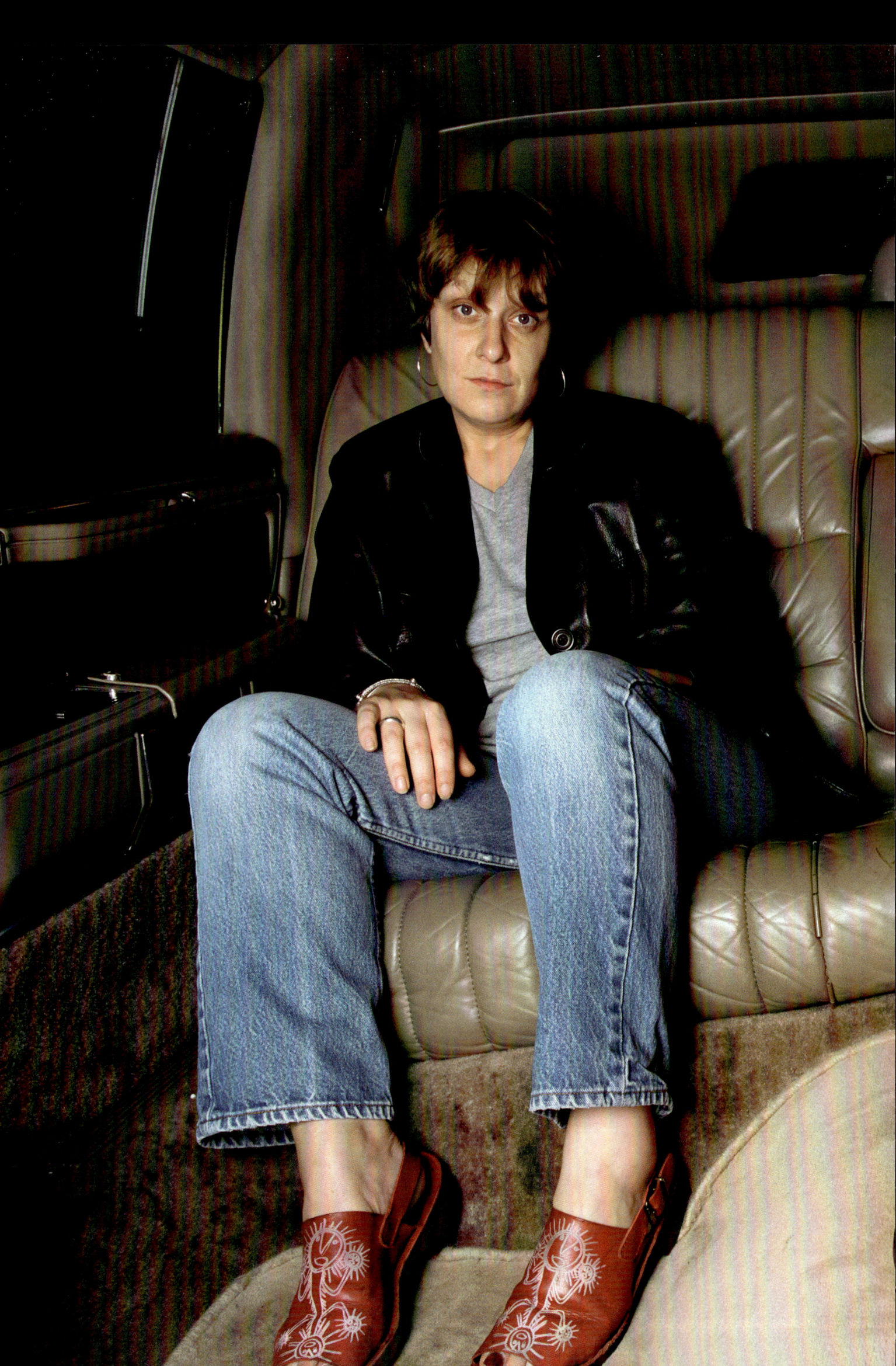

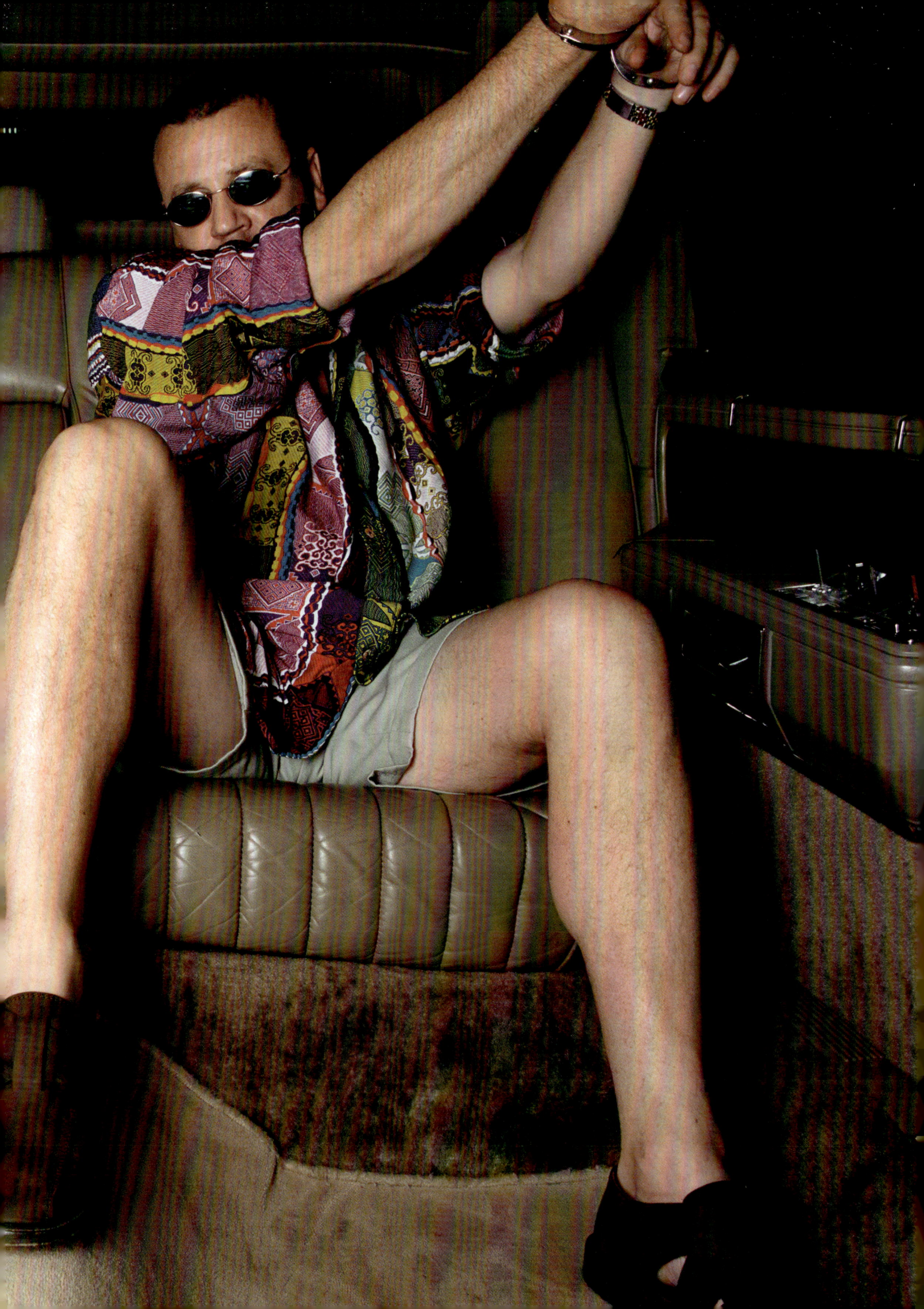

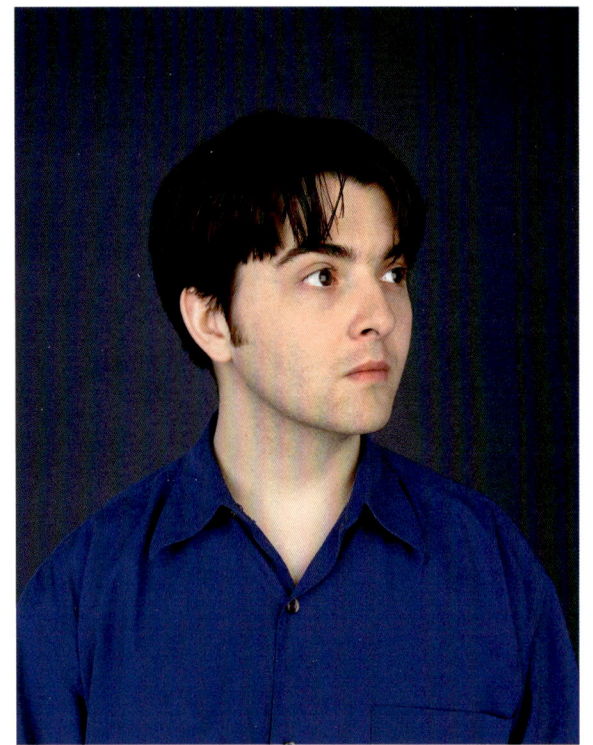

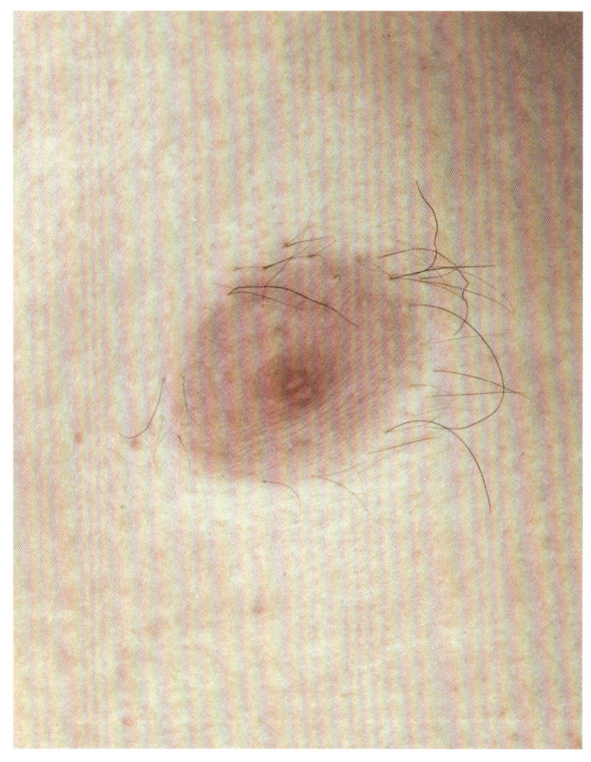

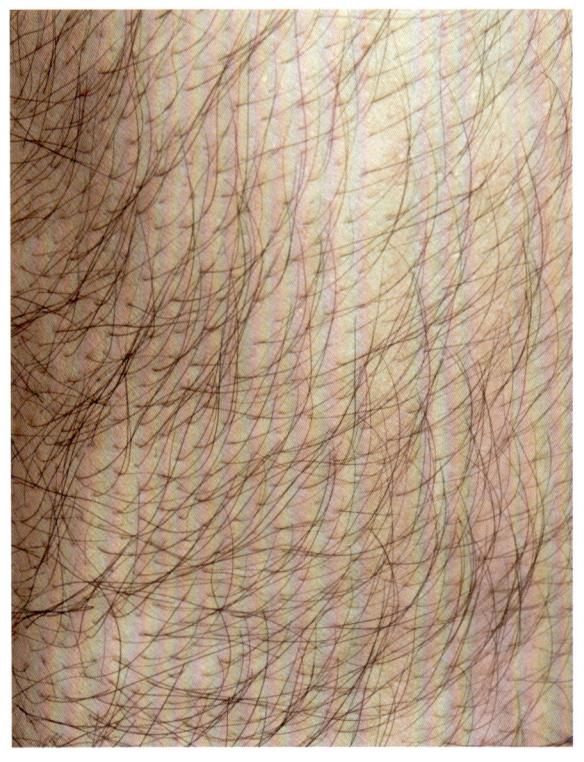

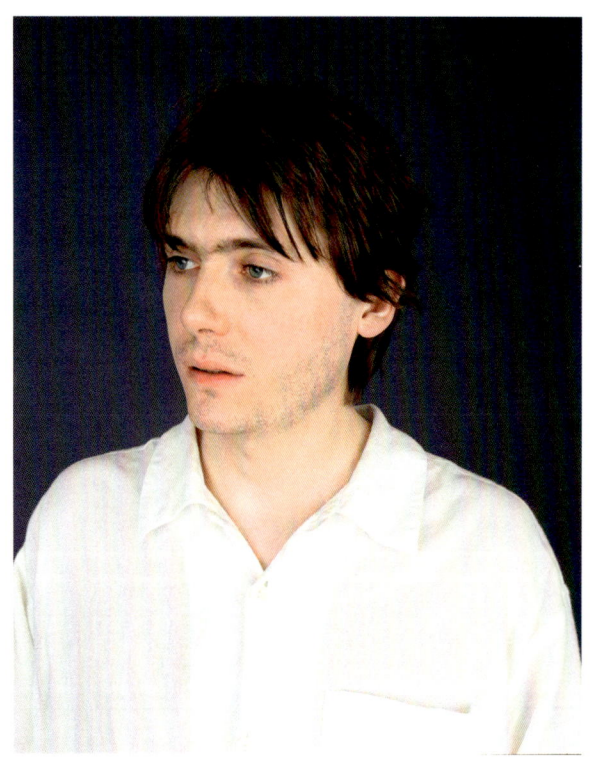

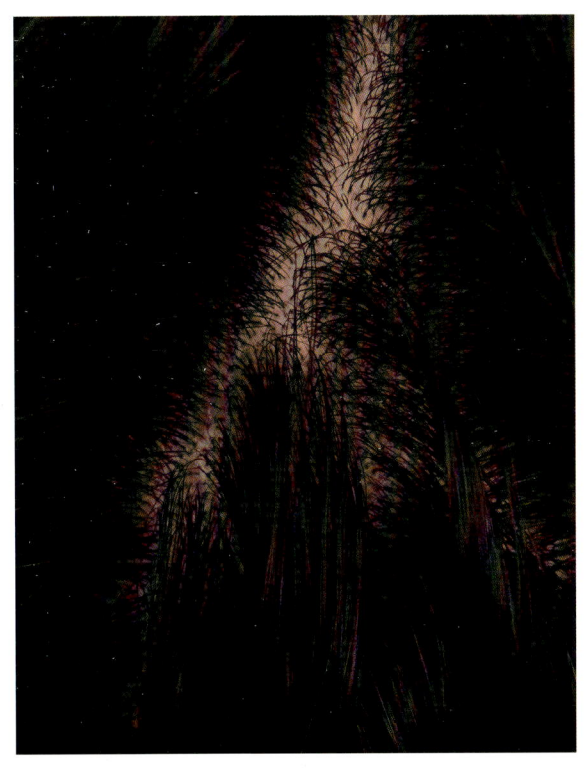
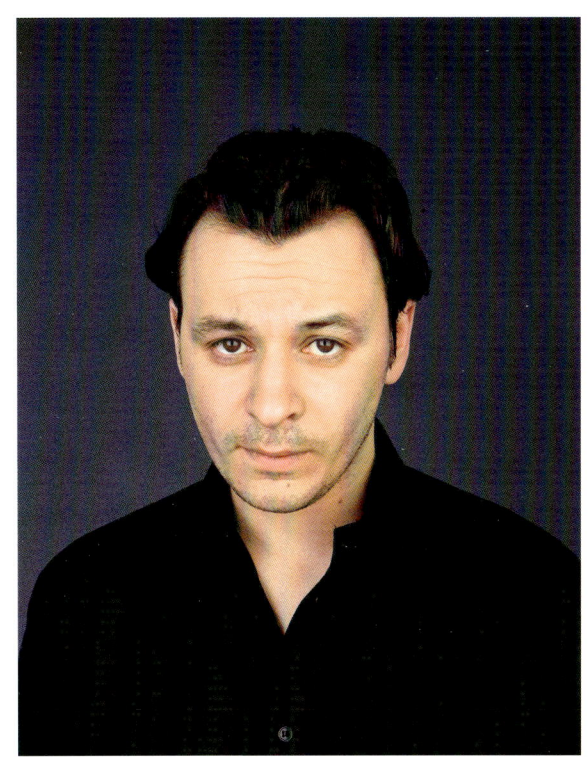
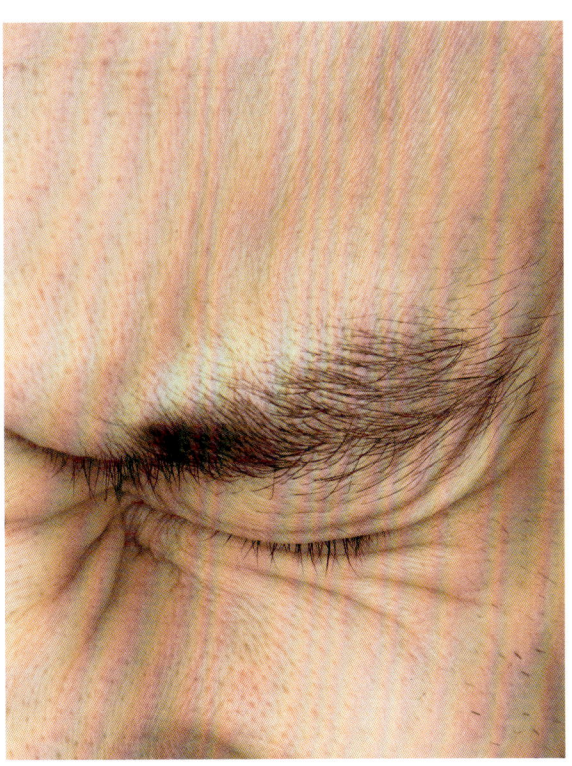
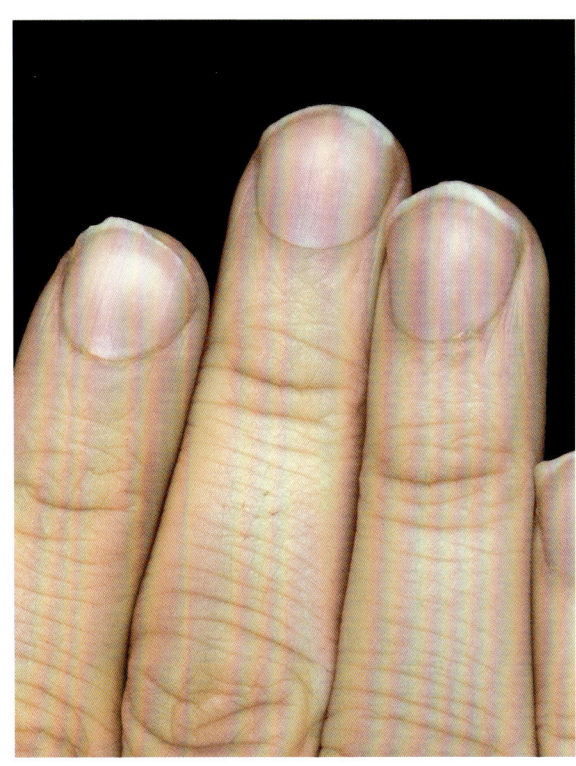

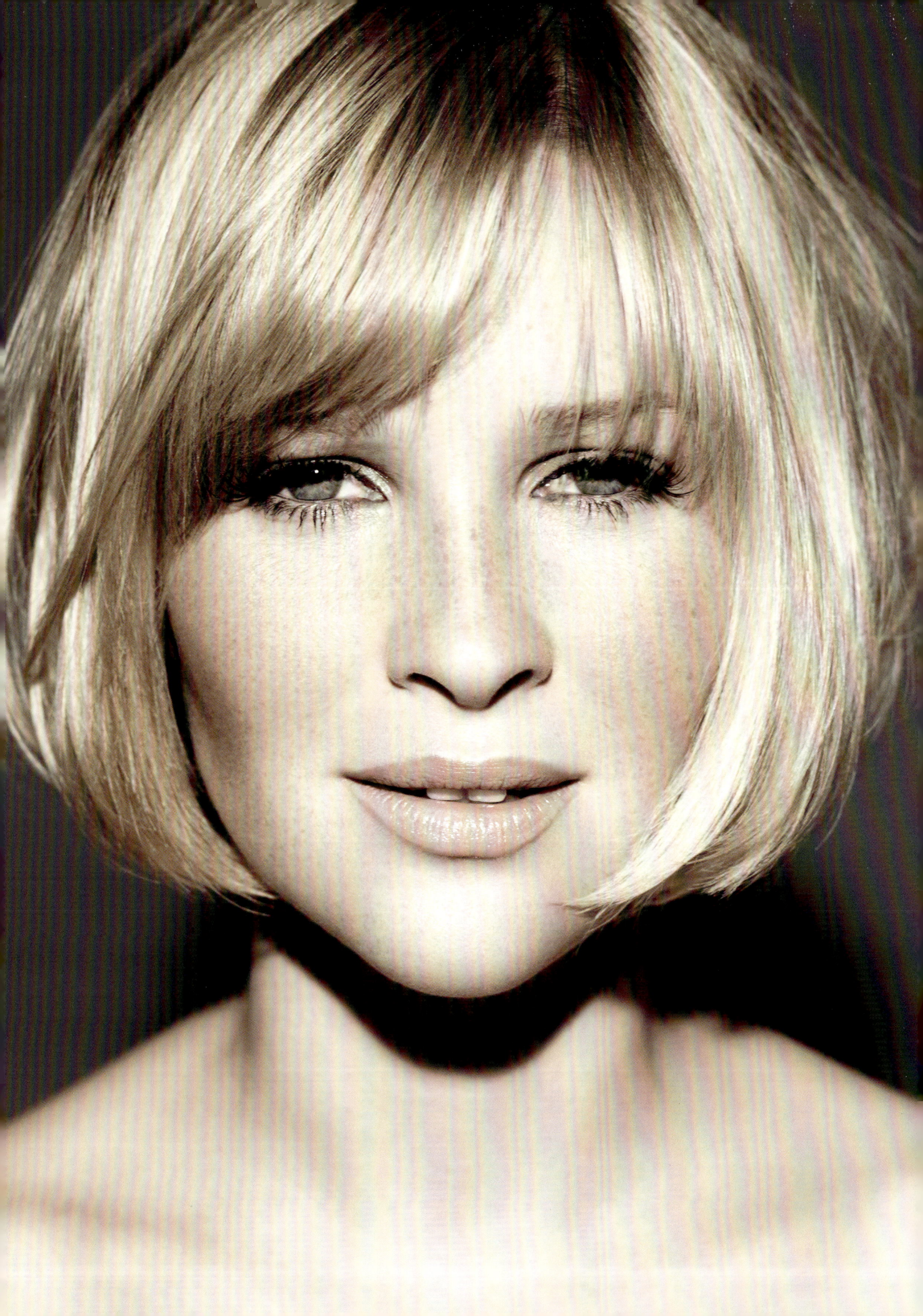

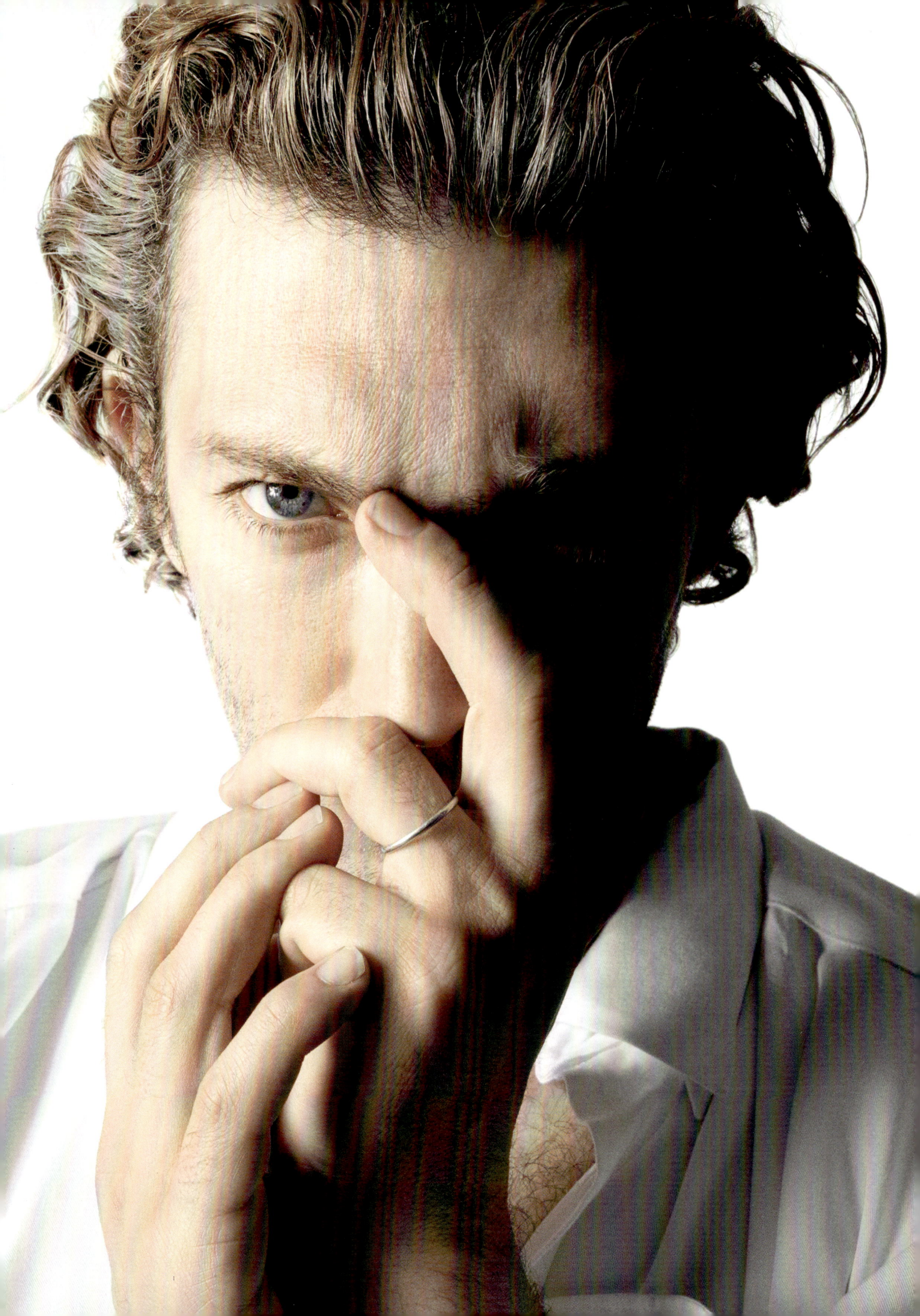

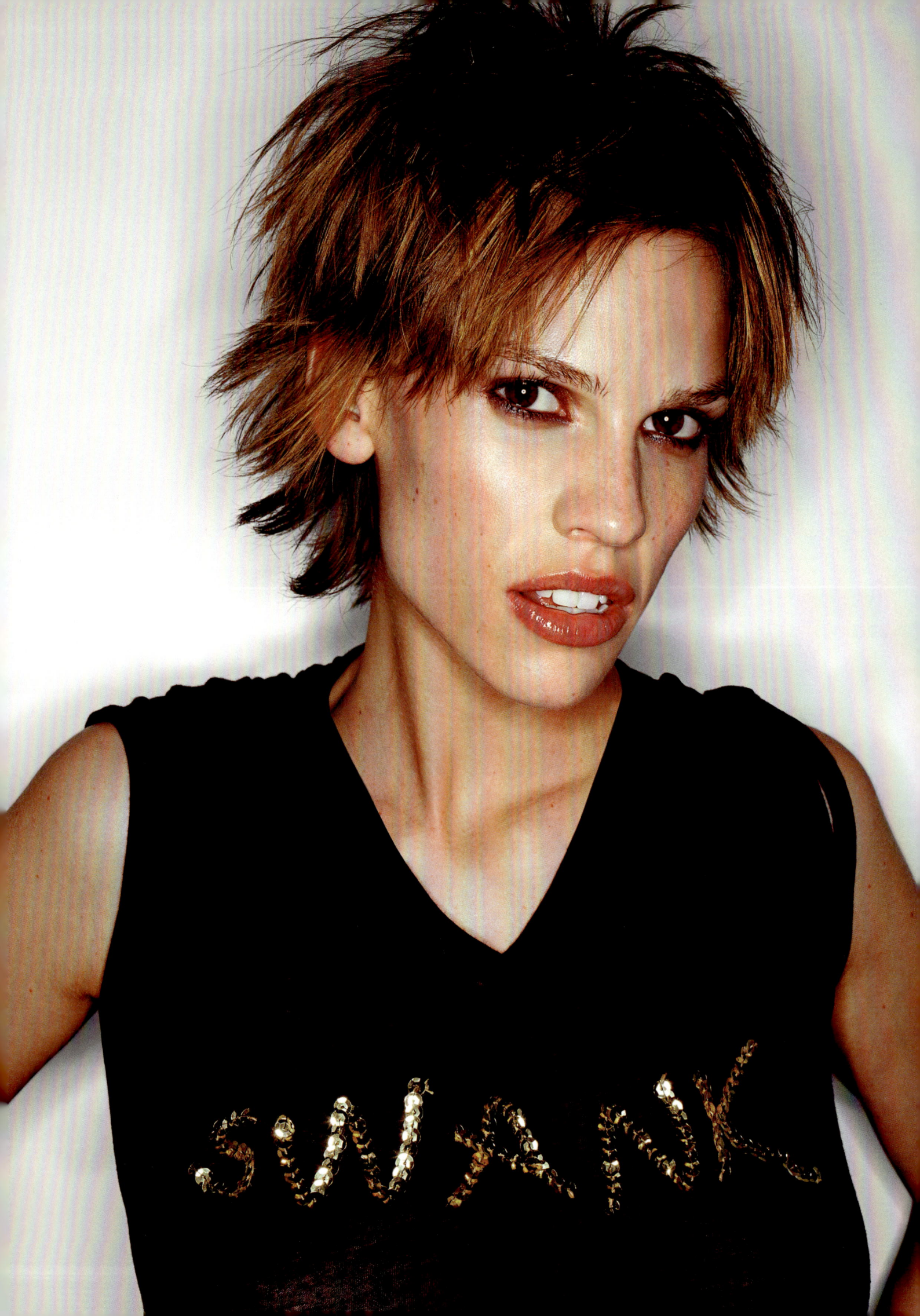

Previous Page - New Blood, New Wave, Issue 98, 2003

Opposite Page - Based on a True Story, Issue 64, 2000

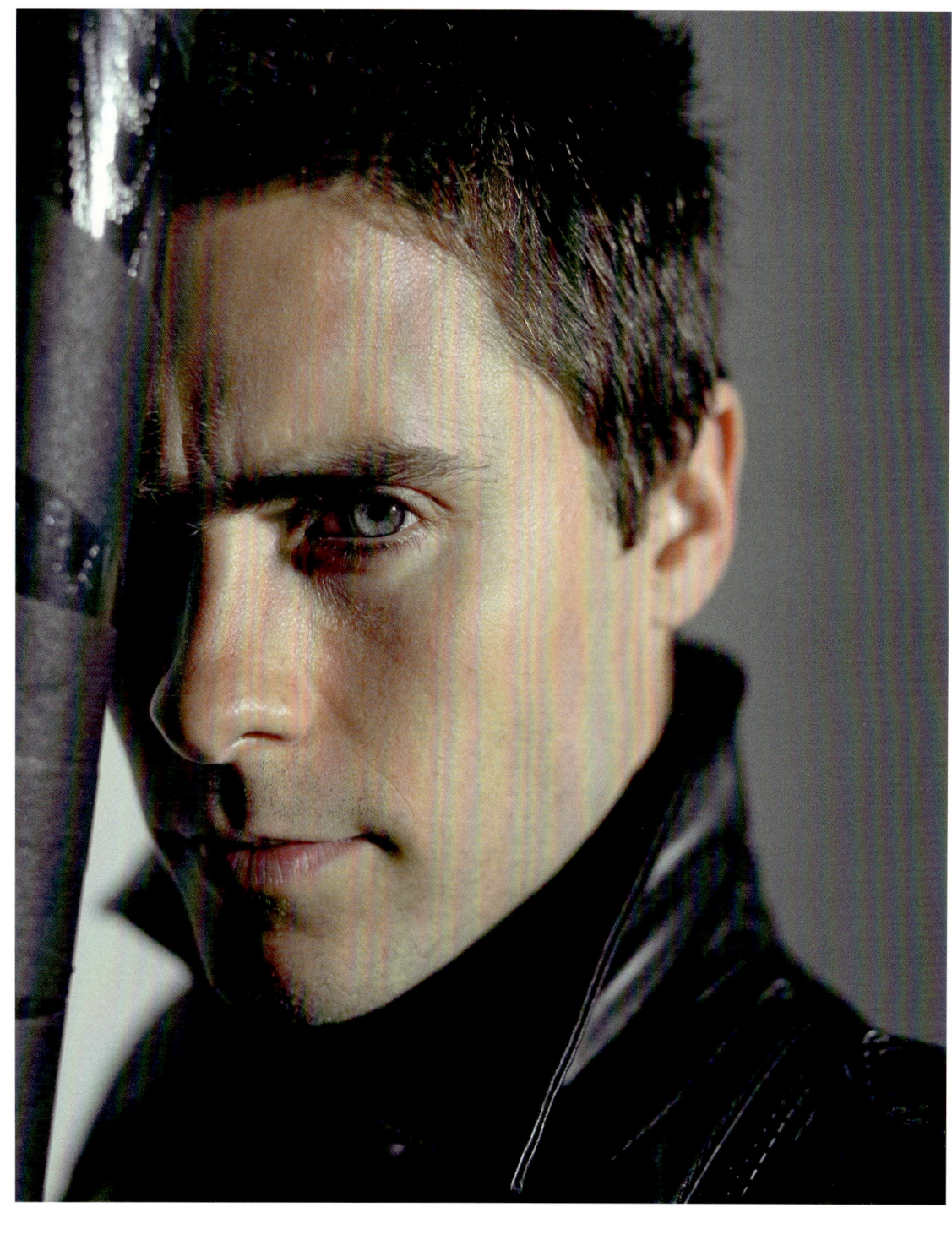

Riot Act, Vol. 2, Issue 30, 2005

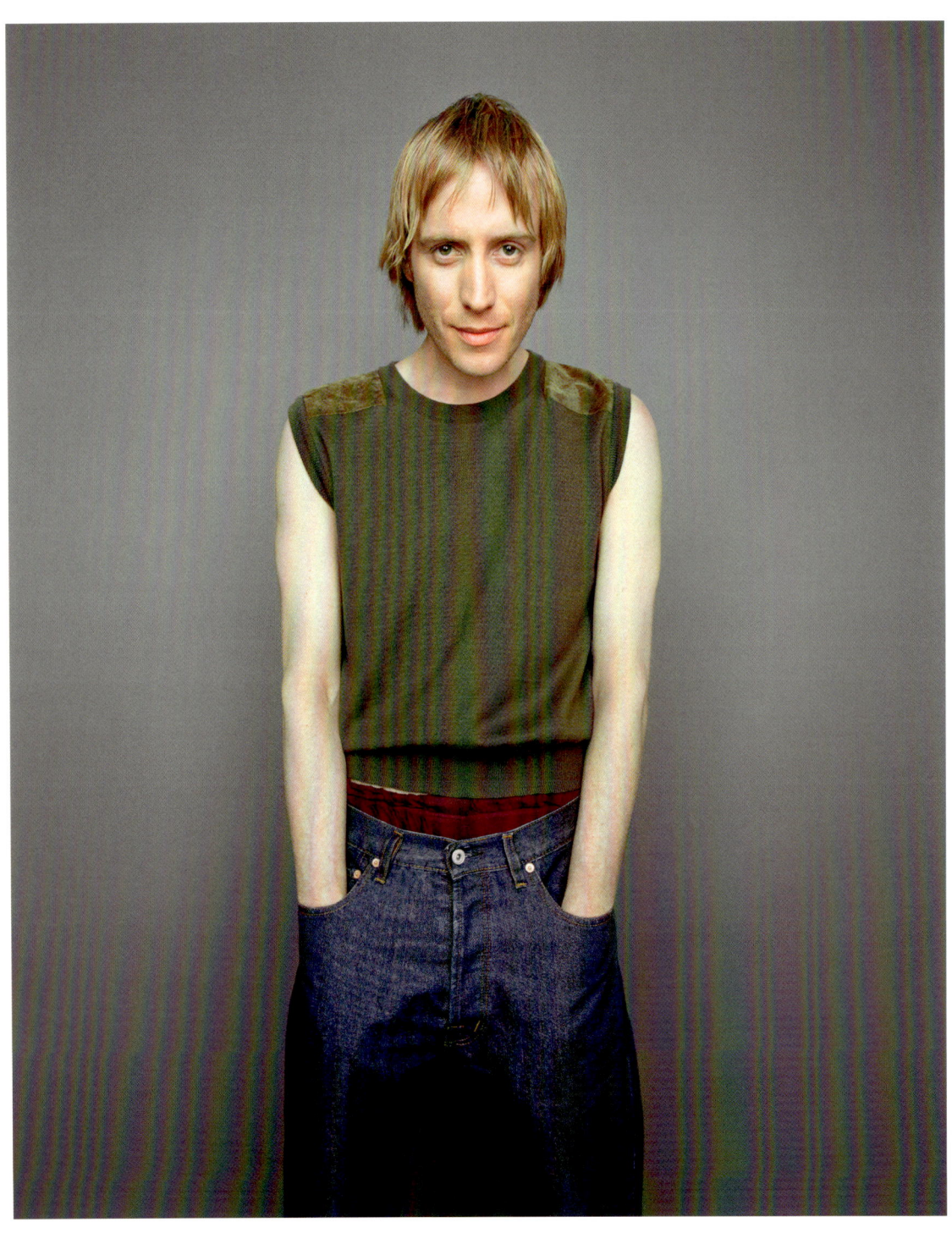

What's the Story?, Issue 31, 1997

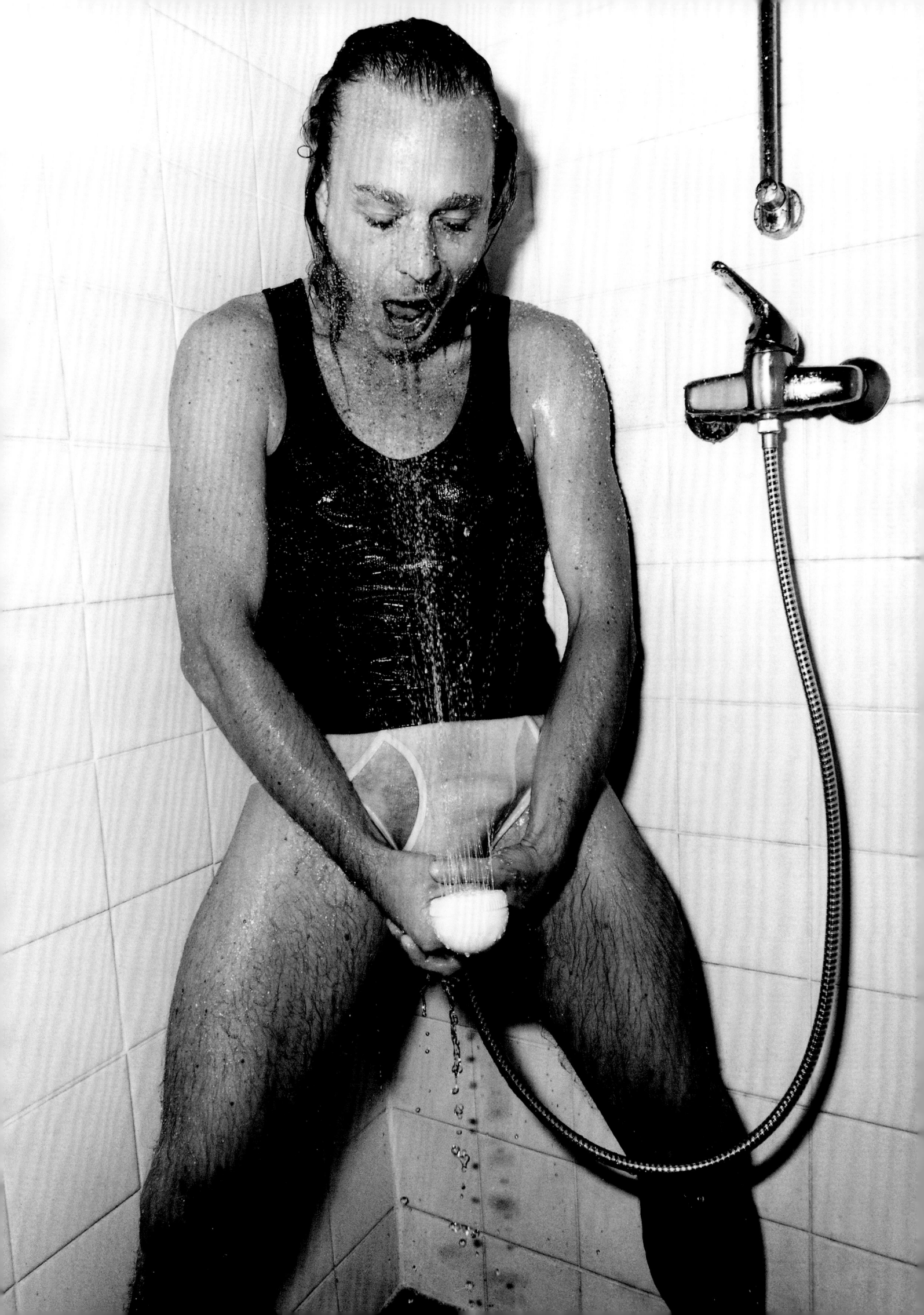

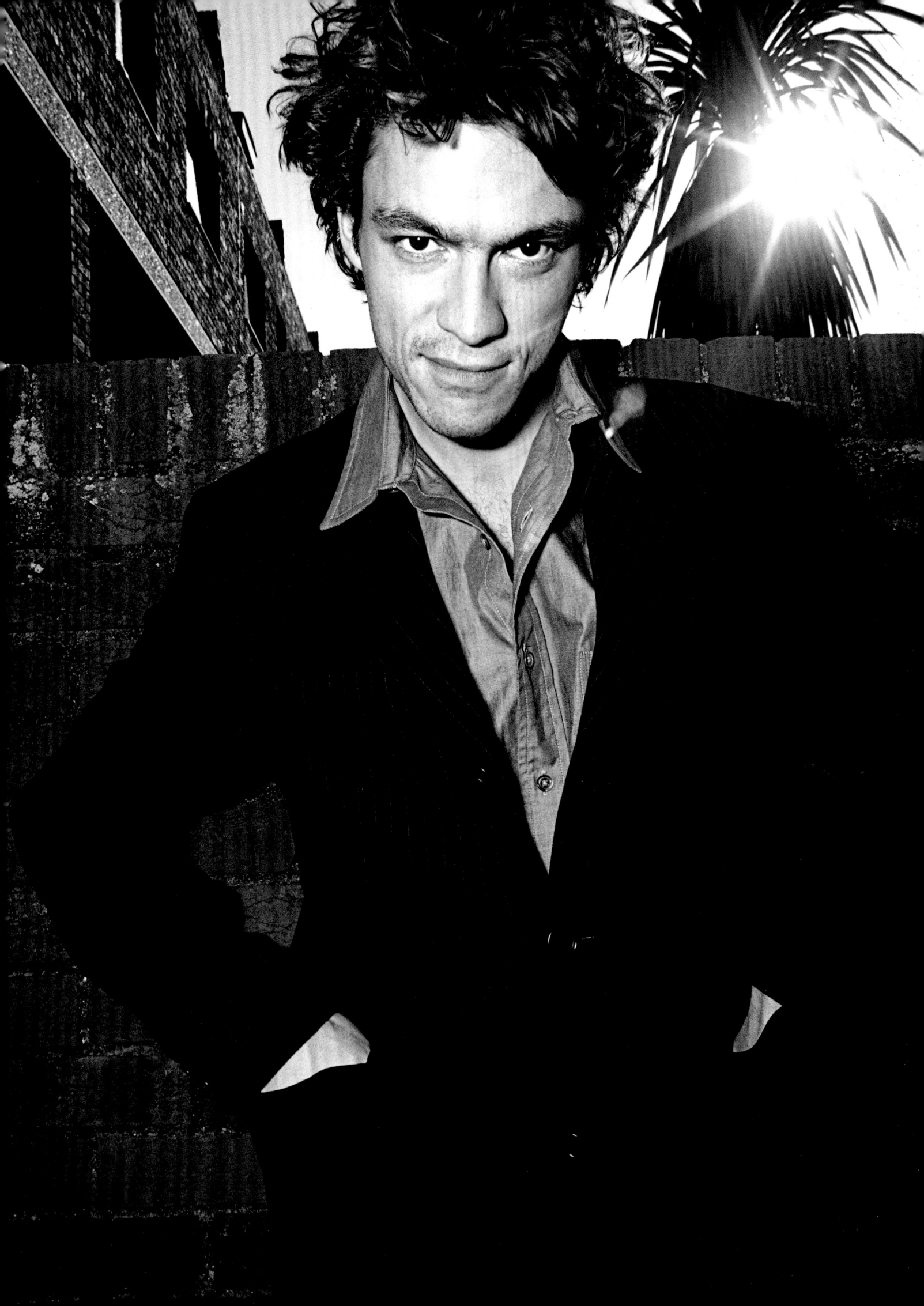

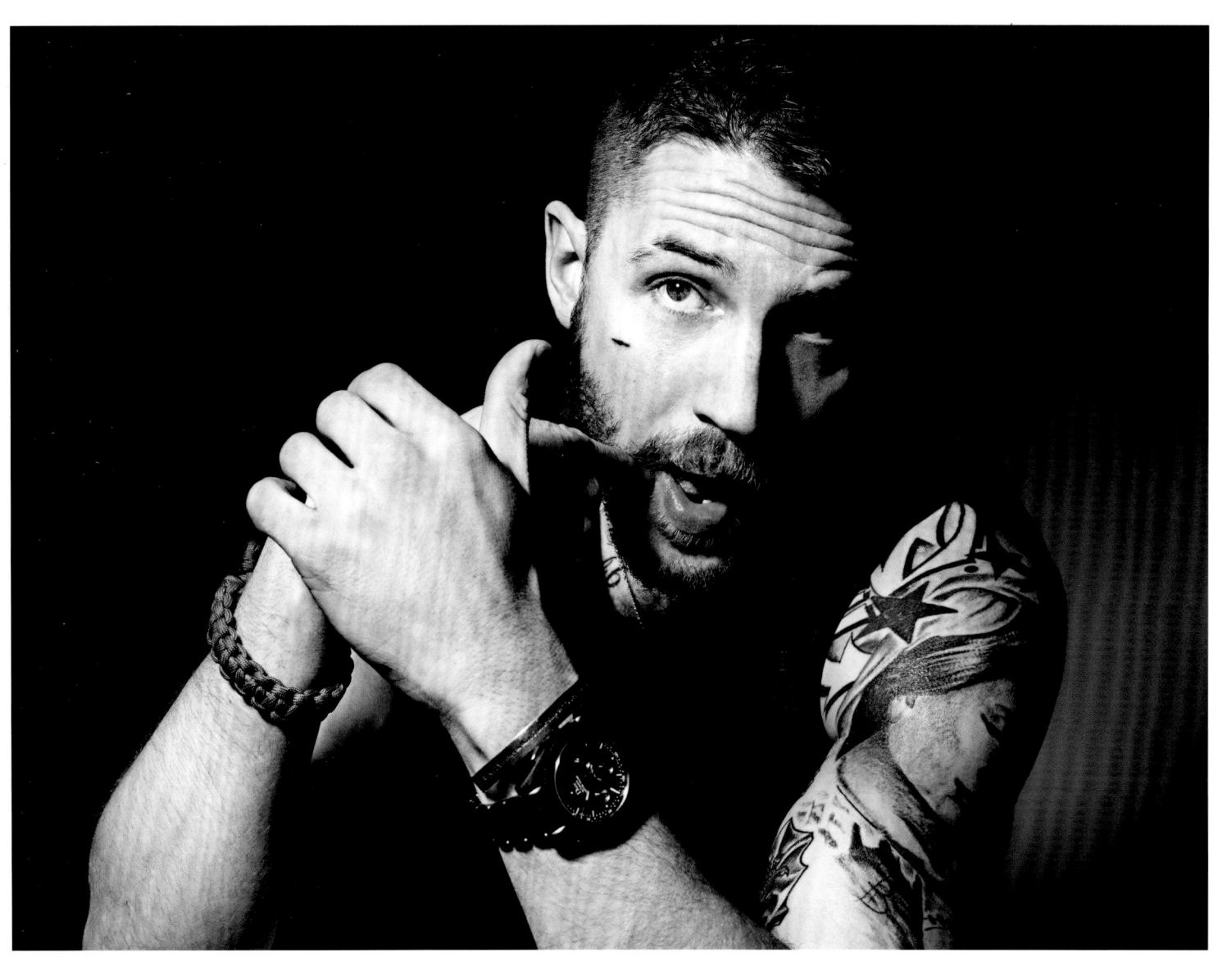

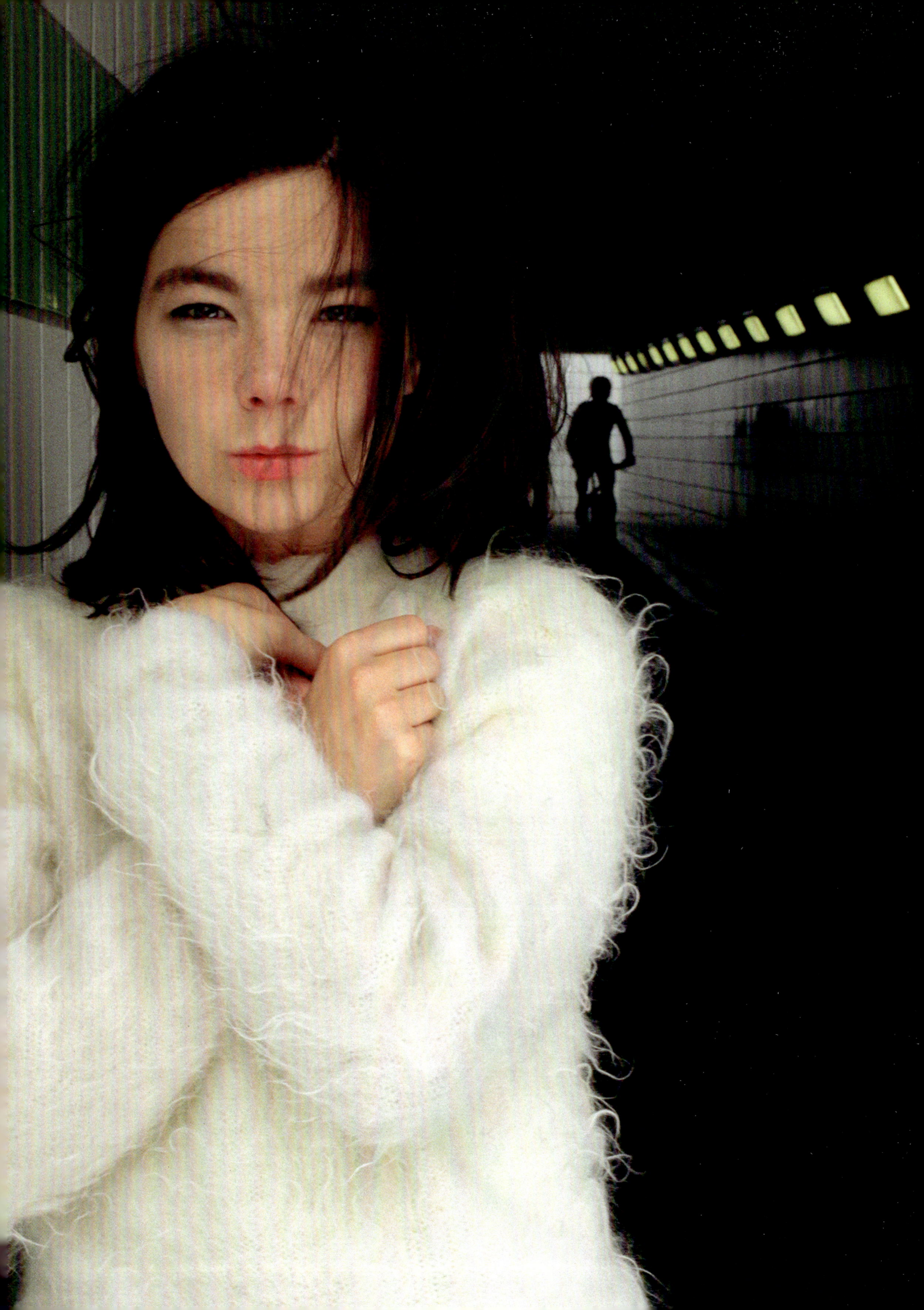

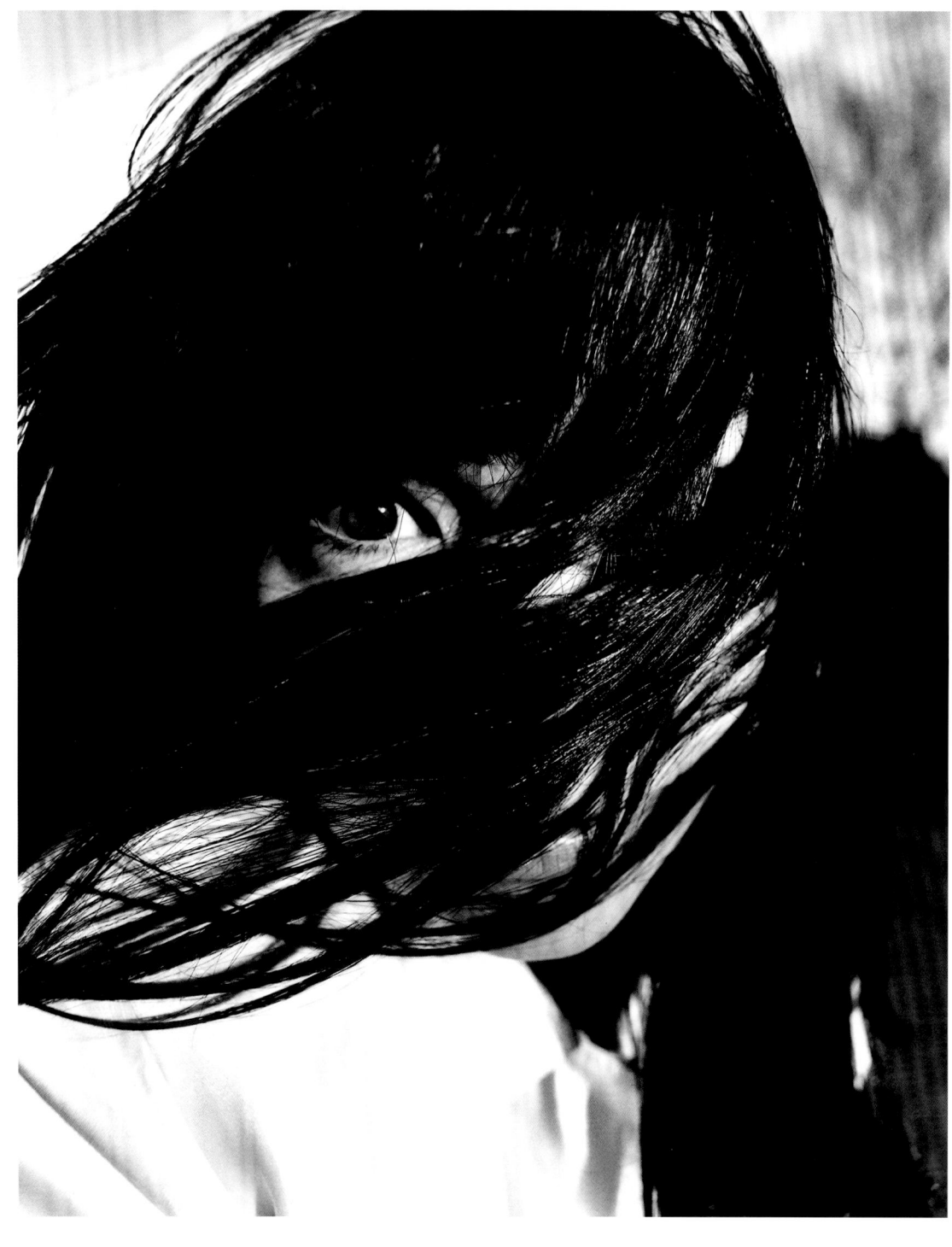

Nanu Nanu Björk Calling..., Issue 16, 1995

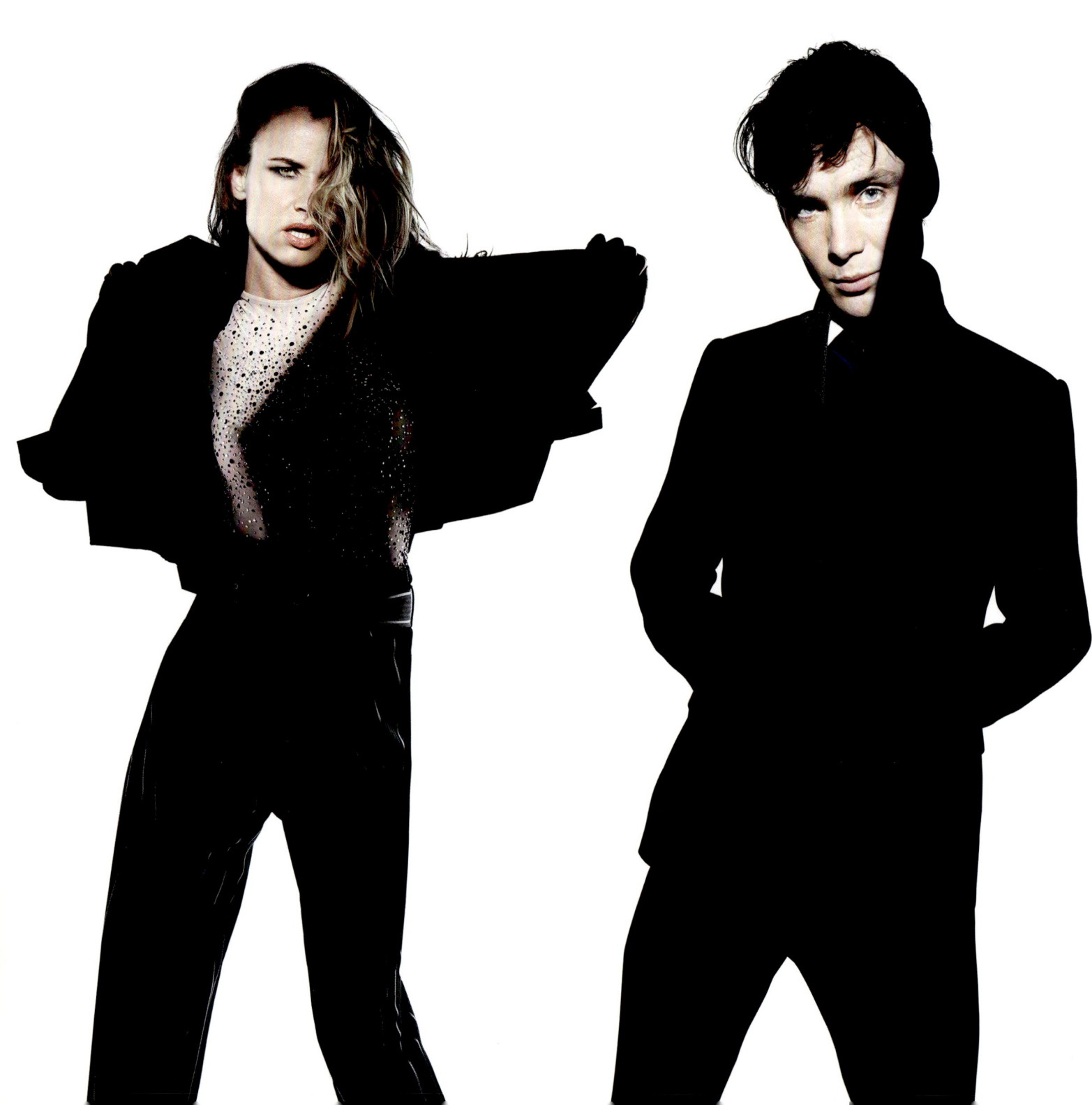

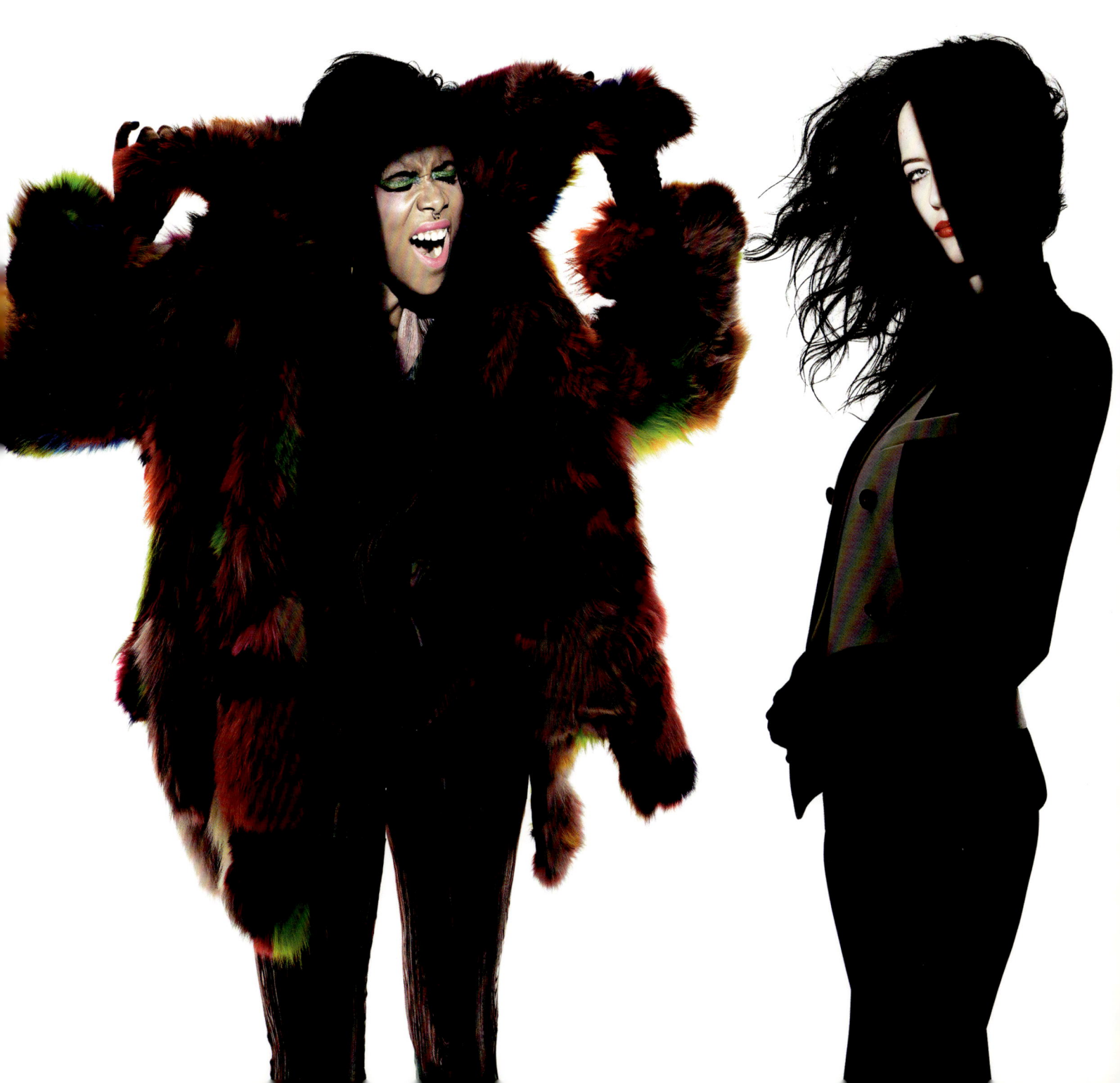

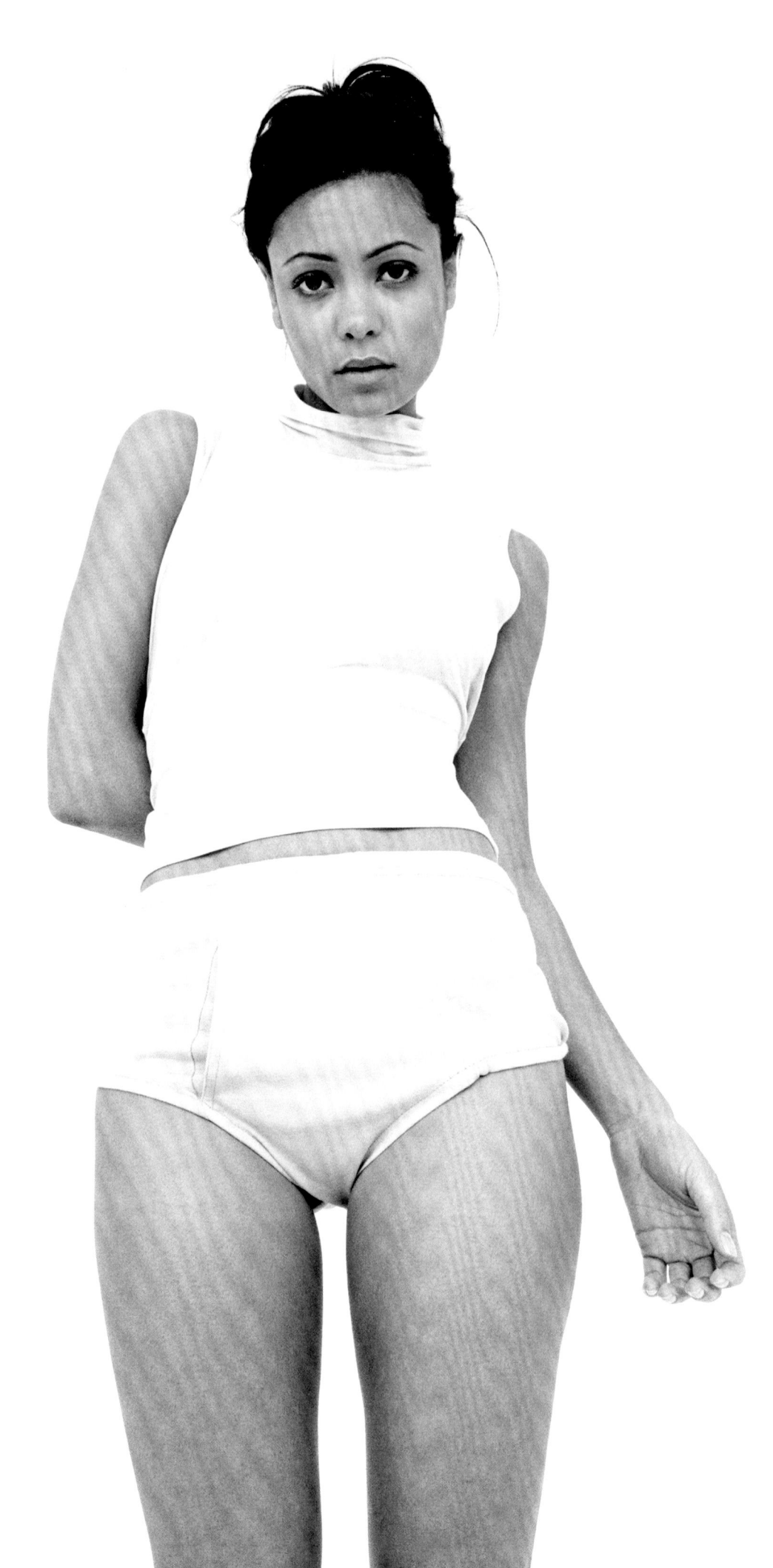

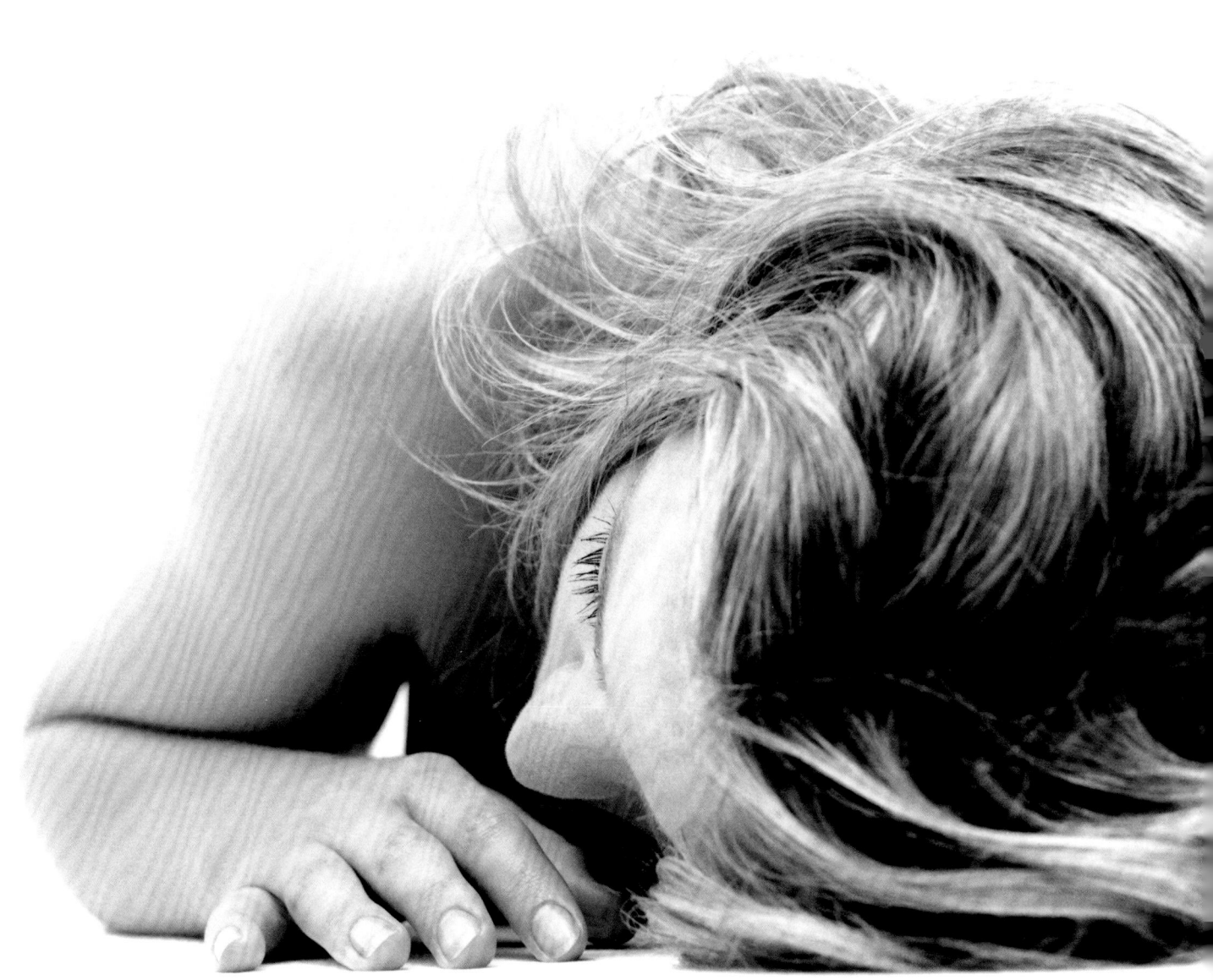

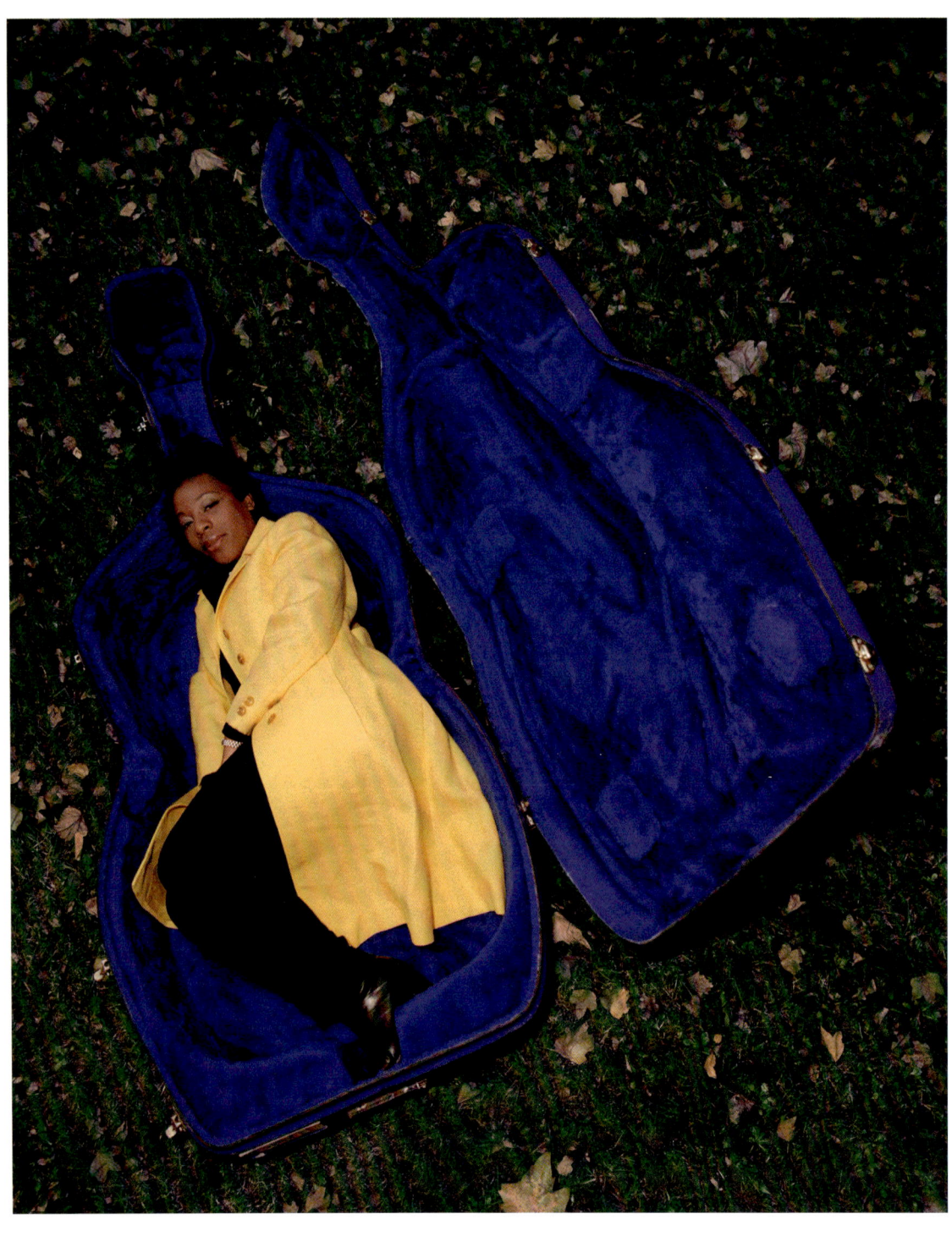

The Cast, Issue 26, 1996

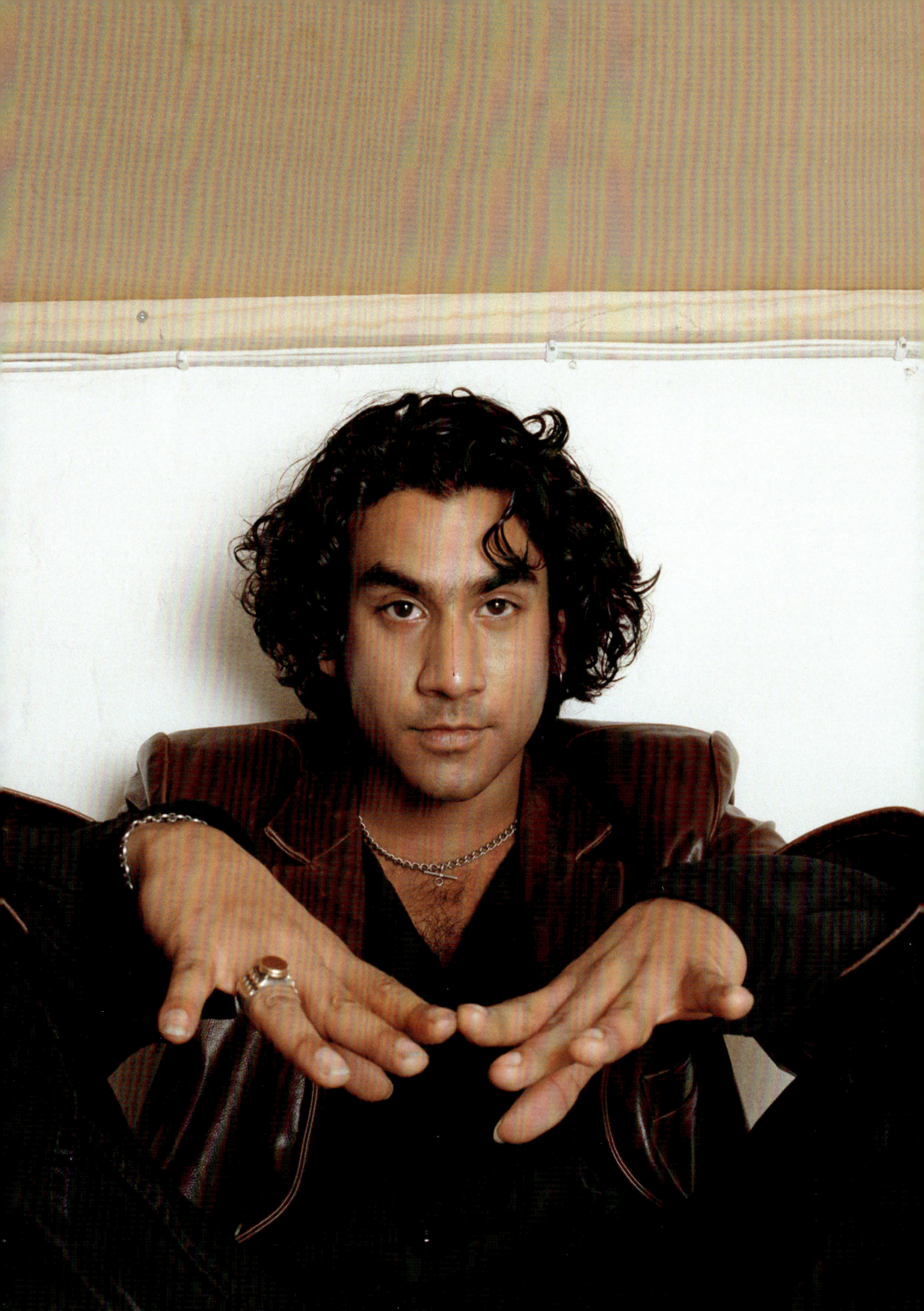

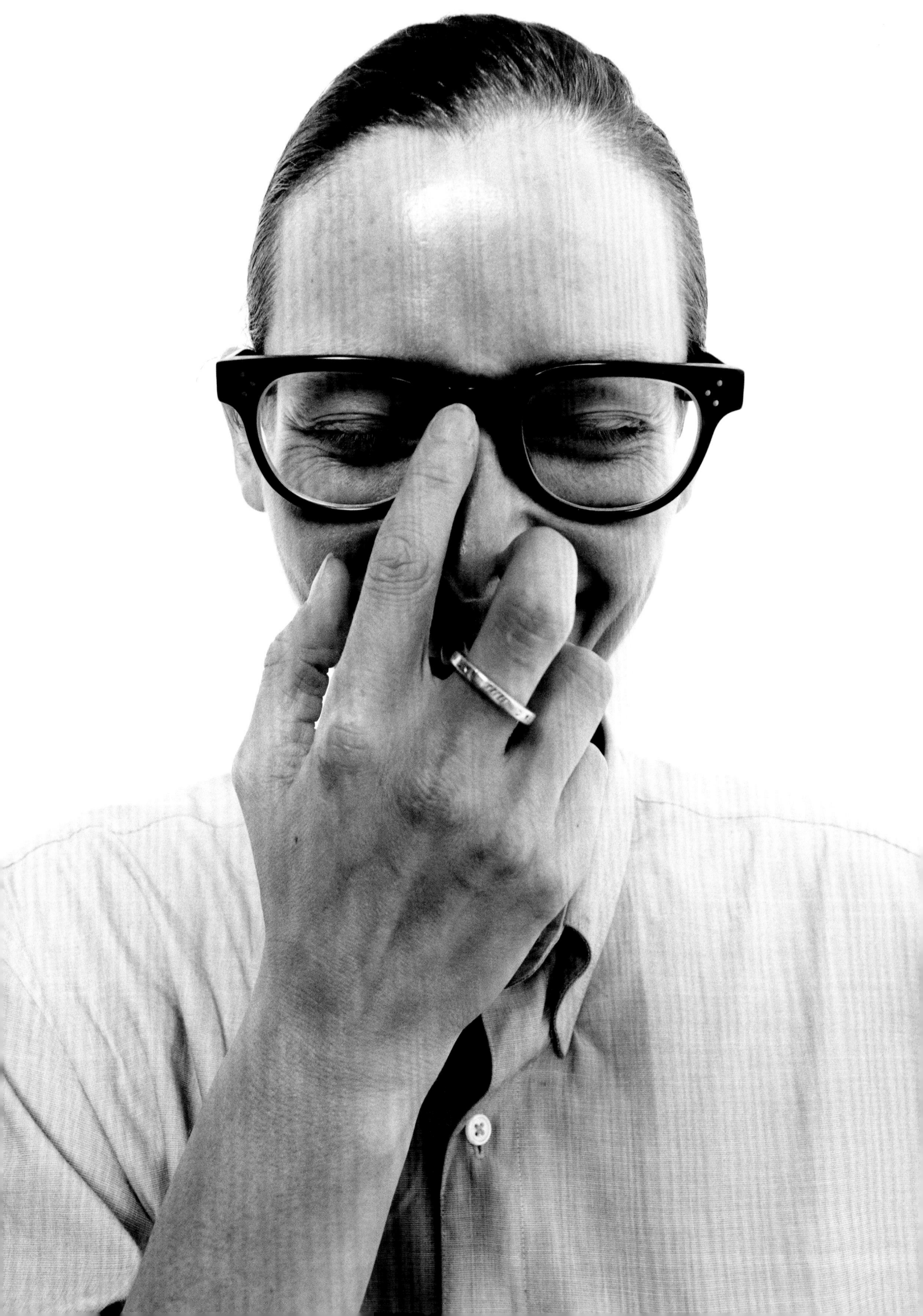

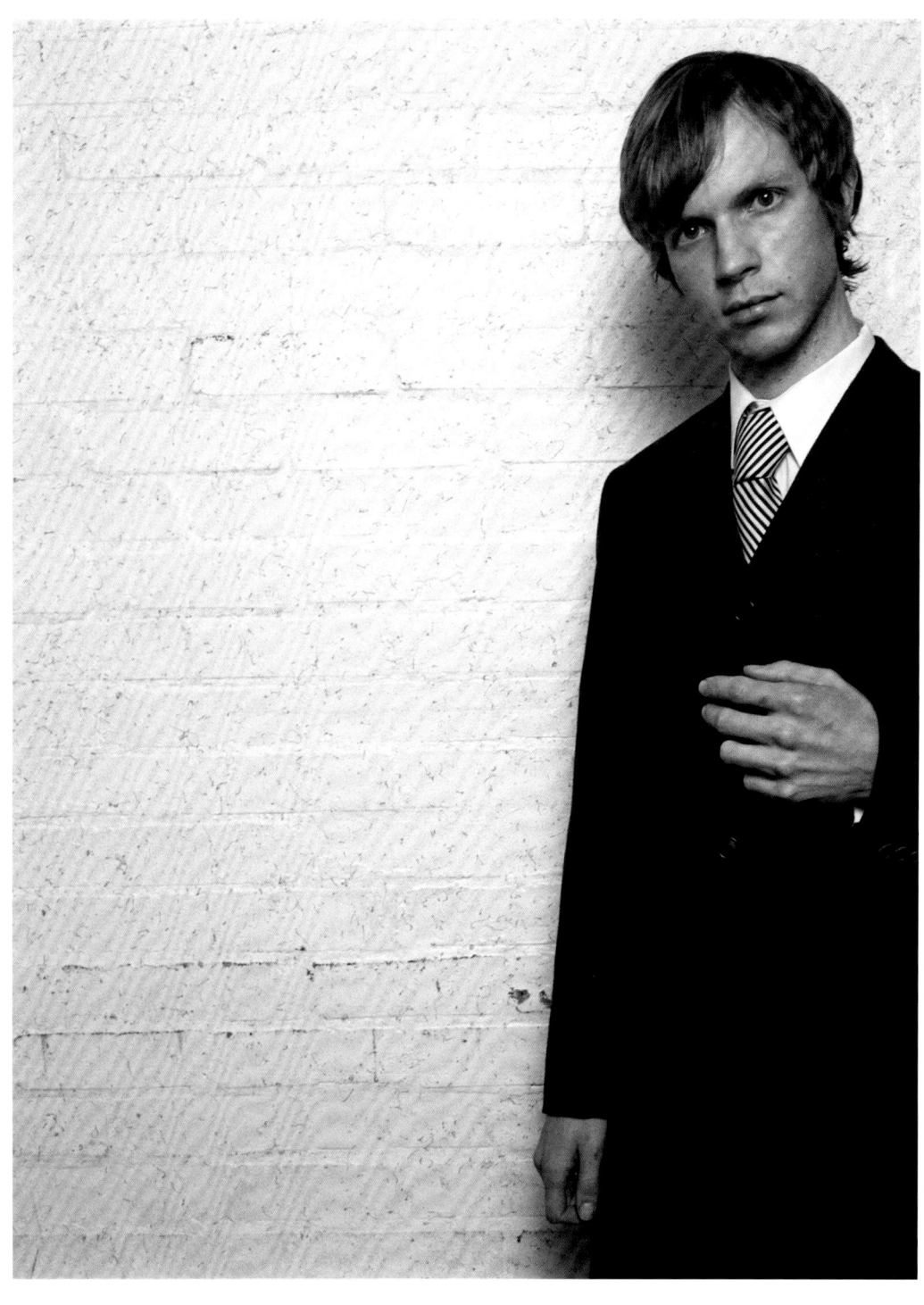

Cool as Fuck, Issue 29, 1997

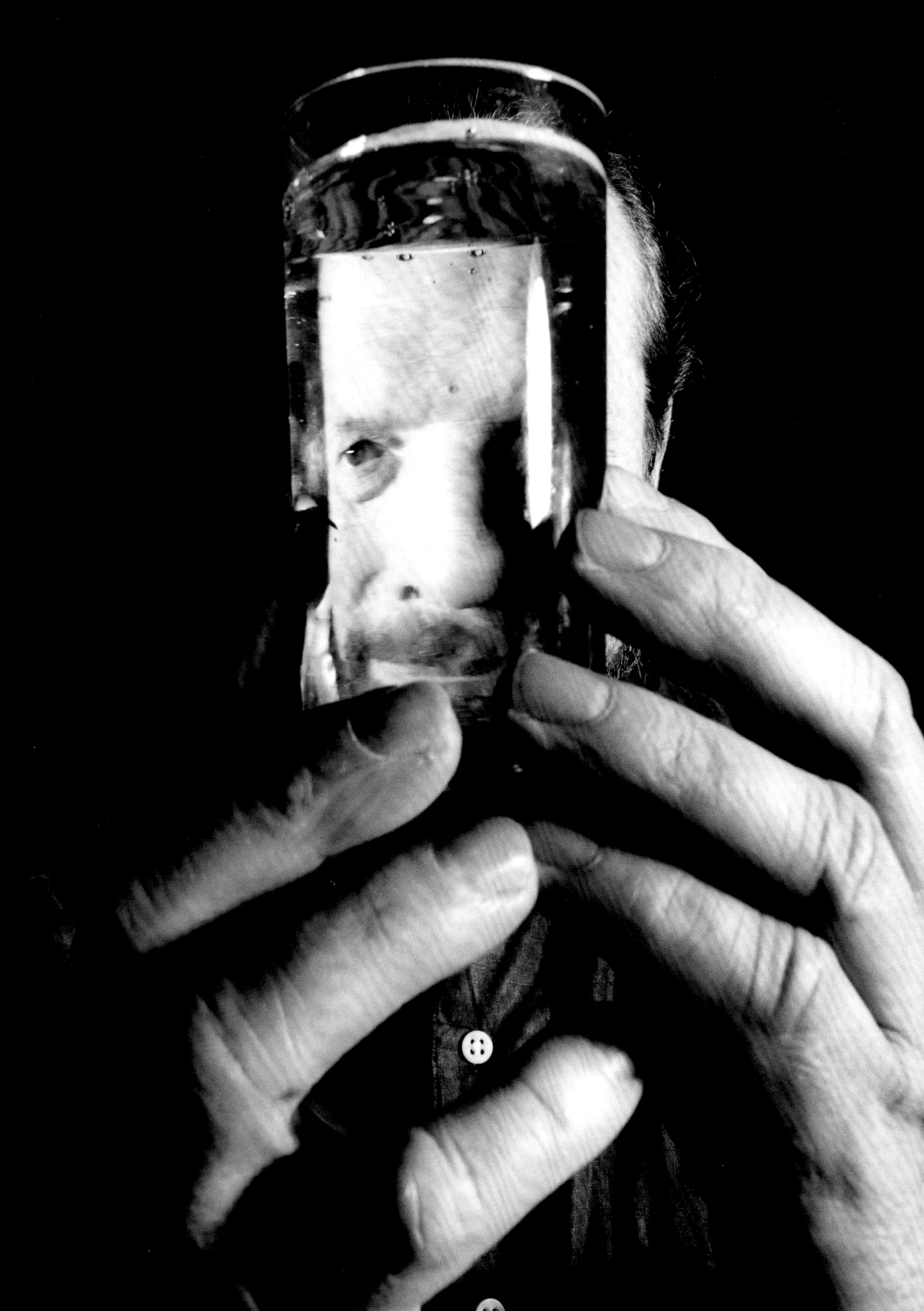

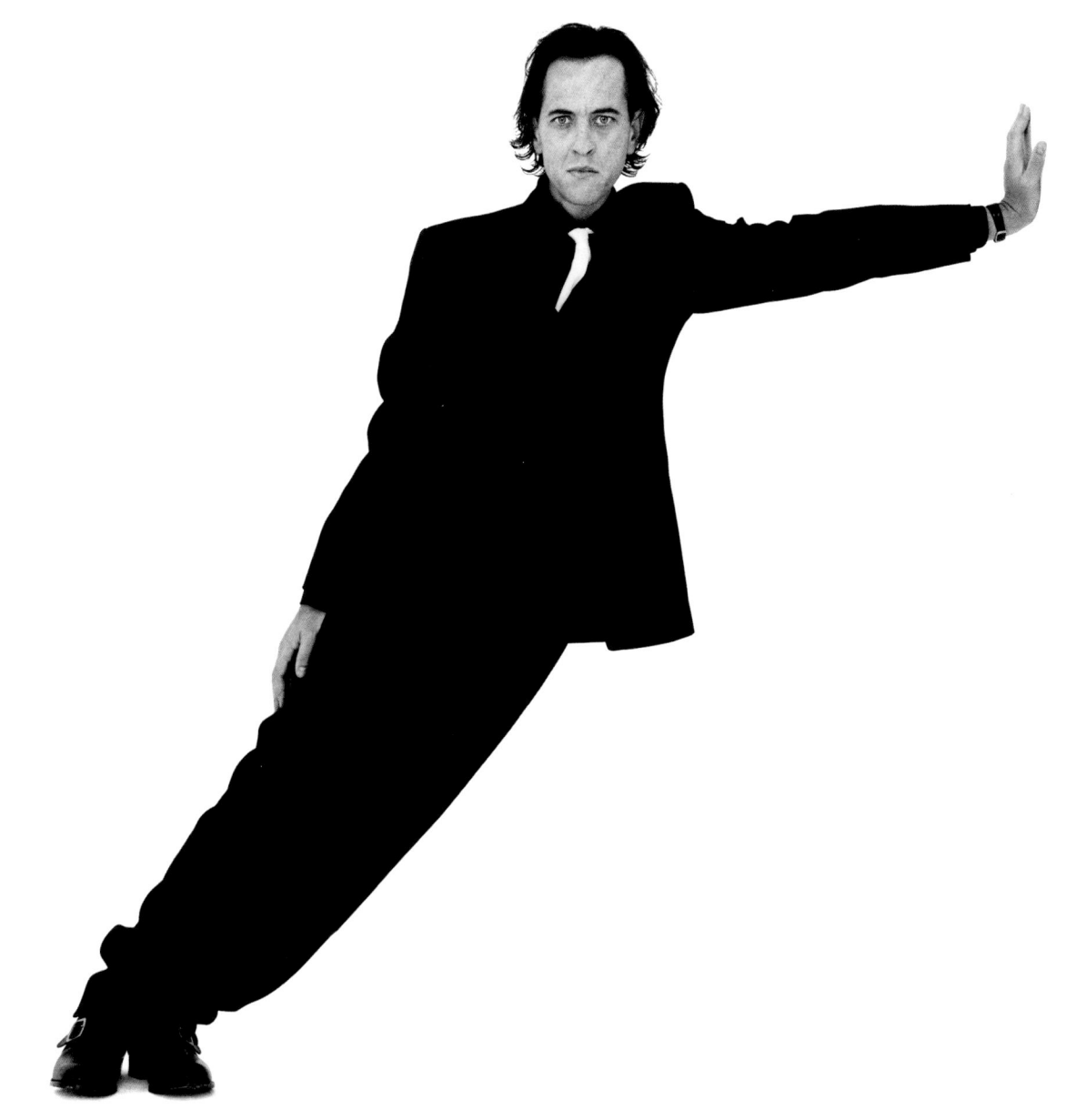

Like a Rhinestone Loudboy, Issue 11, 1995

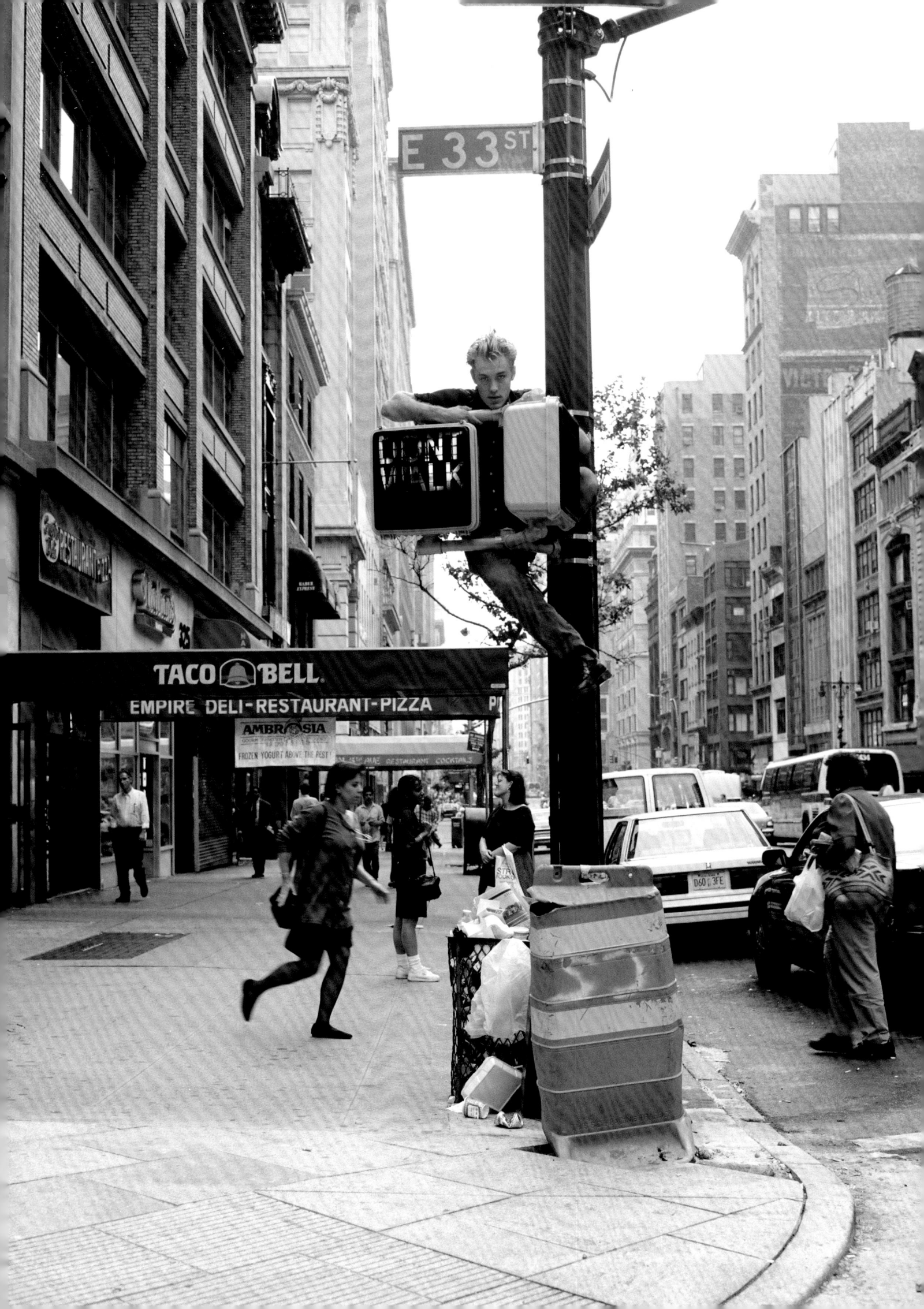

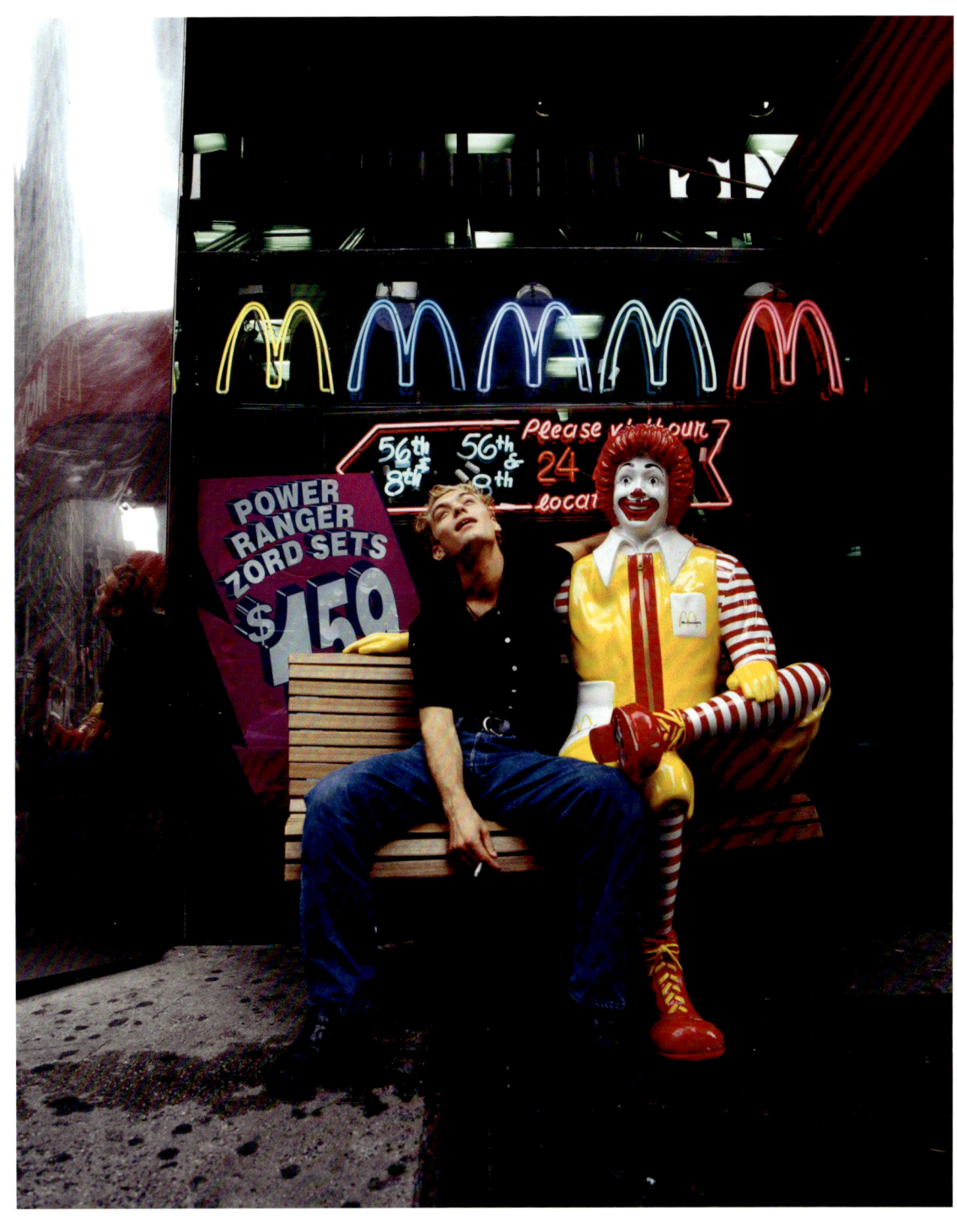

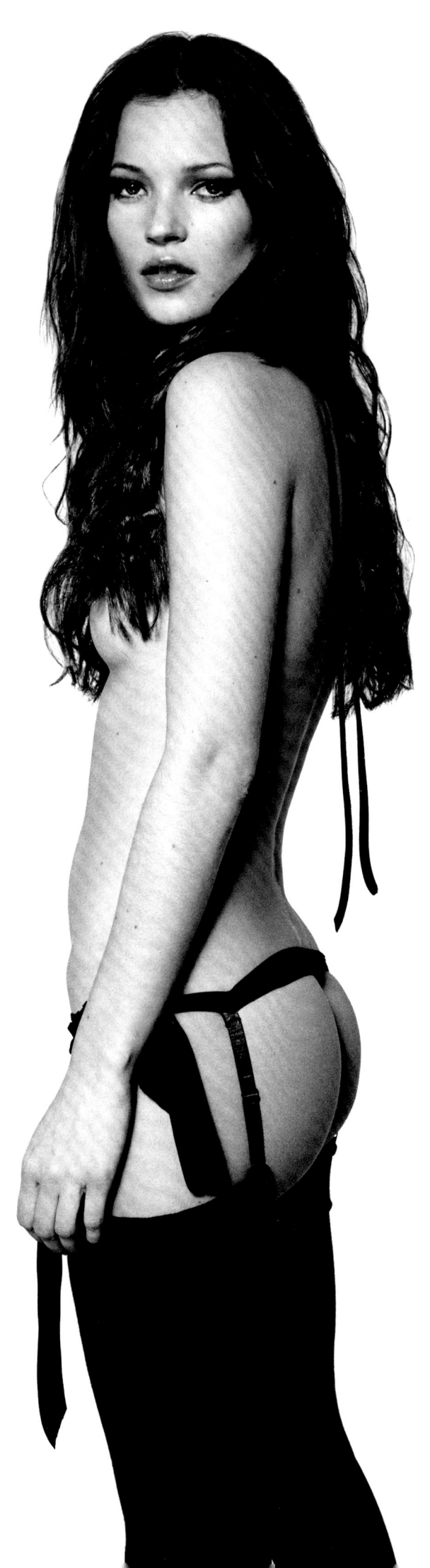

PEOPLE OVER OBJECTS/SUPERMODELS ARE WORTH MORE THAN CLOTHES/I'D RATHER GO NAKED THAN WEAR THAT/I TOLD YOU I WASN'T A FASHION PHOTOGRAPHER...

Ever the contrarian, Rankin's fashion photography is invariably not about clothes. A photographer who has captured more than one generation of supermodel, he has been known to declare "I told you I wasn't a fashion photographer".

In love with people, not objects, this self branding as "unfashionable" allows Rankin's imagery under the veneer of the fashion industry.

Issue 1 of *Dazed & Confused* started loud with this ethos. The first ever *Dazed* cover star being Roy Brown, an openly queer, black model and artist. To look back at the landscape of media in 1991 is to see a time of white-washing and homophobia, yet Rankin and *Dazed & Confused* recognised it was within these communities where fashions and cultures are born.

The first fashion spread within *Dazed & Confused* was *Emperors' New Clothes,*

with models in their underwear, not the styles and trends of the day. And it is interesting to find that within a fashion portfolio from Rankin, nudity and skin are perhaps the prevailing theme.

Kate Moss, stripped down to suspenders, or in a spray painted white vest, puts the fashion industry in focus. With Kate it was her personality that defined the era, it was her body which was lusted after and sold - not the clothes.

For Rankin, fashion itself is often otherworldly, alien, and full of artifice: in *Stranded,* models walk the desert and drink milk from the earth; in *Faking It!* and *Ghost,* the reality of imagery is aesthetically undermined.

Uniting it all is that signature Rankin trait, he is being cheeky, and ultimately, he is letting you in on the joke.

EMPEROR'S NEW CLOTHES

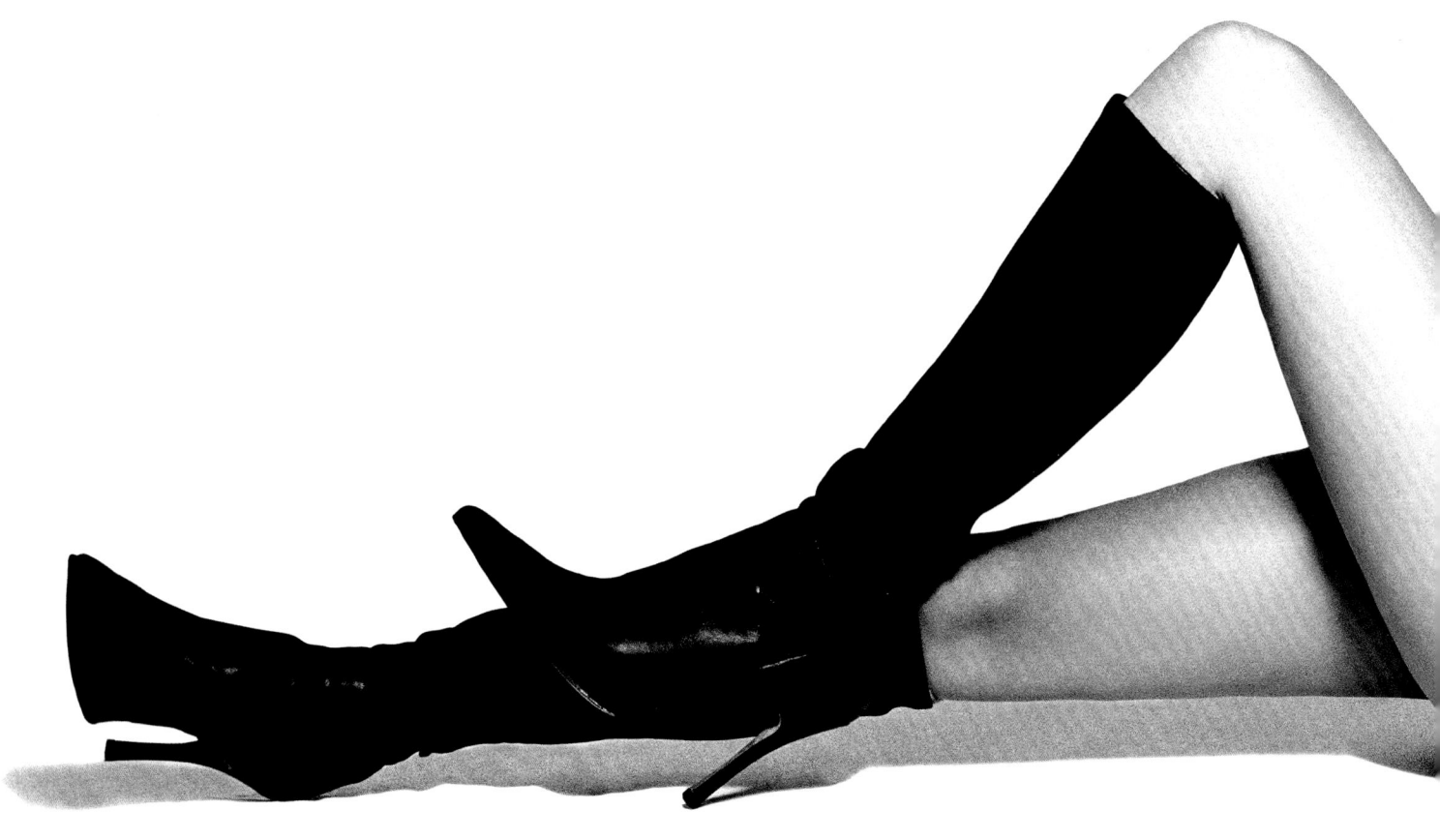

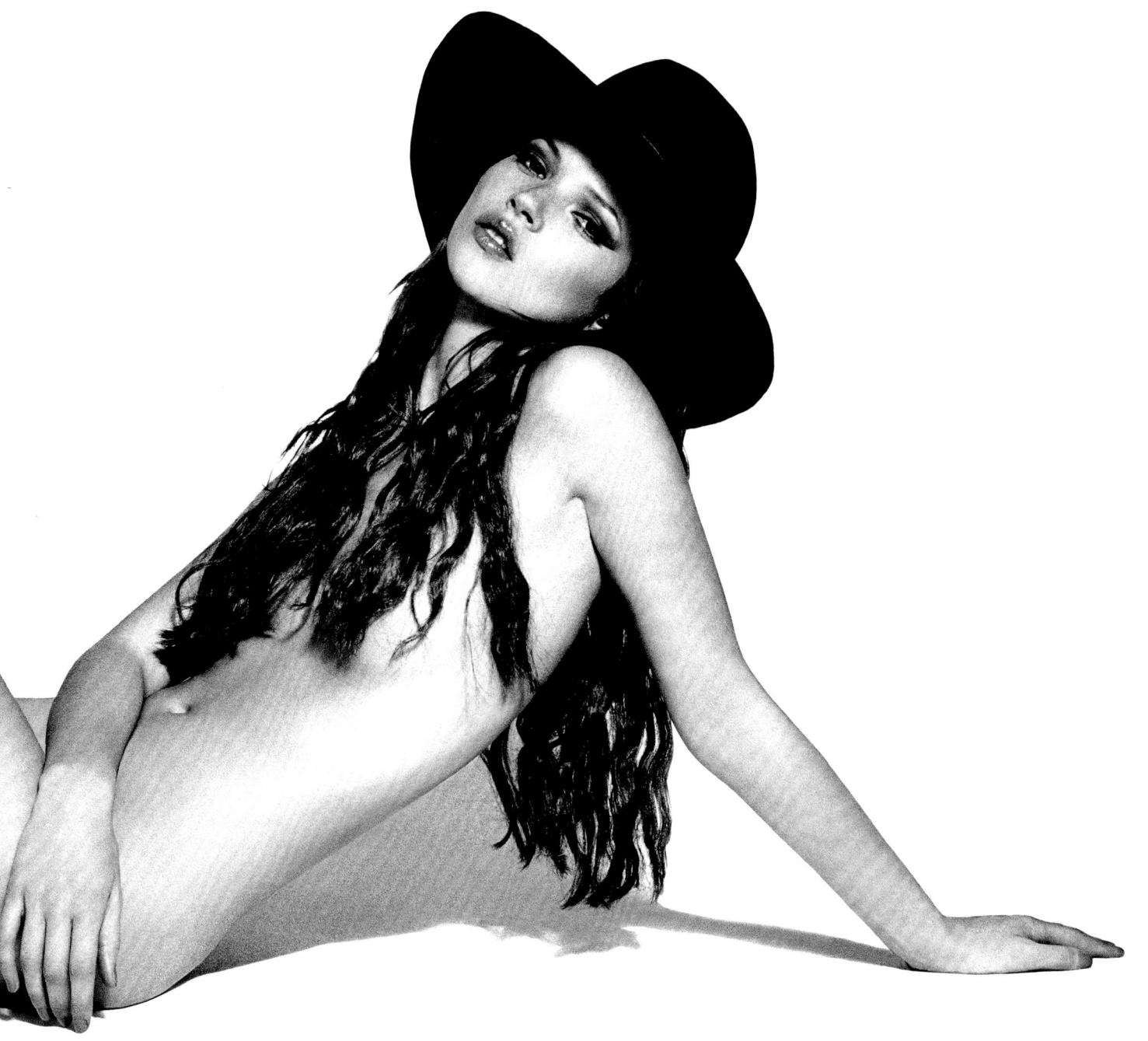

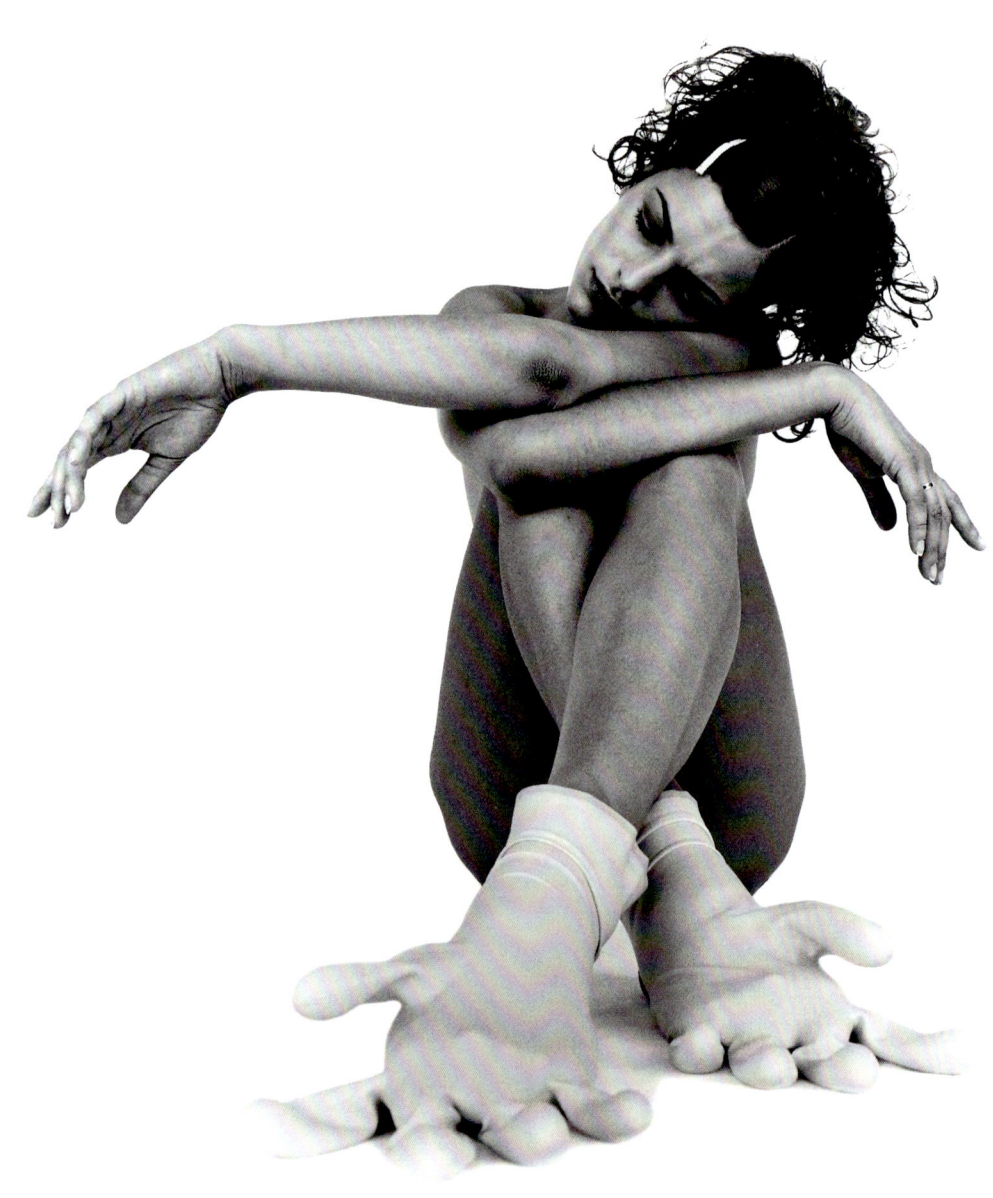

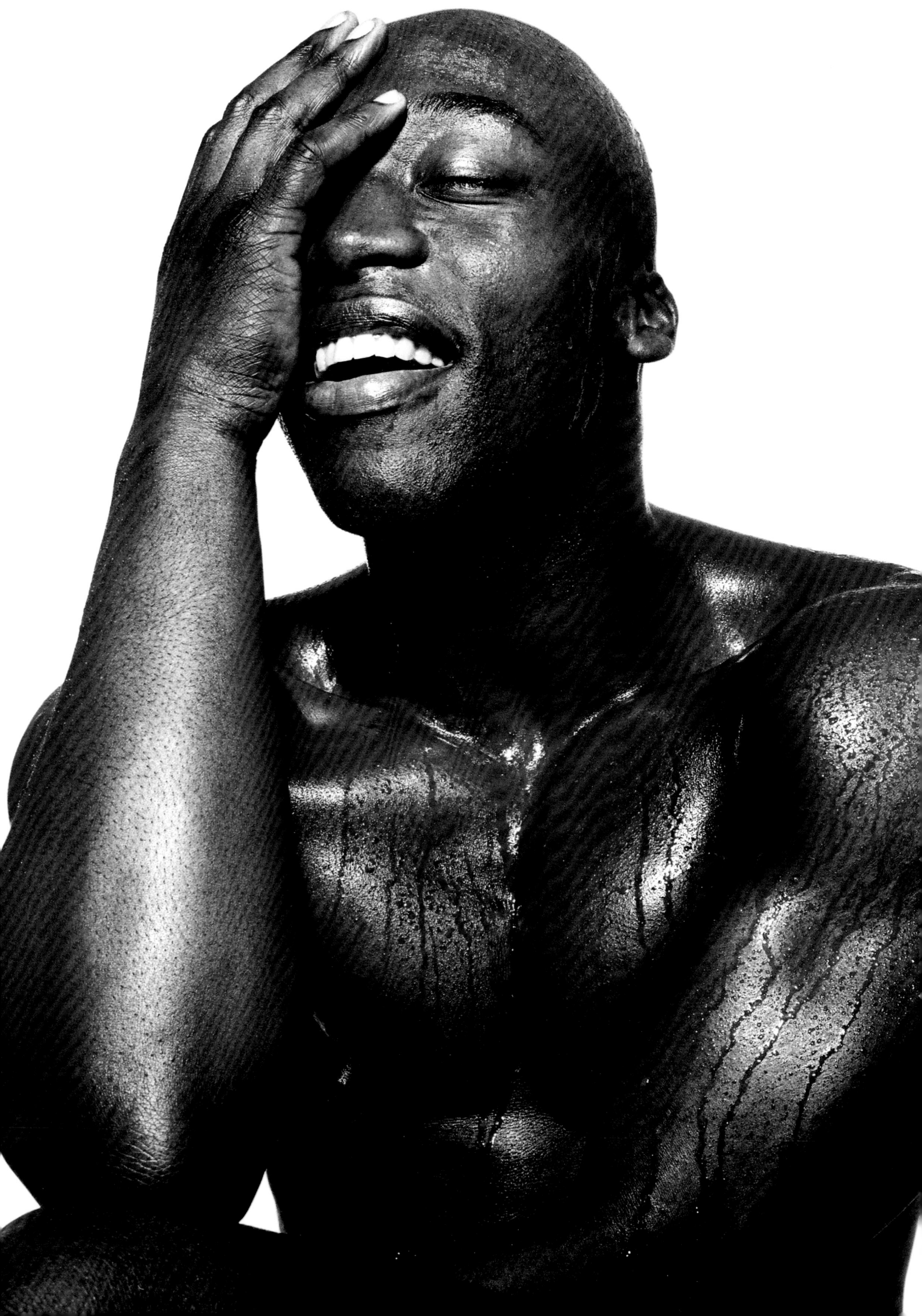

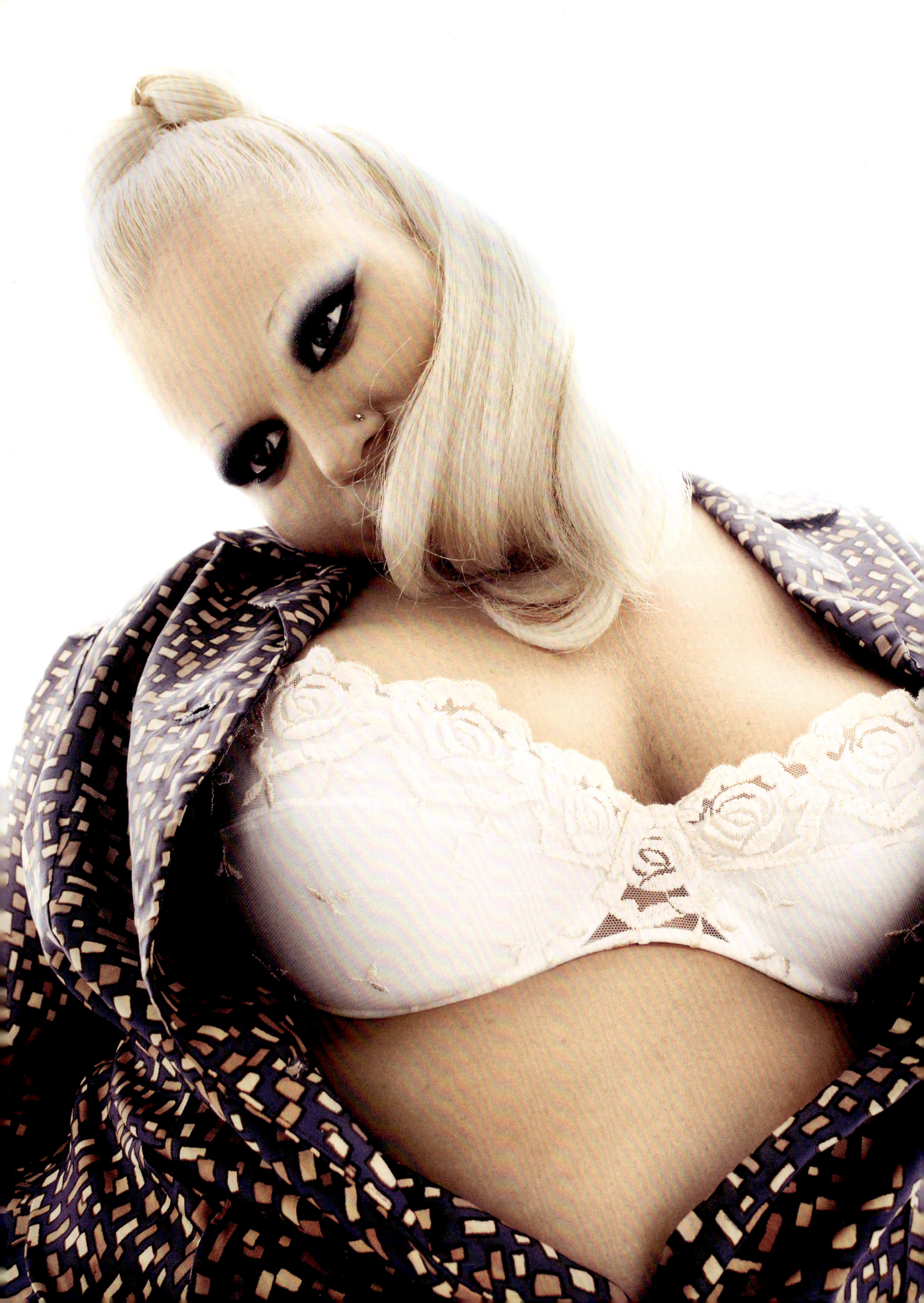

Opposite Page - Big Girl's Blouse, Issue 14, 1995

Next Pages -   What's the First Word That Comes Into Your Head?, Issue 43, 1998
America's Sweetheart, 25th Anniversary Issue, A/W 2016

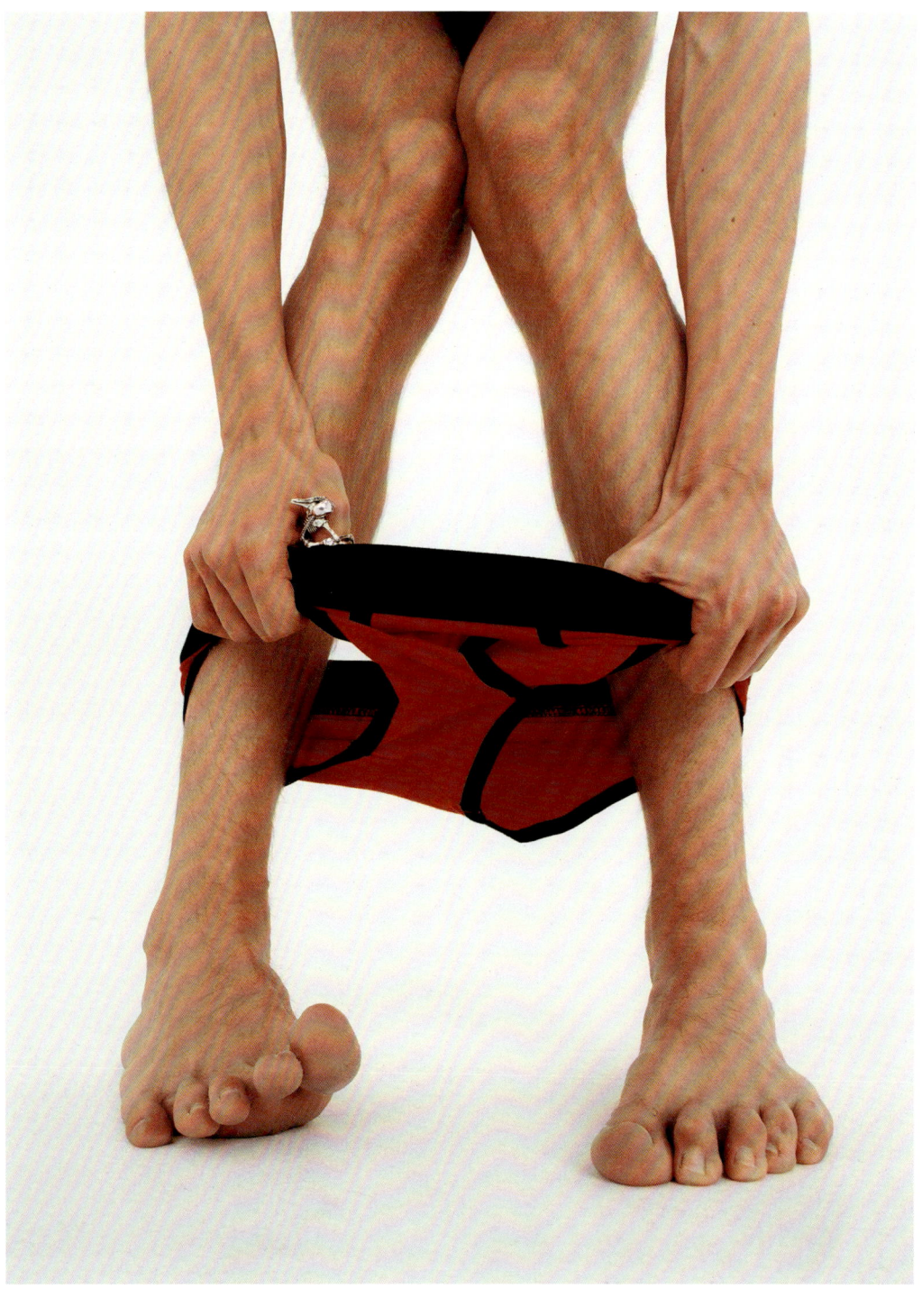

Pack Your Trunks, Issue 17, 1995

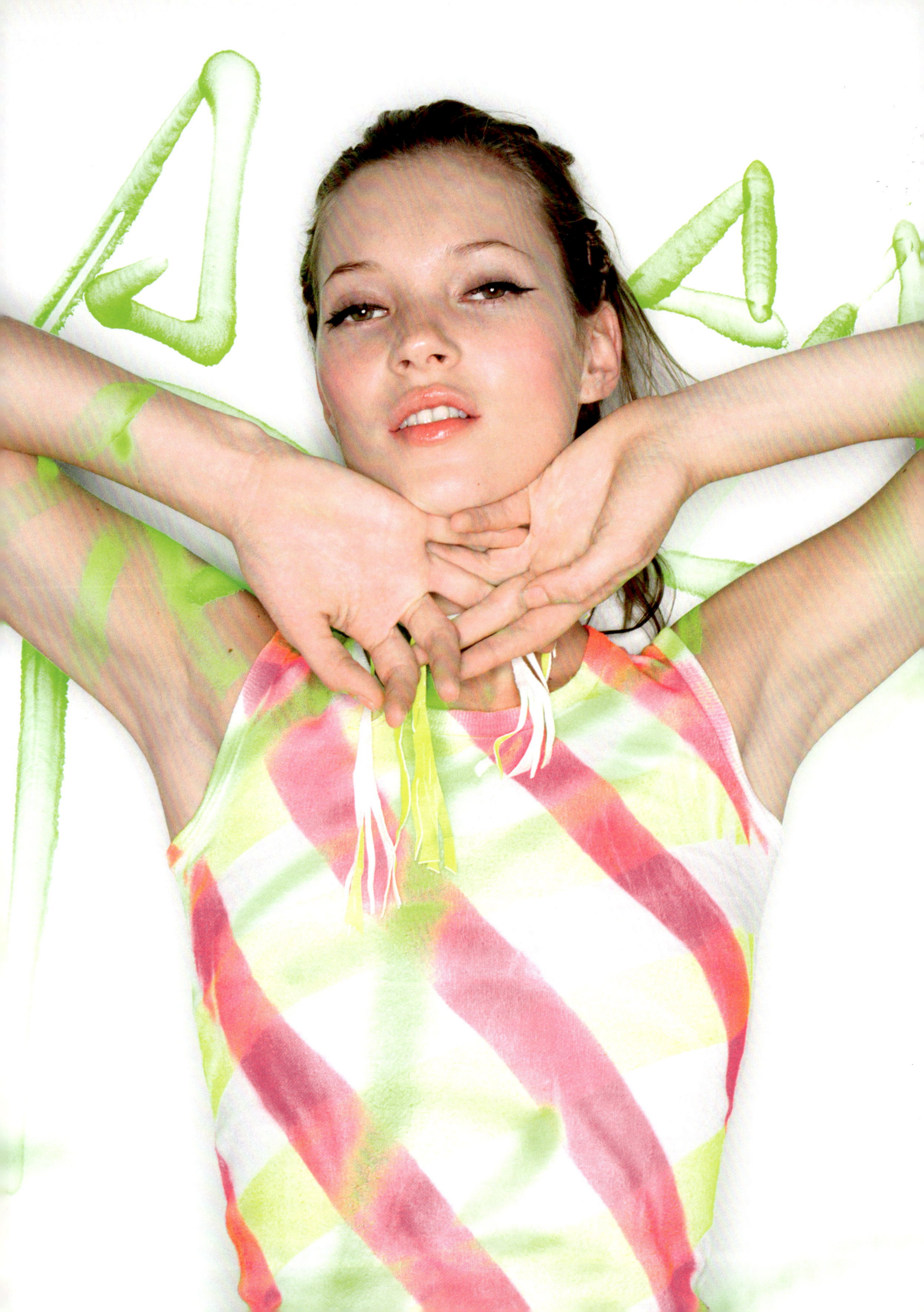

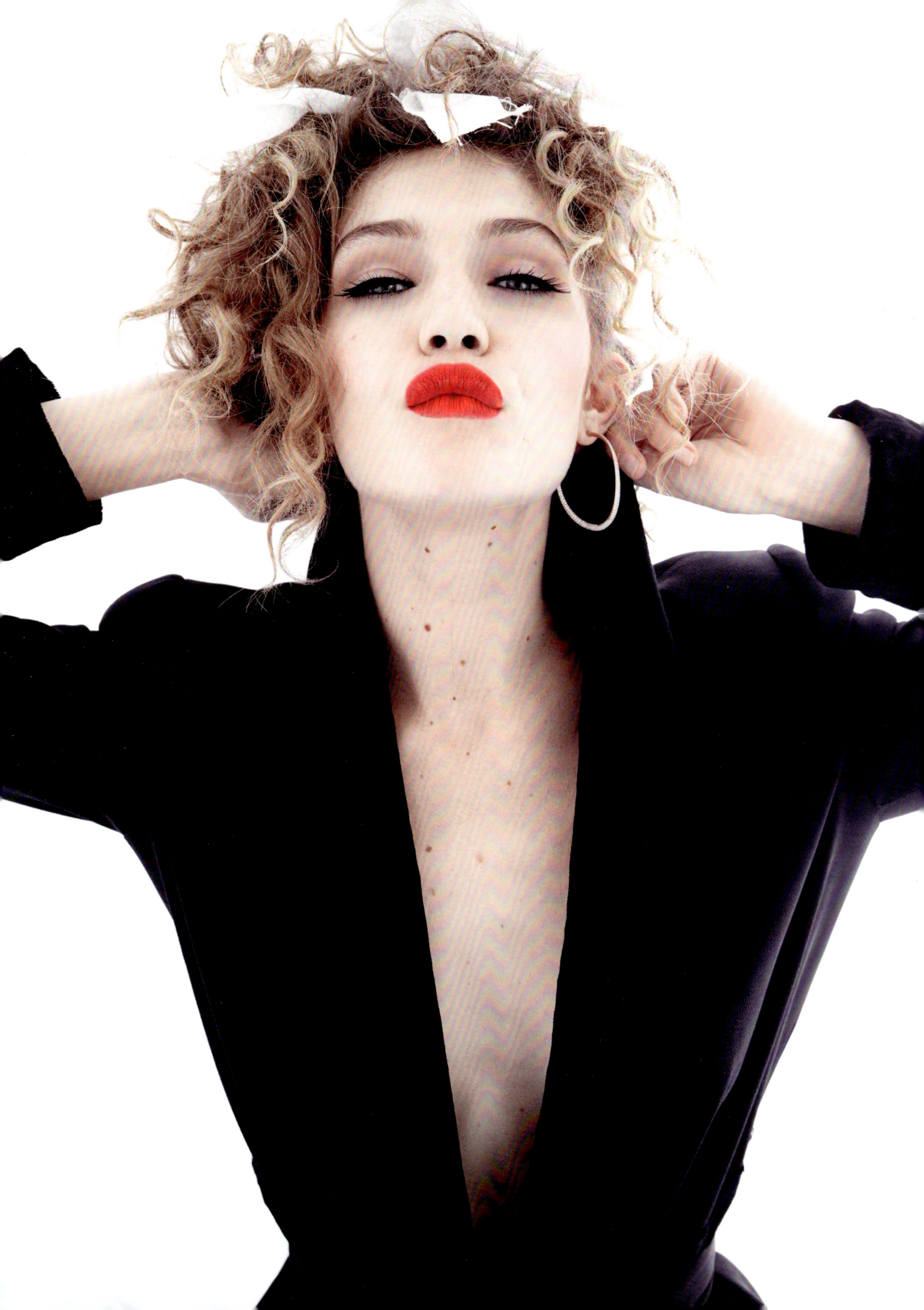

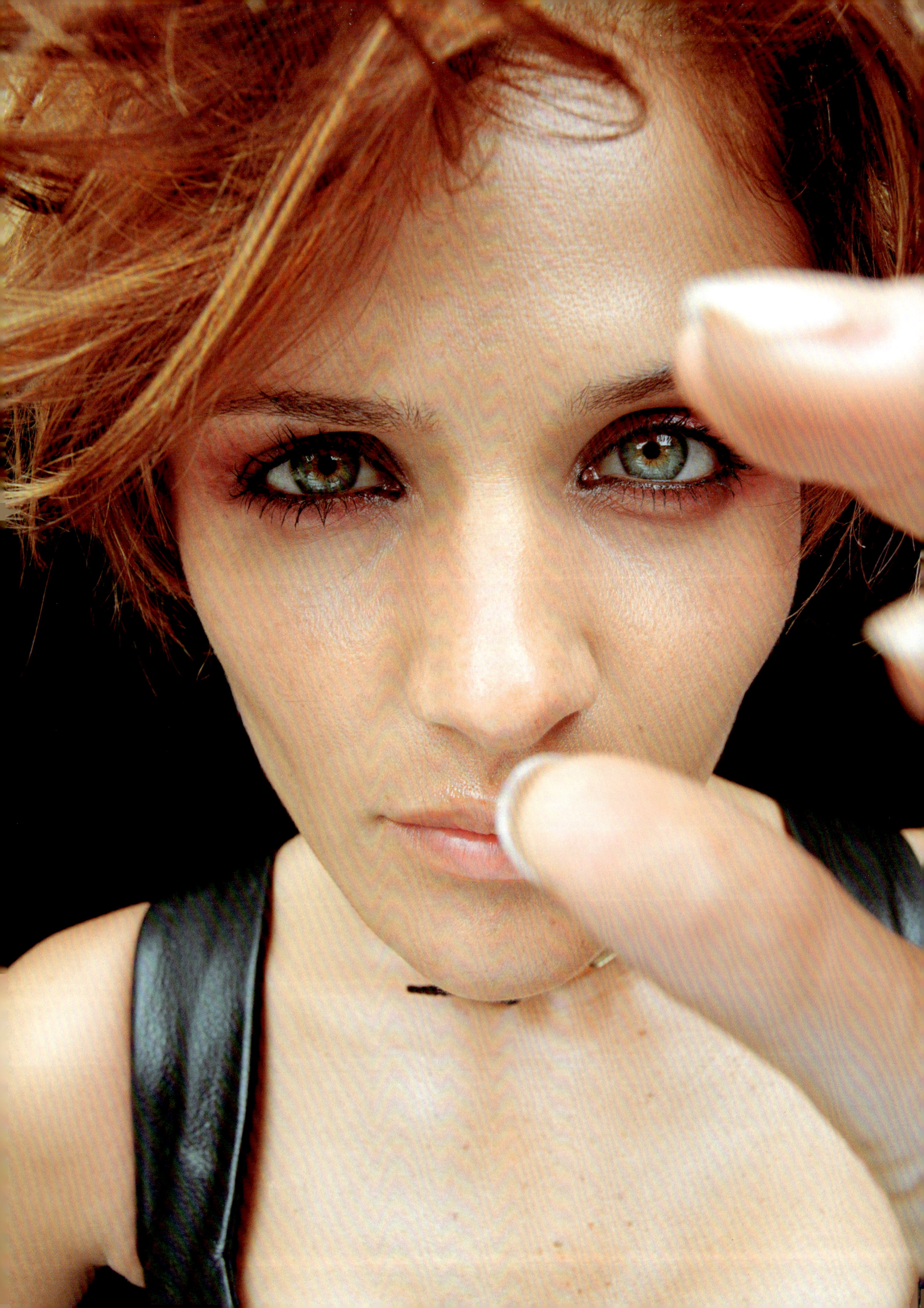

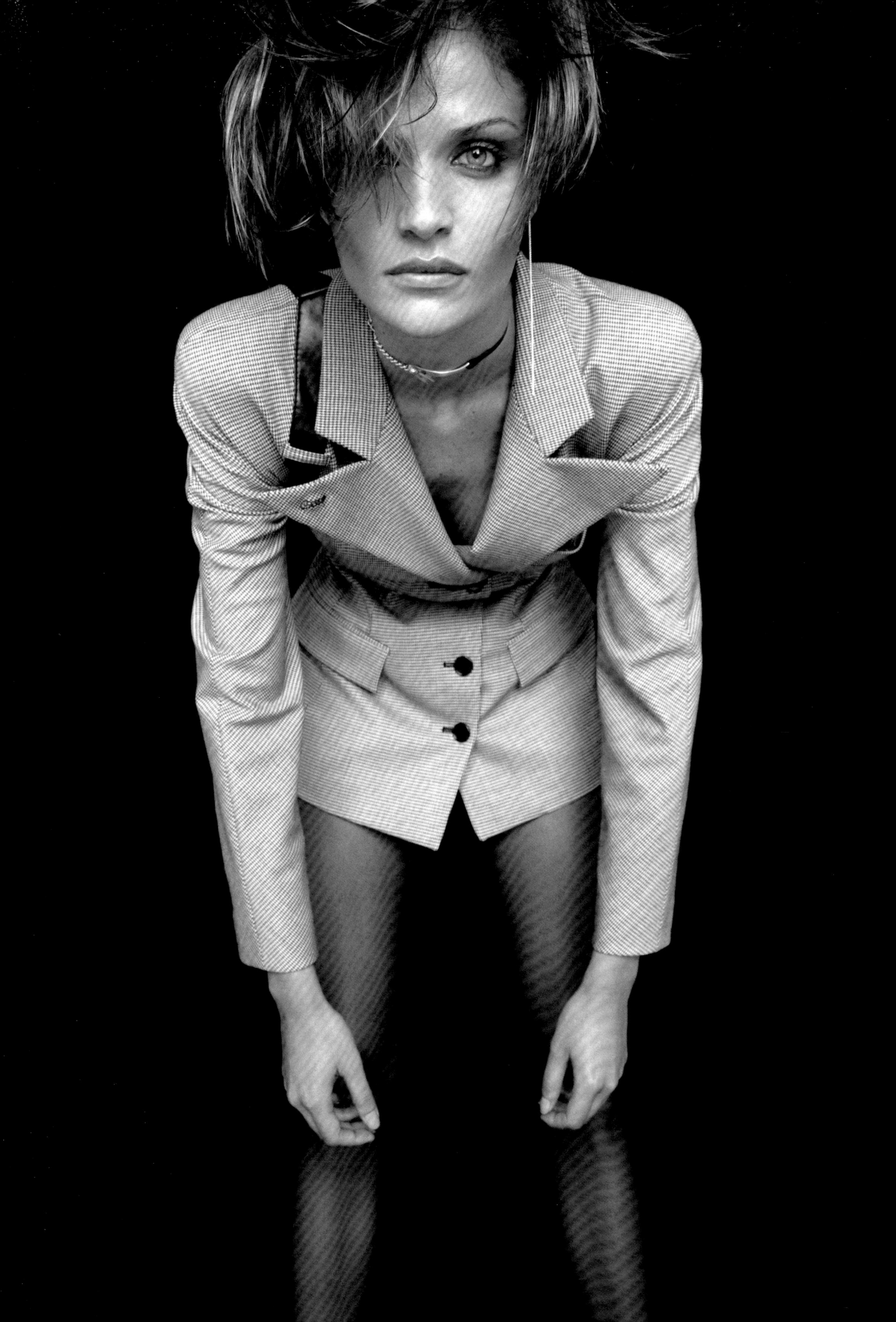

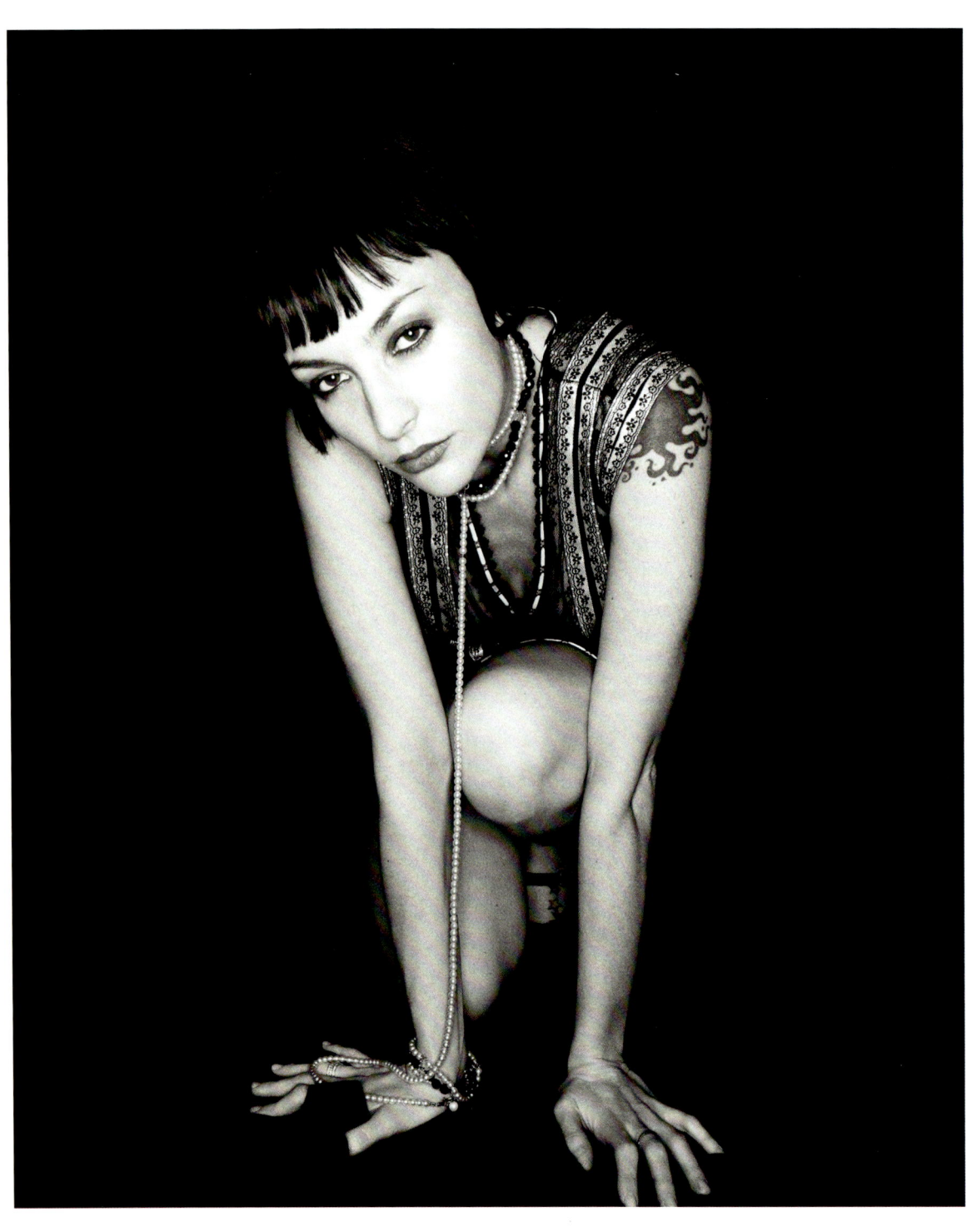

Mother and Pearl, Issue 85, 2002

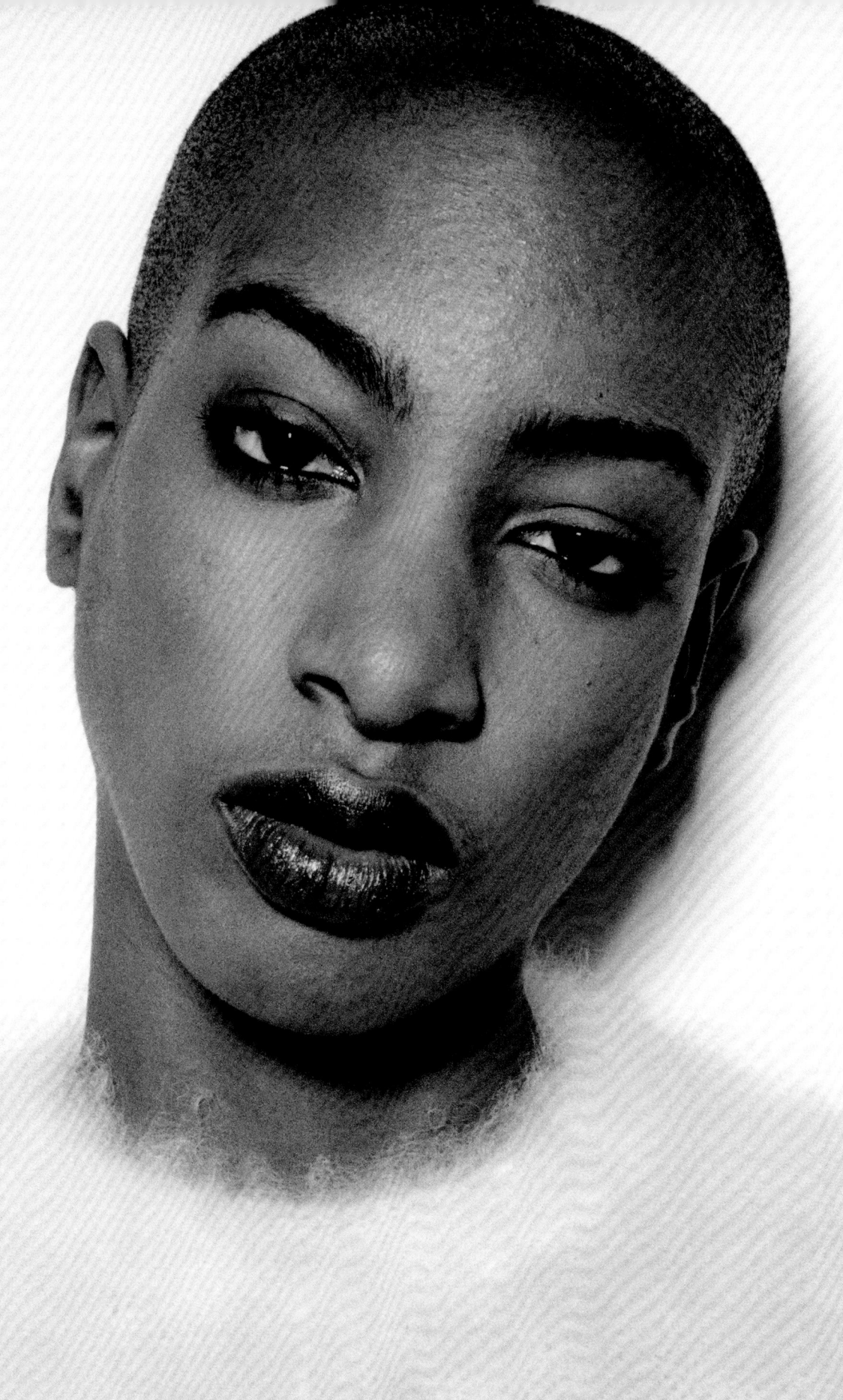

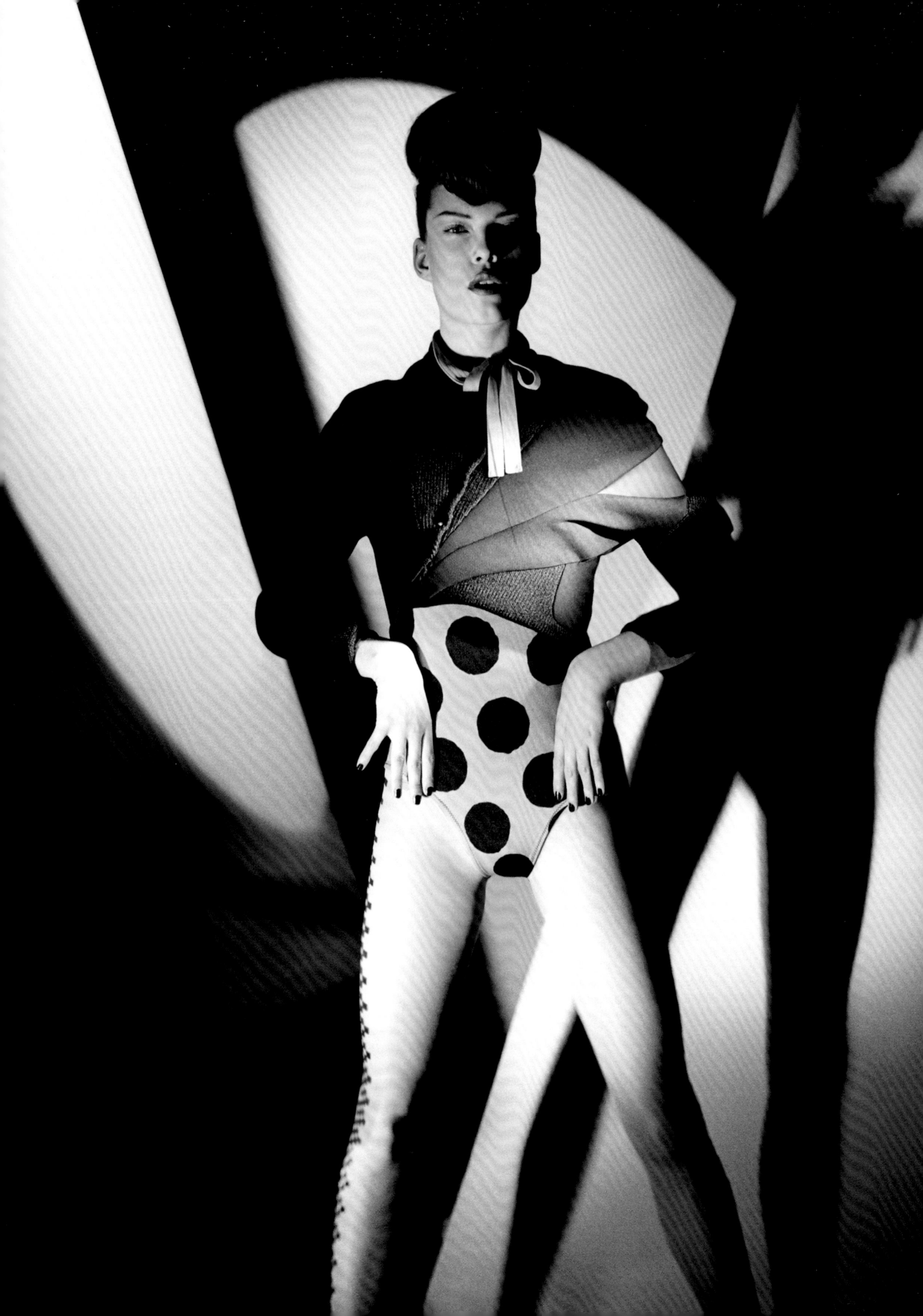

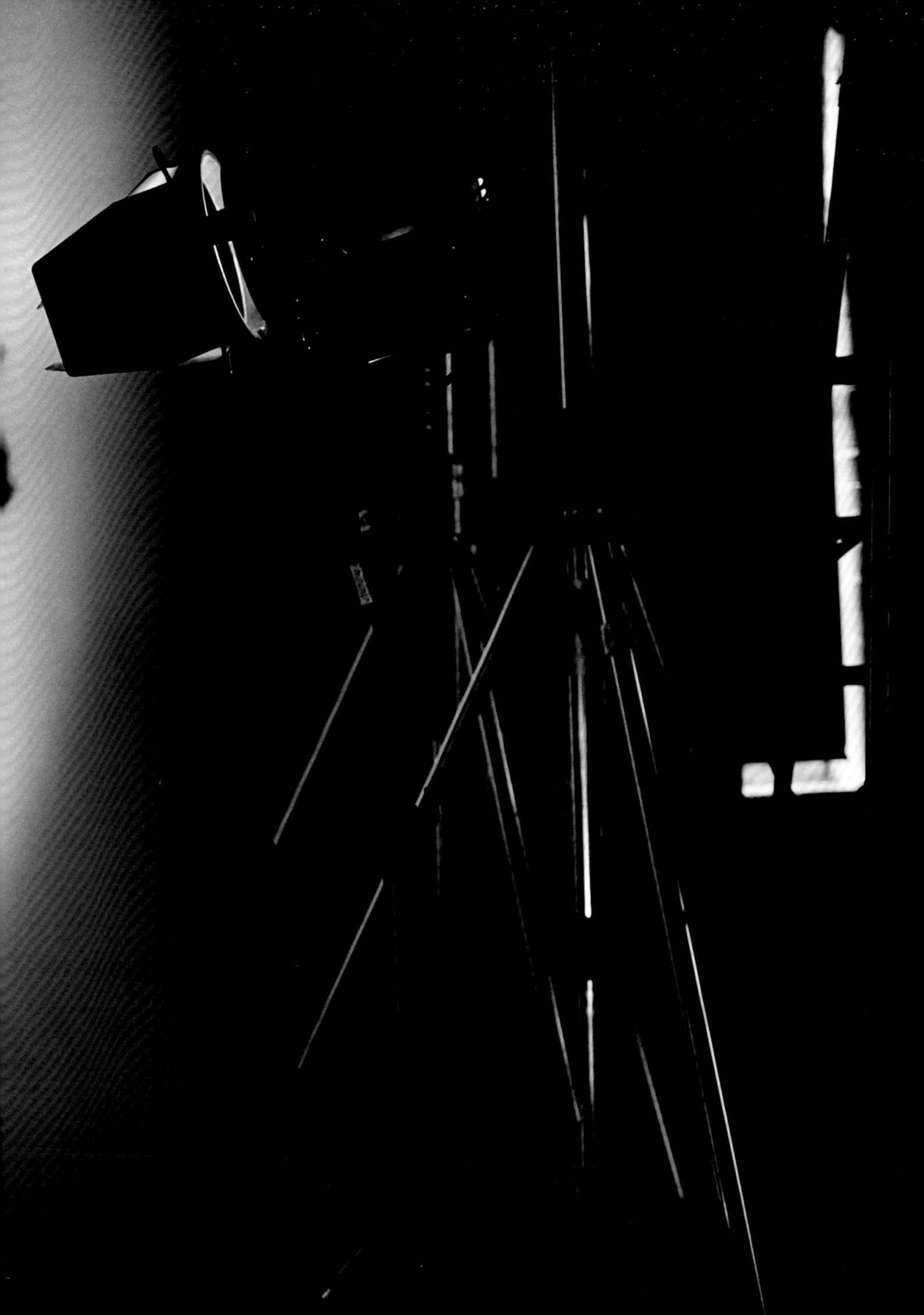

Previous Pages - Celluloid Closet, Vol. 2, Issue 3, 2003

Opposite Page - Two for the Price of One, Issue 12, 1995

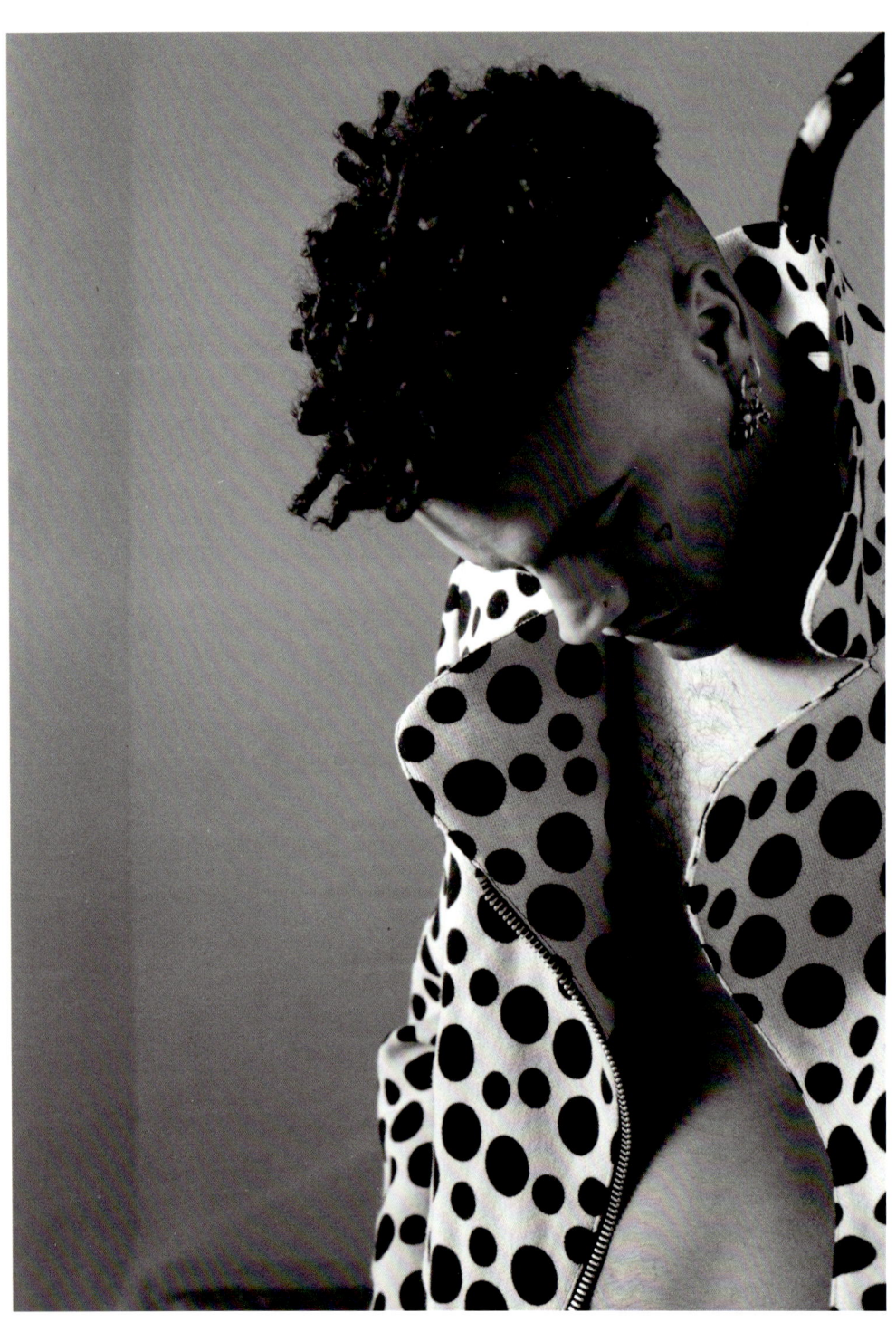

Contribute and Live, Issue 0, 1990

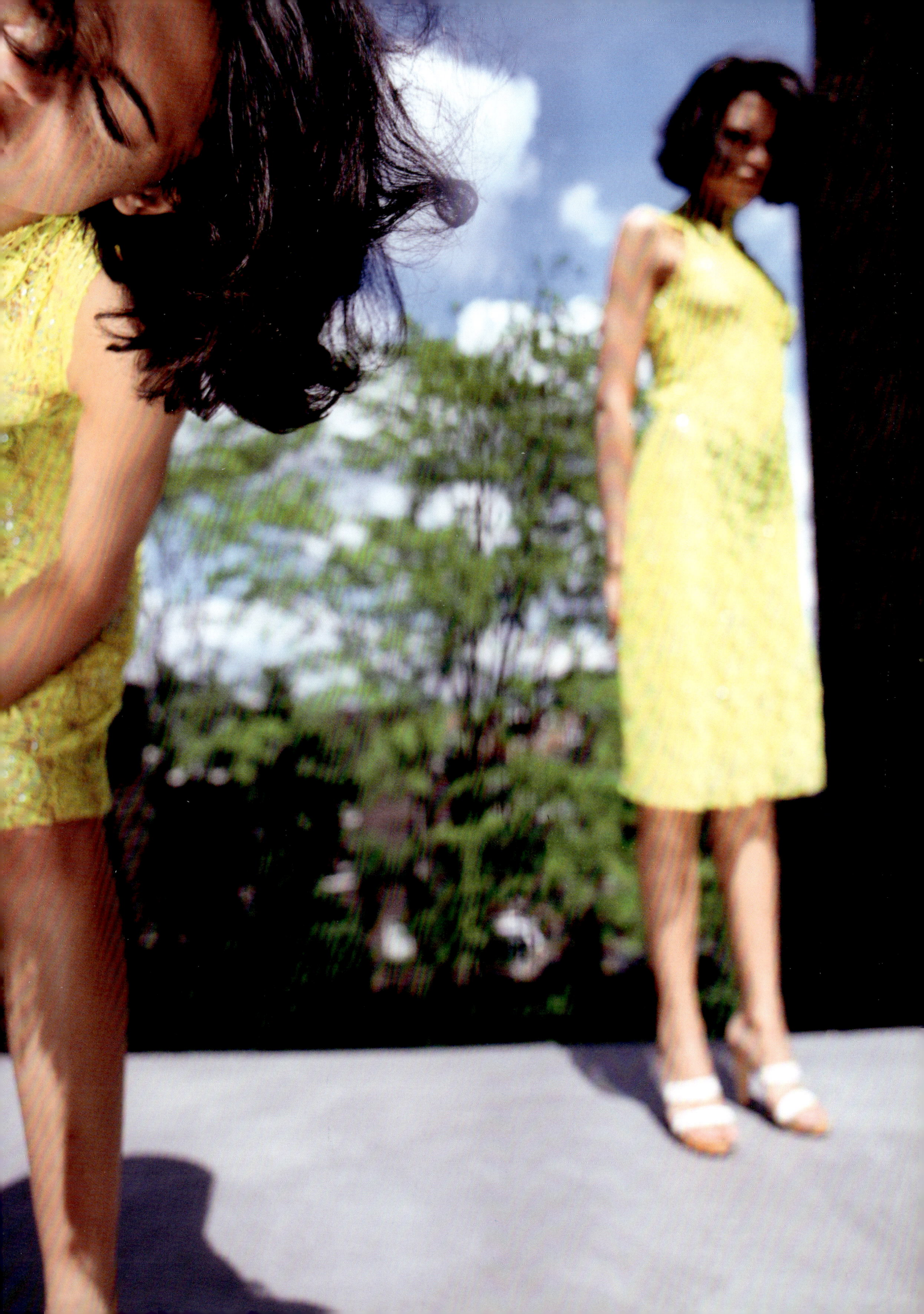

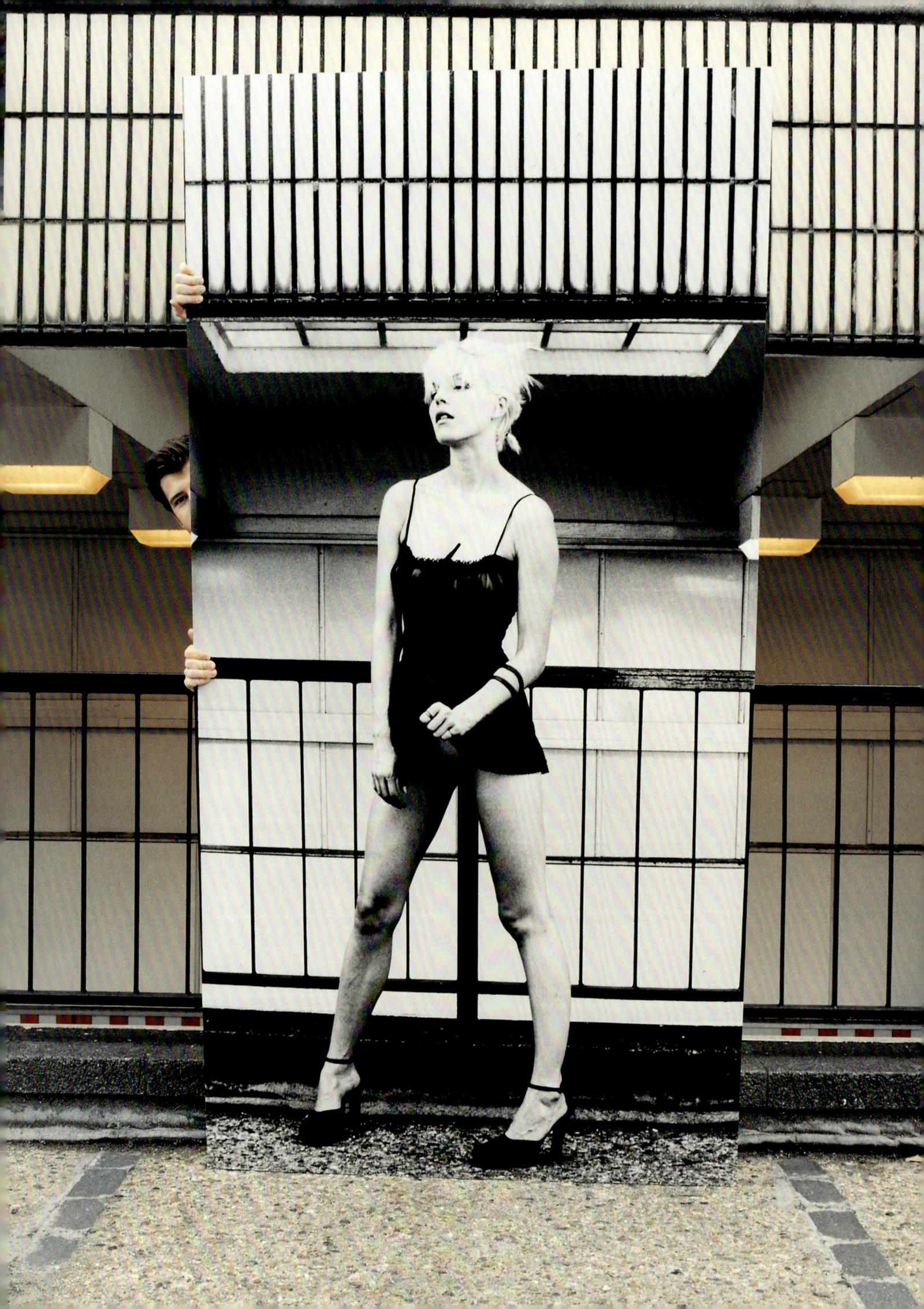

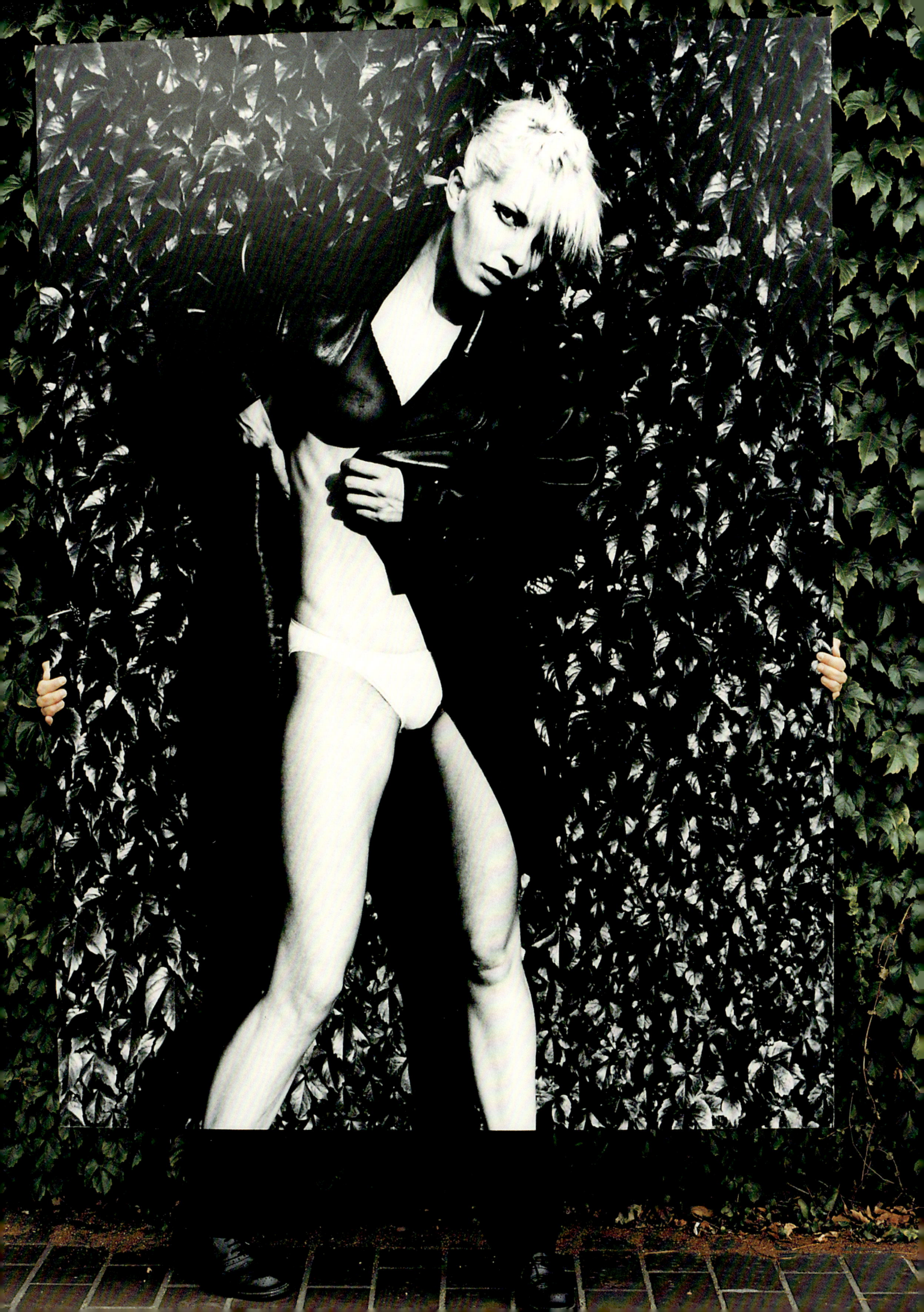

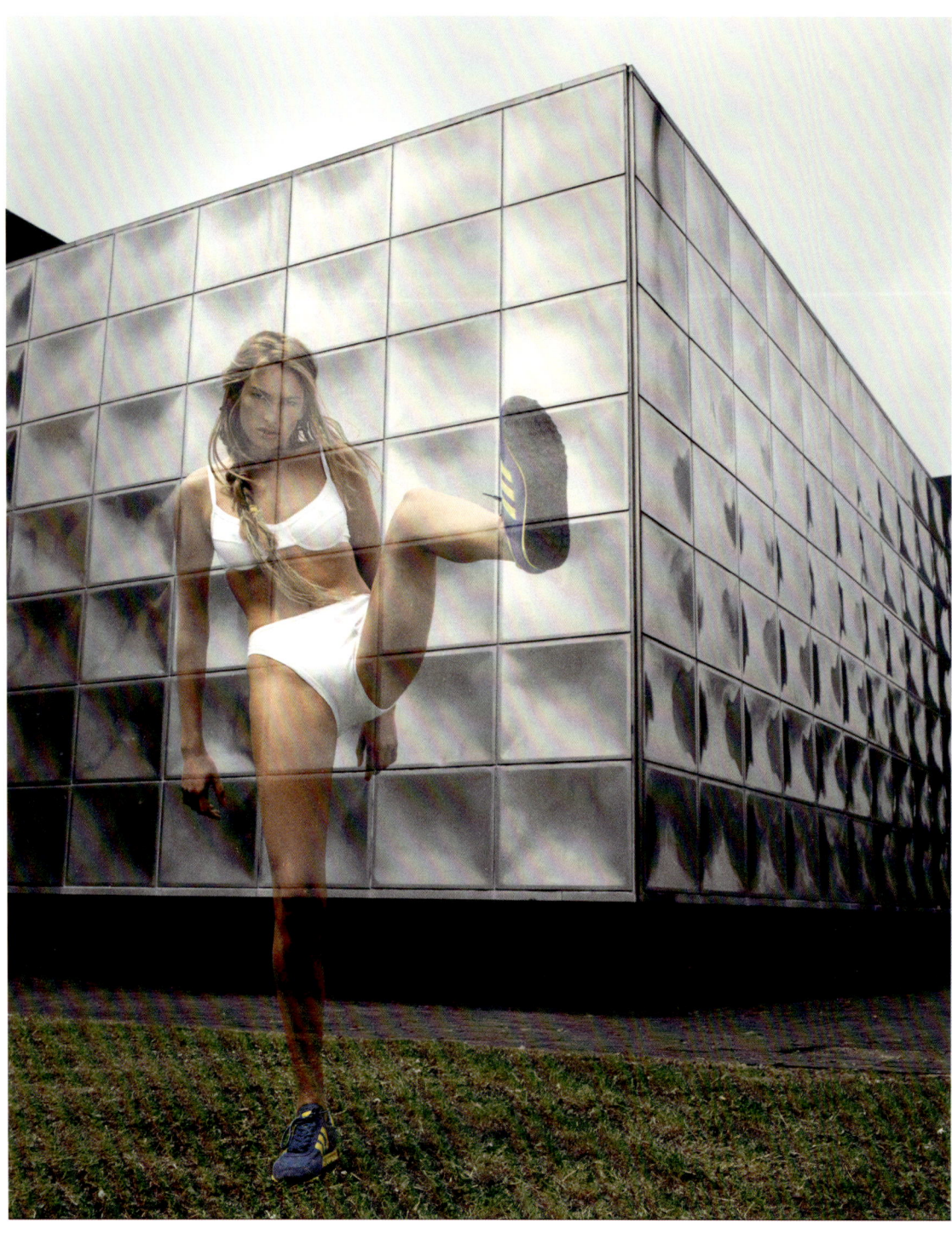

Ghosts, Issue 8, 1994

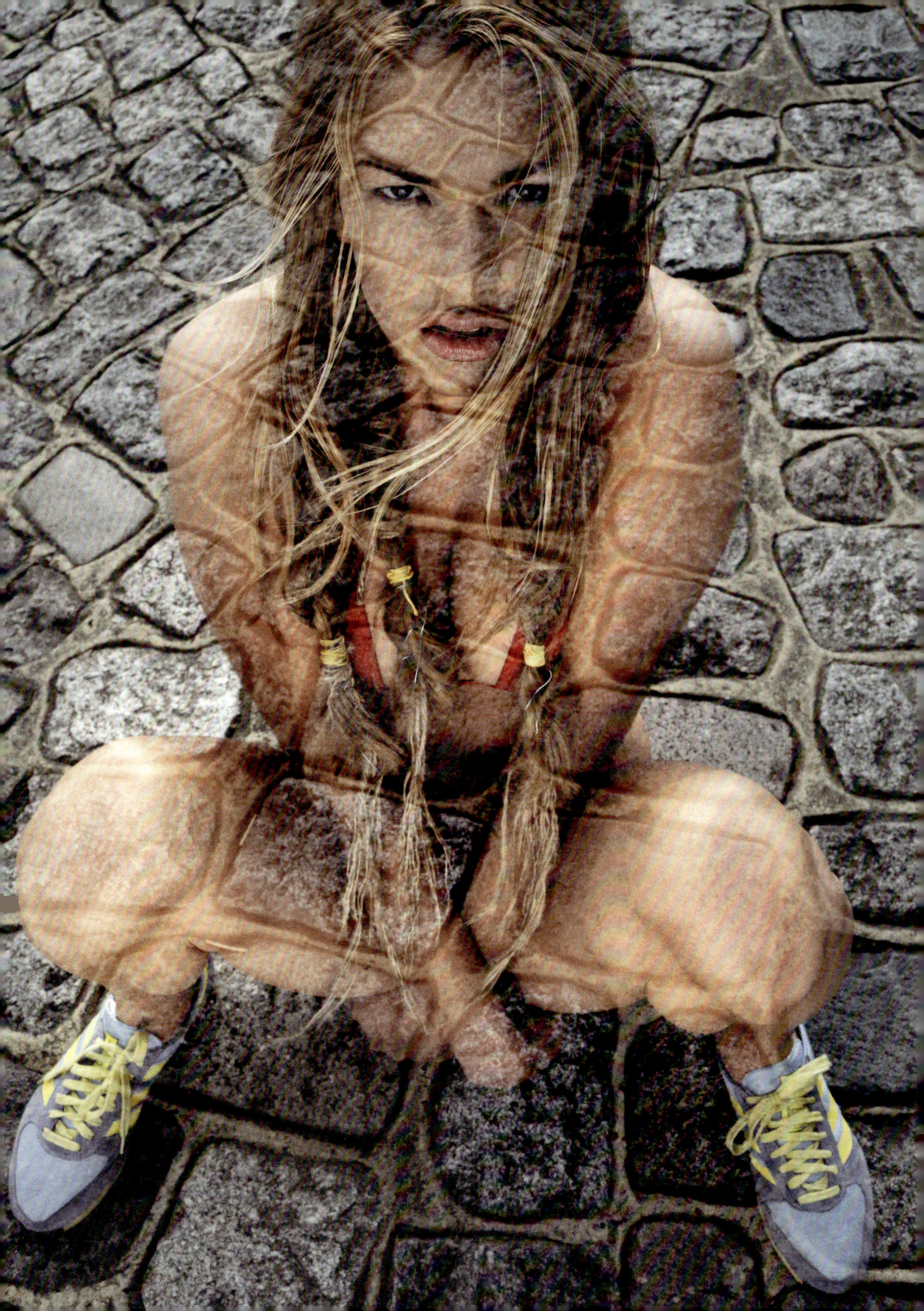

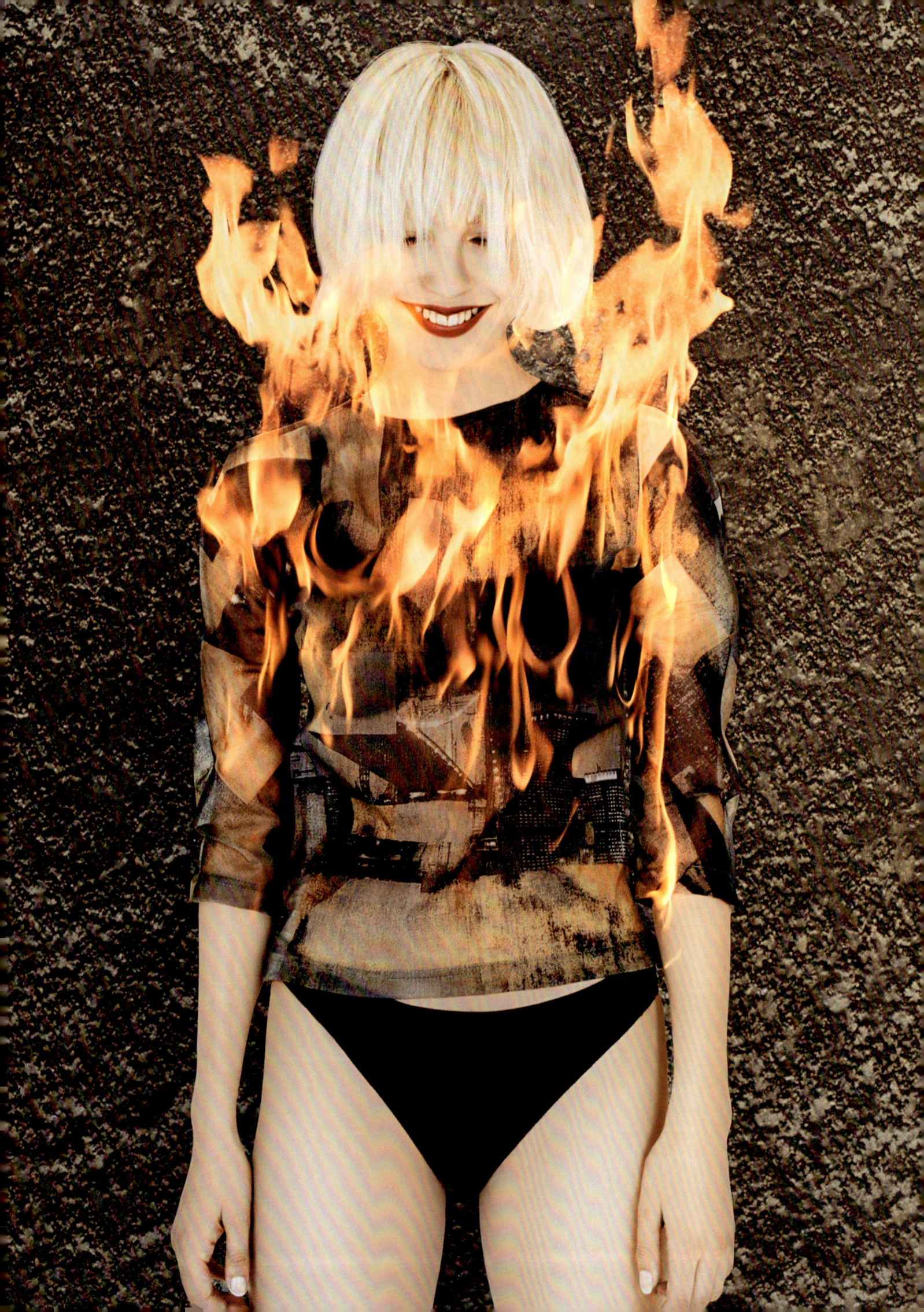

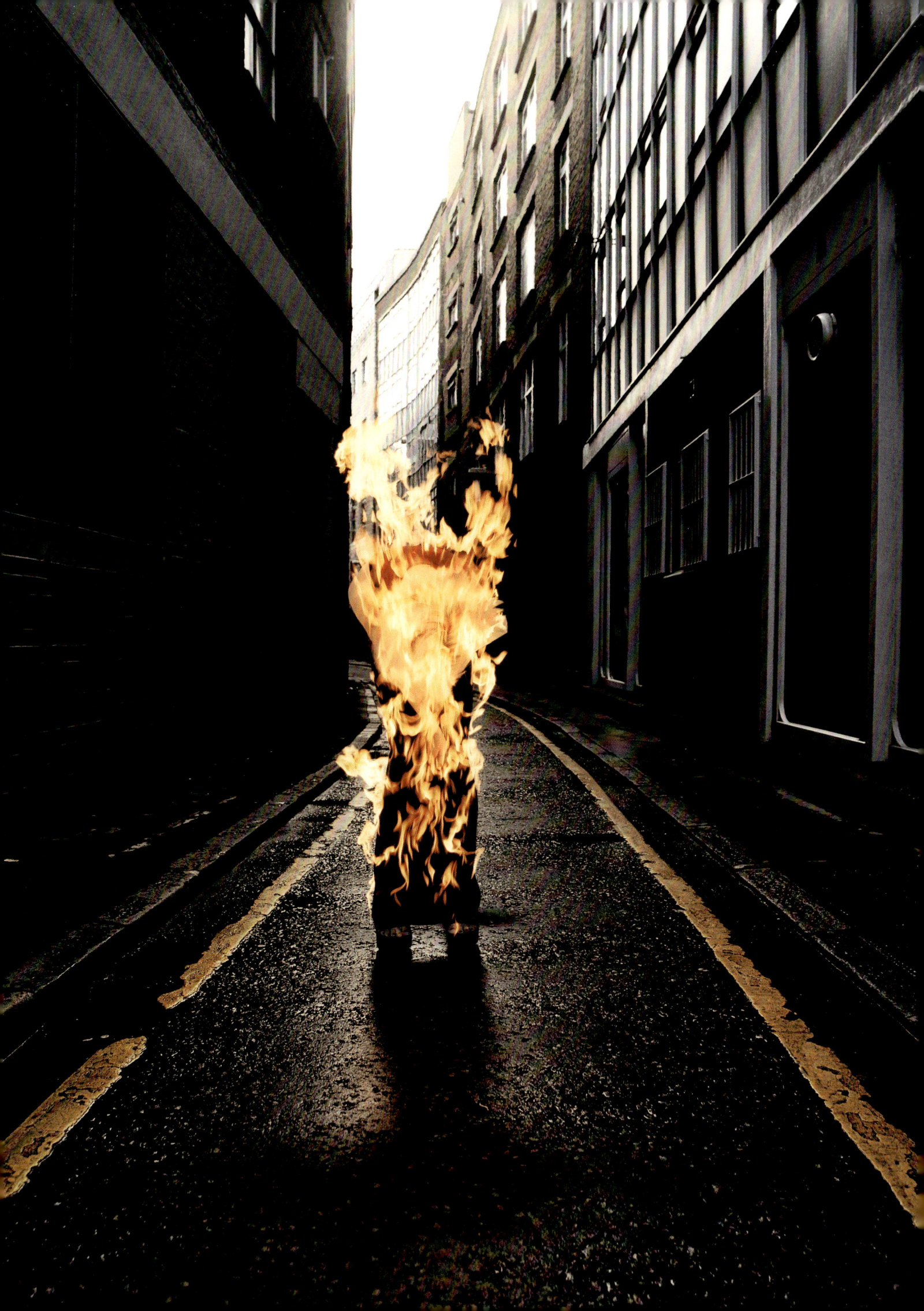

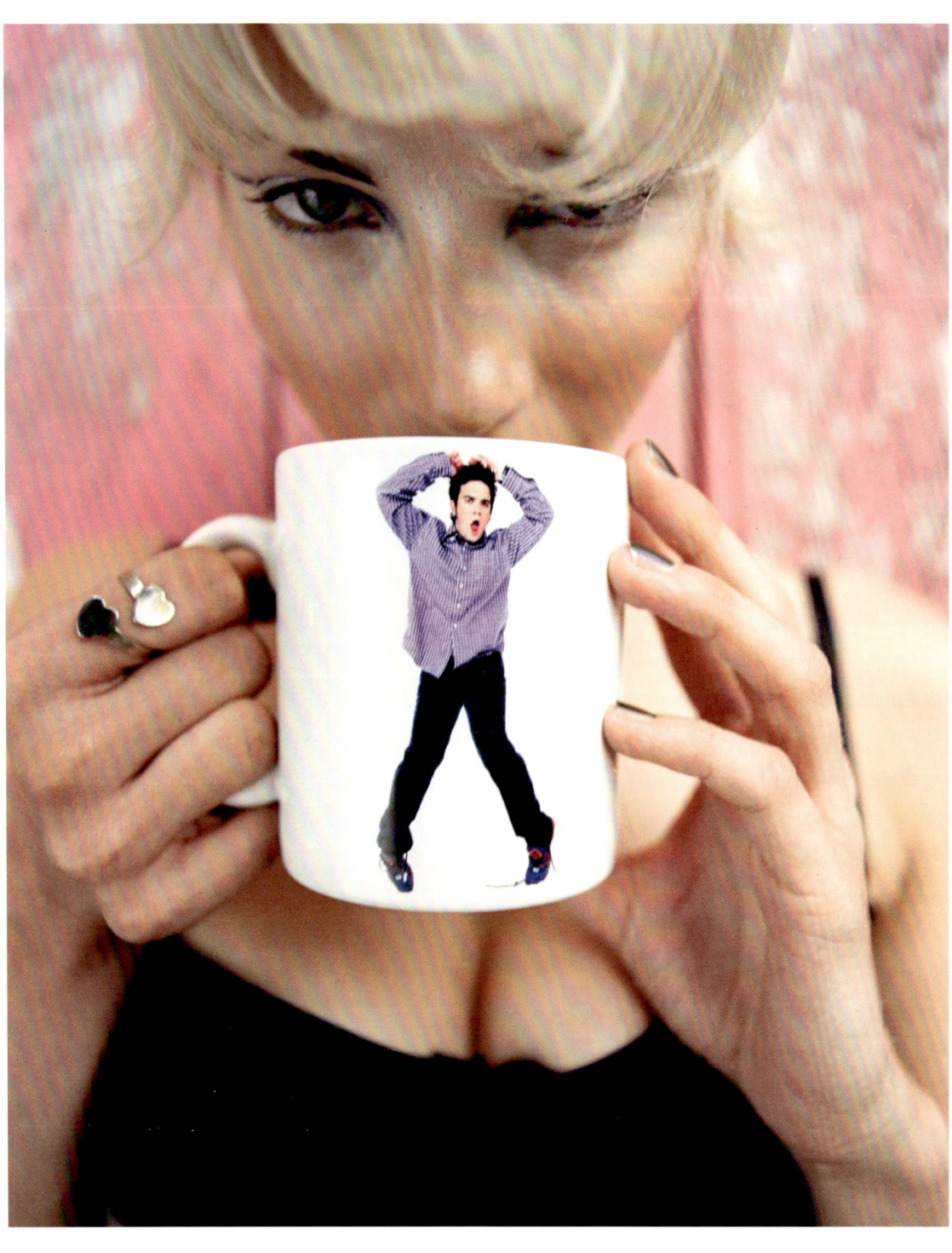

Obsessive Behaviour, Issue 25, 1996

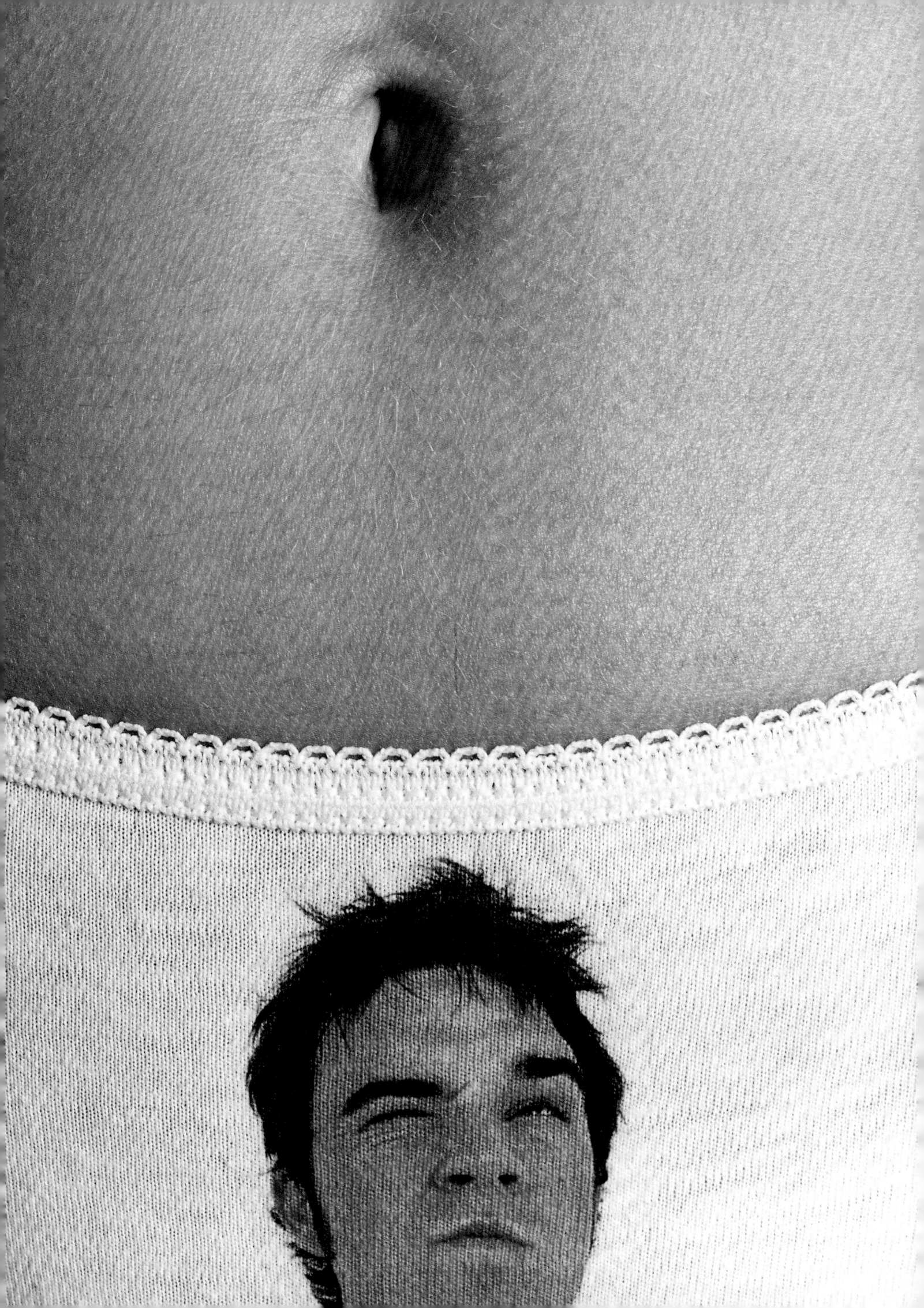

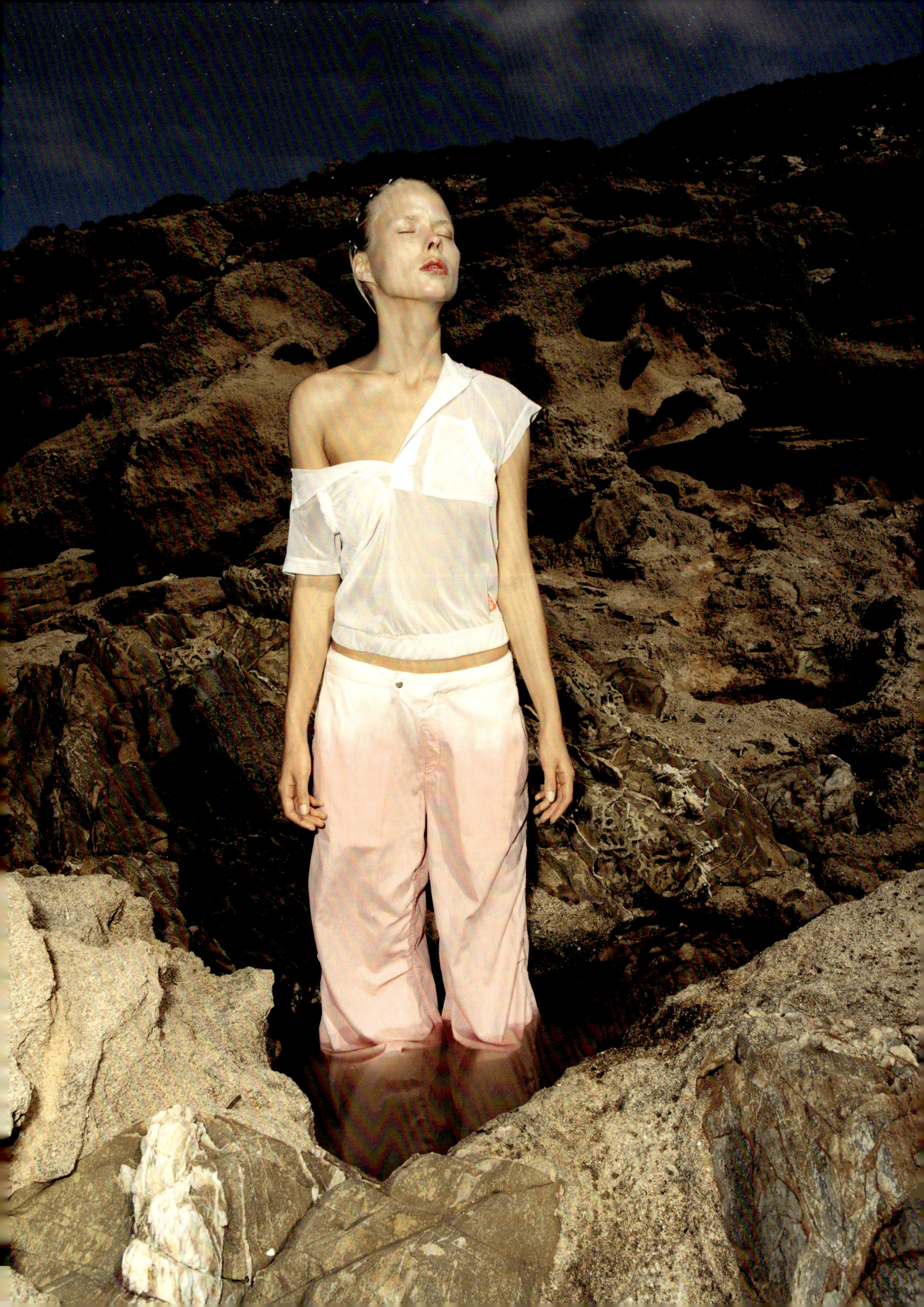

Next Pages - Bra Zilch, Issue 38, 1998

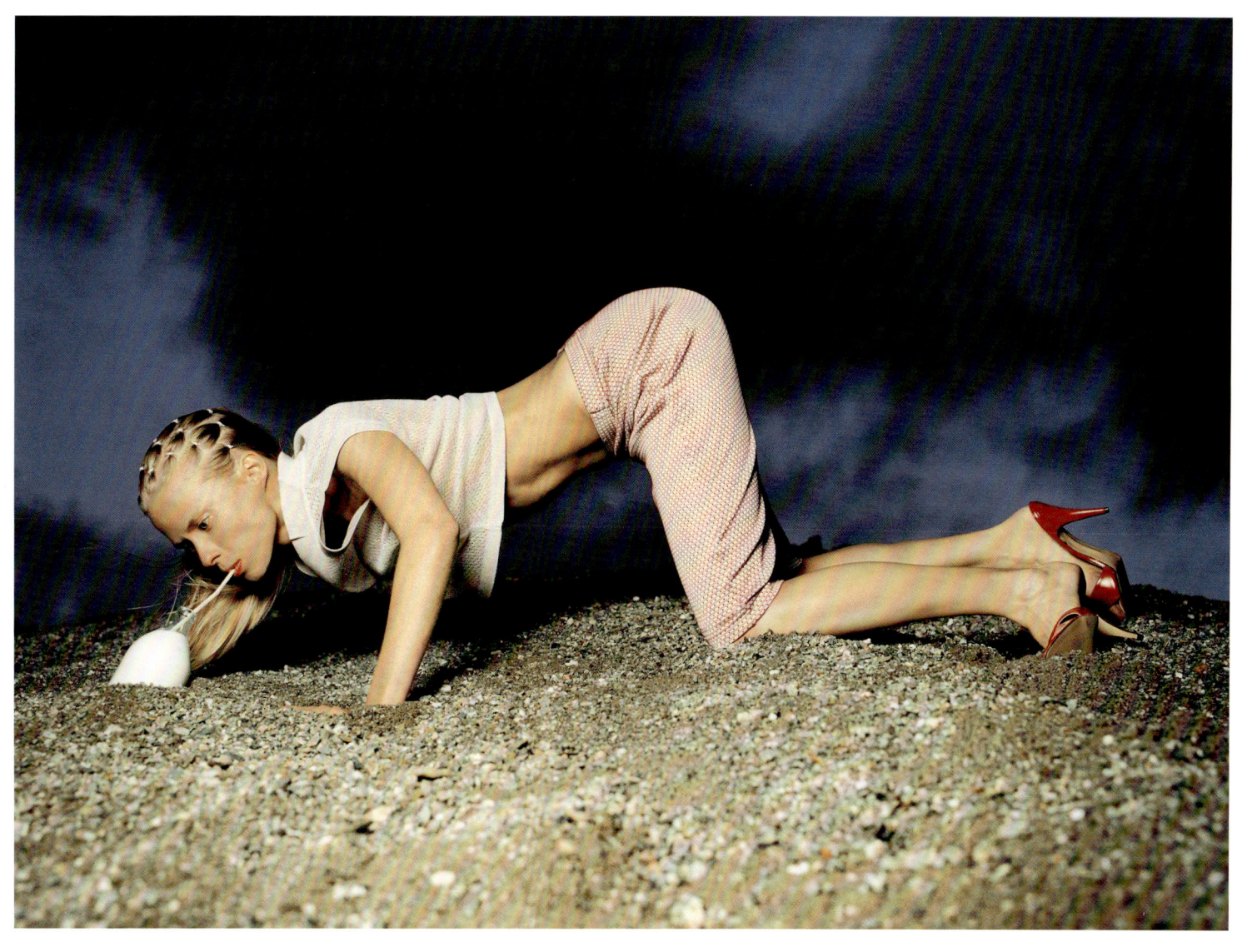

Stranded: Diesel Style Lab S/S, Issue 52, 1999

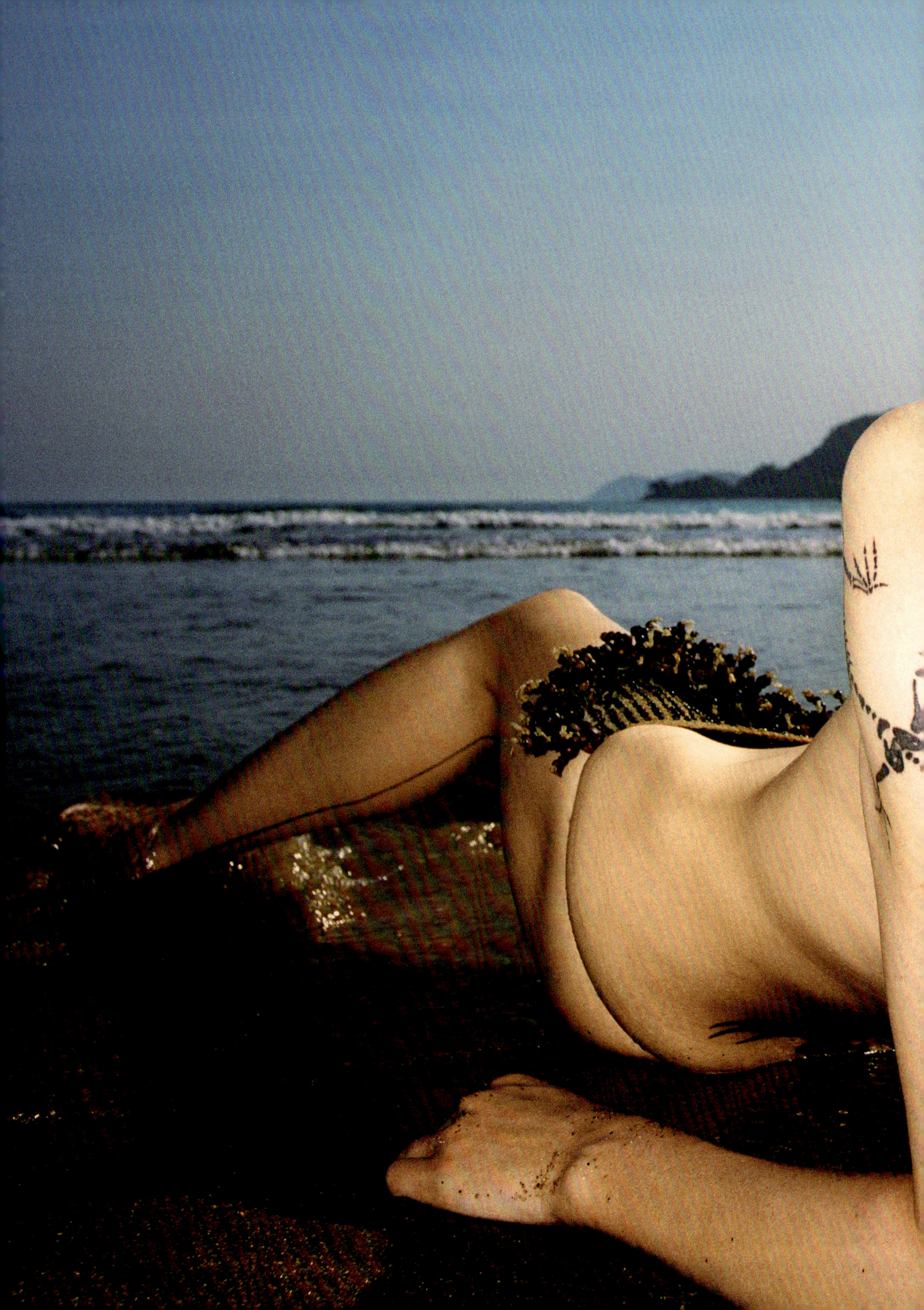

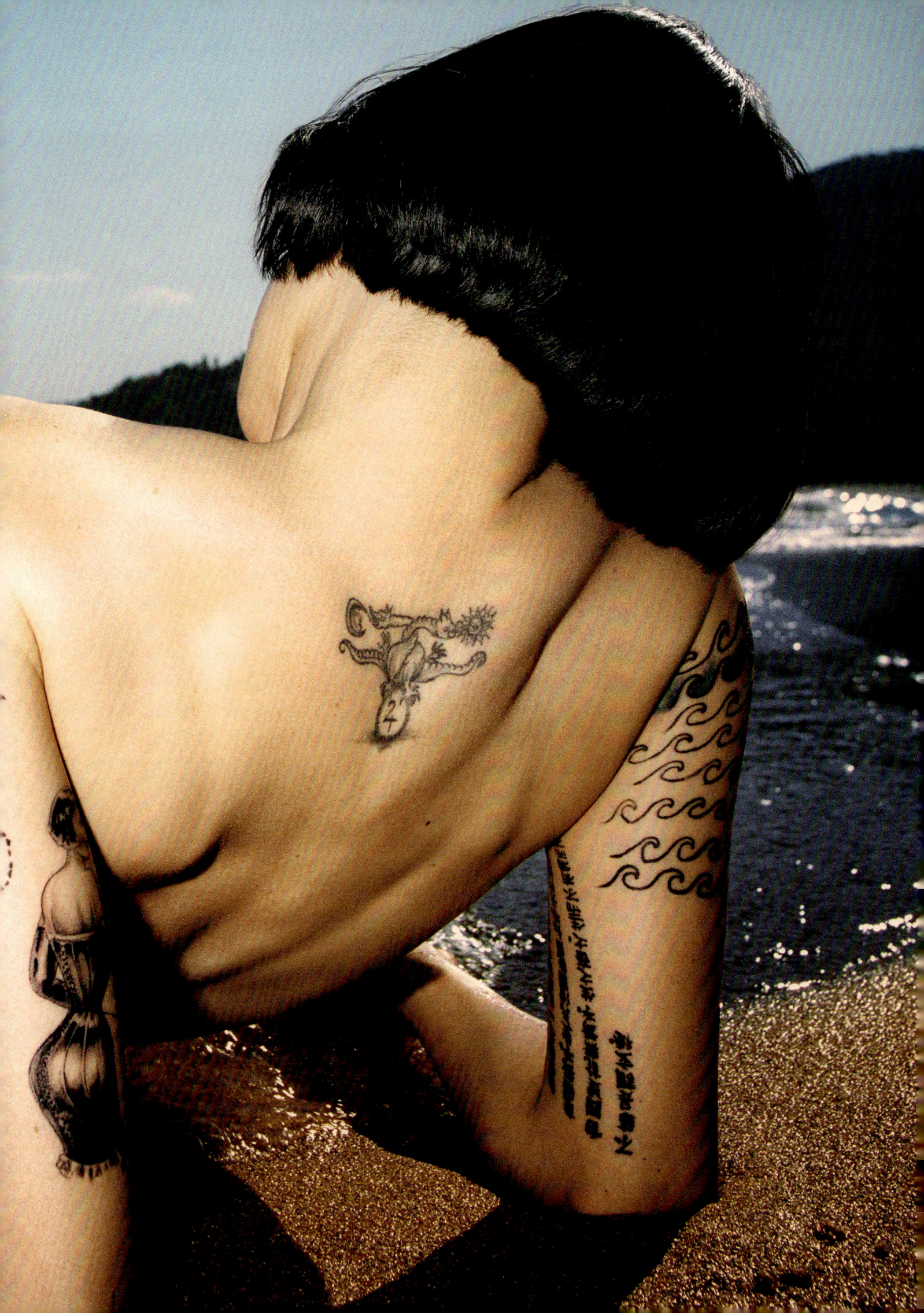

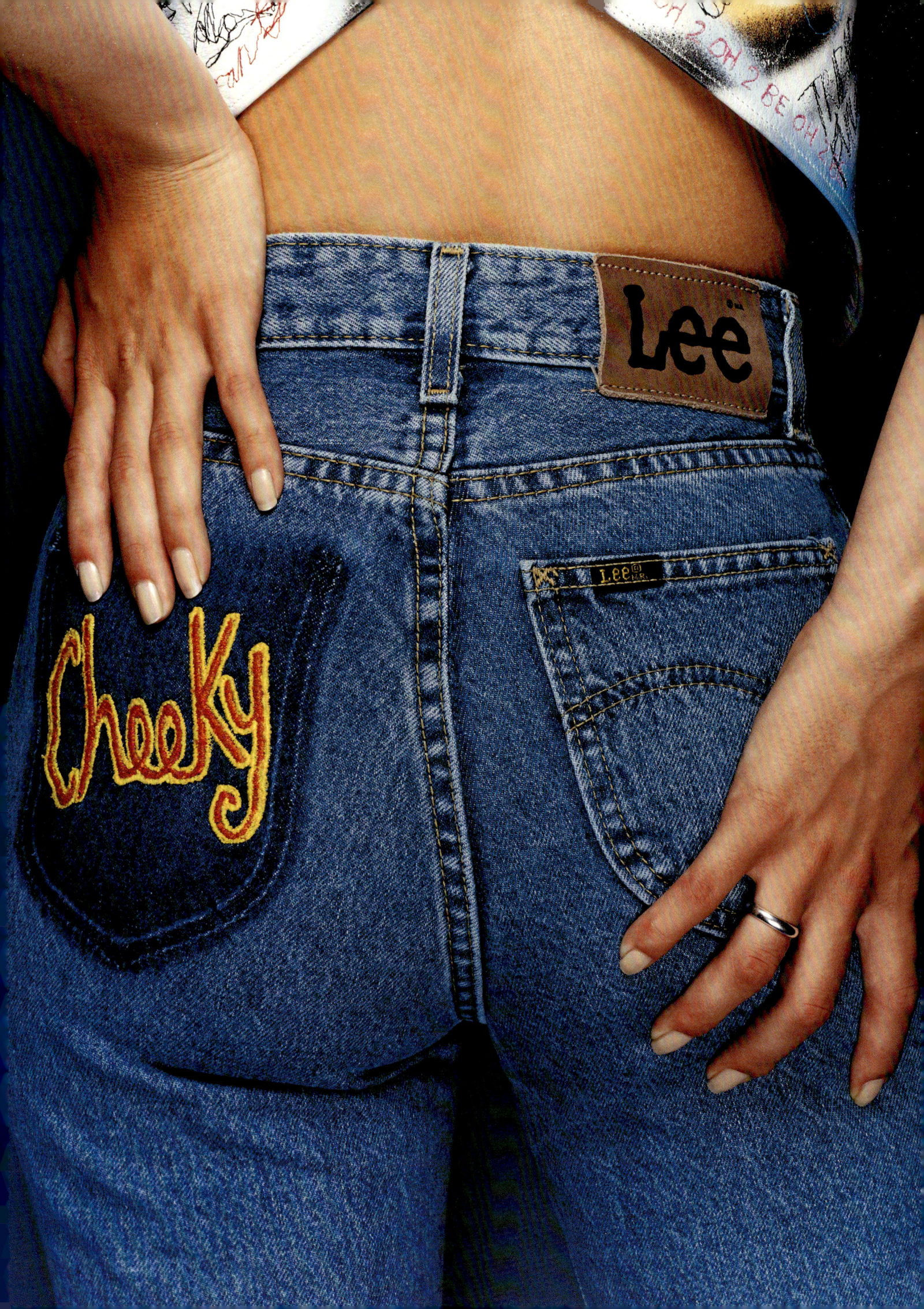

Opposite Page - Cheeky, Issue 56, 1999

Next Pages - Heavy Metal, Issue 10, 1995
Unzipped, Issue 18, 1996

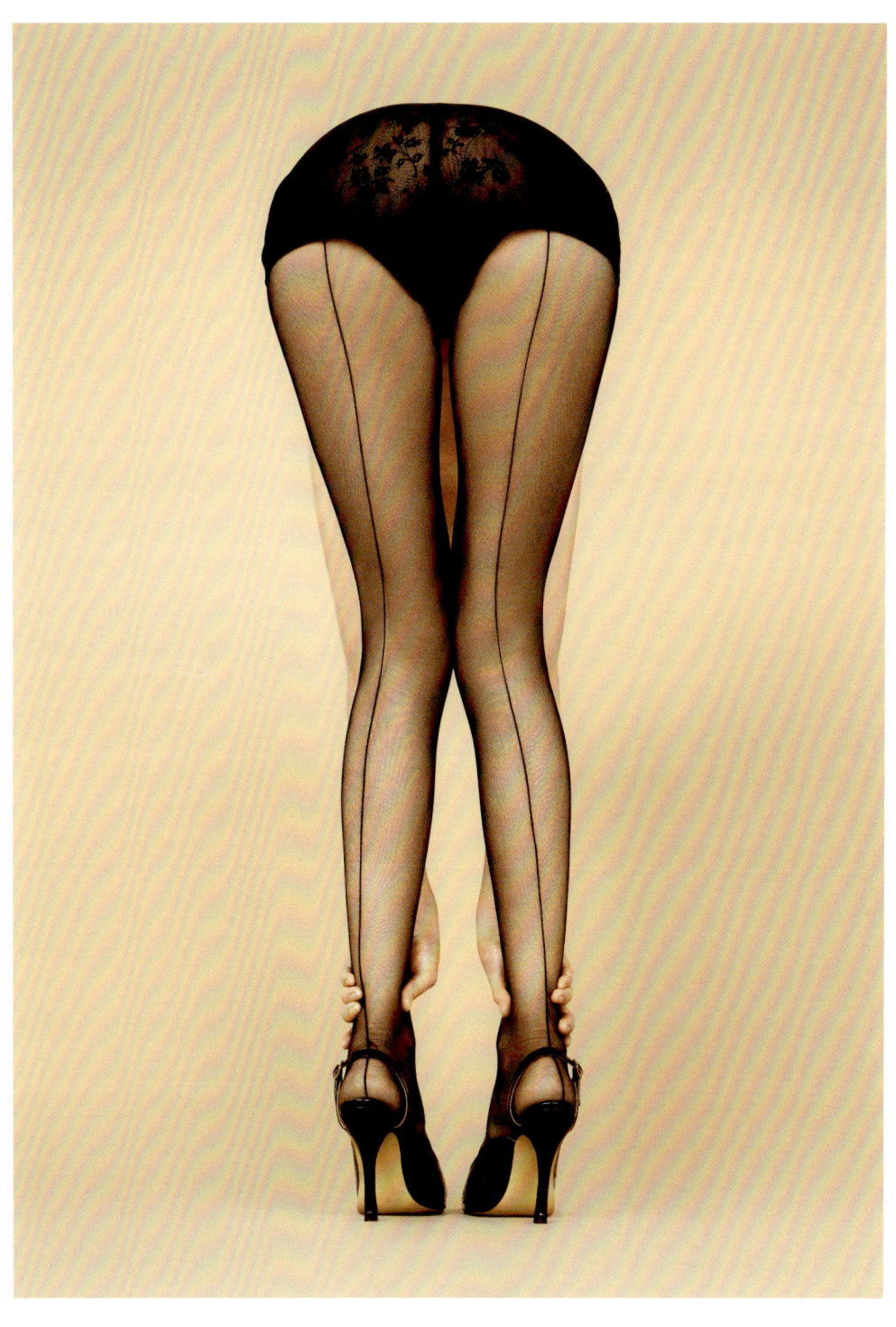

Touch Your Toes, Issue 20, 1996

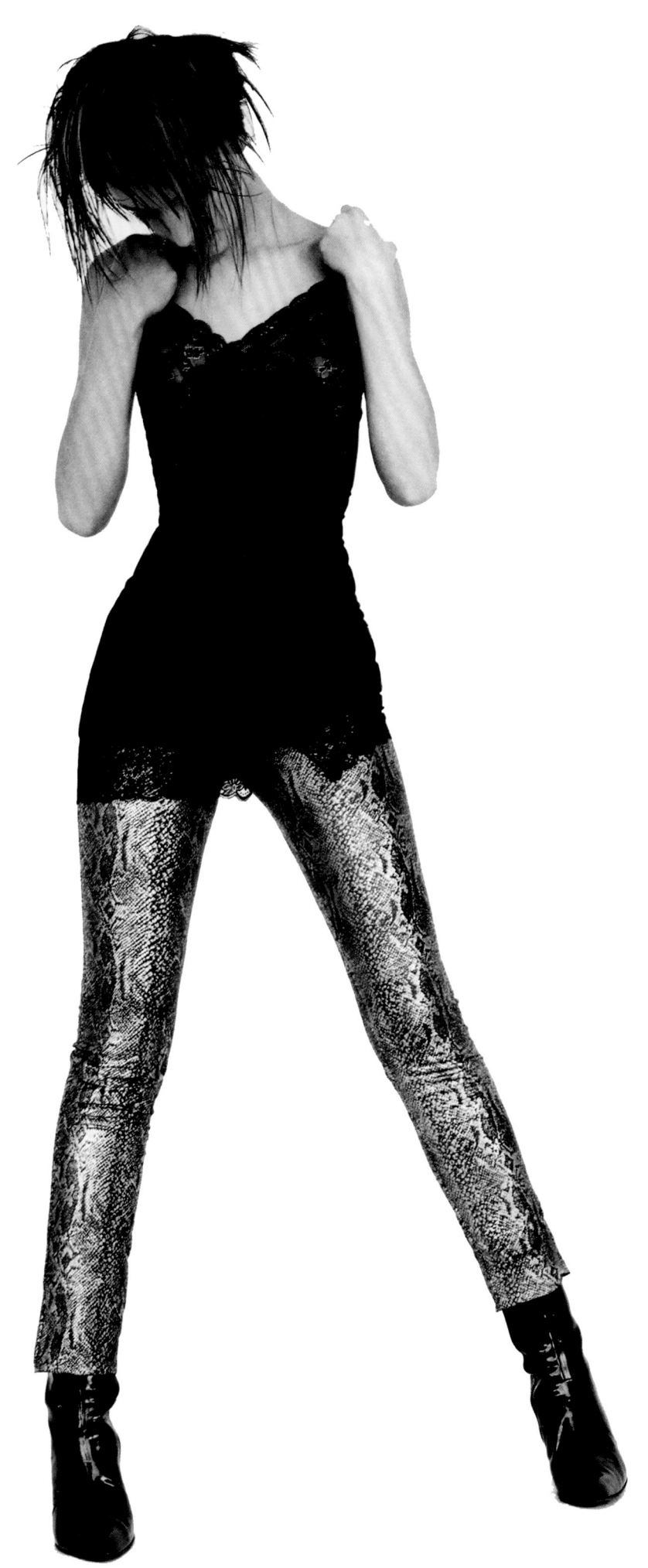

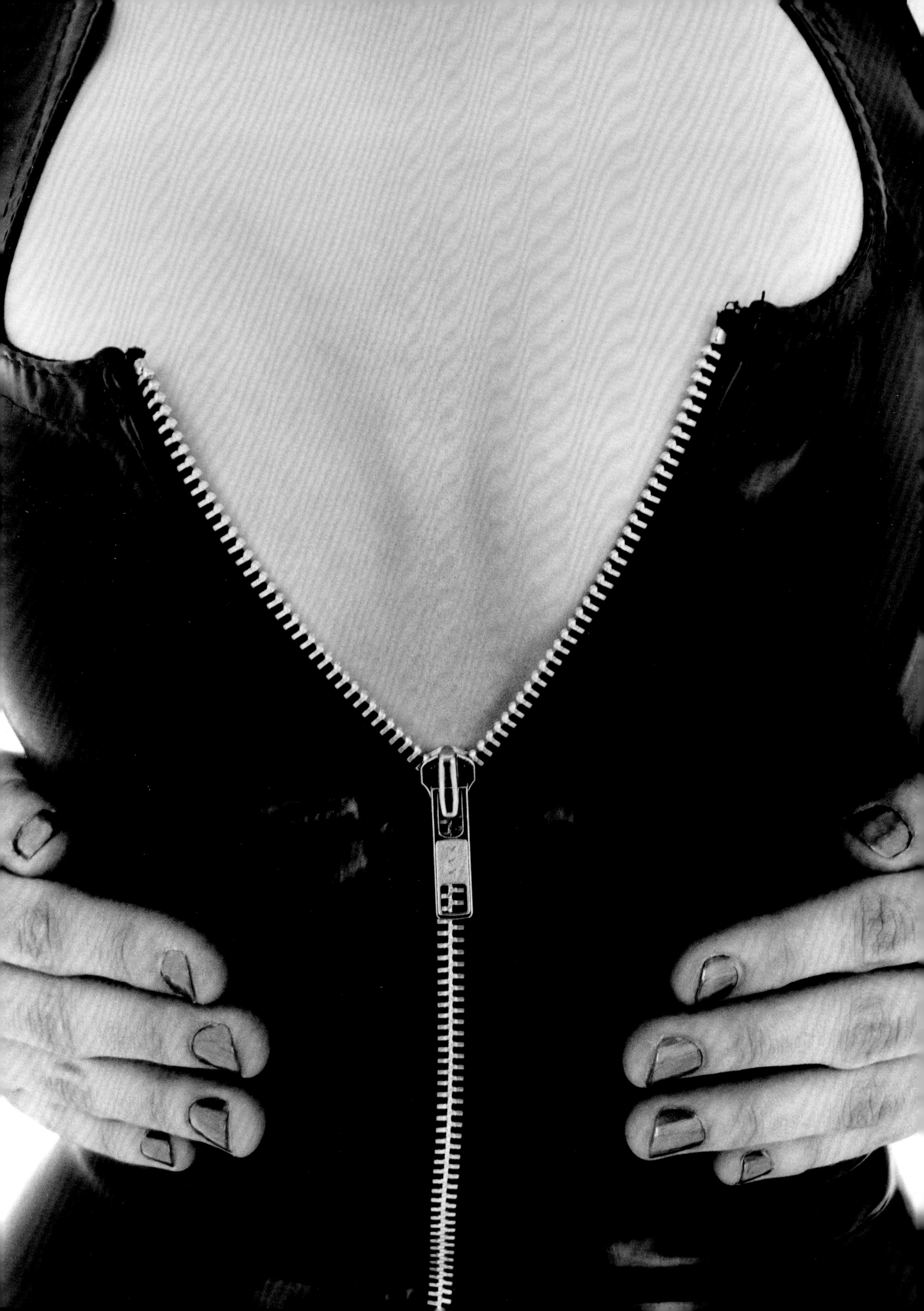

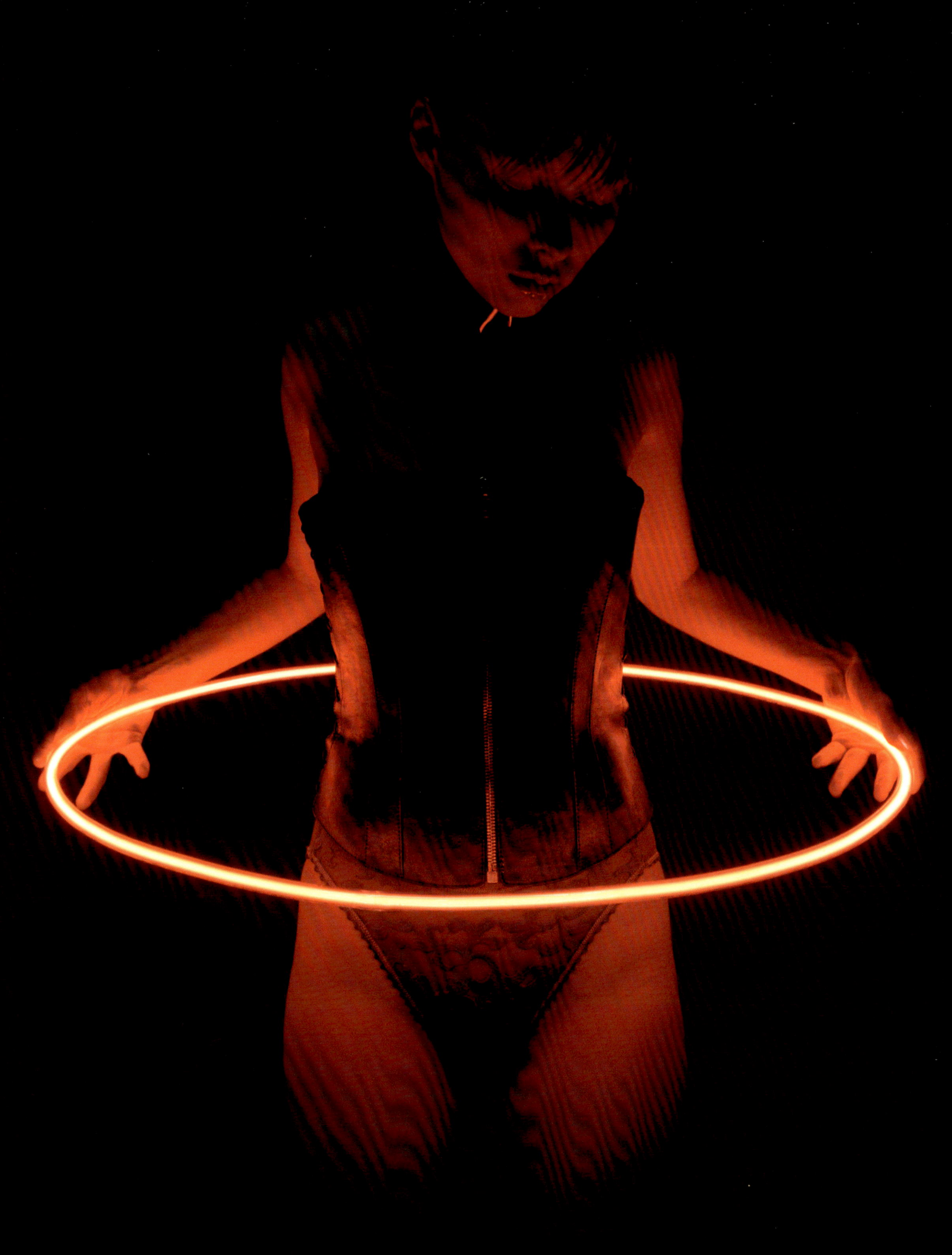

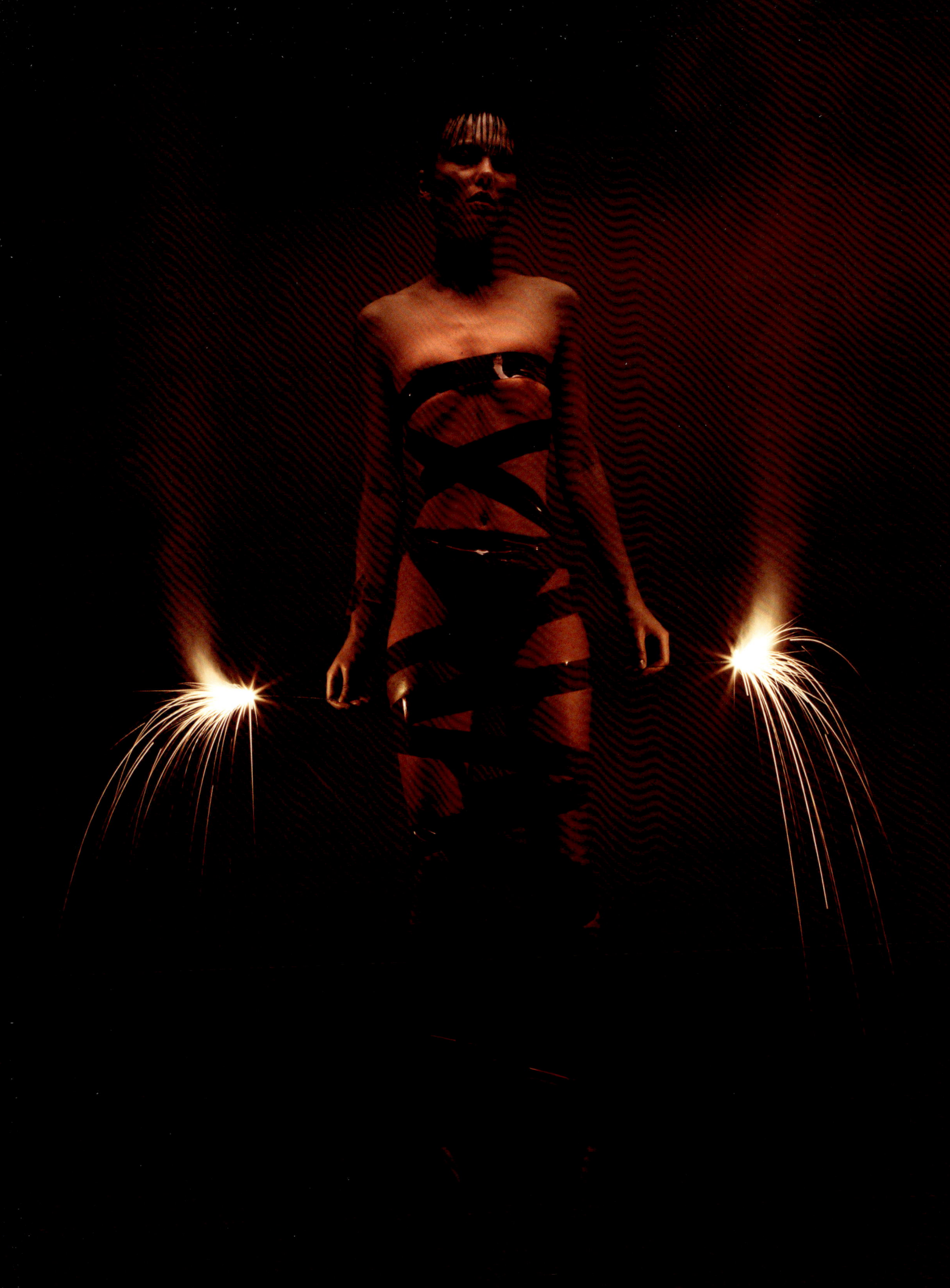

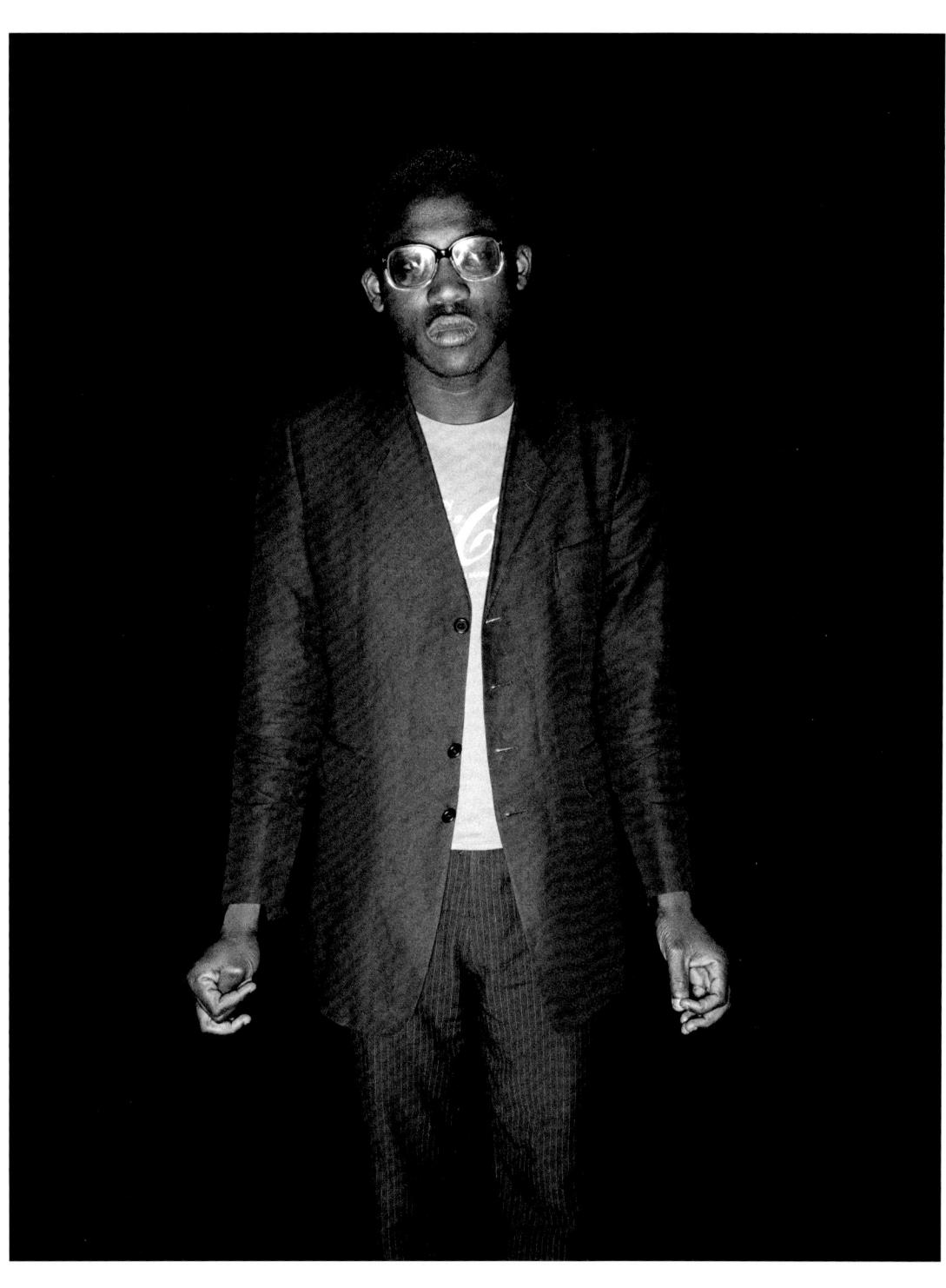

Death Masks, Issue 8, 1994

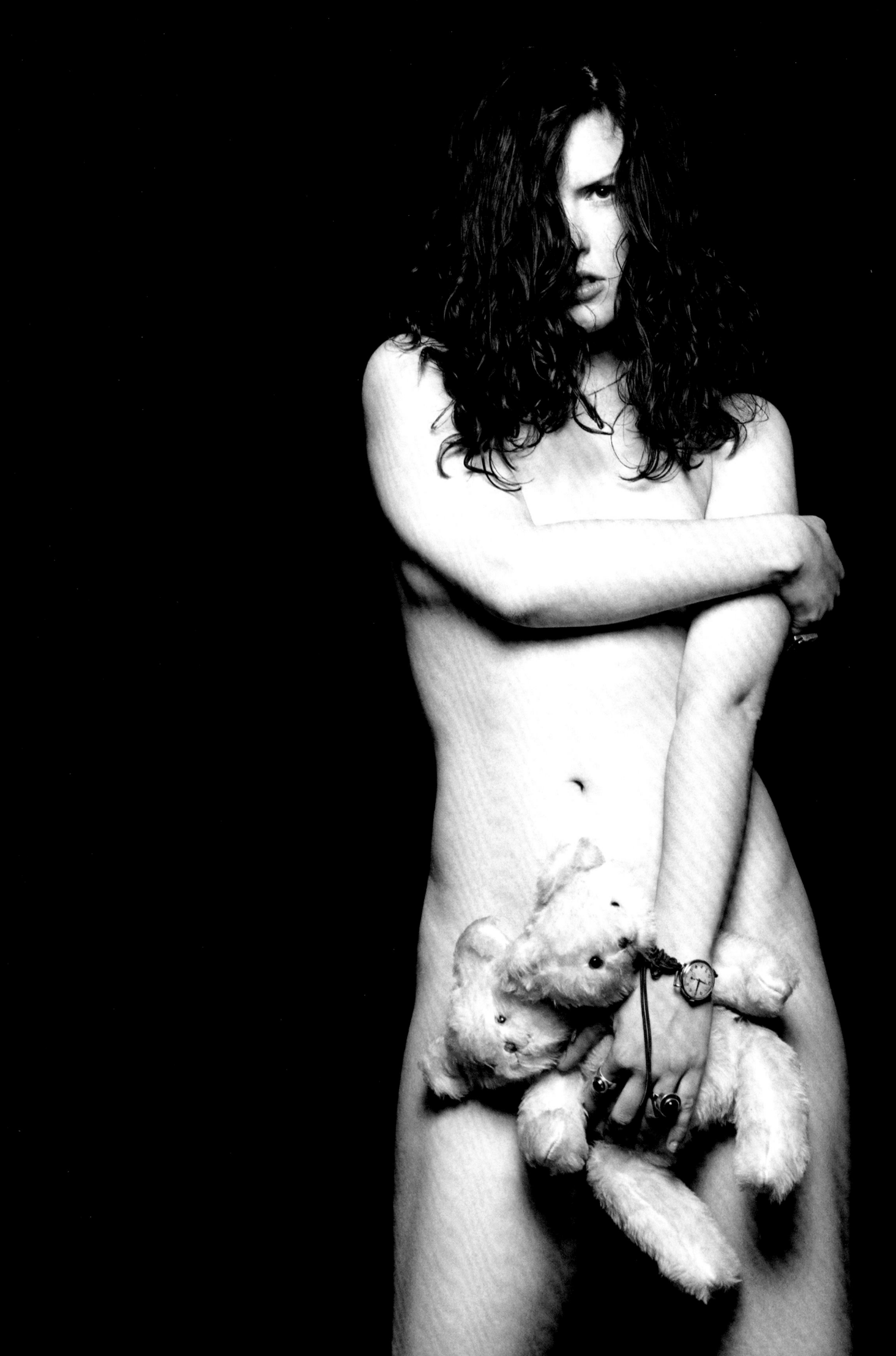

BE YOURSELF/BE SOMEONE ELSE/MAKE A MESS/MAKE IT PERFECT/IT'S ALL SURFACE ATTRACTION...

ABSOLUTELY FLAWLESS?

Rankin always seems to be at his most playful yet cutting when he's poking a hole in reality. We all have expectations of what beauty is, what hair style is right, what make-up looks best - but with Rankin all preconceptions need to be left at the door.

The title, *Absolutely Flawless*? comes from the 2002 cover for issue 85. From a distance, the set of cover stars are your expected beautiful faces: all smooth skin and rosie pink lips. But when up close to the magazine the crosses on the images appear. In this space all retouching is removed, and suddenly freckles, spots and whispy lip hair is revealed. Rankin tears away the digital effects to invite you behind the glamour of a glossy magazine.

Skin texture, so often removed in our Photoshop and social media filter world, is highlighted through extreme close-up in *Sense*. Where the realness of pores and moisture drops ignite all the viewer's senses, and turn model Lisa Ratliffe into a breathing, sweating, touchable human being.

In *Silver Ladies* and *No I.D. Necessary* Rankin questions our understanding of age and glamour. In 1996 Charlotte Connoley, at only 15, was chosen to represent the face of a decade obsessed with youth. Also in 1996, older women spearheaded a *Dazed* fashion editorial - Rankin unquestioningly giving them space alongside supermodels in a youth culture magazine.

But it isn't all about reality in Rankin's beauty work. The fakery of both physical and practical effects on imagery is something he revels in. From icicles to melting models, Rankin creates images of extremes, both aesthetically pleasing yet also questioning how far models and bodies can be pushed for glamour.

Finally though, beauty is clearly fun for Rankin. Make-up is something that can be played with, it changes iconic faces and allows for a surrealism and a trompe-l'œil effect. A true collaborative artist, in Rankin's creative beauty work there is a synergy of model, hair, make-up and photography unparalleled in many careers.

Opposite Page - Touched Up, Issue 85, 2002

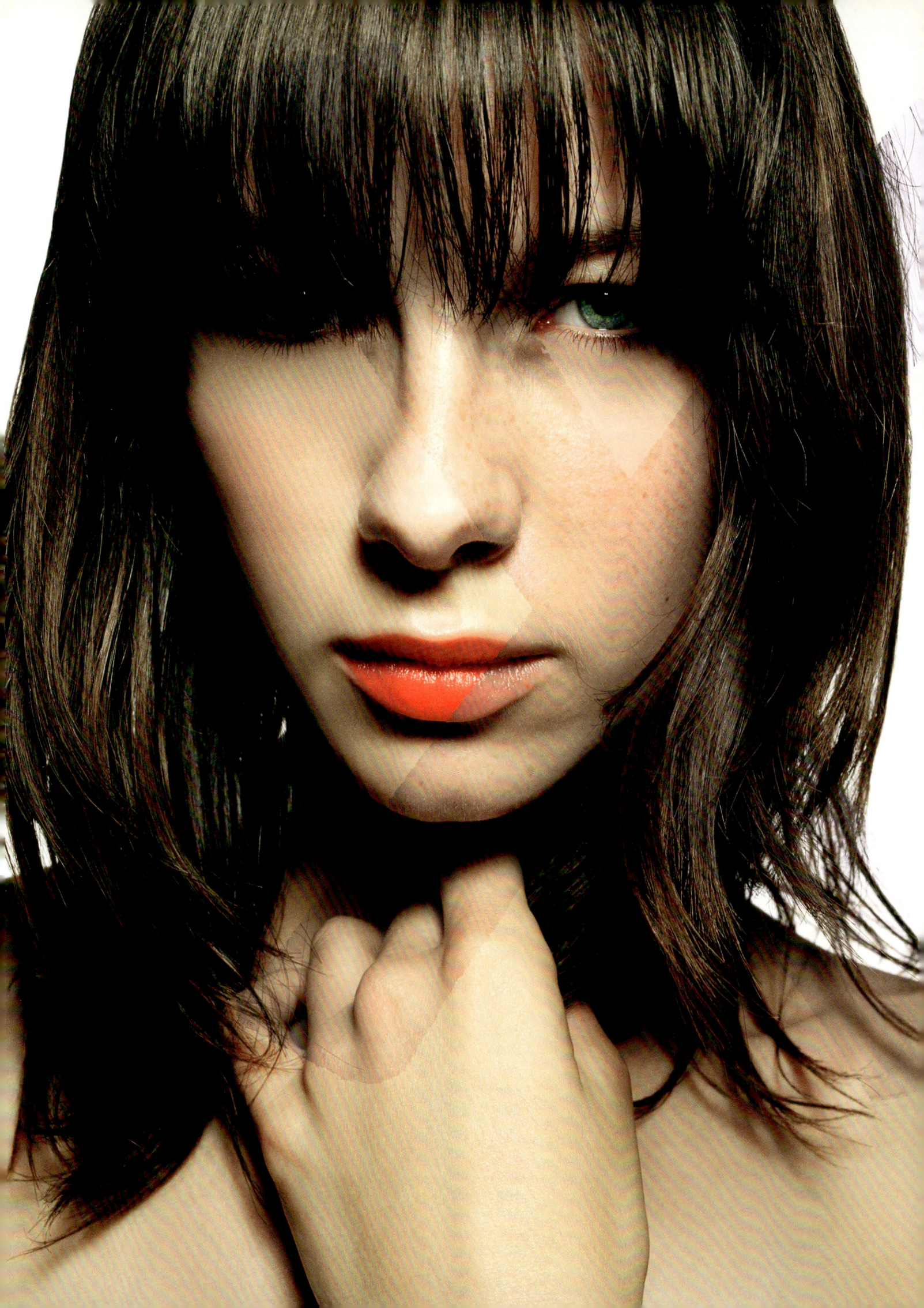

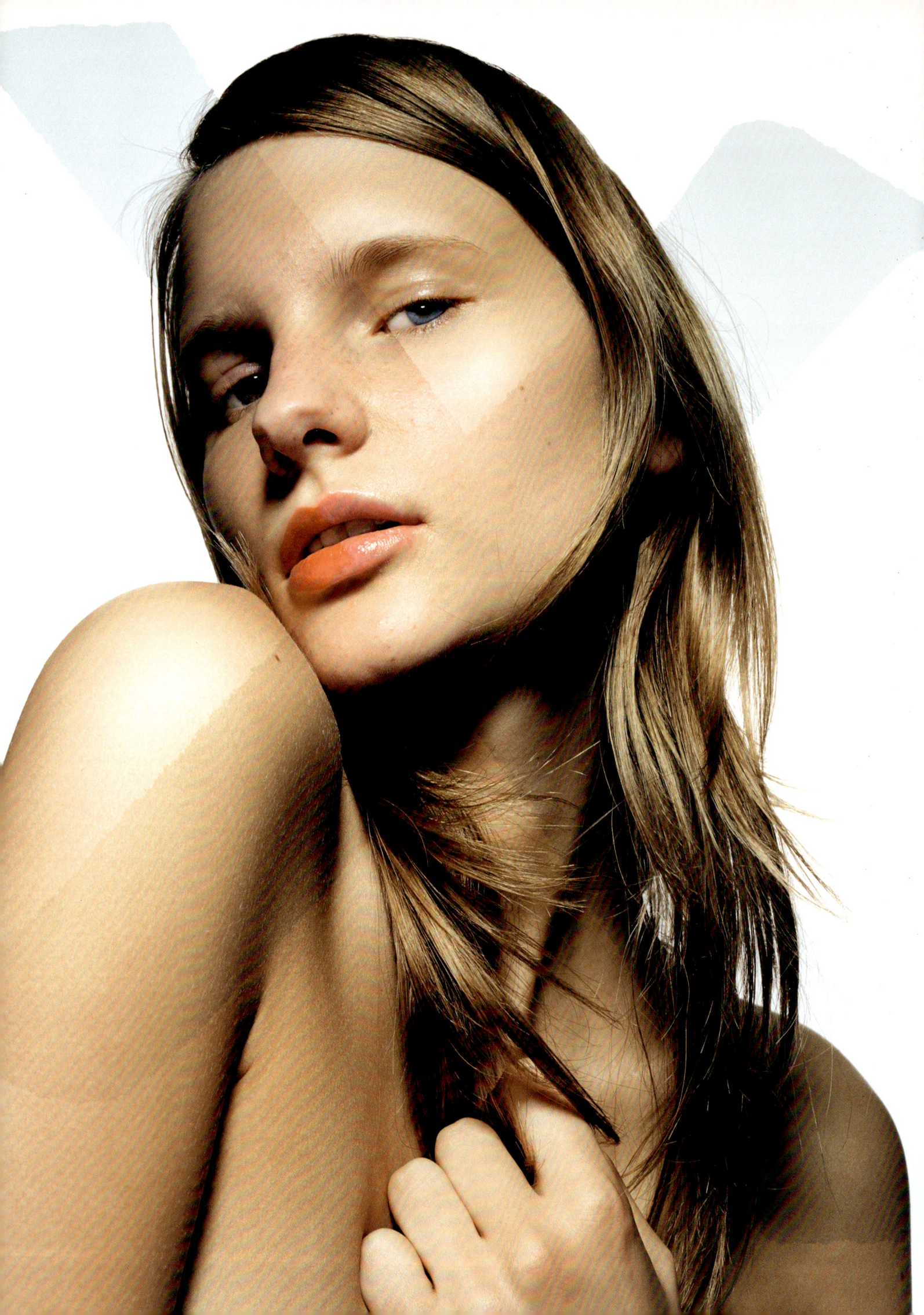

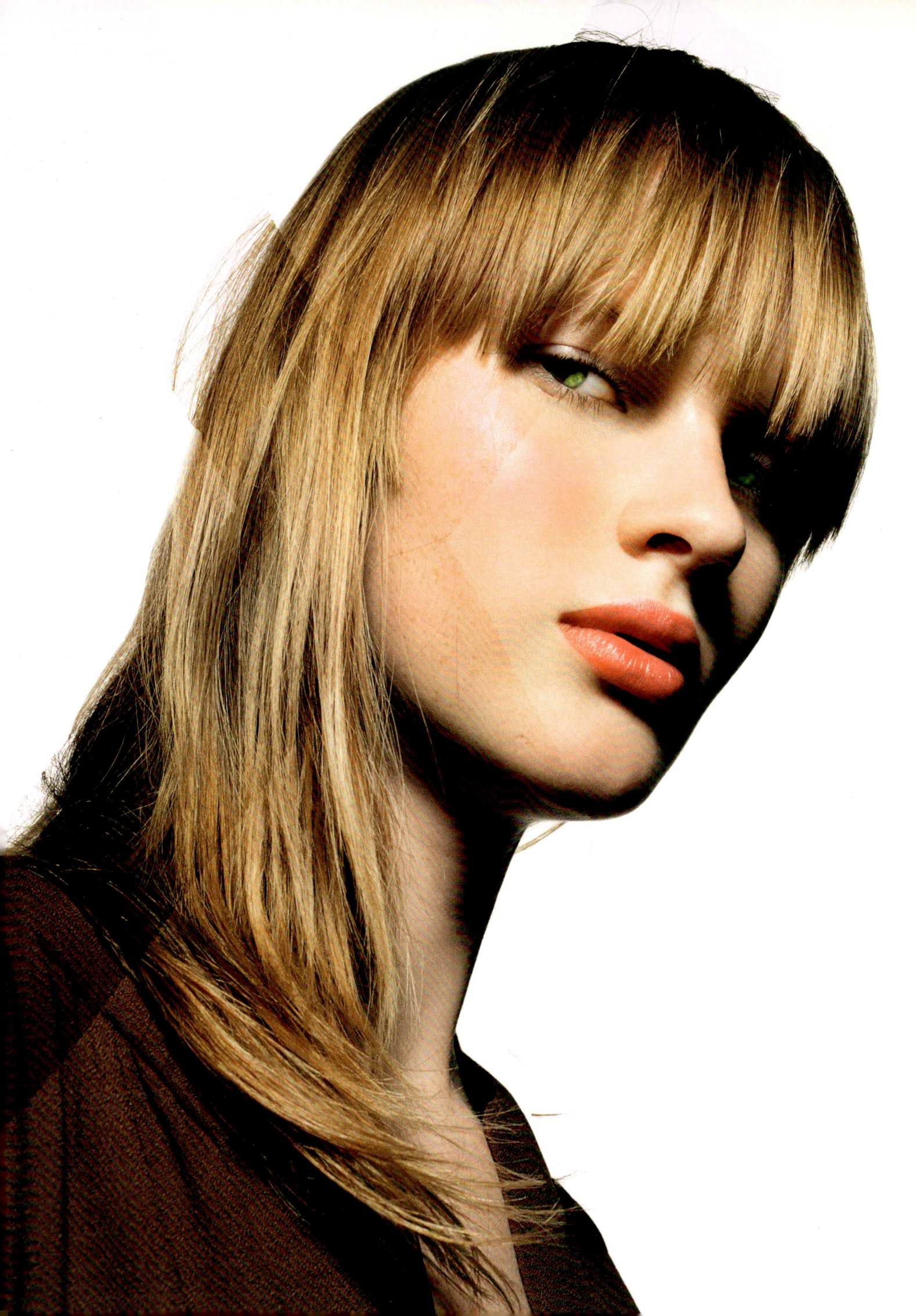

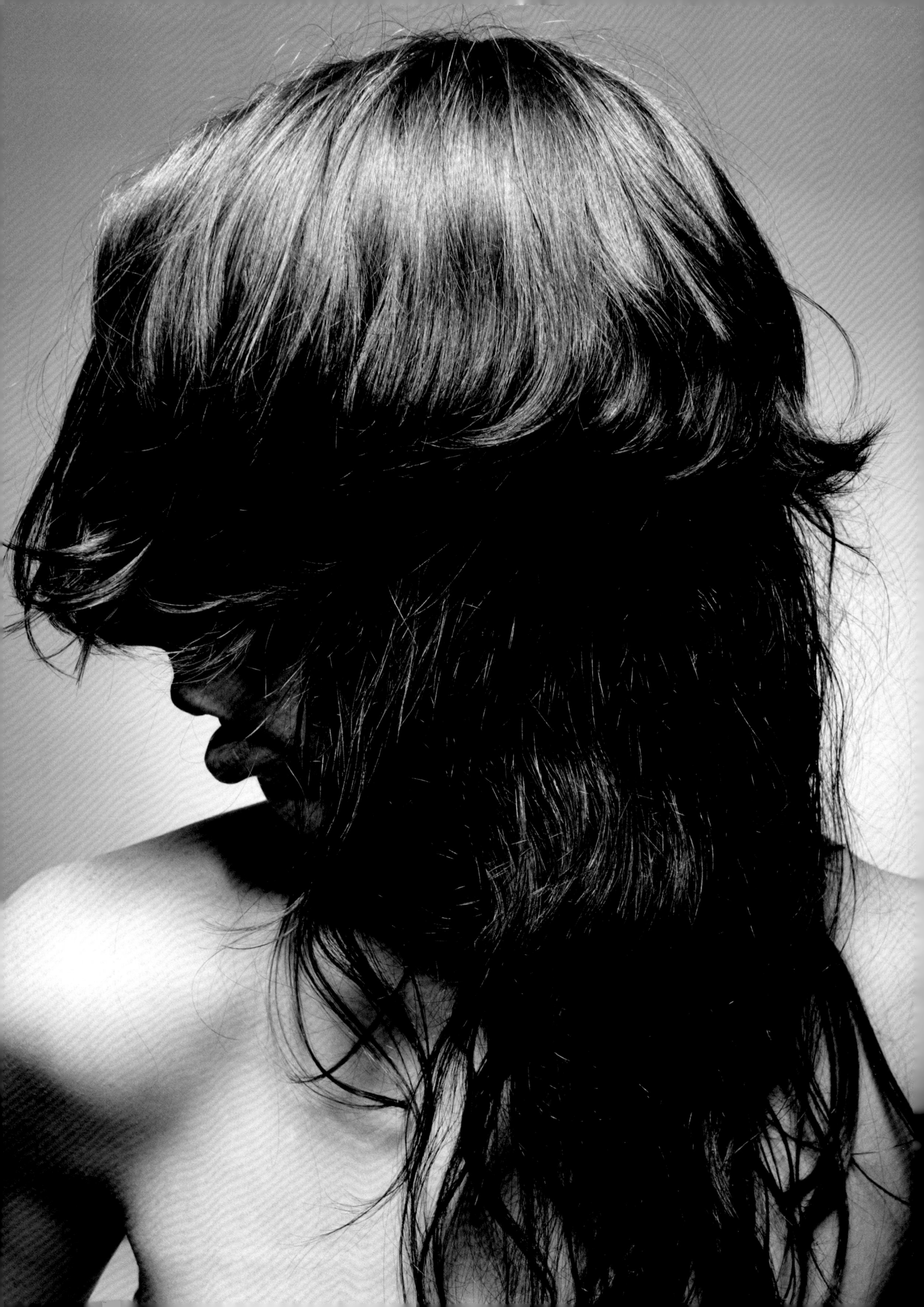

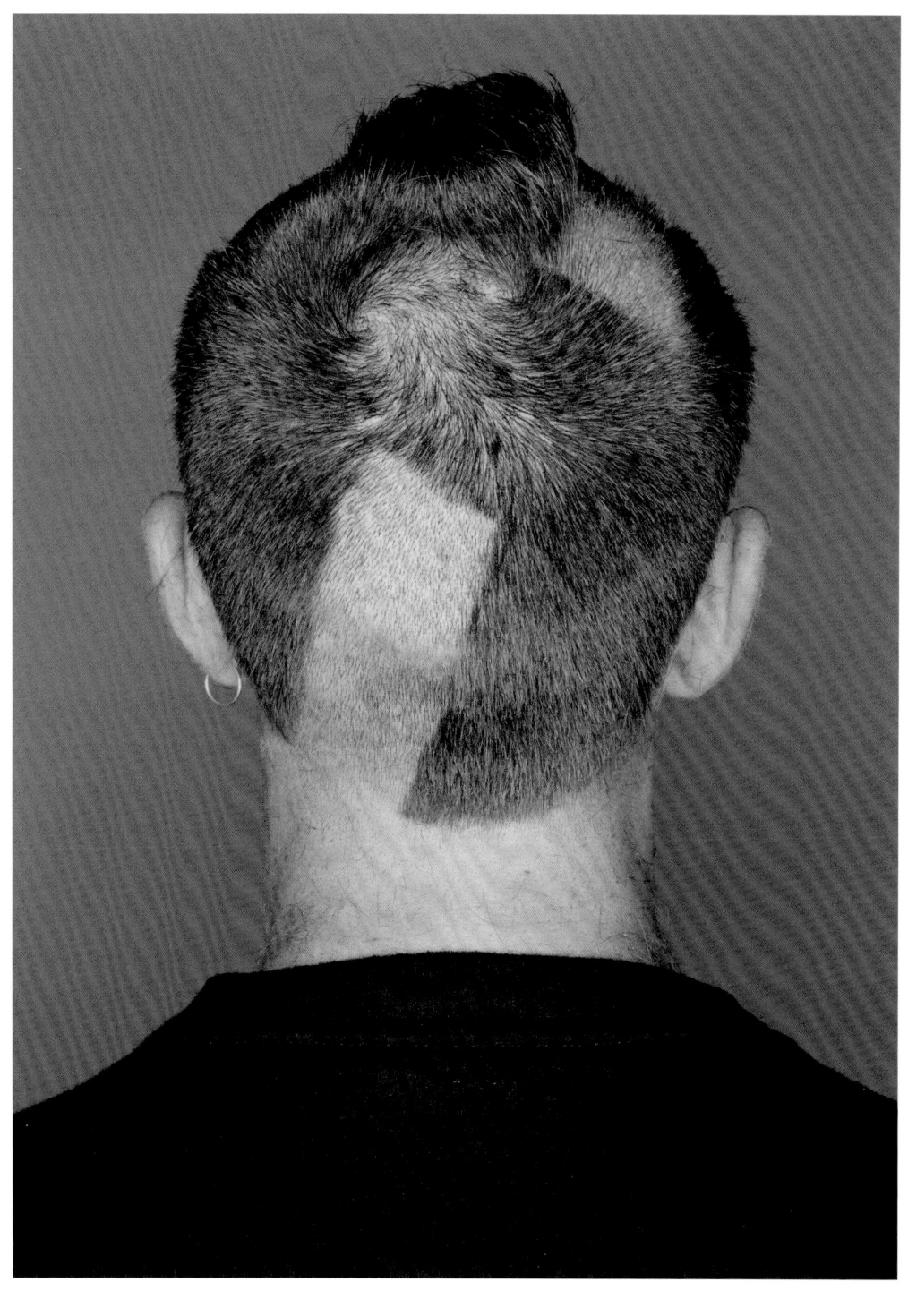

Something For the Weekend, Issue 35, 1997

Opposite Page - Asphyxiation, Issue 44, 1998

Next Pages - Meltdown, Issue 57, 1999
            Baked Alaska: Diesel Style Lab A/W, Issue 45, 1998

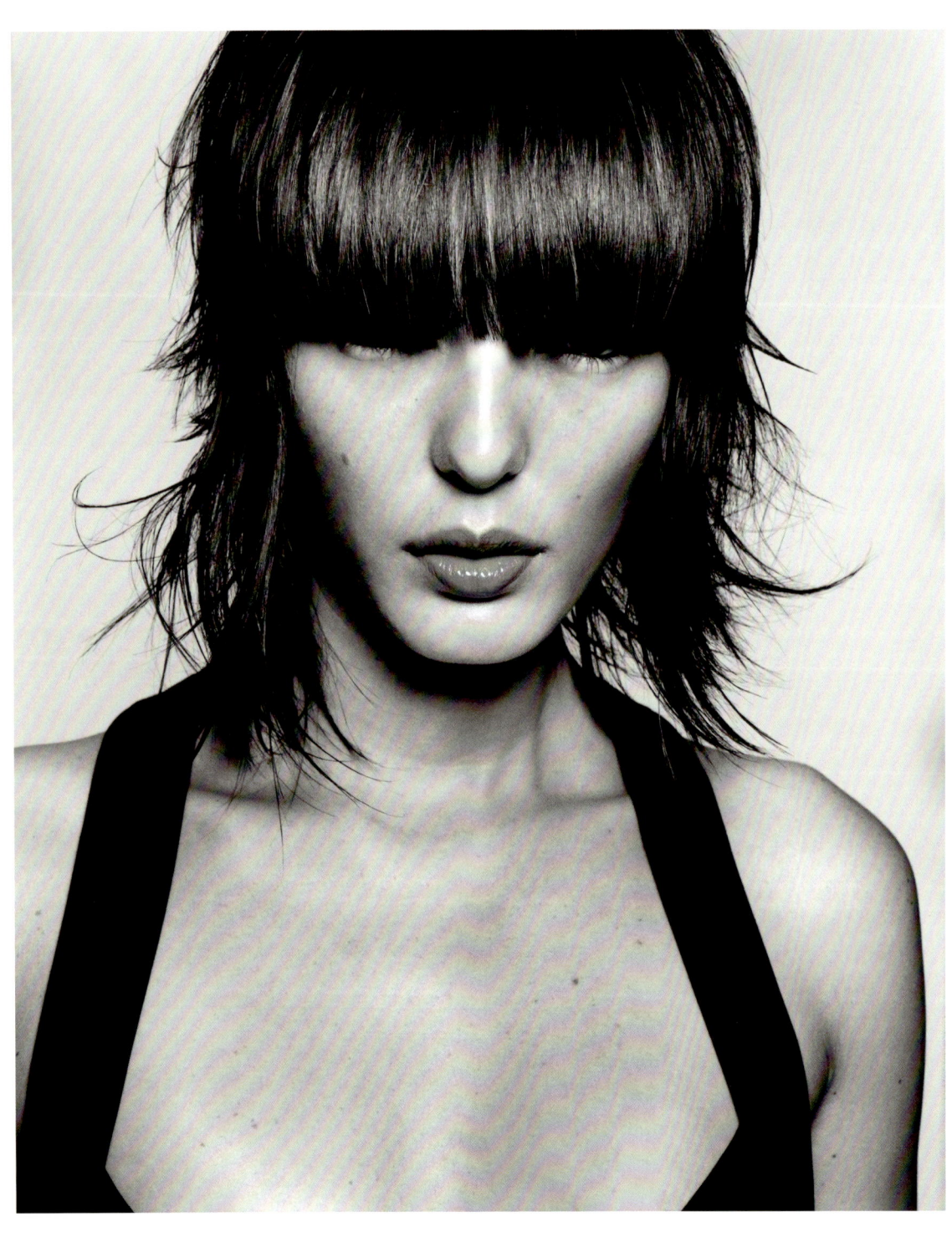

Toni & Guy, Issue 78, 2001

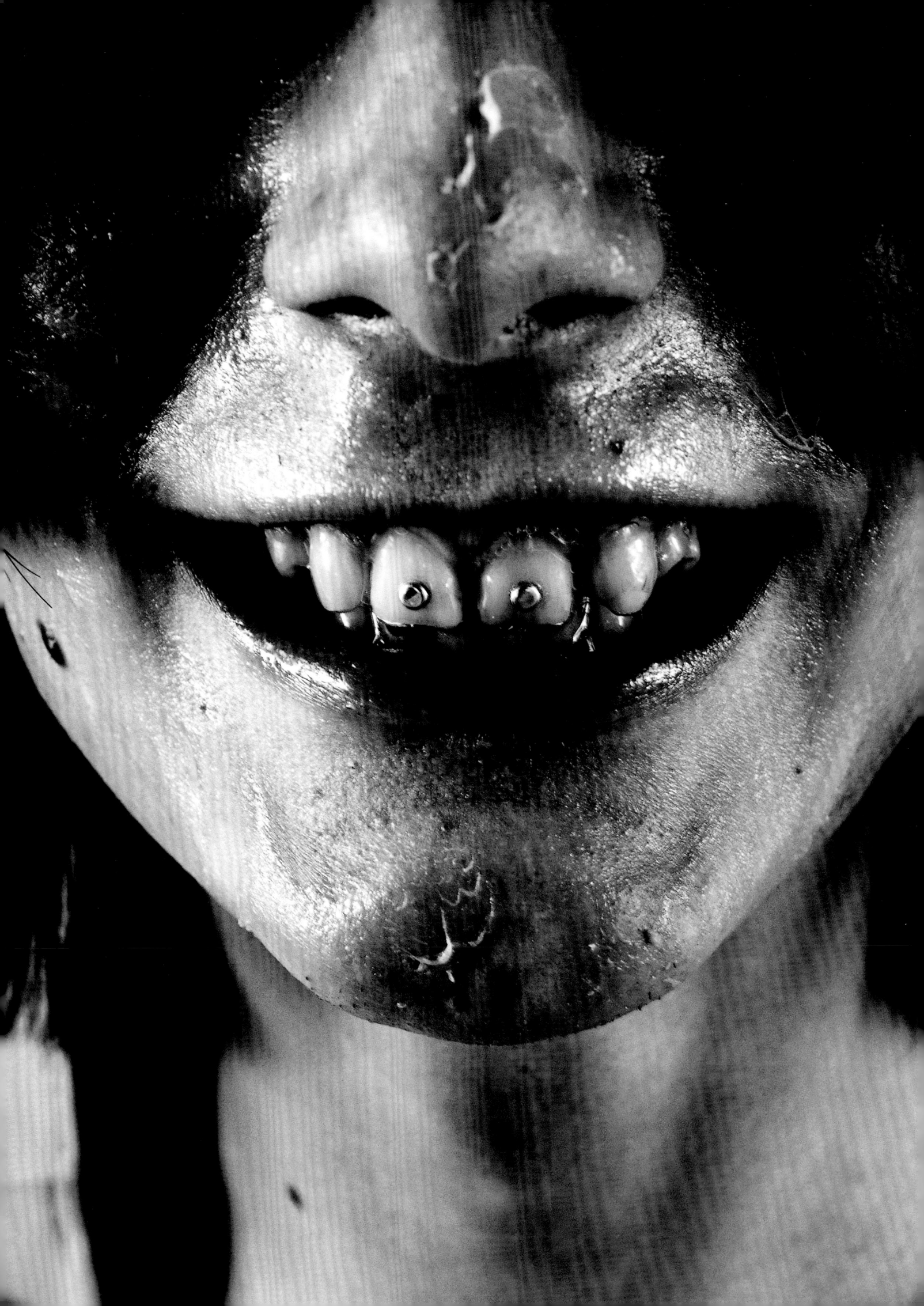

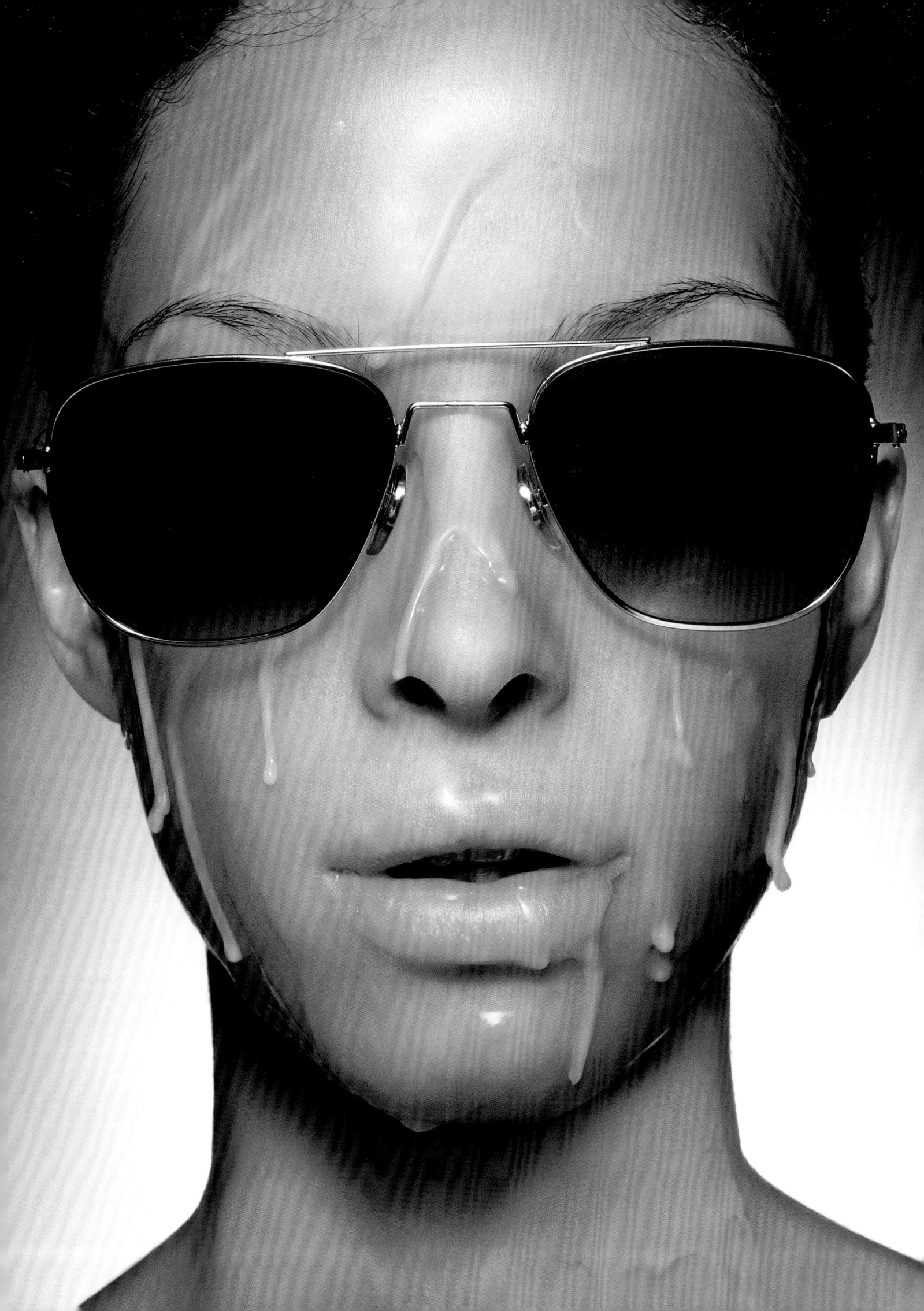

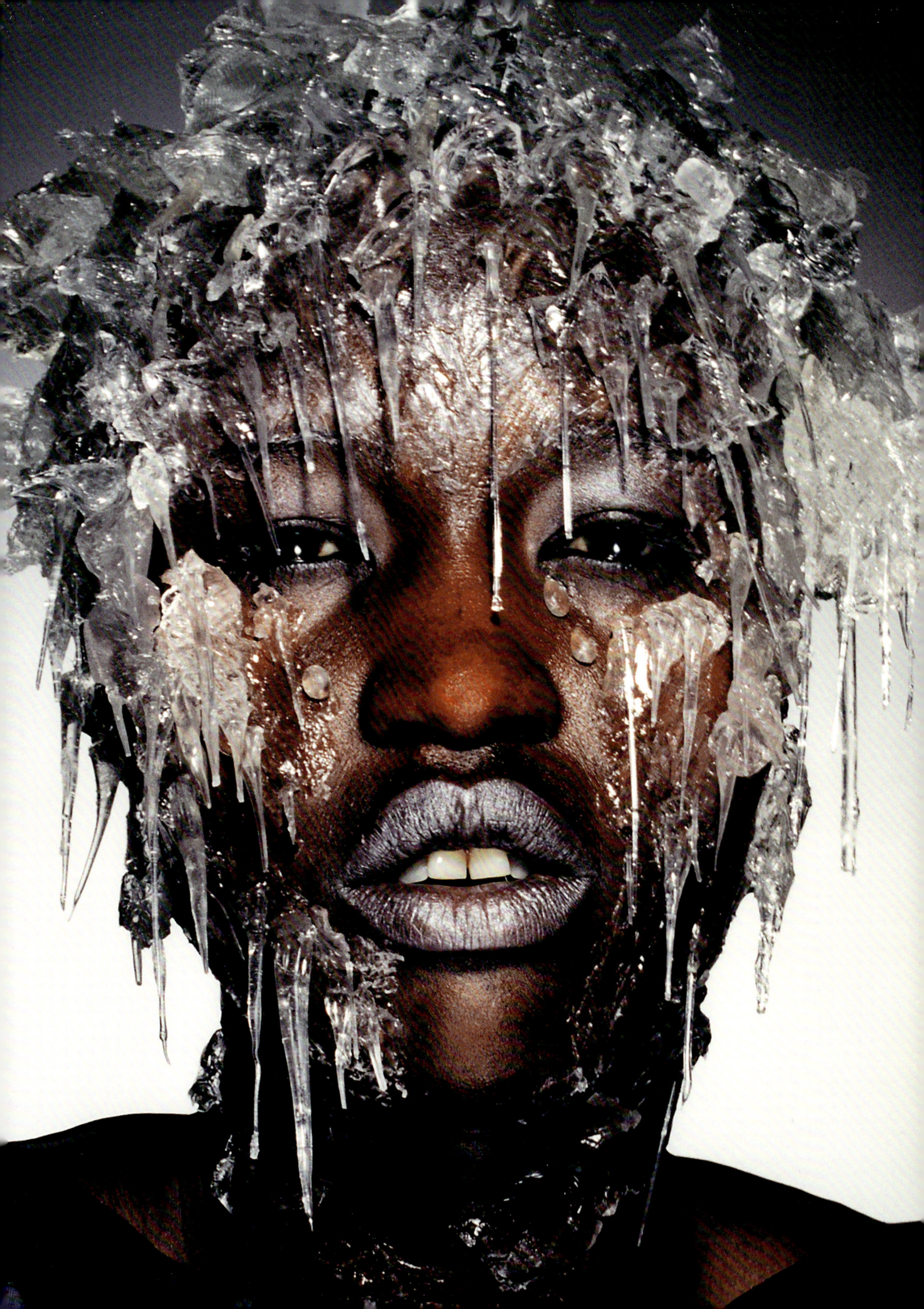

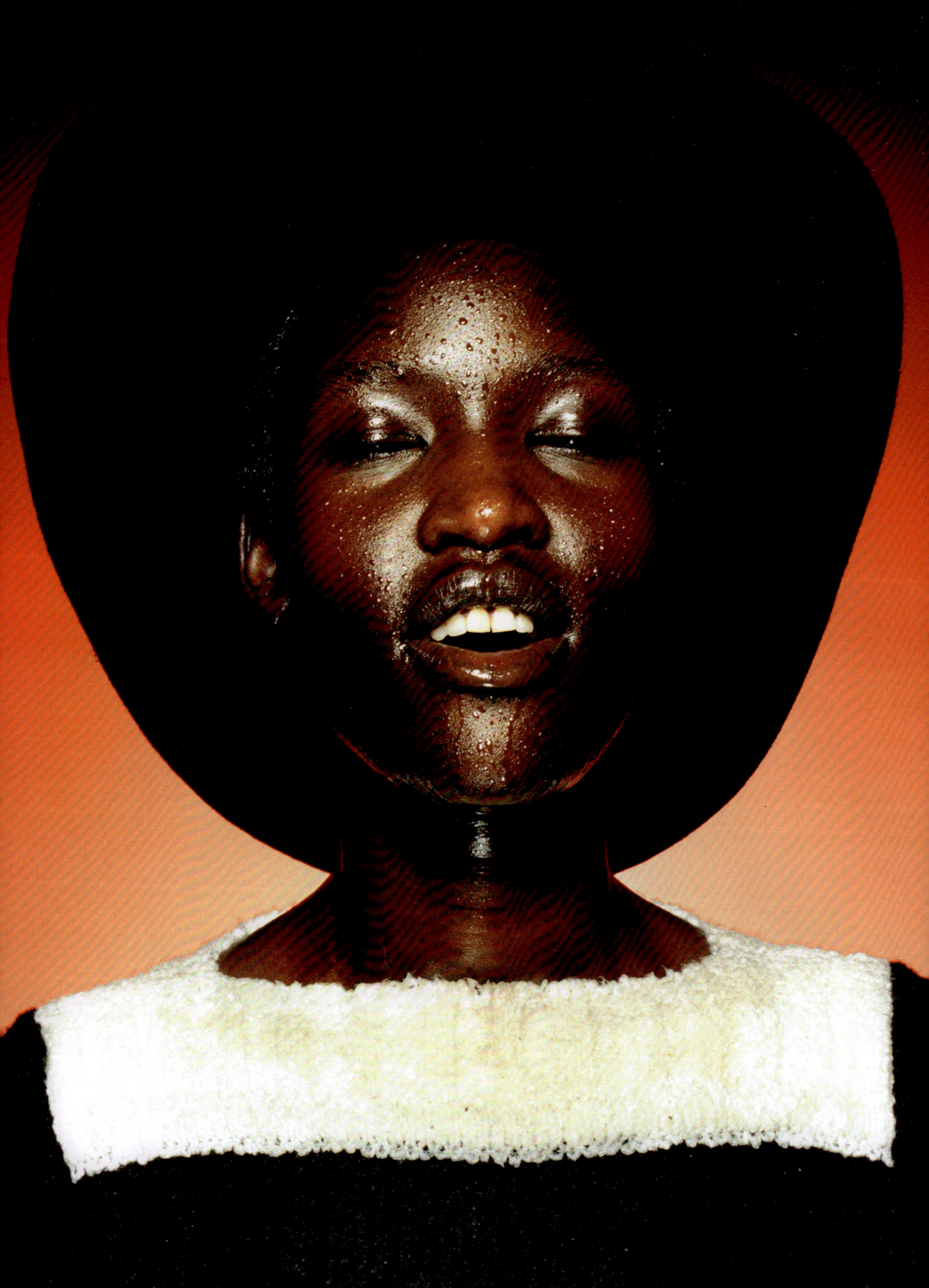

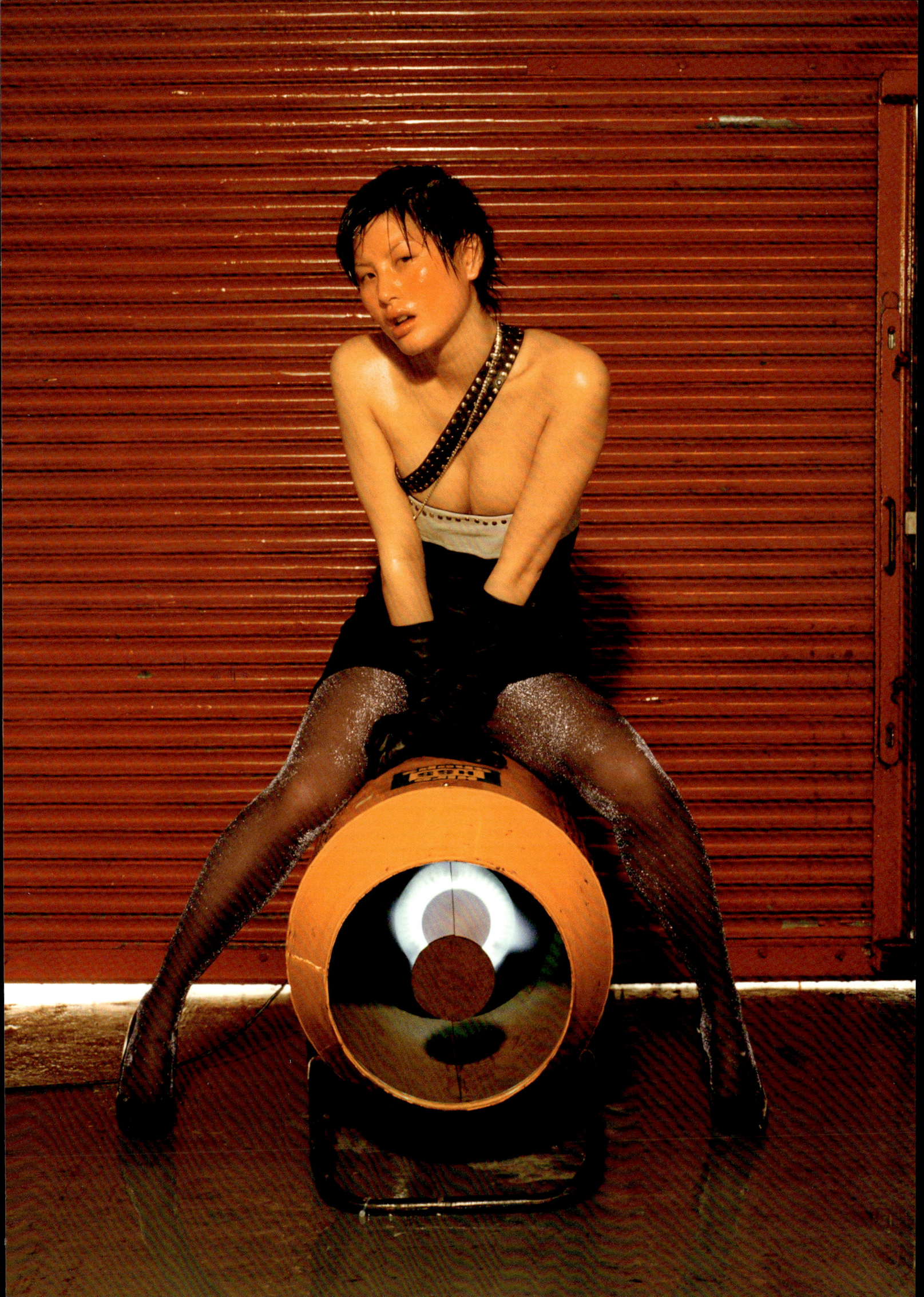

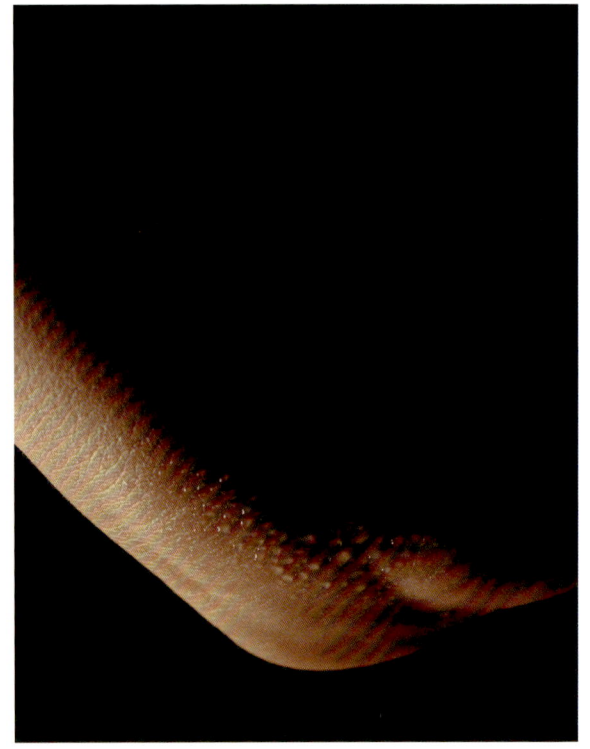
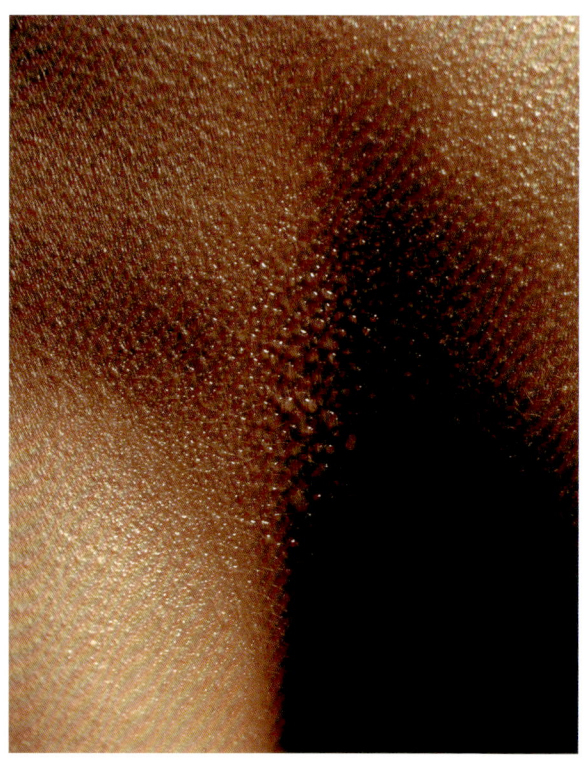
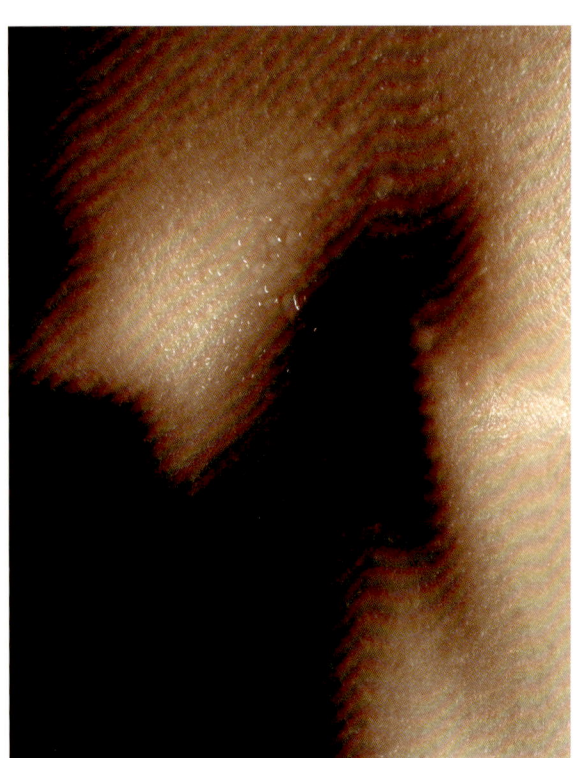
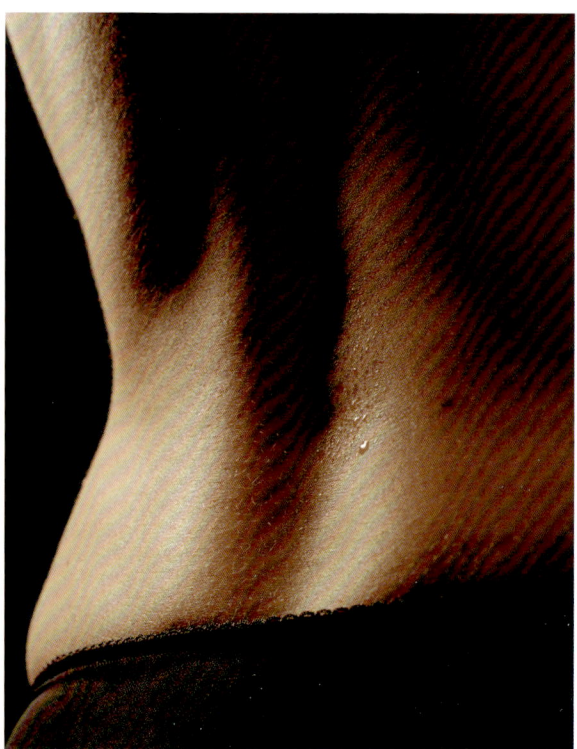

Sense, Issue 72, 2000

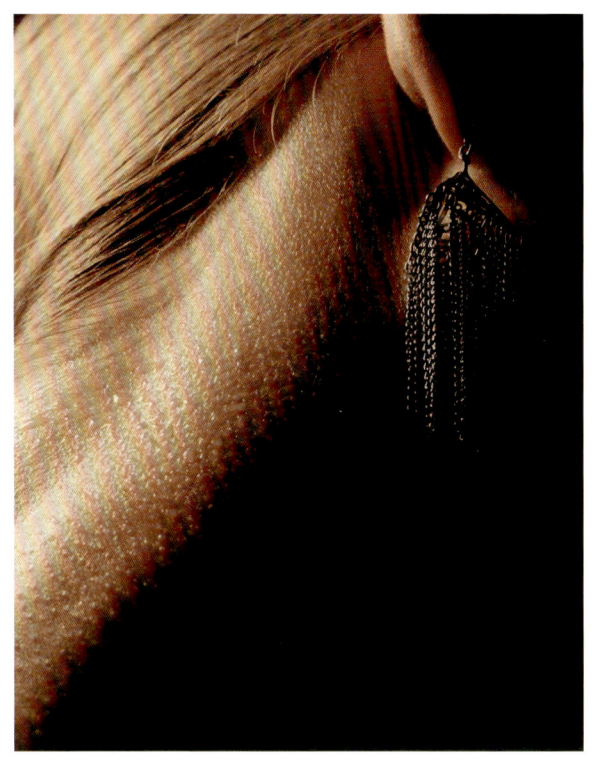
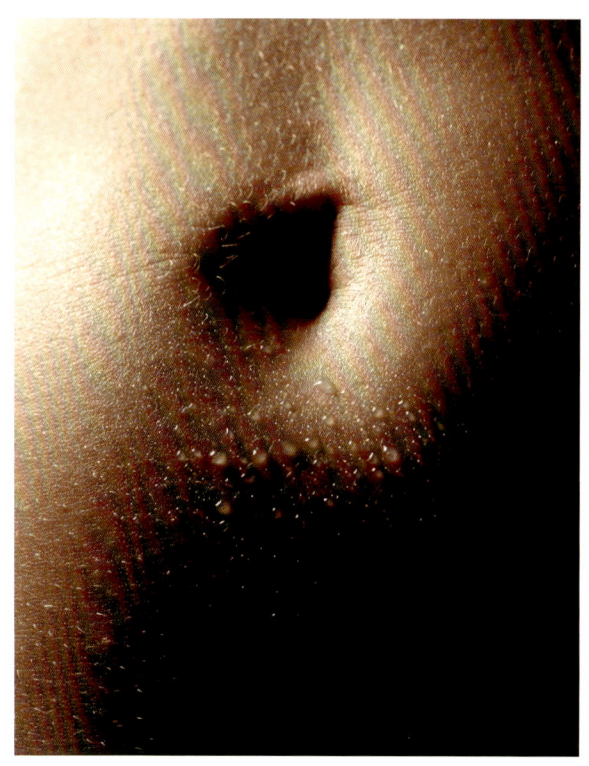
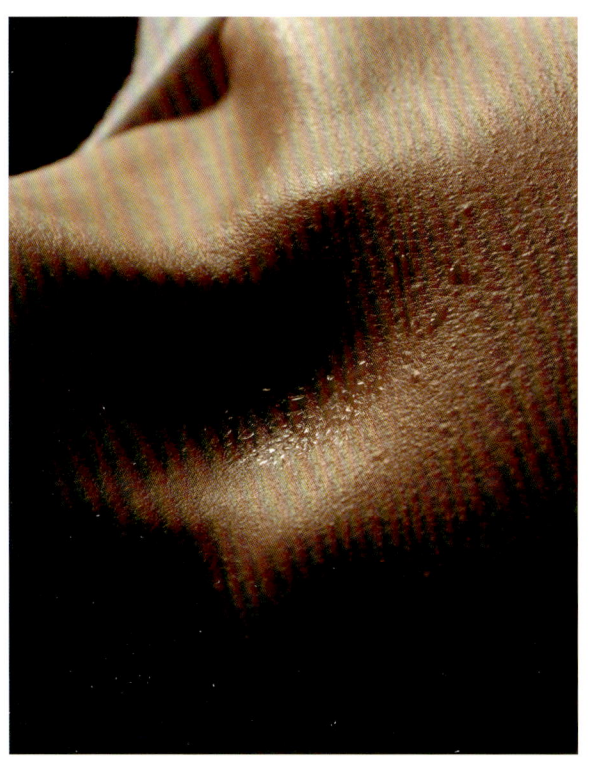
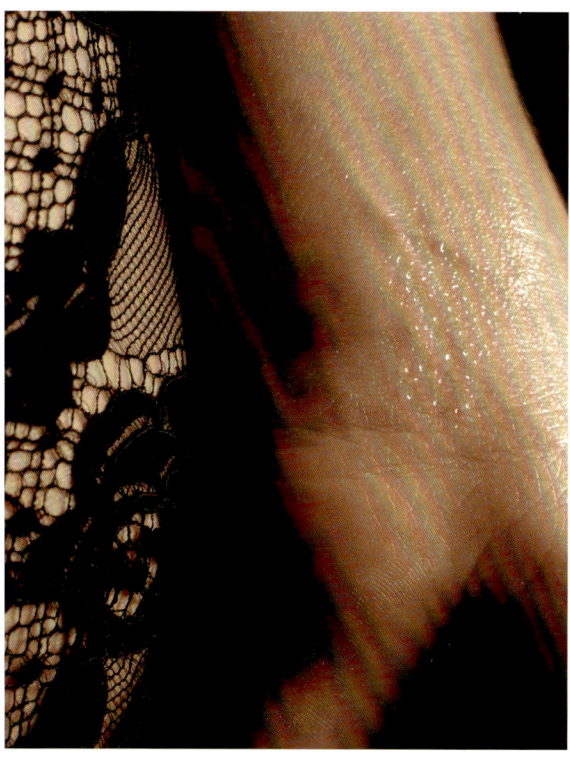

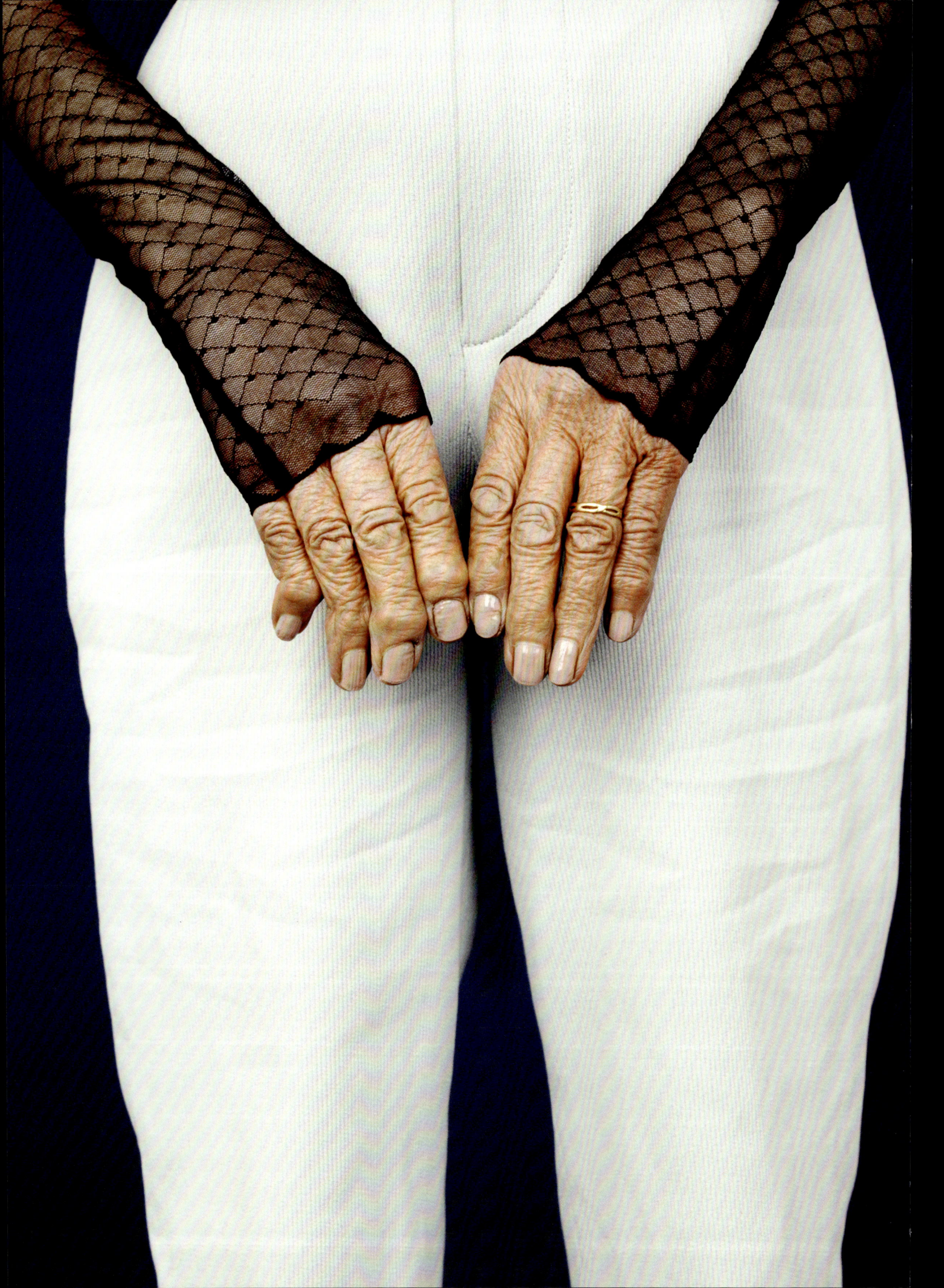

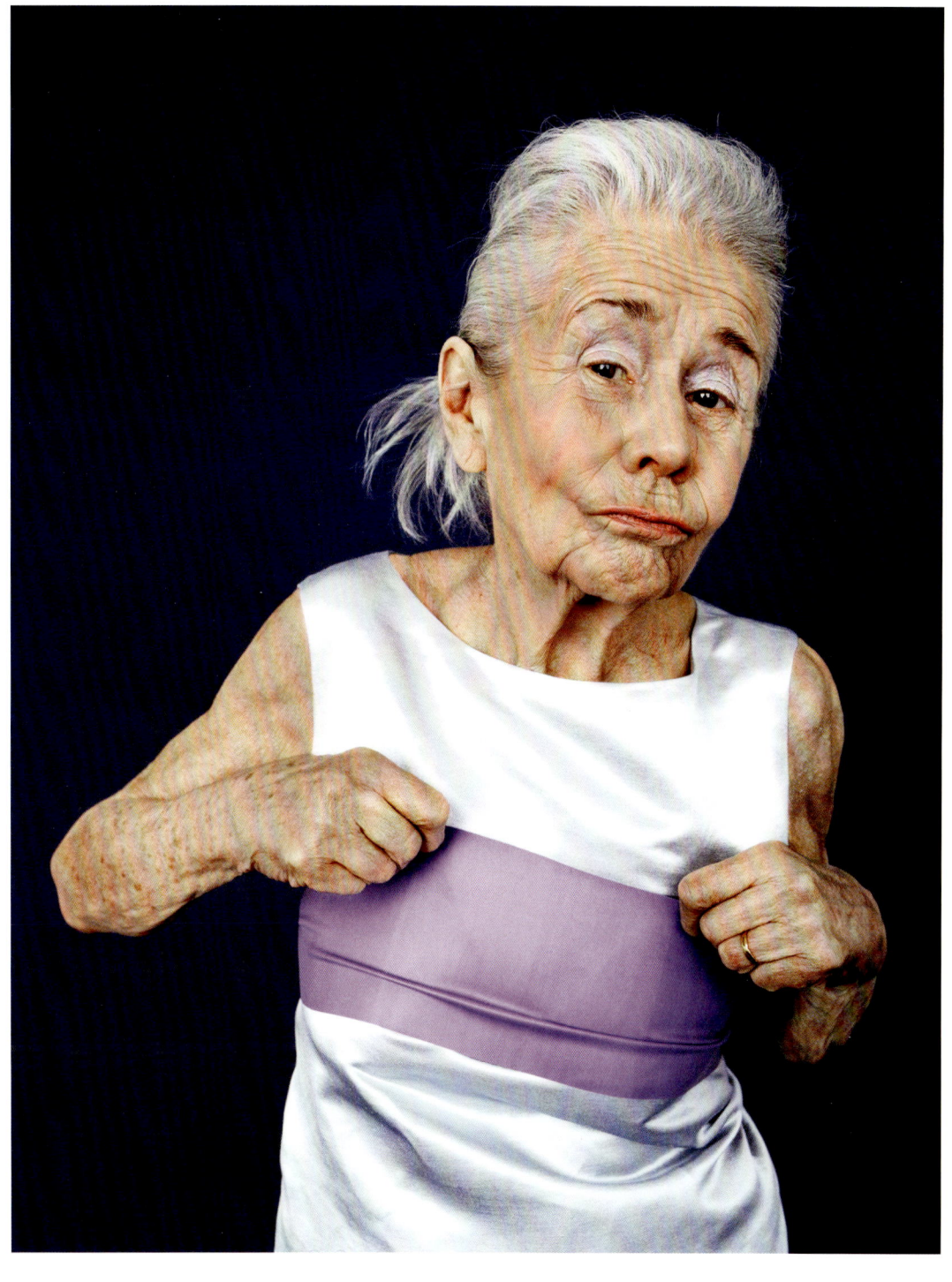

Silver Ladies, Issue 18, 1996

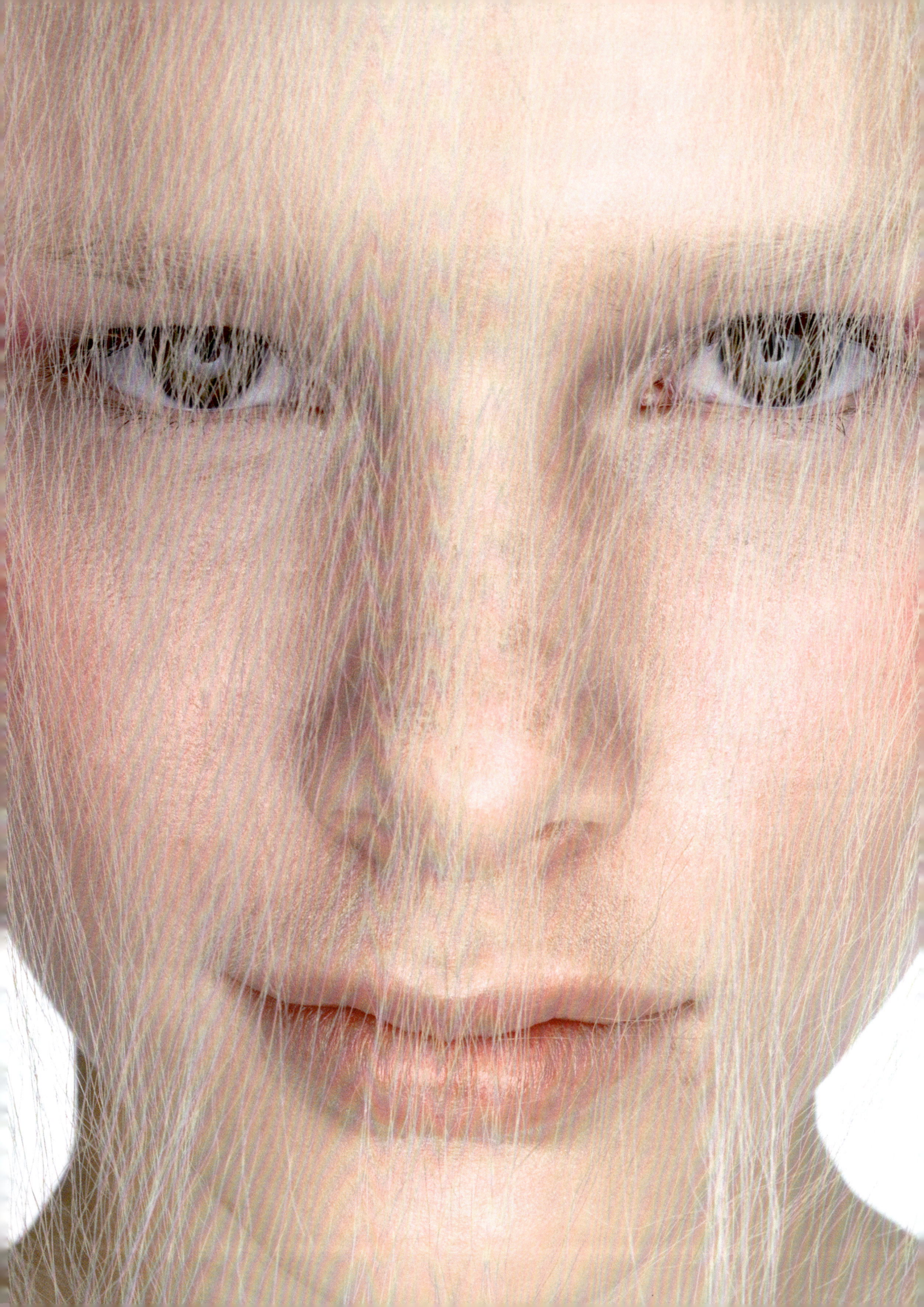

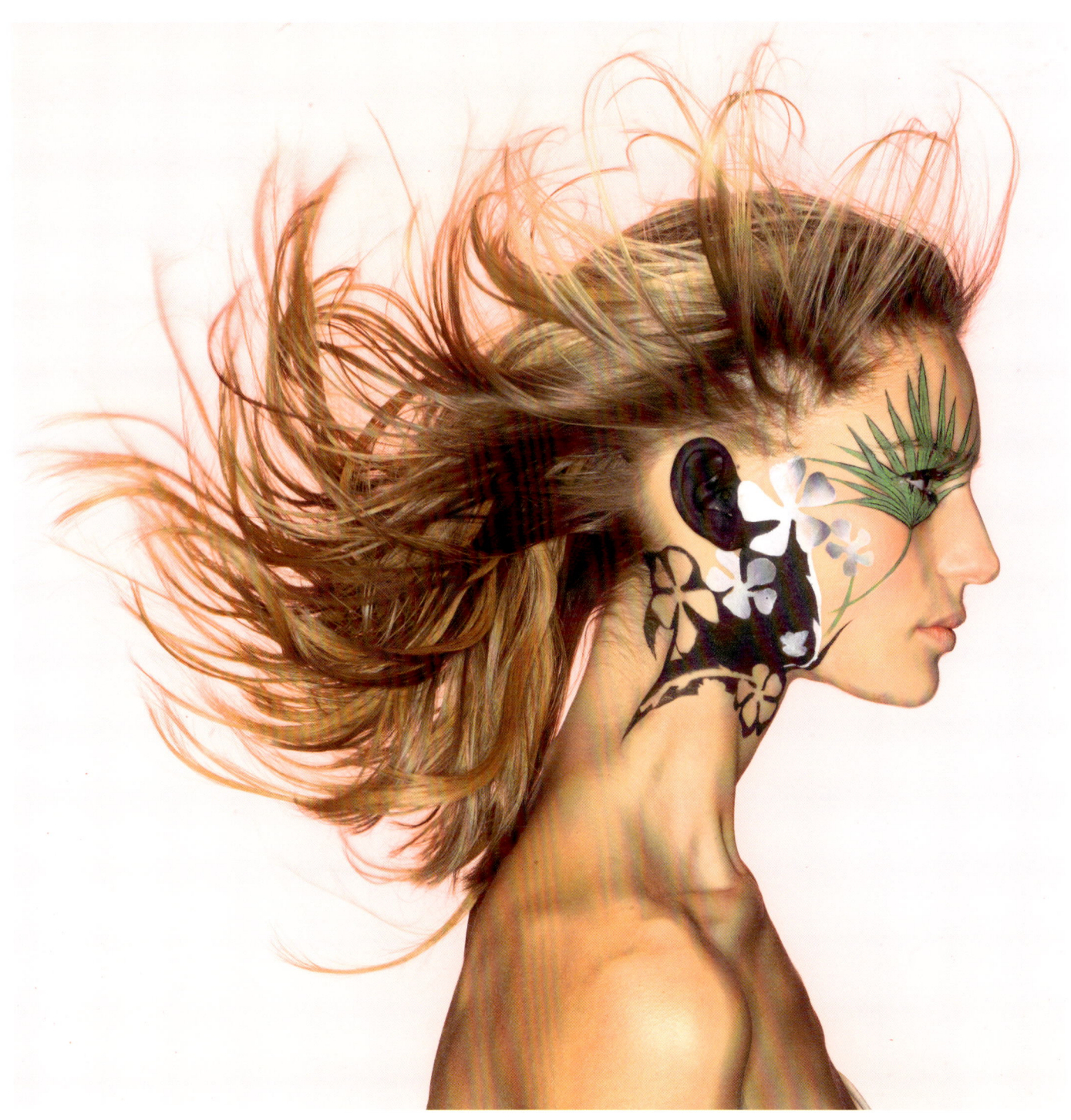

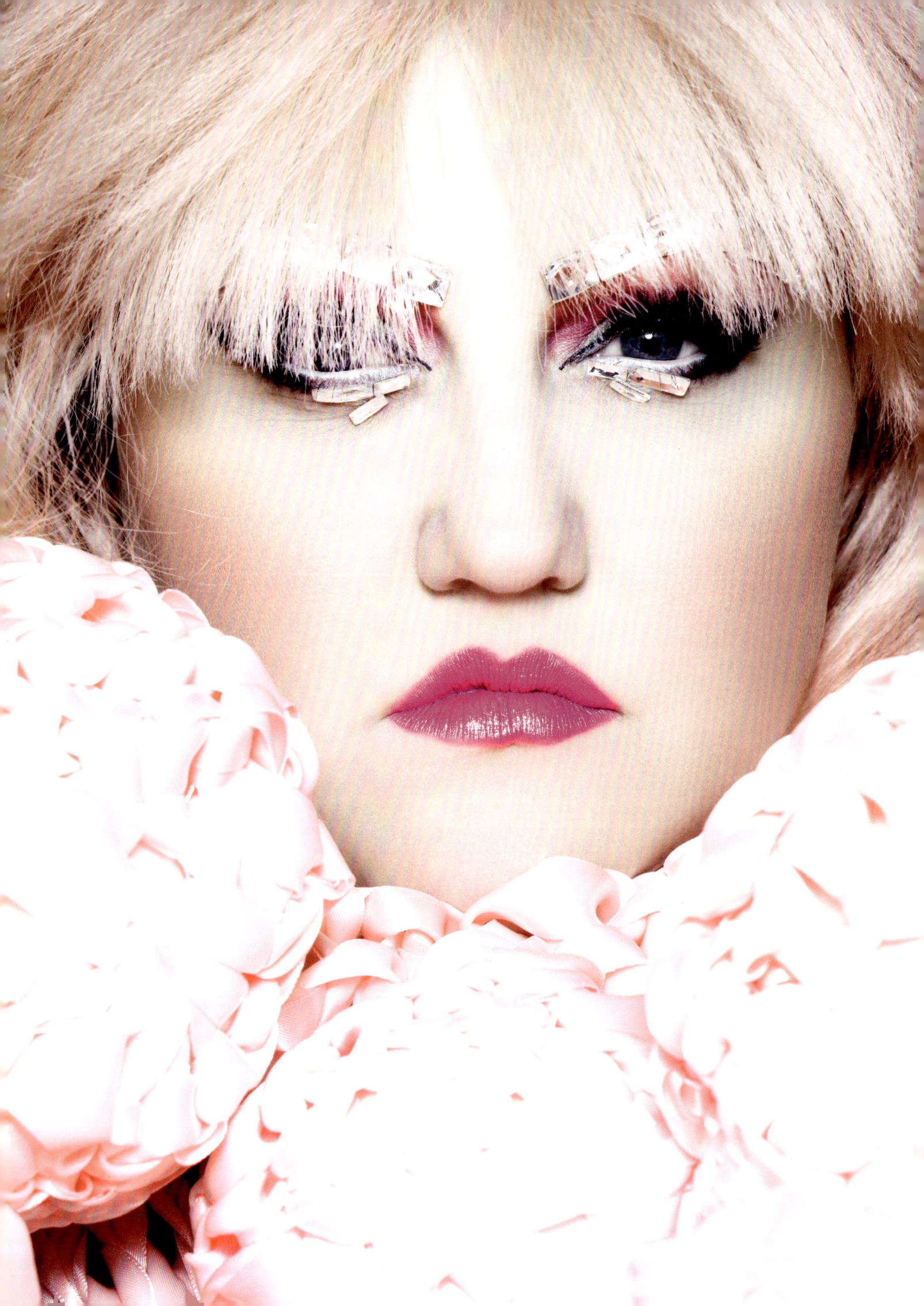

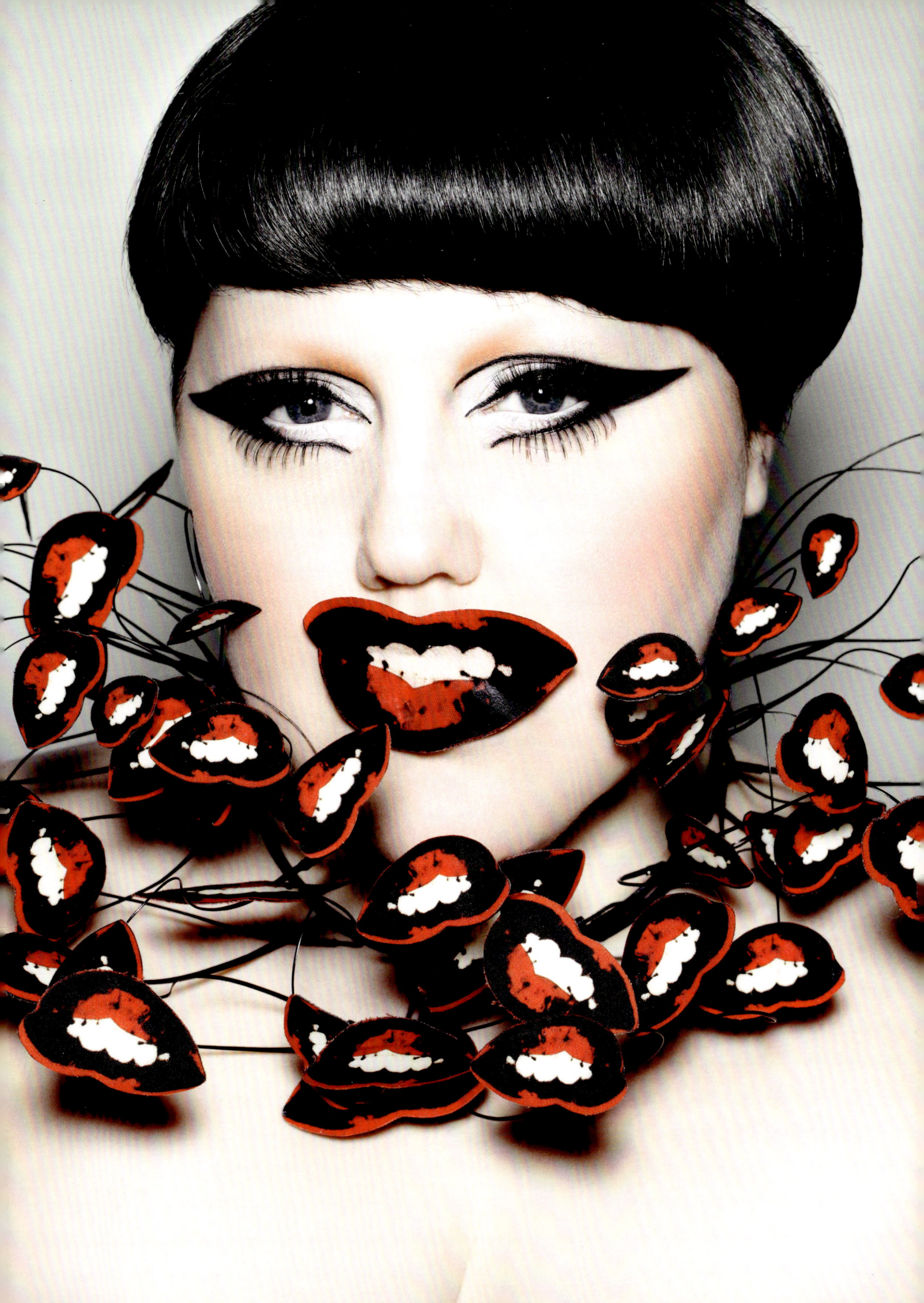

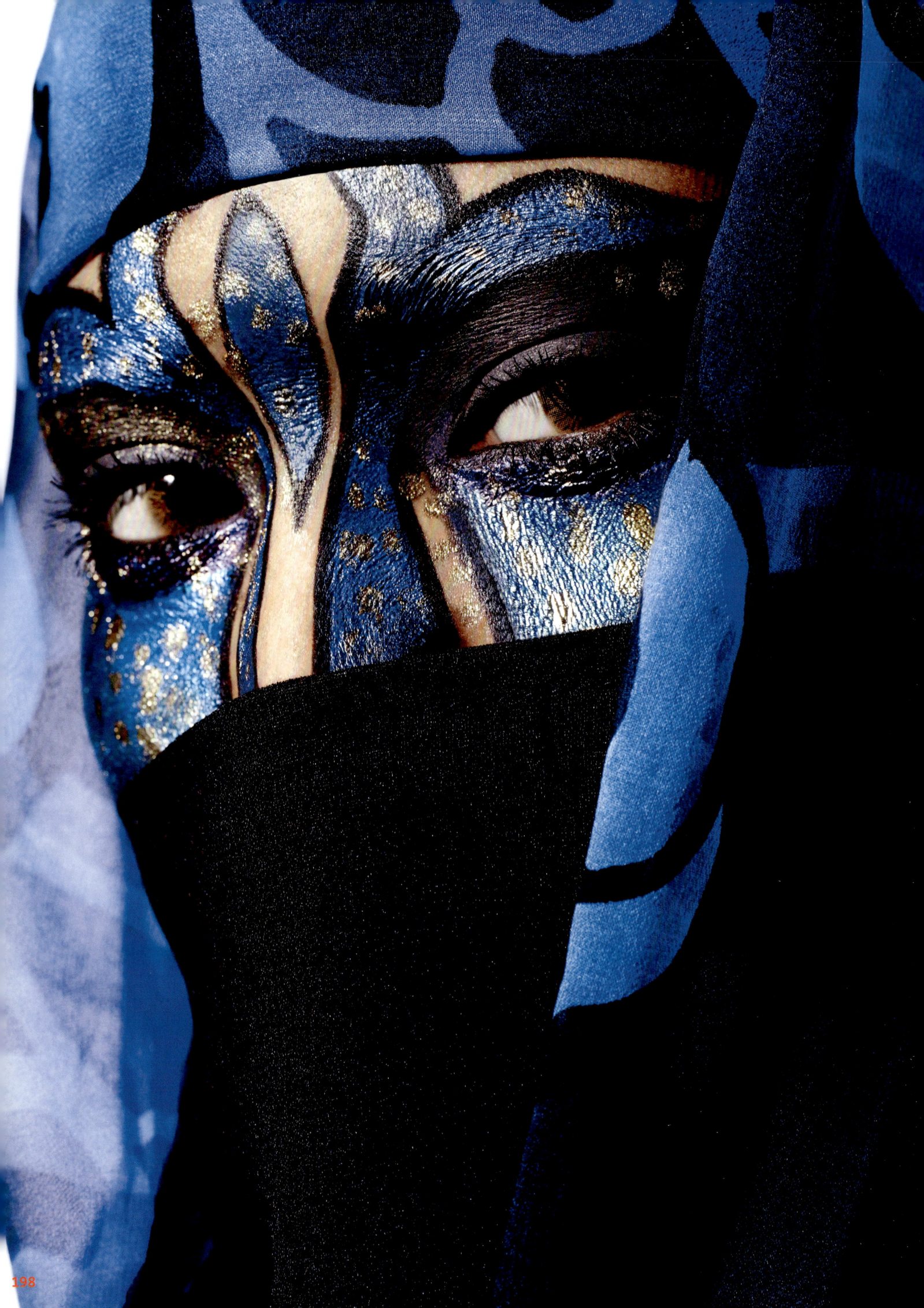

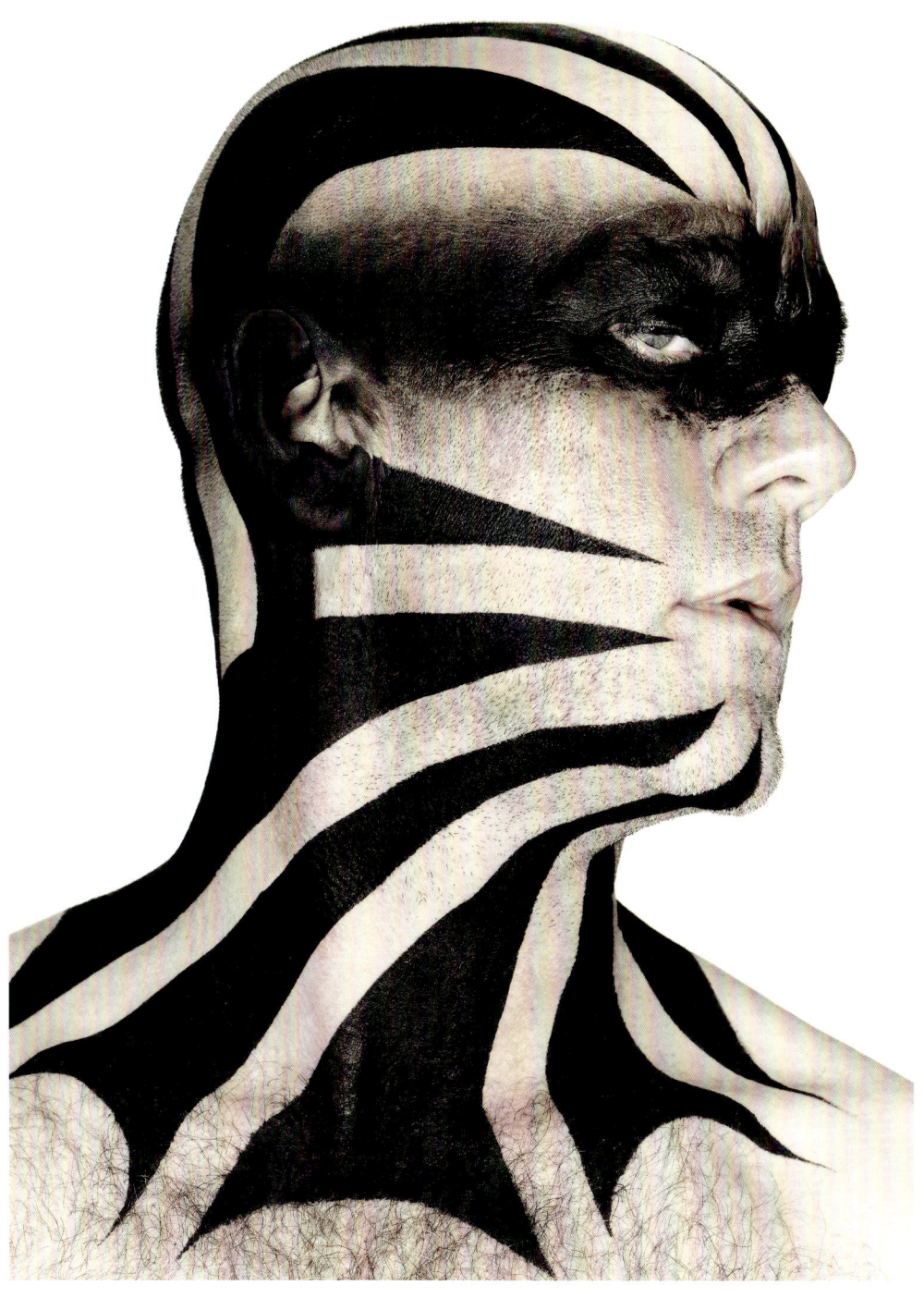

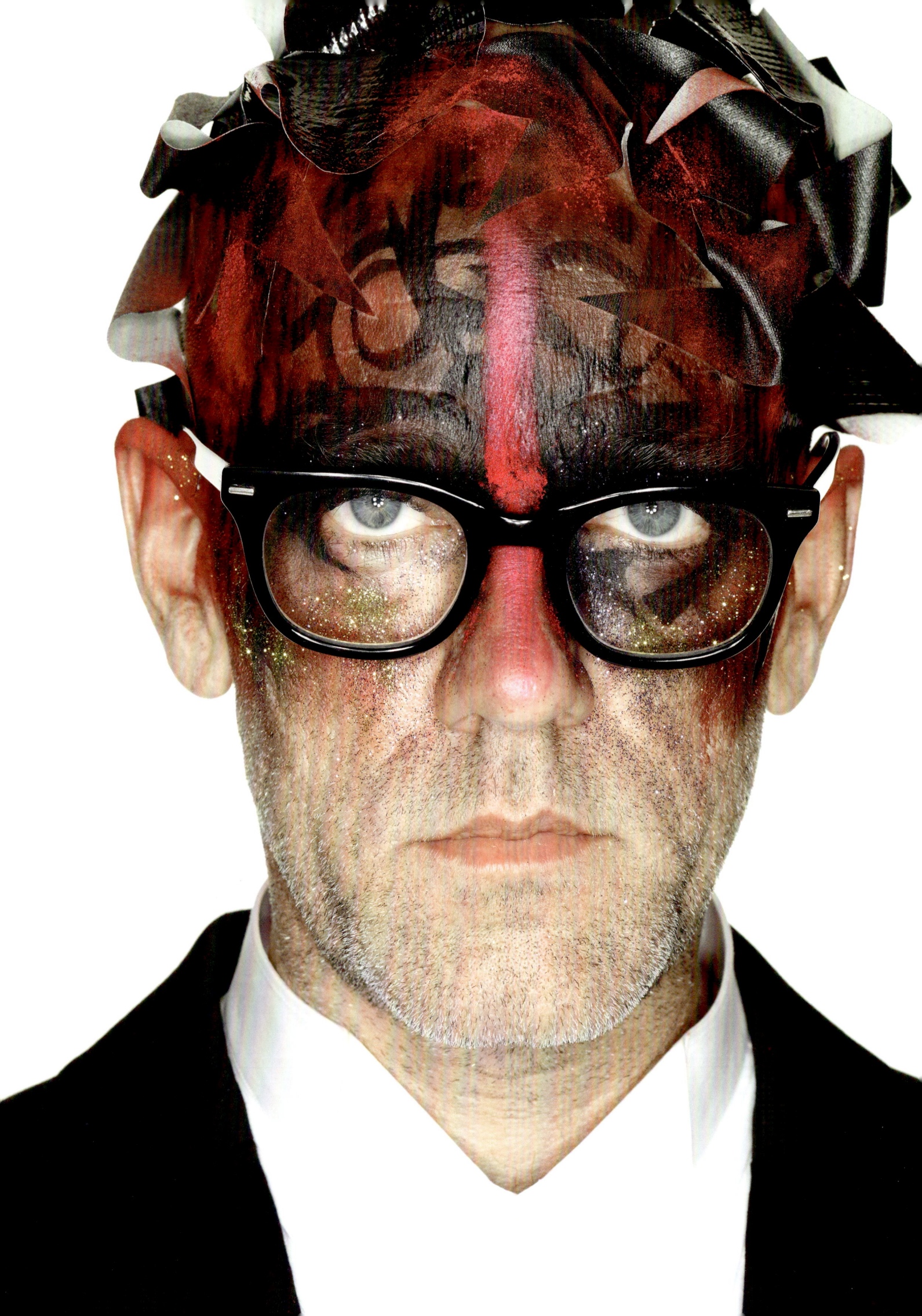

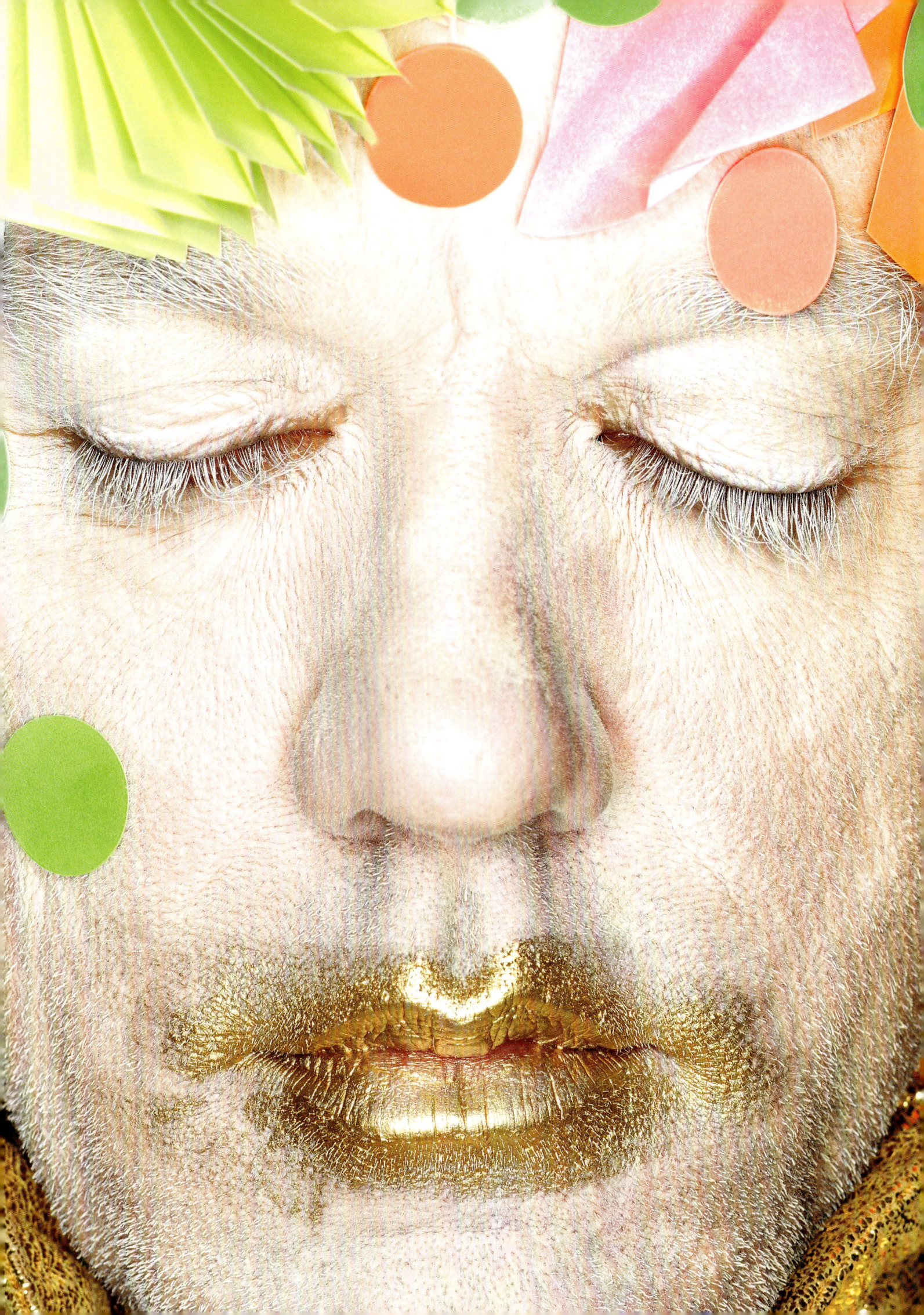

TIMELINE

Contribute and Live

Issue: 0
Year: 1990

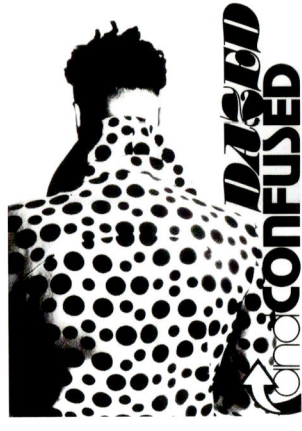

Pseudoheroes

Issue: 0
Year: 1990
Model: Kenny Whymark as Humphrey Bogart / Miles Treacy as Elvis Presley / Albert Evansky as Albert Einstein / Pauline Bailey as Marilyn Monroe
Styling: Model's Own

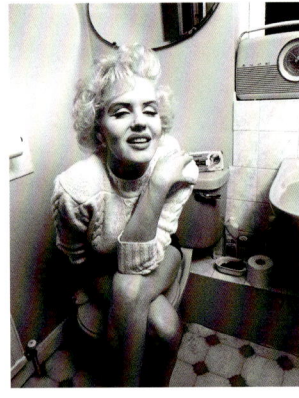

Gilbert & George on George & Gilbert

Issue: 0
Year: 1990
Model: Gilbert & George
Styling: Model's own

Bodylines

Issue: 0
Year: 1990
Model: Sue, Louise
Hair: Darren Stone
Make-up: Cathy Lomax
Styling: Marÿe

The Emperors' New Clothes

Issue: 1
Year: 1991
Model: Keld, Roy Brown, Sue, Rupert Shawn, Antonio, Julian, Ali, Terry, Nour, Kent, Moni LeBon
Hair: Kent, Firyal
Make-up: Firyal

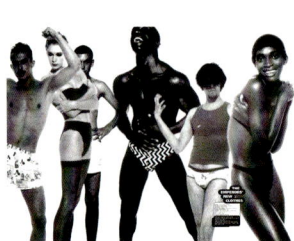

John Godber on John Godber

Issue: 1
Year: 1991
Model: John Godber

"Do You Think Bosoms Will Be In Or Out This Year?"

Issue: The Fashion Supplement
Year: 1992

Have You Heard The One About...

Issue: The Fashion Supplement
Year: 1992
Model: Bella Freud

Blow Up

Issue: The Fashion Supplement
Year: 1992
Model: London Clubbers
Styling: Model's Own

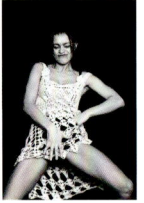 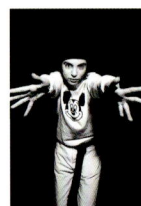

Young Designer Showcase

Issue: The Fashion Supplement
Year: 1992
Model: Nicholas Alexander Dormon / Joie Readman / Eggplant / Jimmy Jumble / Karen Savage

Introducing the Cult Personality of Doctor Stewart

Issue: 2
Year: 1992
Model: Doctor Stewart

Untitled

Issue: 2
Year: 1992

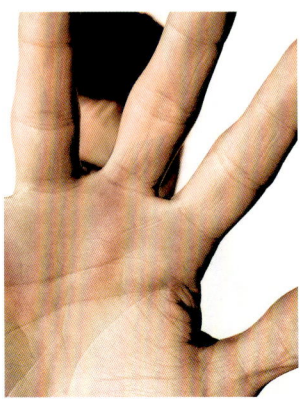

Maur & Barbie Wear

Issue: 2
Year: 1992
Model: Maur Valance & Barbie Superstar
Hair: Pam Wrigley
Make-up: Pam Wrigley
Styling: Katherine Curley

Sex & Death

Issue: 2
Year: 1992
Model: Rebecca Tomlinson aka Bunny Vixen

Are You Ready to Have Your Mind Blown!

Issue: 2
Year: 1992
Model: Peter Cunnah & Al Mckenzie from D:Ream

Ever Get the Feeling You're Being Cheated?

Issue: 3
Year: 1992
Model: Antonina Tramonti

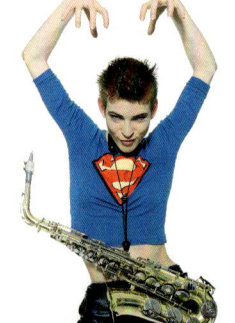

Who's Taking the Mickey?

Issue: 3
Year: 1992

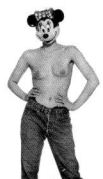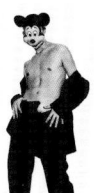

Central Saint Martins B.A. Honours Fashion Degree: Interpretations

Issue: CSM Supplement
Year: 1993
Model: Elaine Thompson / Ingrid / Becky, Kitty, Dawn / Mark Vincent
Make-up: Glen Wood, Nicola Dell

Fashion Sucks

Issue: 4
Year: 1993
Model: Elaine Thompson, Eleanor
Hair: Gavin
Make-up: Shelly Lorcan, Patricia Curry
Styling: Katie Grand

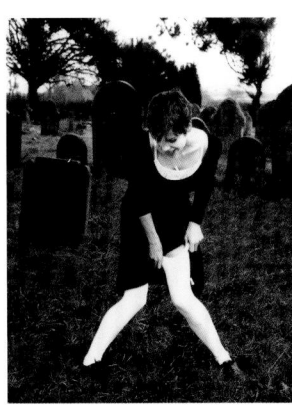

Zenz and the Art of Design Aesthetics

Issue: 4
Year: 1993
Model: Anand Zenz

Twister Conglomerate Bandstand

Issue: 4
Year: 1993
Model: Tom & Marv from Twister Conglomerate Bandstand
Styling: Model's own

It's Been 21 Years Today

Issue: 4
Year: 1993
Model: Pam Hogg / Adrian Webb / Matthew Glamorre / Jo Perfect / Lawrence Hayward & Siobhan from Denim / Johnny / Martin Green
Styling: Model's own

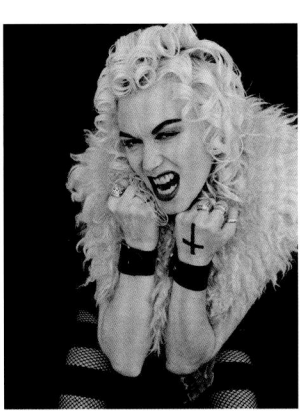

Who Do They Think They Are?

Issue: 4
Year: 1993
Model: Adam Tinley & Simon Monday from The Jet Slags / Mike from Mike Fab-Gere and The Permissive Society

Dance for the Masses

Issue: 4
Year: 1993
Model: Bunty Matthias

Pure Victims

Issue: Exhibitionism Supplement
Year: 1993
Model: Gordon, Jason, Sue, Marie-ann
Make-up: Tish Curry
Styling: Katie Grand

Oui Love You

Issue: 5
Year: 1993
Model: Blair Booth, Phillipe Erb & Trevor Miles from Oui 3

Also Available in Orange

Issue: 5
Year: 1993
Model: Owen, Claire, Alex, Anna / David Kappo / Cameron Richard Young / Mark Jackson / Eleanor Jinks
Hair: Glen Wood
Make-up: Glen Wood

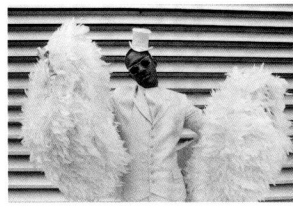

Denim Shot on Vacation

Issue: 5
Year: 1993
Model: Tourists found in London
Styling: Katie Grand

Pretty Vacant

Issue: 5
Year: 1993
Model: Keith Martin, Skinny
Styling: Katie Grand

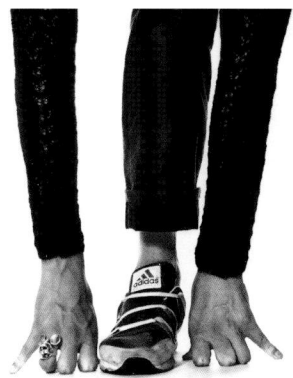

Back to Freality

Issue: 5
Year: 1993
Model: Justin Anderson & Aki Omori from Freaky Realistic

Complete and Unabridged

Issue: 5
Year: 1993
Model: Katie Carr, Jodie Anderson
Hair: Glen Wood
Make-up: Glen Wood
Styling: Katie Grand

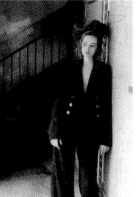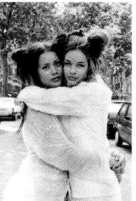

Get A Head

Issue: 5
Year: 1993
Model: Founders of Professor Head

TIMELINE

You Might As Well Face It, You'll Be Addicted To Life

Issue: 5
Year: 1993
Model: Sacha Parsons, Tim O'Riordan & James Harris from Lifes Addiction

Peeping Tom

Issue: 6
Year: 1993
Model: Jason, Fundji Ngelessy, Conran, Moni LeBon, Stephanie Starr
Hair: Glen Wood
Make-up: Glen Wood
Styling: Conran Morrison

Been There, Seen It, Done It!

Issue: 6
Year: 1993
Model: Donna
Hair: Johnny
Make-up: Carl Stanley
Styling: Katie Grand

Access All Areas

Issue: 6
Year: 1993
Model: Jenny from Slapper Magazine

Fashion x5

Issue: 6
Year: 1993
Model: Stephanie
Make-up: Sharon

Have You Heard The One About

Issue: 6
Year: 1993
Model: Eddie Izzard
Make-up: Emma Kotch

No Space

Issue: 6
Year: 1993
Model: Sacha Parsons, Zoe, Jodie, Polly, Emma
Hair: Johnny
Make-up: Sami Jackson, Carl Stanley & Sharon
Styling: Katie Grand & Vanessa Rubio

Bright Lights, Big City

Issue: Mission Impossible: New York and the New Music Seminar Supplement
Year: 1993
Model: Jerry from The Veldt / David Alter, Christopher Curtis, Lance Robertson & Steve Thomas From My Other Self / Shirley Manson from Angelfish / Jennifer Lewis aka Evergreen
Location: New York

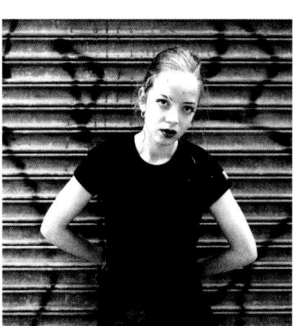

Blow Up! In New York

Issue: Mission Impossible: New York and the New Music Seminar Supplement
Year: 1993
Model: New York Clubbers
Location: Disco 2000 / Nylon / Club USA, NYC

Lifestyles of the Rich & Raucous

Issue: Mission Impossible: New York and the New Music Seminar Supplement
Year: 1993
Model: Gilbert Gottfried & The Ramones
Location: New York

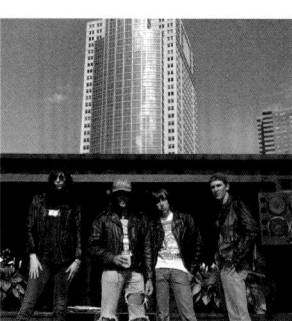

Cool Calling

Issue: Mission Impossible: New York and the New Music Seminar Supplement
Year: 1993
Model: Johnny Brennan & Kamal Ahmed from The Jerky Boys
Location: New York

King of Clubs

Issue: Mission Impossible: New York and the New Music Seminar Supplement
Year: 1993
Model: Peter Gatien
Location: New York

On Lead Guitar...

Issue: Mission Impossible: New York and the New Music Seminar Supplement
Year: 1993
Model: Adam Bomb
Location: New York

Voodoo Chile

Issue: Mission Impossible: New York and the New Music Seminar Supplement
Year: 1993
Model: Darius James
Location: New York

Music Maestro

Issue: Mission Impossible: New York and the New Music Seminar Supplement
Year: 1993
Model: David Morales
Location: New York

Isabella Blow

Issue: 7
Year: 1994
Model: Isabella Blow
Hair: Spencer Gymer
Make-up: Charlotte Tilbury
Styling: Model's own
Location: Click Studios

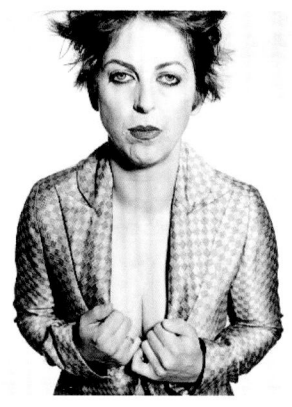

The Next Great British Rock 'N' Roll Star?

Issue: 7
Year: 1994
Model: Beth Orton
Hair: Emma Kotch
Make-up: Emma Kotch
Styling: Katie Grand

In The City

Issue: 7
Year: 1994
Model: Martin Wright, Ian Bendelow, Martin Mittler, Spencer Birtwistle, Stella Grundy & Lil' Anthony from Intastella / Heitham Al Sayed from Senser / Richard Ashcroft from The Verve
Location: Manchester, UK

Blow Up!

Issue: 7
Year: 1994
Model: Manchester Clubbers
Styling: Model's Own

Sign of the Times

Issue: 7
Year: 1994
Model: Gin Godden, Sacha Parsons
Make-up: Emma Kotch
Styling: Katie Grand

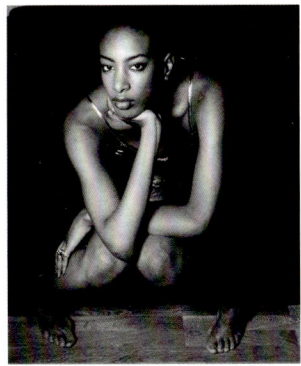

Been There, Seen It, Done It!

Issue: 7
Year: 1994
Model: Jodie Anderson
Hair: Emma Kotch
Make-up: Emma Kotch
Styling: Becky Earley

T.V. is Boring

Issue: 7
Year: 1994
Model: Felina Mia Tramonti
Styling: Katie Grand

Look Me in the Eyes

Issue: 7
Year: 1994
Model: Owen Gaster

No Future

Issue: 7
Year: 1994
Model: Bradford Kids
Location: Bradford, UK

Young British Artists III

Issue: 7
Year: 1994
Model: Jenny Saville / Simon English

Circle Line

Issue: 7
Year: 1994
Model: Jimmy Dixon
Styling: John Spencer

David Begbie

Issue: 7
Year: 1994
Model: David Begbie

Been There, Seen It, Done It!

Issue: 8
Year: 1994
Model: Monica
Hair: Hina Dohi
Make-up: Hina Dohi

Death Masks

Issue: 8
Year: 1994
Model: Katie Grand / Judy Blame / Edward Enninful / Karl Templer / John Bland / Lucinda Alford
Hair: Hina Dohi
Make-up: Hina Dohi
Grooming: Liz Daxtaeur, Jo Peters
Styling: Model's Own

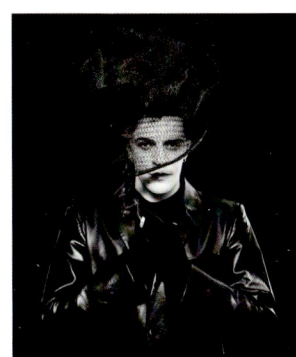

Perpetuating the Myth of the Artist as a Rock and Roll Star

Issue: 8
Year: 1994
Model: Damien Hirst
Styling: Model's Own

Loaded and Ready to Explode

Issue: 8
Year: 1994
Model: Louis Elliot, John Bull, Nick Powell & Julian Fenton from Kinky Machine
Hair: Lynne Barry
Grooming: Lynne Barry
Styling: Katie Grand

Teenage Dream

Issue: 8
Year: 1994
Model: Milla Jovovich

Ghosts

Issue: 8
Year: 1994
Model: Jackie Volker, Kathryn Klugal, John
Hair: Phillipe Balmain
Make-up: Esther Bihore, Fukiko
Styling: Katie Grand

Posh Punks

Issue: 9
Year: 1994
Model: Donovan Leitch from Nancy Boy
Hair: Nicky Whelan
Make-up: Nicky Whelan
Styling: Katie Grand

Mo Wax Than Most

Issue: 9
Year: 1994
Model: James Lavelle

International, Jetset DJ and No Star

Issue: 9
Year: 1994
Model: Sasha

Björk Needs No Introduction...

Issue: 9
Year: 1994
Model: Björk
Location: St Albans, UK

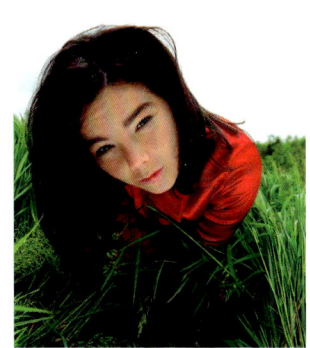

TIMELINE

Inside Out

Issue: 9
Year: 1994
Model: Liz Edwards, Gary Sewell
Hair: Esther Bihore
Make-up: Jo Karsberg
Styling: John Spencer

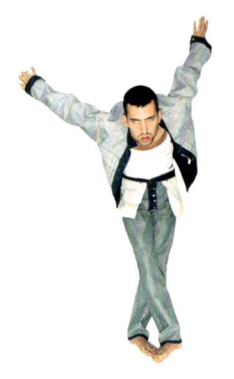

Conflicting Conviction: Alexander McQueen

Issue: 9
Year: 1994
Model: Angelica Boss
Hair: Vanessa Evelyn
Make-up: Vanessa Evelyn
Styling: Katie Grand
Location: New York

Fashion Television In the Box

Issue: 9
Year: 1994
Model: Jade
Hair: Esther Bihore
Make-up: Jo Karsberg
Styling: Katie Grand

Been There, Seen It, Done It!

Issue: 9
Year: 1994
Model: Barney, Ama / Kira
Hair: Vanessa Evelyn, Nicky Whelan
Make-up: Vanessa Evelyn, Nicky Whelan
Styling: Katie Grand, Soltan

Smile, It's Easy!

Issue: 9
Year: 1994
Model: Kitty, Jo, Vic, Lisa, Fred, Marlon, Zak
Styling: Easy Jeans
Location: Prince Street, SoHo, NYC

Things That Make You Go MMM...

Issue: Mission Impossible: Edinburgh and the Fringe Festival Supplement
Year: 1994
Model: Alan Davies / Phil Kay
Location: Edinburgh

'Shots from the Armpit'

Issue: Mission Impossible: Edinburgh and the Fringe Festival Supplement
Year: 1994
Model: Irvine Welsh
Location: Edinburgh

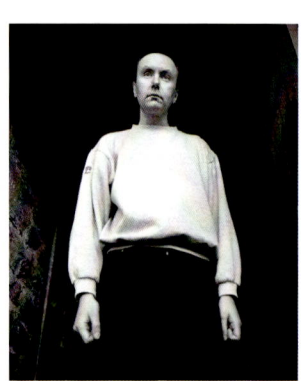

Who Do You Think You're Looking At?

Issue: Mission Impossible: Edinburgh and the Fringe Festival Supplement
Year: 1994
Model: Dave Dorrell / Ian Gelder / Smiley
Location: Edinburgh

Based on a True Story?

Issue: Mission Impossible: Edinburgh and the Fringe Festival Supplement
Year: 1994
Model: Crissy Rock
Location: Edinburgh

The Kylie Bible

Issue: Kylie Minogue Supplement
Year: 1994
Model: Kylie Minogue
Hair: Sharon Ives
Make-up: Sharon Ives
Styling: Katie Grand

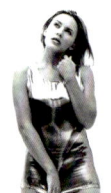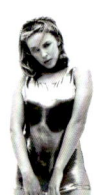

Weep

Issue: 10
Year: 1995
Model: Katie Comer, Katie Carr, James Gooding, Caroline Taylor, Stephanie Green
Hair: Thomas Dunkin
Make-up: Sarah Coleman
Styling: Katie Grand

Auteur American

Issue: 10
Year: 1995
Model: Hal Hartley
Styling: Model's Own

Heavy Metal

Issue: 10
Year: 1995
Hair: Esther Bihore
Make-up: Virginia Young
Styling: Katy England

Been There, Seen It, Done It!

Issue: 10
Year: 1995
Model: Tracey E / Alex Culpin, Richard Davies, Norma Jean Wilow & Jon Solomon from Tiny Monroe

The Patsy Kensit Affair

Issue: 10
Year: 1995
Model: Patsy Kensit
Hair: Vanessa Evelyn
Make-up: Vanessa Evelyn
Styling: Katie Grand

Their Idea of Fun

Issue: 10
Year: 1995
Model: Will Self, Tim Simenom

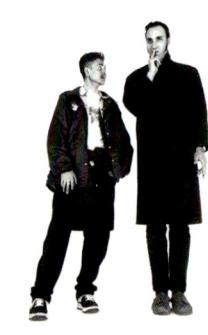

Art Club 2000

Issue: 11
Year: 1995
Model: AC2KUK
Hair: Lisa Fensome
Make-up: Lisa Fensome
Clothes: Vivienne Westwood

Like a Rhinestone Loudboy

Issue: 11
Year: 1995
Model: Richard E. Grant
Styling: Katie Grand

Been There, Seen It, Done It!

Issue: 11
Year: 1995
Model: Sally & Sarah Edwards from Blag Magazine

Space Man

Issue: 11
Year: 1995
Model: Jas Mann from Babylon Zoo
Hair: Nicky Whelan
Make-up: Nicky Whelan
Styling: John Spencer

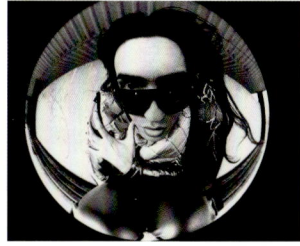

The Desire for Fame

Issue: 11
Year: 1995
Model: Arthur Smith
Styling: Model's Own

Sox

Year: 1995
Model: Sacha Parsons, Louise Tooey, Tabitha Denholdt, Vanessa Rubio
Hair: Gary
Make-up: Laura dos Remedios
Styling: Katie Grand

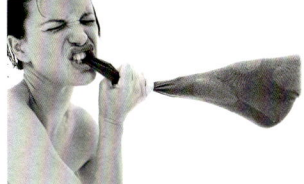

Cross Dressing

Issue: 12
Year: 1995
Model: Liz Edwards, Abe, Amanda, Adia, Kate Hardie, Steph
Hair: Esther Bihore
Make-up: Christopher Ardoff
Styling: Frank

Two for the Price of One

Issue: 12
Year: 1995
Model: Emma Webb, Anita Pallenburg, Rosie, Kina, Jacqueline Wallace, Jake the dog
Hair: Stephen Lacey, Gordon Pinder
Make-up: Jackie Hamilton-Smith, Christopher Ardoff
Styling: Katie Grand

Salad

Issue: 12
Year: 1995
Model: Marijne van der Vlugt, Paul Kennedy, Pete Brown & Rob Wakeman from Salad

It's Not What You Wear It's The Way That You Wear It

Issue: 13
Year: 1995
Model: Kristina Hawkes
Hair: Esther Bihore
Make-up: Maria G2 Luigi
Styling: John Spencer

Too Busy Staying Alive

Issue: 13
Year: 1995
Model: Richard Ashcroft from The Verve

Ask Me Later

Issue: 13
Year: 1995
Model: Kathy Burke
Styling: Model's Own

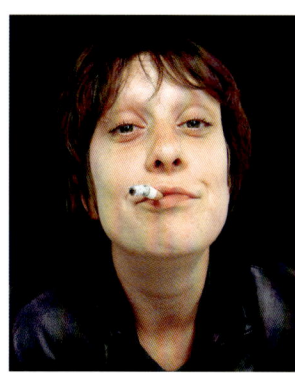

Fashion Extra

Issue: 13
Year: 1995
Model: Claudia M
Hair: Alain Pichon
Make-up: Sharon Dowsett
Styling: Katy England

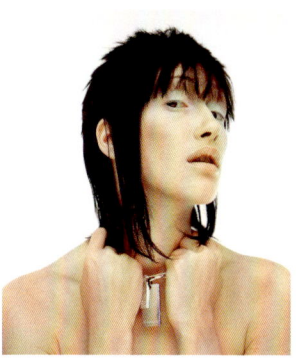

Katrin Cartlidge

Issue: 13
Year: 1995
Model: Katrin Cartlidge

Eye Spy

Issue: 14
Year: 1995
Model: Martha Plimpton

No Different from Anyone Else?

Issue: 14
Year: 1995
Model: David Bowie
Hair: Teddy Antolin
Make-up: Paul Starr
Location: Smashbox Studios, LA

Big Girl's Blouse

Issue: 14
Year: 1995
Model: Jacqueline Wallace, Nicky Clarke
Hair: Adam Bryant
Make-up: Julie Thomas
Styling: Katy England

The World According to...

Issue: 14
Year: 1995
Model: Jas Mann from Babylon Zoo
Hair: Stephen Lacey
Make-up: Nicky Whelan, Mandy Winrow
Styling: Katie Grand

The Changing Faces of...

Issue: 14
Year: 1995
Model: Alister Mackie, Carol-Anne, Margot Dillon, Mystic Mill, Lina Bergman
Hair: Adam Bryant
Make-up: Rachel Howarth
Styling: Katy England

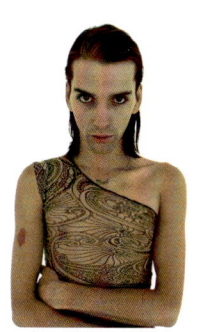

TIMELINE

MMM AAAHH!

Issue: 14
Year: 1995
Model: Móeiður
Júníusdóttir
aka Móa from Bong
Hair: Adam Bryant
Make-up: Emma Kotch
Styling: Charty Durrant

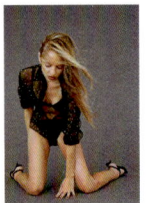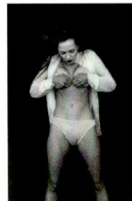

Looking Up

Issue: 14
Year: 1995
Model: Gerard, Lina
Bergman
Hair: Kevin Ford
Make-up: Kevin Ford
Styling: Katie Grand

Wok Weeble Chairs

Issue: 14
Year: 1995
Model: Sarah Smith/
McLoughlin
Styling: Harriet Orman

Hungry?

Issue: 15
Year: 1995
Model: Alex Leigh
Hair: Adam Bryant
Make-up: Sharon Dowsett
Styling: Katie Grand

It's a Wrap

Issue: 15
Year: 1995
Model: Steve Mackie, Nick
Banks, Jarvis
Cocker, Candida
Doyle, Mark
Webber, Russell
Senior from Pulp

Garbage

Issue: 15
Year: 1995
Model: Shirley Manson
from Garbage

Hits from the...

Issue: 15
Year: 1995
Model: Móeiður
Júníusdóttir aka
Móa from Bong

Private & Confidential

Issue: 15
Year: 1995
Model: Lili Taylor

A Law Unto Himself

Issue: 15
Year: 1995
Model: Jude Law
Location: New York, USA

Close Up

Issue: 16
Year: 1995
Model: Marijne van der
Vlugt from Salad
/ Kylie Minogue /
Isabel Monteiro
from Drugstore /
Louise Wener from
Sleeper

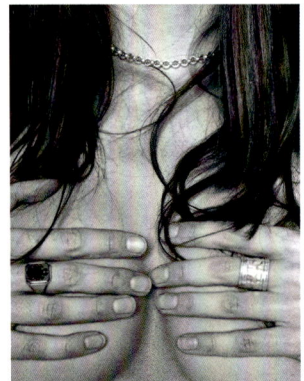

Sad Lad

Issue: 16
Year: 1995
Model: David Newby
Grooming: Emma Kotch
Styling: Alister Mackie

Keep It On!

Issue: 16
Year: 1995
Model: Comfort from
Out of My Hair

Nanu Nanu Björk Calling...

Issue: 16
Year: 1995
Model: Björk
Location: Providence, New
Hampshire, USA

Guess Who?

Issue: 16
Year: 1995
Model: Patsy Kensit
Hair: Adam Bryant
Make-up: Sarah Reygate
Styling: Katie Grand

Benz

Issue: 16
Year: 1995
Model: Tim Shade,
Darkboy, Big Ben
from Benz

It's All a Veneer

Issue: 17
Year: 1995
Model: Kate Groombridge
Hair: Colin Gold
Make-up: Vanessa Evelyn
Styling: Katie Grand
Location: Del's Diner

Talk of the Devil

Issue: 17
Year: 1995
Model: Tori Amos
Hair: Billie Currie
Make-up: Sharon Dowsett
Styling: Katie Grand and
William Baker

Pack Your Trunks

Issue: 17
Year: 1995
Model: James Redmond,
Greg Payne, Steven
Smith, Mark & Myles
Grooming: Val Garland
Styling: Alister Mackie

Ambient Talk, Aether Sound and Music for Babies

Issue: 17
Year: 1995
Model: Howie B

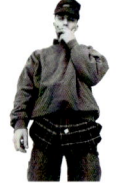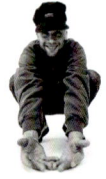

Unzipped

Issue: 18
Year: 1996
Model: Kate Groombridge
Styling: Katie Grand

Outsider as Leading Man

Issue: 18
Year: 1996
Model: Martin Donovan

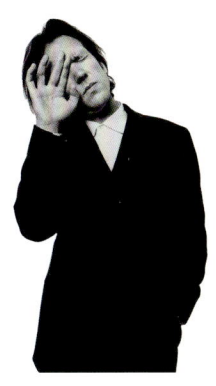

Silver Ladies

Issue: 18
Year: 1996
Model: Margot Dillon, Jean
Hair: Adam Bryant
Make-up: Sharon Dowsett
Styling: Katie Grand
Clothes: Isaac Mizrahi

Ocean Colour The Scene

Issue: 18
Year: 1996
Model: Steve Cradock,
Damon Minchella,
Oscar Harrison &
Simon Fowler from
Ocean Colour Scene
Location: The Royal
Holloway College,
Egham / The White
Room / The Custard
Factory,
Birmingham

Honeycrack

Issue: 18
Year: 1996
Model: Pete Clarke, Mark
McRae, Willy
Dowling, CJ from
Honeycrack

Gone F'shion

Issue: 19
Year: 1996
Model: Kara, Kathleen,
Grey, Laya
Hair: Paul Lopes
Make-up: Julie Begin
Styling: Charlotte
Stockdale
Location: Manumission at
The Palace
Club, Paris

You do it to Yourself

Issue: 19
Year: 1996
Model: Thom Yorke from
Radiohead
Styling: Model's Own

Surveillance

Issue: 19
Year: 1996
Model: Edward Ferguson,
Boppo
Styling: Alister Mackie

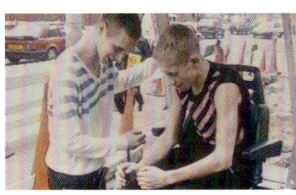

What's Love Got To Do With It?

Issue: 19
Year: 1996
Model: Jon & Helena Marsh
from The Beloved
Nude Model: Steve &
Phyllis

Screaming to be Heard

Issue: 19
Year: 1996
Model: Nut Goscovitch

Straight to the Point

Issue: 20
Year: 1996
Model: Elvis Costello
Styling: Model's Own

Who's That Girl?

Issue: 20
Year: 1996
Model: Chloë Sevigny
Hair: Linda Daniele
Make-up: Christine
Hoffman
Styling: Jennifer Elster

Touch Your Toes

Issue: 20
Year: 1996
Model: Nicole Merry
Hair: Liam Dunn
Make-up: Liam Dunn
Styling: Katie Grand

Close Up and Personal

Issue: 21
Year: 1996
Model: James Dean
Bradfield, Sean
Moore, Nicky
Wire from Manic
Street Preachers
Concept: Mark Farrow

A Private Perspective

Issue: 22
Year: 1996
Model: Neneh Cherry
Hair: Kevin Ford
Make-up: Jackie Hamilton-
Smith
Styling: Katie Grand

Free Spirit

Issue: 22
Year: 1996
Model: Ingrid Schroeder
Hair: Gary Halliday, Mira
Make-up: Alice Ioanna,
Mira
Styling: Katie Grand,
Cathy Edwards

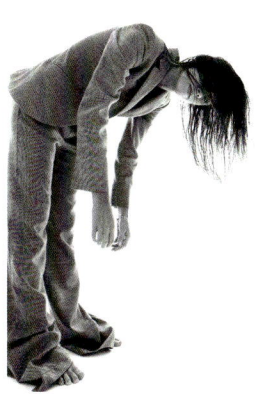

The All-Girl Club

Issue: 23
Year: 1996
Model: Róisín Murphy from
Moloko / Kelli Ali
from Sneaker Pimps
/ Martina Topley-
Bird from Tricky /
Lou Rhodes from
Lamb / Ingrid
Schroeder / Ruth-
Ann Boyle from
Olive / Roba El-
Essawy from Attica
Blues / Skye
Edwards from
Morcheeba / Lesley
Rankine from Ruby
/ Beth Orton /
Andrea Parker /
Nicolette Love
Suwoton
Hair: Esther Bihore
Make-up: Alice Ioanna,
Catherine
Dargenton
Styling: Katie Grand

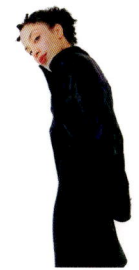

TIMELINE

Snkr Pmps Rgo!

Issue: 24
Year: 1996
Model: Kelli Ali, Liam Howe, Chris Corner from Sneaker Pimps
Hair: Moose
Make-up: Sharon Dowsett
Styling: Katie Grand

M'Donna

Issue: 24
Year: 1996
Model: Donna Matthews from Elastica, Seb Franklin, Sam Talhi, Francesca Goddard, Alison Bender, Lucy Capstick, Edine Talhi, Katie Howerd
Hair: Adam Bryant
Make-up: Sharon Dowsett
Styling: Katy England

Faking It!

Issue: 25
Year: 1996
Model: Natasha Elms
Hair: Moose
Make-up: Sharon Dowsett
Styling: Katie Grand

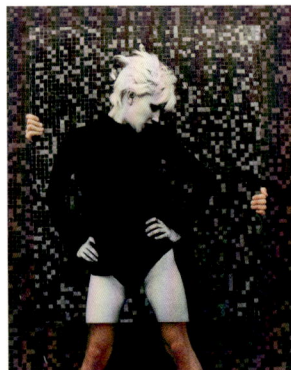

No I.D. Necessary

Issue: 25
Year: 1996
Model: Charlotte Connoley
Hair: Barnabé
Make-up: Sharon Dowsett
Styling: Katy England

Lost & Found

Issue: 25
Year: 1996
Model: Evan Dando from The Lemonheads

Obsessive Behaviour

Issue: 25
Year: 1996
Model: Natasha Elms, Robbie Williams
Hair: Moose
Make-up: Angie Parker
Styling: Katie Grand
Concept: Gerrard Saint

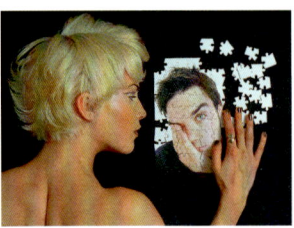

Our Main Man

Issue: 26
Year: 1996
Model: Robert Carlyle
Styling: Alister Mackie, Katie Grand, Miranda Almond

The Cast

Issue: 26
Year: 1996
Model: Richard E. Grant / Brenda Blethyn / Mike Figgis / Steven Mackintosh / Ewen Bremner / Kate Hardie / Emily Mortimer / Charlotte Rampling / Tilda Swinton / Ben Daniels / Aidan Gillen / Marianne Jean-Baptiste / Alan Rickman / Carl Prechezer & Peter Salmi / David Thewlis / Jim Carter & Imelda Staunton / Charles Sturridge / Jared Harris / James Fox / Peter Greenaway / Greta Scacchi / Thandiwe Newton / Kelly Macdonald & Laura Fraser / Martha Fiennes / Philip Ridley / Alan Parker / Bruce Robinson / Georgina Cates / Frances Barber / Minnie Driver / Charlotte Coleman / Iain Robertson / Terry Gilliam / Ian Hart / Katrin Cartlidge / Phil Daniels / Naveen Andrews / Stephen Frears / Kathy Burke & Ray Winstone / Philip Davis / Phyllida Law / Tony Marchant / Kate Winslet / Jude Law / Glen Berry / James Frain / Lee Ross / Nicholas Roeg / Hettie Macdonald / Sara Sugarman & Miranda Richardson / Jonny Phillips / Dominic West / Jim Cartwright / Linus Roache / Derek Jacobi
Hair: Jefferson, Lesley Sayles, Alison Fanning, Charlotte Tilbury, Britta Dicke, Helen Walsh, Carol Hart, Moose, Hina Dohi, Alain Pichon, Glen Woods, Tine Waldensels, Esther Bihore
Make-up: Jefferson, Lesley Sayles, Alison Fanning, Charlotte Tilbury, Britta Dicke, Helen Walsh, Carol Hart, Moraid, Hina Dohi, Glen Woods, Tine Waldensels, Esther Bihore
Styling: Miranda Almond, Alister Mackie, Katie Grand, Lucy Ewing, Martha Taylor, John Spencer, Amanda Gowing

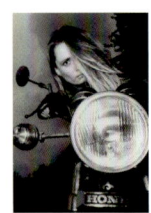
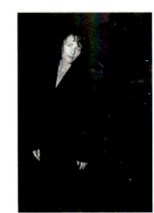
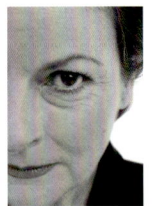
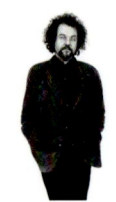
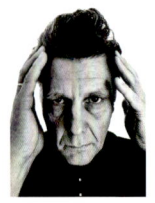
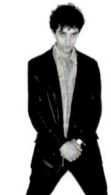
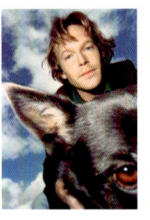
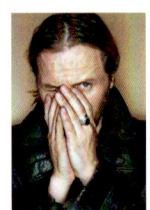
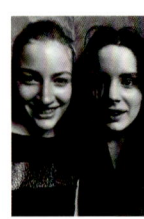
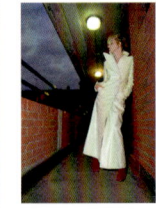
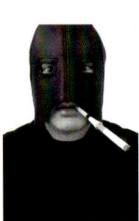
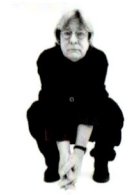
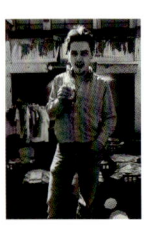
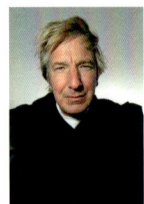

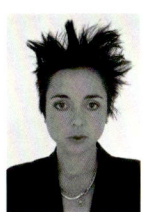
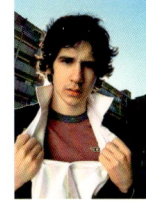
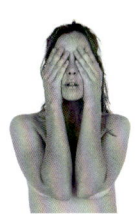
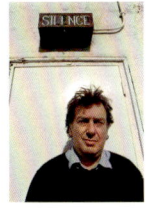
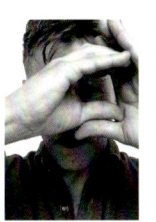
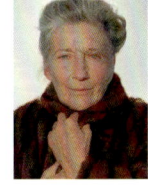
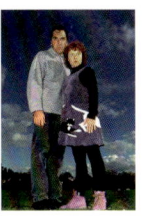
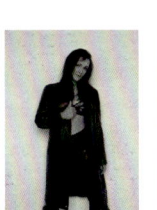
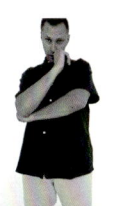
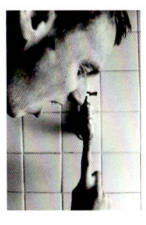

Shooting Star

Issue: 27
Year: 1996
Model: Lili Taylor
Styling: Miranda Almond

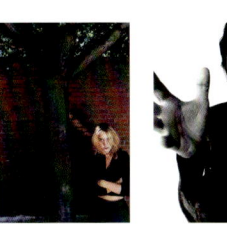

Ragga and the Jack Magic Orchestra

Issue: 27
Year: 1996
Model: Ragnhildur
Gísladóttir from
Ragga and the Jack
Magic Orchestra

In the Meantime

Issue: 27
Year: 1996
Model: Raissa
Hair: Glen Woods,
Helen Walsh
Make-up: Glen Woods,
Helen Walsh
Styling: Miranda Almond

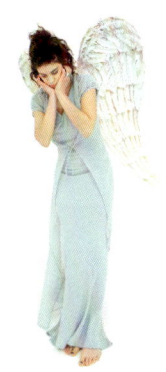

Let's Go Warhol!!!

Issue: 27
Year: 1996
Model: Mary Harron

Jet Set

Issue: 27
Year: 1996
Model: Charlotte Connoley,
Natasha Elms
Hair: Jennie Roberts
Make-up: Glen Woods
Styling: Matt Alas

Ultra Stimulation

Issue: 28
Year: 1997
Model: Finley Quaye
Grooming: Kevin Ford
Styling: Miranda Almond

Cool as Fuck

Issue: 29
Year: 1997
Model: Beck

The Diggers

Issue: 29
Year: 1997
Model: John Eslick, Chris
Mietzitis, Alan
Moffat, Hank Ross
from The Diggers

Plain

Issue: 29
Year: 1997
Model: Laura Palmer
Hair: Paul Lopes
Styling: Charlotte
Stockdale
Make-up: Gina Crozier

The Asian Dance Underground

Issue: 30
Year: 1997
Model: Patrina Morris /
Sanjeev Varma aka
"CoCo", Sanjeve
Rupal & Sanjay
Varma aka "Duke"
from Earthtribe
/ Anju Sharda &
Peter Morris from
The Core
Hair: Moose
Make-up: Liz Pugh
Styling: Miranda Almond

Twisting my Lemon Man

Issue: 30
Year: 1997
Model: Larry Mullen Jr,
Adam Clayton,
Bono & The Edge
from U2
Hair: Helen Dean
Make-up: Helen Dean
Styling: Sharon Blankson

3 Imaginary Boys

Issue: 30
Year: 1997
Model: James Barnett,
Lalo Creme & Ollie
Jacobs from
Arkarna
Hair: Liz Pugh
Make-up: Liz Pugh
Styling: Mark Anthony

Highly Flammable

Issue: 31
Year: 1997
Model: Natasha Elms
Hair: Moose
Make-up: Jackie Hamilton-
Smith
Styling: Miranda Almond

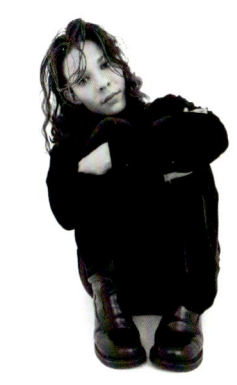

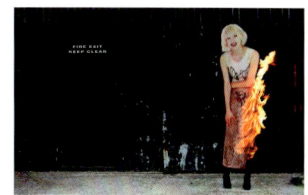

TIMELINE

What's the Story?

Issue: 31
Year: 1997
Model: Rhys Ifans
Grooming: Charlotte
　　　　　Tilbury
Styling: Miranda Almond

Folk Explosion

Issue: 31
Year: 1997
Model: Terry Callier &
　　　　Beth Orton

Jaguar

Issue: 31
Year: 1997
Model: Julian Carr,
　　　　Malcolm Carson &
　　　　Tam Johnstone from
　　　　Jaguar
Grooming: Jenny Roberts
Styling: Miranda Almond

Are You Alright?

Issue: 32
Year: 1997
Model: Terry Hall

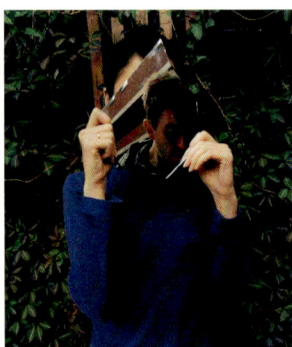

C'mon, Let's Have It

Issue: 32
Year: 1997
Model: Richard Ashcroft,
　　　　Simon Jones, Pete
　　　　Salisbury, Simon
　　　　Tong & Nick McCabe
　　　　from The Verve
Styling: Model's Own

Non-Stop Moveable Freak Show...

Issue: 32
Year: 1997
Model: Jamie, Allan, Liam
　　　　& Simon from Geek
Grooming: Glen Woods,
　　　　　　Kinuko
Hair: Paula Weir
Styling: Miranda Almond

No Fear

Issue: 33
Year: 1997
Model: Luke Bullen,
　　　　Nikolaj Juel, Mark
　　　　Aston & James
　　　　Denham from Addict
Hair: Simon Bayliss
Make-up: Kate Lee

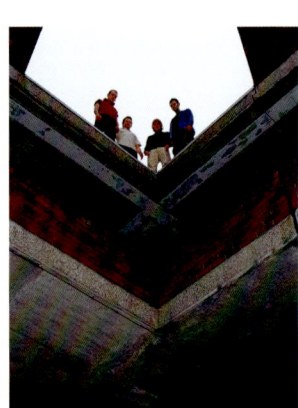

Flesh for Fantasy

Issue: 33
Year: 1997
Model: Helena Christensen
Hair: Malcolm Edwards
Make-up: Val Garland
Styling: Katie Grand

The Boys Are Back In Town

Issue: 34
Year: 1997
Model: Toby Slater, Wayne
　　　　Murray & Ben
　　　　Etchells from Catch
Hair: Mira
Grooming: H.B.
Styling: Katie Grand

Pop Art: Revolution for your Breakfast

Issue: 34
Year: 1997
Model: Damien Hirst
Grooming: Mira
Styling: Alister Mackie

The King is Alive

Issue: 35
Year: 1997
Model: Richard Fearless
　　　　from Death in Vegas

'aving It

Issue: 35
Year: 1997
Model: Charlie Creed-Miles

Something for the Weekend

Issue: 35
Year: 1997
Hair: Jonny Drill
Model: Matt, Avi Koifman,
　　　　Matt, Minky,
　　　　Rebecca, Margaret
　　　　Laing

Class of '97

Issue: 35
Year: 1997
Model: John Squire & Chris
　　　　Helme from
　　　　Seahorses /
　　　　Louise Wener
　　　　from Sleeper /
　　　　Skin from Skunk
　　　　Anansie / Talvin
　　　　Singh / Tim
　　　　Burgess from The
　　　　Charlatans / Thom
　　　　York, Jonny
　　　　Greenwood, Colin
　　　　Greenwood, Philip
　　　　Selway & Ed
　　　　O'Brien from
　　　　Radiohead / Tricky
　　　　/ Nick Banks,
　　　　Jarvis Cocker,
　　　　Candida Doyle,
　　　　Steve Mackie &
　　　　Mark Webber from
　　　　Pulp / Sean Moore,
James Bradfield &
Nicky Wire from
Manic Street
Preachers / Donna
Matthews & Justine
Frischmann from
Elastica / Richard
Ashcroft from The
Verve / Kelli Ali
from Sneaker Pimps
/ Damon Albarn
from Blur / Roba
El-Essawi, Charlie
D'afro & Tony
Nwachukwu from
Attica Blues / Lou
Rhodes & Andy
Barlow from Lamb /
Andrea Parker

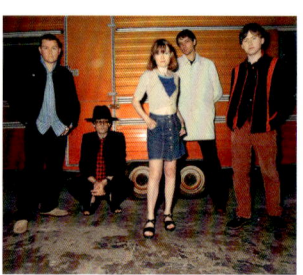

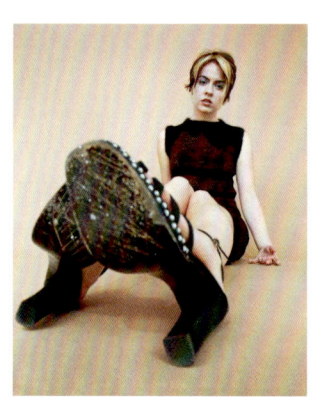

03 Minute Heroes

Issue: 35
Year: 1997
Model: Stephane Sednaoui
　　　　/ John Hardwick /
　　　　Pedro Romhanyi /
　　　　Walter Stern /
　　　　Jonathan Glazer
　　　　/ Wiz / Michel
　　　　Gondry / Nick
　　　　Abrahams & Mikey
　　　　Tompkins aka Trash
　　　　2000 / Dom Hawley
　　　　& Nick Joffey

Take Over TV...

Issue: 36
Year: 1997
Model: Swindeli, Mr Blonde, Browns Focus, Dr Jives, Stu Boy Stu, Snaykee & Roy Frost from Manbreak
Hair: Justin Mann
Make-up: Kate Lee
Styling: Charlotte Stockdale

Girls on Film

Issue: 36
Year: 1997
Model: Samantha Morton / Emily Watson / Katrin Cartlidge / Kate Hardie / Marianne Jean-Baptiste
Hair: Kevin Ford, Malcolm Edwards, Liz Martins, Jenny Roberts
Make-up: Charlotte Tilbury, Jackie Hamilton-Smith
Styling: Miranda Almond

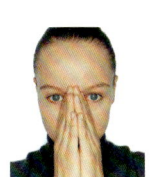 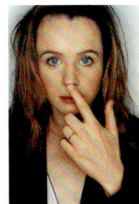

Hard Act to Follow

Issue: 37
Year: 1997
Model: Sophie Ellis-Bextor from Theaudience
Hair: Moose
Make-up: Kate Lee
Styling: Katie and Polly

Natalie Imbruglia

Issue: 37
Year: 1997
Model: Natalie Imbruglia
Styling: John Bland

Empire Strikes Back

Issue: 37
Year: 1997
Model: Adam Yauch & Mike D from The Beastie Boys

Hide & Seek

Issue: 37
Year: 1997
Model: Bobbie Gillespie from Primal Scream

Bra Zilch

Issue: 38
Year: 1998
Model: Marina Dias
Hair: Danilo Mazzuca
Make-up: Danilo Mazzuca
Styling: Cesar Fassina

Air Max

Issue: 38
Year: 1998
Model: Jean-Benoit Dunckle, Nicolas Godin from Air

Split Personalities

Issue: 39
Year: 1998
Model: Andrew "Mushroom" Vowles, Robert "3D" Del Naja & Grant "Daddy G" Marshall from Massive Attack
Grooming: Peter Gray
Styling: Mark Griffiths

The Spotlight's On...

Issue: 39
Year: 1998
Model: Emma Townshend
Hair: Lesley McMenamin
Make-up: J Maskrey
Styling: Miranda Almond

Get Your Mojo Working

Issue: 40
Year: 1998
Model: Aidan Gillen
Styling: Miranda Almond

Tear Along the Dotted Line

Issue: 40
Year: 1998
Model: Natalie Imbruglia
Hair: Peter Gray
Make-up: Charlotte Tilbury
Styling: Alice McCall

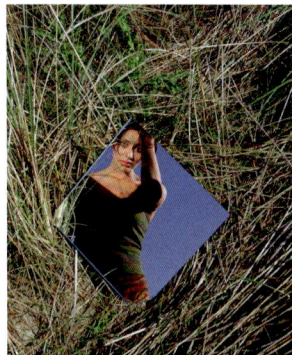

Famous Forever

Issue: 41
Year: 1998
Model: Peter Holmström, Courtney Taylor-Taylor, Zia McCabe & Eric Hedford from The Dandy Warhols
Hair: Mira
Make-up: Liz Martins
Styling: Simon Robins

Getting Into Gear

Issue: 42
Year: 1998
Model: Felix Taylor, Sam Hazeldine, James Powell, Erik Bower & John Ruscoe from Mover
Grooming: Liz Martins
Styling: Miranda Richardson

Tell 'Em About the Money

Issue: 42
Year: 1998
Model: Mark Ramos Nishita aka Money Mark

H is For

Issue: 43
Year: 1998
Model: Daniel Glendining, Tom Glendining, Clovis Taylor & Nick Watts from Headswim
Grooming: Kevin Ford
Styling: Miranda Almond

What's the First Word that Comes into Your Head?

Issue: 43
Year: 1998
Model: Kate Moss
Hair: Malcom Edwards
Make-up: Charlotte Tilbury
Styling: Katie Grand
Spray Paint: Peter Corrie

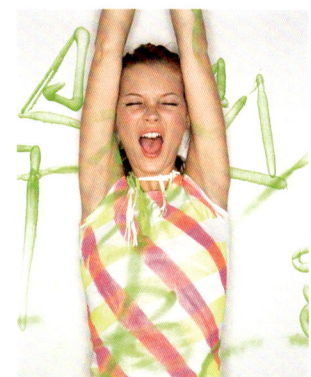

Asphyxiation

Issue: 44
Year: 1998
Model: Alissa Bennett, Sampsa
Hair: Carina Finnstrom
Make-up: Brenda Touhy
Styling: Sally O'Sullivan

TIMELINE

PJ Harvey

Issue: 45
Year: 1998
Model: Polly Jean Harvey aka PJ Harvey

What's in a Name?

Issue: 45
Year: 1998
Model: Mary Cassidy, Svet, Ben Blakeman & Del from Agnes
Hair: Terese Broccoli
Make-up: Jackie Hamilton-Smith
Styling: Miranda Almond

Baked Alaska: Diesel Style Lab A/W

Issue: 45
Year: 1998
Model: Josephine Rukia, Edward Ferguson, Jaimee Gong, Karta
Hair: Alain Pichon
Make-up: Val Garland
Styling: Diesel Creative

Mirren Mirren on the Wall

Issue: 46
Year: 1998
Model: Helen Mirren
Hair: Lesley McMenamin
Make-up: Sam Bryant
Styling: Cathy Edwards

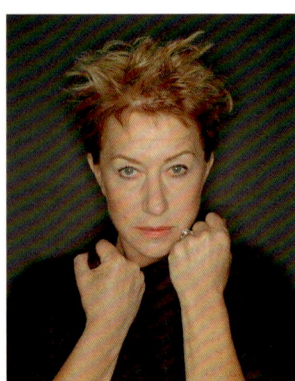

For Folk's Sake

Issue: 46
Year: 1998
Model: Noah Francis Johnson & Rayne from Johnson
Hair: Lesley McMenamin
Make-up: Liz Daxhaur
Styling: Miranda Almond

Everyone's Someone

Issue: 46
Year: 1998
Model: Kele Le Roc
Hair: Sherman Hawthorne
Make-up: Nadia Adorni
Styling: Miranda Almond

She's Got a Devil's Haircut on her Mind

Issue: 47
Year: 1998
Model: Beth Orton
Hair: Peter Gray
Make-up: Jackie Hamilton-Smith
Styling: Simon Robbins

Take It Away

Issue: 47
Year: 1998
Model: Astrid Williamson
Hair: Peter Gray
Make-up: Jackie Hamilton-Smith
Styling: Mark Anthony

The Eagle Has Landed

Issue: Desert Eagle Discs Supplement
Year: 1998
Model: Nik Nak / Homocide / Rebel Baz / Shari Syze-Up
Styling: Tabitha Simmons, Miranda Almond

What's The Difference Between Beautiful and Sexy?

Issue: 48
Year: 1998
Model: Angela Lindvall
Hair: Peter Gray
Make-up: Ashley Ward
Styling: Katie Grand
Concept: David Sebbha

Glow in the Dark

Issue: 48
Year: 1998
Model: Gina Rae, Jim Sutherland & Silvia Rae from The Lanterns
Hair: Lesley McMenamin
Make-up: Christian McCullogh
Styling: Tabitha and Cathy

Transperm

Issue: 49
Year: 1998
Model: Audrey, Lydia
Hair: Peter Gray
Make-up: Max Delorme
Styling: Yvonne Sporre

The Mood I'm In

Issue: 49
Year: 1998
Model: Anja Garbarek
Hair: Mark Anderson
Make-up: Jackie Hamilton-Smith
Styling: Miranda Almond

You're Making Me Hot

Issue: 49
Year: 1998
Model: Debbie Harry, Jimmy Destri, Clem Burke & Chris Stein from Blondie
Hair: Malcom Edwards
Make-up: Jackie Hamilton-Smith
Styling: Alister Mackie

Sexy Boys

Issue: 50
Year: 1999
Model: Philippe "Zdar" Cerboneschi & Hubert "Boombass" Blanc-Francard from Cassius / Laura Morgan, Louise Hargreaves, Kaja Wunder, Carin, Lin, Miele, Ulla, Essi, Sarah Wietzel
Hair: Peter Gray
Make-up: Sam Bryant, Christian McCulloch
Styling: Miranda Almond
Cut Out Photography: Simon Fly

Pop Psychology

Issue: 50
Year: 1999
Model: Kate Holmes & Xan Tyler from Technique
Hair: Mark Anderson
Make-up: Jackie Hamilton-Smith
Styling: Paul Frecker

You Bend

Issue: 50
Year: 1999
Model: Micky Hicks, Sara Daykin
Hair: Peter Gray
Make-up: Max Delorme
Styling: Yvonne Sporre

This is Where It's At

Issue: XFM 104.9 London Fashion Week Guide
Year: 1999
Model: Sophie Dahl
Hair: Lesley McMenamin
Make-up: Charlotte Tilbury

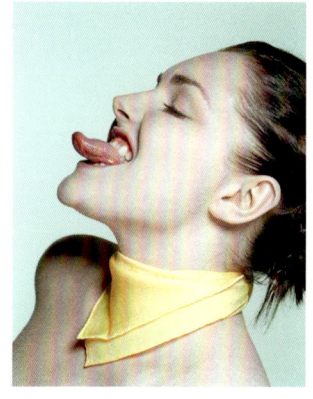

Viva La Revolution

Issue: 51
Year: 1999
Model: Kate Moss
Hair: James Brown
Make-up: Charlotte Tilbury
Styling: Katie Grand

Turn the Dark On

Issue: 52
Year: 1999
Model: Sanna Saastamoinen, Laura Kay
Hair: Colin Gold
Make-up: Emma Lovell
Styling: Jo Phillips

Slipslide Away

Issue: 52
Year: 1999
Model: Jennifer Turner, Jason Lader, & Adam MacDougall from Furslide
Hair: Mark Anderson
Make-up: Jackie Hamilton-Smith

Spare Parts

Issue: 52
Year: 1999
Model: Sanna Saastamoinen, Ivor, Amy Lunt, Nancy Hagen, Sveta
Hair: Paul Persival, Peter Gray
Make-up: Max Delorne, Christian McCulloch
Prosthetics: Kate J Thompson
Styling: Yvonne Sporre

Stranded: Diesel Style Lab S/S

Issue: 52
Year: 1999
Model: Laura Kay, Sanna Saastamoinen, Edward Ferguson, Sascha
Hair: Peter Gray
Make-up: Charlotte Tilbury
Styling: Diesel Creative

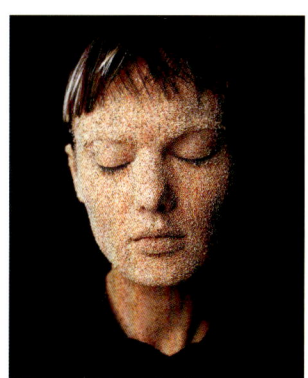

Hostess with the Mostess

Issue: Dazed & INCredible Supplement
Year: 1999
Model: Jo Whiley

Tear It Up and Start Again

Issue: 53
Year: 1999
Model: Nick Laird-Clowes aka Trashmonk

Synthetic Pleasures

Issue: 53
Year: 1999
Model: Jude Law, Ewan McGregor, Sadie Frost, Sean Pertwee
Hair: Peter Gray
Make-up: Jackie Hamilton-Smith
Styling: Miranda Almond

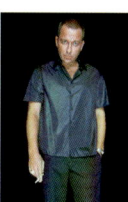

I Want It All

Issue: 53
Year: 1999
Model: Victoria Hogg
Hair: Peter Gray
Make-up: Jackie Hamilton-Smith

Where the Horizon Meets the Sea

Issue: Dazed & INCredibe Supplement
Year: 1999
Model: Goldie
Styling: Miranda Almond

Play the Fandango

Issue: 54
Year: 1999
Model: William Orbit
Sculpture: Jake & Dinos Chapman

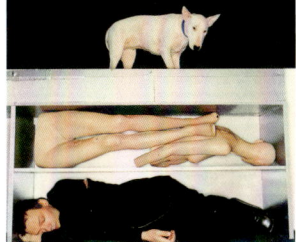

Heart Of the Matter

Issue: 54
Year: 1999
Model: Kate Hardie
Hair: Lesly McMenamin
Make-up: Christian McCulloch, Bobbie Brown
Styling: Heather Mary Jackson

It's All About You

Issue: 54
Year: 1999
Model: John Simm
Styling: Miranda Almond

Genuine Draft

Issue: 54
Year: 1999
Model: Harland Miller

My Story

Issue: 55
Year: 1999
Model: Kevin Rowland
Hair: Jay Fahey
Styling: Model's Own

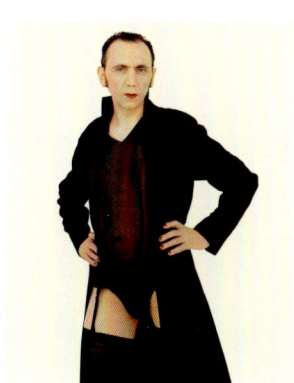

Sound Off

Issue: Dazed & INCredible Supplement
Year: 1999
Model: Trevor Nelson
Grooming: Sam Bryant, Mark Anderson
Styling: Miranda Almond

TIMELINE

Do You Remember...

Issue: 56
Year: 1999
Model: Lisa Marie
Hair: Malcolm Edwards
Make-up: Val Garland
Styling: Alister Mackie
Art Direction: Giles
            Deacon

Boys Who Like Girls

Issue: 56
Year: 1999
Model: Damon Albarn, Dave
        Rowntree, Graham
        Coxon & Alex James
        from Blur
Hair: Mark Anderson
Grooming: Sam Bryant
Styling: Miranda Almond
Image Manipulation:
        Justine Foord

Cheeky

Issue: 56
Year: 1999
Models: Chantal, Tilly,
        Kamilla, Anna,
        Madelaine, Sarah
        Wietzel
Make-up: Emma Lovell
Styling: Miranda Almond

Off the Main Stream

Issue: Dazed & INCredibe
        Supplement
Year: 1999
Model: Gilles Peterson
Grooming: Sam Bryant
Styling: Miranda Almond

The Things You Do When You're Bored

Issue: 57
Year: 1999
Model: Shelby Lynne
Hair: Oliver Wood
Make-up: Christian
        McCulloch
Styling: Miranda Almond

Meltdown

Issue: 57
Year: 1999
Model: Lauren Gold,
        Amanda
Hair: Mark Anderson,
        Shinya Nakayama
Make-up: Charlotte
        Tilbury
Styling: Miranda Almond
Model Casts: John
        Schoonraad
Retouching: Colin Humme

Emiliana

Issue: 57
Year: 1999
Model: Emiliana Torrini
Hair: Peter Gray
Make-up: Charlotte
        Tilbury
Styling: Mat Ryalls

From Take That To Now

Issue: Mark Owen Special
        Supplement
Year: 1999
Model: Mark Owen
Make-up: Hina Dohi
Styling: Alister Mackie,
        Katie Grand, Jo

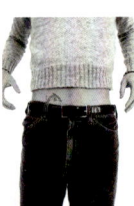 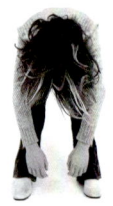

Guerilla Funk!

Issue: 58
Year: 1999
Model: Iza aka La Femme
        Fatale, Paulus
        aka Falcon,
        Canavese aka
        L'assassine,
        Ochowiak aka Mad
        Mich & Mellino aka
        El Diablo from Les
        Négresses Vertes
Styling: Heather Mary
        Jackson

Hell's Angels

Issue: 59
Year: 1999
Model: Melanie Blatt,
        Natalie Appleton,
        Nicole Appleton &
        Shaznay Lewis from
        All Saints
Hair: Alex Price
Make-up: Justin Henry
Styling: Heather Mary
        Jackson

Songs in the Key of Life

Issue: 61
Year: 1999
Model: Matthew James
        Firth aka MJ
        Cole, Elisabeth
        Troy
Hair: Shinya Nakayama
Make-up: Emma Lovell
Styling: Miranda Almond

Making Bass Noises

Issue: 61
Year: 1999
Model: Samantha Morton
Styling: Model's Own

Vidal Sassoon

Issue: 62
Year: 2000
Model: Sanna
        Saastamoinen, K,
        Jessy, Cheryl
Hair: Peter Gray
Make-up: Charlotte
        Tilbury, Val
        Garland

Just Say "Bo!"

Issue: Dazed & INCredibe
        Supplement
Year: 2000
Model: DJ Spoony, Timmi
        Magic & Mikee B
        from The Dreem Teem
Grooming: Jessie
Styling: Miranda Almond

Feel It

Issue: 63
Year: 2000
Model: Aron, Chris
        Farrell, Mebrak
        Tareke, Zora Star,
        David, Jocelyn,
        James Rousseau,
        Lulla, Tanja,
        Jamie Del Moon
Hair: Alain Pichon
Make-up: Val Garland
Styling: Alister Mackie

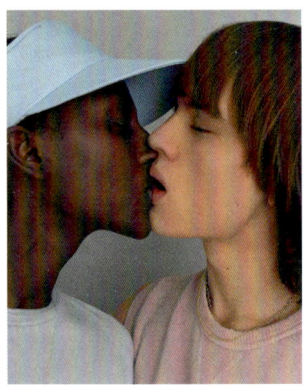

Based on a True Story

Issue: 64
Year: 2000
Model: Hilary Swank
Hair: Clyde Haygood
Make-up: Jeanine Lobell
Styling: Maria Serra

Revolution in the Head

Issue: 68
Year: 2000
Model: Michael Stipe from
        R.E.M.
Make-up: Lisa Eldridge
Styling: Alister Mackie

The Menswear Issue

Issue: 68
Year: 2000
Model: Ben North
Styling: Alister Mackie

Give the Drummer Some

Issue: 70
Year: 2000
Model: Charlie Watts from The Rolling Stones

Lone Star

Issue: 71
Year: 2000
Model: Shea Seger
Hair: Shinya Nakayama
Make-up: Jackie Hamilton-Smith
Styling: Miranda Almond

Sense

Issue: 72
Year: 2000
Model: Lisa Ratliffe
Hair: Richard Scorer
Make-up: Wendy Rowe
Styling: Miranda Almond

Mathmos - Let There Be Light

Issue: 72
Year: 2000
Model: Valeria, Anna L
Hair: Shinya Nakayama
Make-up: Jackie Hamilton-Smith

Queen B

Issue: 73
Year: 2001
Model: Jane Birkin
Hair: Shinya Nakayama
Make-up: Emma Lovell

Double Edged...

Issue: 74
Year: 2001
Model: Aidan Gillen

Vision 1: Zoe Manzi

Issue: 75
Year: 2001
Model: Zoe Manzi
Hair: Shinya Nakayama
Make-up: Lisa Houghton

Year Zero

Issue: 76
Year: 2001
Model: Jodell, William, Kieran, Daniel, Charmaine, Levi, Jennifer, Ben, Daniel, Rory, Taya, Amelia, Danté, Leona, August-Jade, Gromit, Emma, Jeanette, Jack, Tavia, Twinkle, Beccy, Amber, Moe, Joe, Rio
Hair: Shinya Nakayama

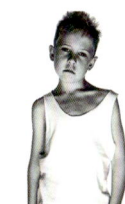

Toni & Guy

Issue: 78
Year: 2001
Model: Caroline Roy, Liv, Joanne Grittiths, Hen Yani, Vivi, Georgina
Hair: Antony Moscolo, Steve Terry, Nick Irwin, Gary France
Make-up: Pat Moscolo
Styling: Miranda Almond

Faked & Confused

Issue: 79
Year: 2001
Model: Navi King
Retouching: Becky

Wanted: Reasons to Combat the Doom and Gloom...

Issue: 85
Year: 2002
Model: Anne
Hair: Cher Savery
Make-up: Liz Draxhaur

Mother and Pearl

Issue: 85
Year: 2002
Model: Pearl Lowe

Touched Up

Issue: 85
Year: 2002
Model: Claire Elliot, Anne Vyalitsyna, Lisa Lauwaert, Caitriona, Rassa
Hair: Sascha Breuer
Make-up: Lisa Houghton
Styling: Miranda Almond

25 Ways to Wear Spring Summer 2002

Issue: 87
Year: 2002
Styling: Miranda Almond
Clothes: Gucci

The Cover Story

Issue: 87
Year: 2002
Model: Harland Miller
Styling: Model's Own
Location: Harland Miller's Studio

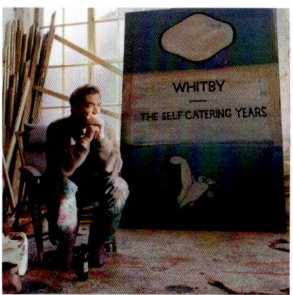

100% of Me

Issue: 89
Year: 2002
Model: Ms. Dynamite
Hair: Paul Hanlon
Make-up: Pep Gay
Styling: Cathy Edwards, Nicola Formichetti

The Space Between Us

Issue: 89
Year: 2002
Model: Imogen Heap & Guy Sigsworth from Frou Frou
Hair: Paul Hanlon
Make-up: Lisa Houghton

Elvis Lives

Issue: 91
Year: 2002
Model: Marios Schwab, Nicola Formichetti, Lizzie Finn, Remi, Leah Wood, Elizabeth Jagger, Sara Burn, Emma Cook, Sally Vicars, Katie Hillier, Magnus Unnar, Kim Jones
Hair: Paul Hanlon
Make-up: Lisa Houghton
Styling: Miranda Almond

Fashion Made Me Hardcore

Issue: 94
Year: 2002
Model: Michelle Hicks
Hair: Alain Pichon
Make-up: Peter Philips
Styling: Hector Castro

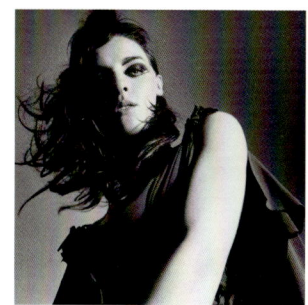

TIMELINE

Toni & Guy: UK Tour

Year: 2002
Model: Toni & Guy UK
  Hair Stylists
Styling: Model's Own

Out of the Dark

Issue: 98
Year: 2003
Model: Jake Gyllenhaal
Grooming: Gigi Hale
Styling: Nicola
  Formichetti

New Blood, New Wave

Issue: 98
Year: 2003
Model: Vincent Cassel
Hair: Tomo Jidai
Make-up: Shinobu
Styling: Sarah Cobb

Boys to the Front of the Queue

Issue: 98
Year: 2003
Model: Chiwetel Ejiofor /
  Marc Warren / Leo
  Gregory / Noel
  Fielding / Ashton
  Kutcher / Pharrell
  Williams / James
  Ransone aka PJ /
  Tyrone & Jesse
  Wood / Chris
  Teckkam from Ten
  Benson / Aidan
  Gillen / Patrick
  Wolf / Shay / Kit
  Lawrence / Jay
  Massacret / Leo
  Houlding / Jakob
  Dylan / Christian
  Coulson / Charlie
  Creed-Miles /
  Jose Antonio Parla
  aka Ease /
  Martin Compston
Make-up: Shinobu
Hair: Tomo Jidai
Grooming: Lorena Lopez,
  Andrea
  Helgadottir
Styling: Nicola
  Formichetti

Start from Zero

Issue: 99
Year: 2003
Model: Madeleine
  Blomberg, Wade
  Crescent
Hair: Peter Gray
Make-up: Petros
  Petrohilos
Styling: Cathy Edwards,
  Nicola
  Formichetti
Clothes: Junya Watanabe

Nothing But Daylight Between Us

Issue: Vol. 2, Issue 1
Year: 2003
Model: Pharrell Williams

Celluloid Closet

Issue: Vol. 2, Issue 3
Year: 2003
Model: Louise Pedersen
Hair: Alain Pichon
Make-up: Val Garland
Styling: Hector Castro

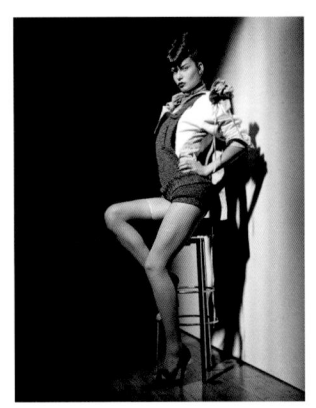

Model, Actress, Whatever

Issue: Vol. 2, Issue 3
Year: 2003
Model: Darcy Donavan,
  Julie Strain,
  Lizzy Strain,
  Susan Holmes
  McKagan, Heather
  Elizabeth Parkhurst
Styling: Sebastien Clivaz

Always Check the Label: Wall of Sound

Issue: Vol. 2, Issue 5
Year: 2003
Model: Mark Jones & Marc
  Lessner from
  E-Klektik,
  Est'elle, Derek
  Dah Large from
  Ceasefire, Stuart
  Price aka Jacques
  Lu Cont from
  Les Rythmes
  Digitales and Zoot
  Woman, Adam
  Blake & Jonny
  Blake from Zoot
  Woman, John
  Gosling aka Mekon,
  Alex Gifford &
  Will White from
  Propellerheads,
  Jon Carter, George
  Jones, Fee Doran
  aka Mrs Jones,
  Theo Keating aka
  DJ Touché from The
  Wiseguys, Daniel
  Peppe aka Themroc,
  Tony Rotton aka
  Blak Twang,
  Torbjørn
  Brundtland & Svein
  Berge from
  Röyksopp

Pete Yorn Bangs the Drums

Issue: Vol. 2, Issue 7
Year: 2003
Model: Pete Yorn
Grooming: Stevie Purcell
Styling: Lara Ferros

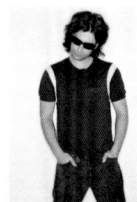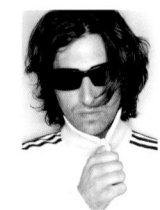

Natalie Press

Issue: Vol. 2, Issue 10
Year: 2004
Model: Natalie Press

Talking About a Revolution

Issue: Vol. 2, Issue 10
Year: 2004
Model: Gael García Bernal
Hair: Tomo Jidai
Make-up: Alex Box
Styling: Nicola
  Formichetti

Eyespy: Free Tibet

Issue: Vol. 2, Issue 11
Year: 2004
Model: Natasha Vojnovic
Hair: Eugene Souleiman
Make-up: Alex Box
Styling: Tal Brener

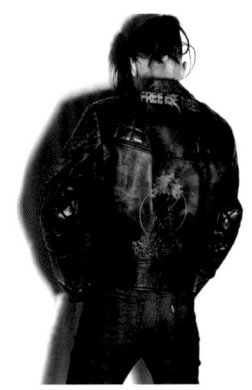

Aural Delight

Issue: Vol. 2, Issue 11
Year: 2004
Model: Gemma Fox /
  Shystie / Cmone
  / Lady Sovereign /
  Nina Jayne / Alex
  Cartañá / Keisha
  White / Belle
  Montenegro
Hair: Dejan
Make-up: Shinobu
Styling: Deep Kailey

Whirlygig

Issue: Vol. 2, Issue 12
Year: 2004
Model: Renee Meijer
Hair: Oscar Quesada
Make-up: Sam Bryant
Styling: Cathy Edwards
Art Direction: Shona Heath

The Sun Always Shines on Kirsten

Issue: Vol. 2, Issue 13
Year: 2004
Model: Kirsten Dunst
Hair: Giovanni Giuliano
Make-up: Jillian Dempsey
Styling: Nina, Clare Hallworth

The Iron Maiden

Issue: Vol. 2, Issue 13
Year: 2004
Model: Melissa Auf Der Maur
Hair: Lanini Reeves
Make-up: Kate Lee
Styling: Magda Berliner

Future + Positive

Issue: Vol. 2, Issue 15
Year: 2004
Model: Thoko Masilela, Muntu Masombuka, Ishmail Ngozo, Diliue Nkosi, Mlungisi Dlamini, Machobane Morake, Natasha Cornelius, Fezeka Poswayo, Kedibone Morifi, Sphiwe Shezi, Nonhlanhla Ntyeza, Portia Joyce, Mpho Babusi, Tebogo Nobela, Nonpumelelo Mbele, Dereck Louw, Clive Mathebula
Hair: Marilyn Du Preez
Make-up: Marilyn Du Preez
Styling: Karen Langley
Location: South Africa

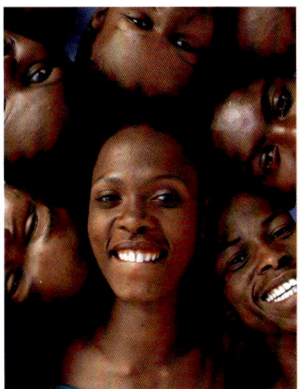

Prince Charming

Issue: Vol. 2, Issue 18
Year: 2004
Model: Ben Whishaw
Grooming: Gareth Von Cuylenburg
Styling: David St. John-James

Creatures of the Cut

Issue: Vol. 2, Issue 20
Year: 2004
Model: Ivana Laurence, Becca Grouer, Hanna Rantala, Lina Scheynius, Kate Woodiwiss, Roberta Bonfils
Hair: Alain Pichon
Make-up: Michelle Campbell

Way Down Here

Issue: Vol. 2, Issue 24
Year: 2005
Model: Nick Littlemore aka Panu/ Myles Heskett, Andrew Stockdale & Chris Ross From Wolfmother / Oliver Ackland / Mini Graff / Susiem Chong & Nic Briand / Tim Hoey & Dan Whitford From Cut Copy / Amelia Liddi
Location: Sydney, Australia

Smack Down

Issue: Vol. 2, Issue 26
Year: 2005
Model: Dave Grohl from Foo Fighters
Grooming: Deborah Ferullo

Riot Act

Issue: Vol. 2, Issue 30
Year: 2005
Model: Jared Leto
Grooming: Mai Quynh
Styling: Cher Coulter

Golden Touch

Issue: Vol. 2, Issue 32
Year: 2005
Model: Jamie Foxx
Hair: Deirdre Dixon
Make-up: Lalette Littlejohn
Styling: Dawn Haynes

#Head to Head

Issue: Vol. 2, Issue 34
Year: 2006
Model: Damien Hirst / Antony Genn & Martin Slattery from The Hours

Brilliant Disguise

Issue: Vol. 2, Issue 38
Year: 2006
Model: Irina
Hair: Steven Lowe
Make-up: Alex Box
Nails: Nonie Creme

Winter Light

Issue: Vol. 2, Issue 41
Year: 2006
Model: Eugenia
Hair: Alain Pichon
Make-up: Florrie White
Styling: Sarah Richardson

Booty Cool

Issue: Vol. 2, Issue 41
Year: 2006
Model: Justin Timberlake
Grooming: Kim Verbeck
Styling: Nicola Formichetti

Risky Business

Issue: Vol. 2, Issue 42
Year: 2006
Model: Tuuli Shipster
Hair: Lyndell Mansfield
Make-up: Florrie White
Styling: Sarah Cobb

Fashion: Paule Ka

Issue: Vol. 2, Issue 45
Year: 2007
Model: Natalie Press
Hair: Soren Bach
Make-up: Michelle Campbell
Styling: Sarah Cobb

Silhouettes

Issue: Vol. 2, Issue 52
Year: 2007
Model: Tuuli Shipster
Hair: Tomo Jidai
Make-up: Michelle Campbell
Styling: Karen Langley

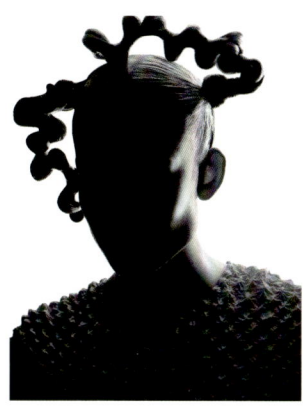

Filthy and Gorgeous

Issue: Vol. 2, Issue 53
Year: 2007
Model: Selma Blair
Hair: Chris McMillan
Make-up: Kara Yoshimoto Bua
Nails: Ashlie Johnson
Styling: Katie Shillingford

TIMELINE

Kiss The Flame

Issue: Vol. 2, Issue 55
Year: 2007
Model: Andressa Fontana, Jensen
Hair: Laini Reeves
Make-up: Melanie Inglessis
Styling: Katie Shillingford

The End of the World as we Know It

Issue: Vol. 2, Issue 59
Year: 2008
Model: Michael Stipe from R.E.M.
Make-up: Alex Box
Styling: Jason Farrer

Born Kicking

Issue: Vol. 2, Issue 61
Year: 2008
Model: Thierry Henry
Grooming: Victor Alvarez
Styling: David St John James

Painted Veils

Issue: Vol. 2, Issue 62
Year: 2008
Model: Adrianna, Amina, Isabelle, Momeena, Rosanna, Zhang, Stephanie
Hair: Gow Tanaka
Make-up: Ayami Nishimura
Styling: Katie Shillingford

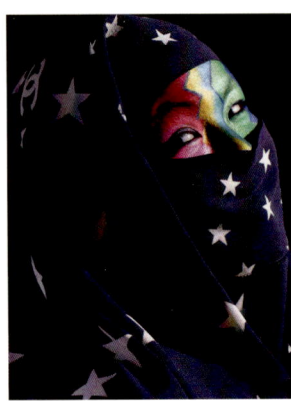

Fresh Faced

Issue: Vol. 2, Issue 68
Year: 2008
Model: Joanna Page
Hair: Gow Tanaka
Make-up: Louise Constad

Far Out!

Issue: Vol. 2, Issue 70
Year: 2009
Model: Natasha Khan aka Bat for Lashes
Make-up: Ayami Nishimura
Hair: James Pecis
Styling: Katie Shillingford

Stand and Deliver

Issue: Vol. 2, Issue 73
Year: 2009
Model: Beth Ditto, Nathan Howdeshell aka Brace Paine & Hannah Blilie from Gossip
Hair: Lyndell Mansfield
Make-up: Peter Philips
Styling: Robbie Spencer

In the Spotlight

Issue: Vol. 2, Issue 84
Year: 2010
Model: Sky Ferreira
Make-up: Ayami Nishimura
Hair: Sascha Breuer
Nails: Julie Luoug
Styling: Scott Robert Clark

Naked is Dekan Backwards

Issue: Vol. 2, Issue 85
Year: 2010
Bodycast: Tuuli Shipster

South Africa 2010

Issue: Vol. 2, Issue 86
Year: 2010
Model: Nontsikelelo Veleko aka Lolo Veleko / Mpumi Mcata, Molefi Makananise, Lindani Buthelezi aka L-R Linda, & Tshepang Ramobar from BLK JKS

On The Attack

Issue: Vol. 2, Issue 87
Year: 2010
Model: Mathangi Arulpragasam aka M.I.A
Hair: Alex Brownsnell
Make-up: Ayami Nishimura
Nails: Kim Treacy
Styling: Katie Shillingford

Big Talk

Issue: Vol. 2, Issue 89
Year: 2010
Model: Toby Kebbell
Grooming: Sascha Breuer
Styling: Scott Robert Clarke

Rosie: Ten Wild Personas

Issue: Vol. 2, Issue 90
Year: 2010
Model: Rosie Huntington-Whiteley
Make-up: Kathy Jeung
Hair: Yiotis Panayiotou
Styling: Maryam Malakpour

Make Her Feel Music.

Issue: Dazed & Confused Korea, Issue 36
Year: 2011
Model: Daisy Lowe
Hair: Sascha Breuer
Make-up: Linda Öhrström
Styling: Scott Robert Clarke

A Taste for Danger

Issue: Vol. 2, Issue 94
Year: 2011
Model: Andrea Riseborough
Hair: Tracie Cant
Make-up: Ayami Nishimura
Nails: Adam Slee
Styling: Katie Shillingford

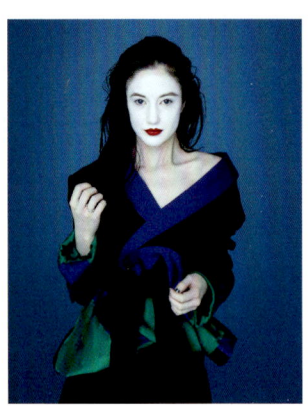

Tough Nut

Issue: Vol. 3, Issue 1
Year: 2011
Model: Tom Hardy
Grooming: Liz Taw
Styling: Scott Robert Clarke

20 + 20

Issue: Vol. 3, Issue 4
Year: 2011
Model: Alicia Keys / Emeli Sandé / Björk / Eddie Jefferys & Jason Morrison from 16bit / Bobby Gillespie from Primal Scream / Faris Badwan & Rachel Zeffira from

Cat's Eyes / Chloë Sevigny / Lizzi Bougatsos from Gang Gang Dance/ Cillian Murphy / Craig Roberts / Damien Hirst / Judd Trump / Damon Albarn from Blur & Gorillaz / Yukimi Nagano from Little Dragon / Eva Green / Jordan Scott / Gael García Bernal / Verónica Echegui / Harmony Korine / Dan Colen / Jarvis Cocker from Pulp / Frances Castle / Juliette Lewis / James Walbourne / Kate Moss / Josephine de la Baume from Sing Tank / Kelis / Jamie Woon / Michael Stipe from R.E.M. / Jeremy Shaw / Milla Jovovich / Luke Evans / Pharrell Williams / Maxine Ashley / Polly Jean Harvey aka PJ Harvey / Claire Foy / Jamie Hince & Alison Mosshart from The Kills / Melissa Rigby from S.C.U.M / Tilda Swinton / Justin Bond

Hair: Serge Normant, Kenna, Raphael Sally, Chi Wong, Martin Cullen, Ashley Javier, Christian Eberhard, Syd Hayes, Tomo Jidai, Lisa Eastwood, Karen Adler, Christian Wood, Roxie Dott, James Brown, Liz Taw, Jenny Cho, Yoichi Tomizawa, Chi Wong, Duffy, Brent Lawler, Rankin

Make-up: Dotti, Kate Lindsay, Gemma Smith-Edhouse, Lotten Holmqvist, Lisa Houghton, Linda Hay, Ayami Nishimura, James O'Riley, Andrew Gallimore, Sally Branka, Karen Adler,

Su Han, Kristen Piggott, Lisa Eldridge, Melanie Inglesses, Francelle, Petros Petrohilos, Christian McCulloch

Grooming: James Rowe, Kenichi, Dennis Gots, Panos Papandrianos, Diana Schmidke, Johnny Castellands

Nails: Deana Blackwell, Trish Lomax, Nichola Joss, Anatole Rainey

Styling: Yuki James, Bay Garnett, Robbie Spencer, John McCarty, Steven Westgrath, Tracey Nicholson, Elizabeth Fraser-Bell, Celestine Cooney, Soraya Dayani, Agata Belcen, Laura Duncan, Cathy Edwards, Katie Shillingford, Joanna Schlenzka, Ryan Hastings, Sally Lyndley, John McCarty

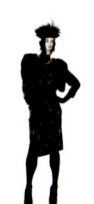
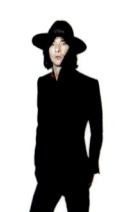
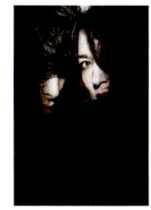
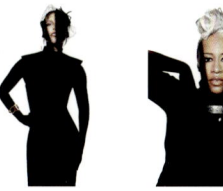

Rankin Selects Anna Calvi

Issue: Vol. 3, Issue 4
Year: 2011
Model: Anna Calvi
Hair: James Brown
Make-up: Kristen Piggott
Styling: Nell Kalonji

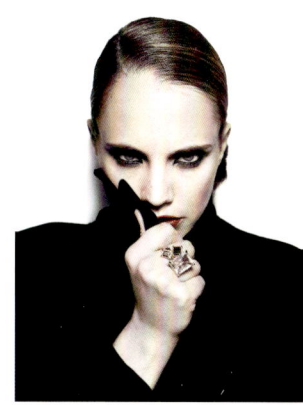

Graffiti Dreams

Issue: Vol. 3, Issue 4
Year: 2011
Model: Josephine Skriver
Hair: Martin Cullen
Make-up: Ayami Nishimura
Styling: Katie Shillingford
Spray Paint: Jack Murray

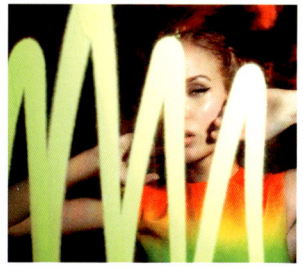

Born Free

Issue: Vol. 3, Issue 20
Year: 2013
Model: Saoirse Ronan
Hair: Raphael Salley
Make-up: Ayami Nishimura
Nails: Zarra Celik
Styling: Cathy Edwards

Wild at Heart

Issue: Vol. 3, Issue 29
Year: 2014
Model: Carey Mulligan
Hair: Ben Cooke
Make-up: Ayami Nishimura
Nails: Zarra Celik
Styling: Cathy Edwards

Take a Stand: Dazed Fashion Forum

Issue: Vol. 4, A/W 2015
Year: 2015
Model: Isamaya Ffrench, Ryan Lo, Claire Barrow
Hair: Cyndia Harvey
Make-up: Thomas de Kluyver
Styling: Emma Wyman

Unravelled: Dazed x Woolmark Prize

Year: 2016
Model: Carmen Kass, Danny Beauchamp
Hair: Sharmaine Cox
Make-up: Marco Antonio
Styling: Anna Hughes-Chamberlain

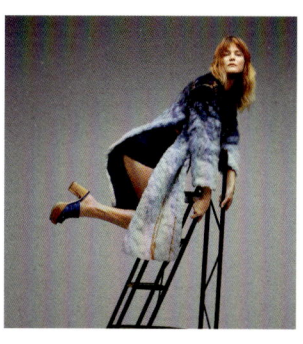

America's Sweetheart. Gigi Hadid Lives in your Wildest Dreams.

Issue: 25th Anniversary Issue, A/W 2016
Year: 2016
Model: Gigi Hadid
Hair: Luke Hersheson
Make-up: Lisa Eldridge
Nails: Chisato Yamamoto
Styling: Katie Grand

THANKS

It's always difficult to thank people, there are so many people who deserve a mention. So this book is dedicated to everyone who we worked with, or featured in, *Dazed*.

They were heady days and we were just kids. We made so many mistakes and essentially grew up in public, but I'm very proud of what the magazine became.

But here's a few special mentions: Sandra Barron, Cathy Edwards, Katy England, Robert Montgomery, Lotte Ould, Phil Poynter, Matt Roach, Mark Sanders, Steve Savigear, Ian C Taylor, and Stuart White.

Then there are those whithout whom *Dazed* would not have been possible:

To Jefferson and the madness of our *Dazed* days. It's no secret that our magazine and partnership made me the photographer I am today. Thank you.

A special thanks will always go out to Katie Grand, for the adventure, creativity and style you brought with you. You taught me so much.

Finally, the biggest shout-out needs to be to my sister Susanne. You were always the sensible one between us, and *Dazed* (not to mention me personally) owes you a massive debt of gratitude for everything you've given it.

Big love to you all!

Rankin x

Opposite Page - The Cast, Issue 26, 1996

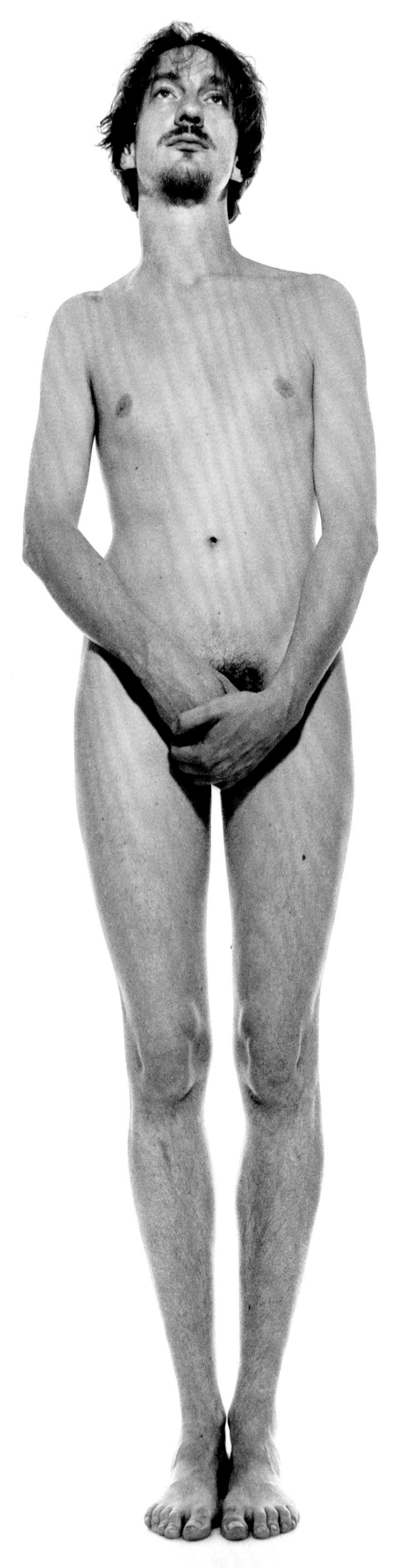

COPYRIGHT

Publisher: Rankin Publishing Ltd.
Photography: Rankin
Editor: Ellen Stone
Texts: Rankin / Ellen Stone
Design: Public Offerings Ltd.
Archive Research: Holly Allan, Felix
                  Allan, Calum Watson
Post Production: True Black Studio
Printed by: MM ArtBook

First published on the occasion of *The Dazed Decades* exhibition at Scharpoord Cultural Centre, Knokke-Heist, Belgium, 25 March - 11 June 2023.

ISBN: 978-1-7392910-1-3
© Rankin, 2023

Front Cover - Nanu Nanu Björk Calling..., Issue 16, 1995
Back Cover - Touch Your Toes, Issue 20, 1996